Population, Politics, and the Future of Southern Asia

Population, Politics, and the Future of Southern Asia

Edited by
W. Howard Wriggins and James F. Guyot

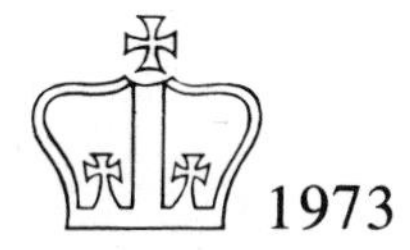

1973
Columbia University Press / New York and London

This study was prepared under the auspices of the Southern Asian Institute, Columbia University, New York. The Southern Asian Institute seeks a deeper knowledge of that vast and tumultuous area stretching from Pakistan in the West to Indonesia and the Philippines in the East. To understand the problems facing its leaders and diverse peoples requires sustained study and research. Our publications are intended to contribute to that better understanding.

Library of Congress Cataloging in Publication Data
Main entry under title:
Population, politics, and the future of southern Asia.

Papers presented at a conference on population, the human condition, and politics in southern Asia, held at Columbia University in Nov. 1971, and sponsored by the Southern Asian Institute of Columbia University.

Includes bibliographical references.

1. South Asia—Population—Congresses. 2. South Asia—Politics and government—Congresses. 3. Urbanization—South Asia—Congresses. 4. Youth—South Asia —Congresses. I. Wriggins, William Howard, 1918– ed. II. Guyot, James Franklin, 1932–, ed. III. Columbia University. Southern Asian Institute.
HB3635.P66 301.32′9′54 73-8673
ISBN 0-231-23756-2
ISBN 0-231-03757-0 (pbk)

Printed in the United States of America

The Contributors

SHAHID JAVED BURKI did not attend the conference, but his chapter, part of a larger study on Pakistan, is close to the center of our concern and therefore was included here. He was born in India, his family migrating to Rawalpindi, Pakistan, at partition. He was a Rhodes Scholar, receiving an M.A. in Economics. In 1964 he was appointed Director of West Pakistan's Rural Works Programme. In 1967 he was a Public Service Fellow at the J. F. Kennedy School of Public Administration at Harvard. His books include *Basic Democracies, Rural Development and Social Welfare* (Government of West Pakistan); *A Study of Chinese Communes* (Harvard University); and *Social Groups and Development: The Case of Pakistan* (forthcoming, from which the materials in this essay have been drawn).

CORA DUBOIS received her Ph.D. from the University of California, Berkeley, in Anthropology. She has long been concerned with the relations between culture and personality. Her field work in Indonesia led to *The People of Alor* (1944) and, following government service during World War II, she published *Social Forces in Southeast Asia* (1949). For ten years she has been observing at very close hand social, cultural, and economic changes in Bhubaneswar, the capital of Orissa in India. She has been President of the American Anthropological Association and the Association of Asian Studies.

DONALD K. EMMERSON is Assistant Professor of Political Science at the University of Wisconsin. He spent 1967–1969 in Indonesia researching elite political culture and lecturing on social science topics and received his Ph.D. from Yale in 1972. His publications include "Bureaucratic Alienation in Indonesia: The Director General's Dilemma" in R. William Liddle's *Political Participation in Modern Indonesia* (Yale, 1973); and he edited a volume on *Students and Politics in Developing Nations* (Praeger, 1968). He is currently exploring questions of growth, equity, and participation in development.

SIDNEY GOLDSTEIN, Professor of Sociology and Director of the Population Studies and Training Center at Brown University, is a demographer who has specialized in the study of internal migration and urbanization. He served as Demographic Adviser to the Institute of Population Studies of Chulalongkorn University, Bangkok, Thailand, where he has participated in the design and execution of the National Longitudinal Survey of Social, Economic, and Demographic Change. He has served as consultant to a number of United States and United Nations agencies and has authored numerous books, monographs, and articles dealing with migration, fertility, and urbanization in the developed and developing world.

JAMES F. GUYOT, a Research Associate at the Southern Asian Institute and Associate Professor of Political Science at Baruch College, CUNY, is a specialist on bureaucratic behavior in varying environments. He is co-author of *Asian Bureaucratic Systems Emergent from the British Imperial Tradition,* has written articles on "Creeping Urbanism in Malaysia" and "The 'Clerk Mentality' in Burmese Education" and recently co-edited *The Military as Political Elites in Asia: A Review of Performance.* He was an examiner with the U.S. Civil Service Commission prior to earning his Ph.D. at Yale and more recently has been Manager of Personnel Research at the Port Authority of New York and New Jersey. In between he served on faculties at Swarthmore, the University of Connecticut, UCLA, and Columbia, with visiting appointments at the University of Malaya and the University of Pennsylvania. His field research experiences in the Soviet Union, Burma, and Malaysia, as well as the raising of three children, have been shared with his wife, a fellow political scientist.

DR. C. H. S. JAYEWARDENE is a medical doctor and criminologist with an M.D. degree from the University of Ceylon and a Ph.D. in Sociology and Criminology from the University of Pennsylvania. His major works include *Fertility Trends in Ceylon* and *Family Planning in Ceylon,* co-authored with Professor O. E. R. Abhayaratne. His main interest, however, has been the study of criminology with special emphasis on the cultural aspects of violence. He has taught Forensic Medicine at the University of Ceylon and at present is Professor of Criminology at the University of Ottawa.

GAVIN W. JONES was adviser to the Economic Development Board of the Government of Thailand until 1972. He received his Ph.D. from Australian National University in 1966. His writings include "Australia's Immigration Policy: Some Malaysian Attitudes," *Australian Outlook,* December 1965; "The Economic Effect of Declining Fertility in Less Developed Countries," *Population Council Occasional Papers,* 1969. He was co-author, with S. Selvaratnam, of *Population Growth and Economic Growth in Ceylon* (Colombo, Hausa, 1972), and has written a number of additional articles and monographs on demographic and economic development issues.

He is presently Representative of the Population Council and Advisor to the Demographic Institute in Djakarta, Indonesia.

NATHAN KEYFITZ is Professor of Sociology and Demography at Harvard University with a B.Sc. from McGill University and a Ph.D. in Sociology from the University of Chicago. He was Director of the Columbo Plan Bureau in Sri Lanka, 1956–1957, and had advised the governments of Burma, India, Indonesia, Chile, Argentina, and Canada on their censuses, statistical development, and demographic analysis. He has written numerous articles on these and related subjects and is editor of *Theoretical Population Biology.* He is currently working on a manuscript, *Applied Mathematical Demography,* to be published by John Wiley in 1974.

APRODICIO A. LAQUIAN is Associate Director, Social Sciences and Human Resources, International Development Research Centre, Ottawa. His Doctorate in Political Science was from MIT. He has written a number of studies on urban questions, including: *The City in Nation-Building: Politics and Administration in Metropolitan Manila* (Manila, 1966); *Slums are for People: The Barrio Magsaysay Pilot Project in Philippine Community Development* (East West Center Press, 1971) and has edited *Rural-Urban Migrants and Metropolitan Development.* (Toronto, 1971).

KENNETH W. THOMPSON is Vice-President of the Rockefeller Foundation and was, before joining the Foundation in 1955, a member of the political science faculties of Northwestern University and the University of Chicago. He is author of, among other studies, *Foreign Assistance: A View from the Private Sector; American Diplomacy and Emergent Patterns; Political Realism and the Crisis of World Politics;* and *Christian Ethics and the Dilemmas of Foreign*

Policy. He is co-author of *Man and Modern Society* (with Karl de Schweinitz), *Foreign Policies in a World of Change* (with Joseph E. Black), *Conflict and Cooperation Among Nations* (with Ivo Duchacek), and *Principles and Problems of International Politics* (with Hans J. Morgenthau). He has contributed to numerous other books and professional journals.

MYRON WEINER is Professor of Political Science and senior staff member of the Center for International Studies, Massachusetts Institute of Technology. His books on South Asia include *Party Building: The Indian National Congress, State Politics in India,* and *Politics of Scarcity*. He is author of "Political Demography: An Inquiry into the Political Consequences of Population Change," in *Rapid Population Growth* (National Academy of Science). He is currently at work on a book on the socio-political consequences of internal migration in India under a grant from the Behavioral Sciences Branch of the National Institutes of Mental Health. Professor Weiner is chairman of the Population Policy Seminar Project of the National Academy of Sciences and is a member of the Technical Advisory panel of the Population Reference Bureau.

VINCENT H. WHITNEY received his Ph.D from the University of North Carolina, and has taught sociology at Wesleyan, Brown, and the University of Pennsylvania, where he was Chairman of the Sociology Department. He is now Professor of Sociology and Demography and Director of the Population Studies Center, University of Pennsylvania, and a Senior Staff Consultant to the Population Council for the Far East. He has written numerous articles on aspects of demography, including "Population Distribution," "Population in Theories of Economic Development," "The Significance of Changes in World Population Growth," etc. Among other professional activities, he is also a member of the Technical Advisory Committee on Population, U.S. Bureau of the Census; a member of the Population, Research and Training Committee, National Institutes of Health; and Consulting Editor of *Demography*.

W. HOWARD WRIGGINS is Professor of Political Science and Director of the Southern Asian Institute at Columbia University. He received his Ph.D. in International Relations from Yale, and has taught at Yale, Vassar College, and the School of Advanced International Studies, Washington. He served in the Library of Congress, the Policy Planning Council of the Department of State, and was a

Senior Member of the National Security Council staff before joining Columbia in 1967. He has published *The Status of the United Nations Secretariat: Role of the Administrative Tribunal* (with Edwin Bock); *Ceylon, Dilemmas of a New Nation* (Princeton, 1960); *The Ruler's Imperative* (Columbia, 1969); and a number of articles on politics, development, and international relations of Southern Asia. He is presently at work on a study of the bases of international bargaining between industrialized and "third world" countries.

Preface

Population growth and related demographic changes during the next two or three decades will pose major challenges to the world's political leaders and peoples. Achieving a humane distribution of social benefits within and among nations, sustaining effective political systems, assuring the orderly growth of productive capabilities, and maintaining peaceful relations among the nations of the world will all be made more difficult by population changes now in process. Rapid population growth and related changes will severely limit what political leaders can do and magnify the burdens peoples will have to bear.

These challenges are particularly acute in Southern Asia, an area of impoverished masses, extreme socio-economic contrasts, uneven organizational capabilities, and often inchoate political systems.

Seeking to direct the serious attention of the social sciences to the complex interactions between population change and politics, the Southern Asian Institute of Columbia University convened a conference on Population, the Human Condition and Politics in Southern Asia in November 1971. Here some sixty representatives from social science disciplines considered these problems over a three-day period. We first examined basic demographic changes under way in Southern Asia and then focused on two areas of major interest: (1) the general processes and effects of urbanization, and (2) the particular difficulties and opportunities engendered by substantially larger youth cohorts.

In chapter 1, the editors present a preliminary sketch of the many ways in which population change and politics interact, forming a complex pattern of interdependence difficult to disentangle. Written after the conference, this chapter is intended to help the reader understand the political context within which the demographic changes have been taking place and to perceive more readily the difficulties governments face in coping with these complexities. Believing that a solid base of demographic analysis was necessary for our consultations, we asked two associates of the Population Council, Vincent Whitney, Director of the University of Pennsylvania Population Studies Center, and Gavin Jones, based in Bangkok, to provide in Part I (chapter 2) an overview of basic demographic dynamics in the area. Their paper also examines relationships between rapid population growth and economic development.

Part II takes up various aspects of urbanization, one of the processes where the interplay of demographic change and politics tends to be most critical. Introducing this section in chapter 3, Sidney Goldstein, Director of Brown University's Population Research and Training Center, discusses the demographic characteristics of Bangkok. He provides information on the socio-political sources and consequences of Bangkok's rapid rise to its preponderant position in Thailand and a ratio of primacy far above other primate cities in the region. Growing social and political tensions in the Southeast Asian cities of Manila, Djakarta, and Kuala Lumpur are discussed in chapter 4 by Aprodicio Laquian, Associate Director of Social Science of the International Development Research Center in Ottawa. In chapter 5, Shahid Javed Burki, a member of the Civil Service of Pakistan, describes and analyzes migration patterns in Pakistan. He draws on government publications and his own surveys in considering the sources and political consequences of urbanization. In chapter 6, Myron Weiner, of the Political Science Department of the Massachusetts Institute of Technology, examines the socio-political consequences in India of the migration of peoples from one cultural and linguistic area to another. He shows how governmental policy and the pulls of economic development induce migrations which then generate antagonisms of substantial import.

Part III surveys the successive youth cohorts from several perspectives. It is introduced in chapter 7 by Nathan Keyfitz, Professor of Demography and Sociology at Harvard. He assesses the size and the unprecedented increase of Indonesia's younger age groups and speculates on how the combination of increased numbers and changing youth values is posing new challenges—and opportunities—to the existing political regime and social system. In chapter 8 Donald Emmerson of the University of Wisconsin's Department of Political Science draws on original survey data to analyze what he calls the "status-generation gap" between students and establishment in Indonesia, which has its counterpart in most countries of the area. In chapter 9 Cora DuBois of Harvard's Department of Anthropology considers the relationships between schooling, youth, and modernization in northeast India, an area she has observed for many years, and suggests that the interconnections are more complex and subtle than might be imagined. In chapter 10, C. H. S. Jayewardene, of the University of Ottawa's Department of Criminology and Howard Wriggins of Columbia University's Southern Asian Institute seek to link demographic changes and political events through a number of intervening variables in an effort to explain the youth protest in Ceylon in 1971.

Our focus on population change and politics in the Southern Asian segment of the Third World in no way denies that population growth in the industrialized world also presents problems, both for the richer nations and for the world at large. Nor is our emphasis on challenges and difficulties intended to obscure the positive opportunities associated with changes in the size and character of national populations. Our choice of the particular themes for analysis arose from a joint consideration of both important issue areas and effective avenues for analysis. We hope that our organized examination of some of the finely textured relationships between population and politics will suggest worthwhile lines of social science inquiry. Such an undertaking may also enable policy-makers in the area to better understand the bases for decisions they will have to make in the future.

Columbia University
New York City
July 1973

W. Howard Wriggins
James F. Guyot

Acknowledgments

The editors are deeply indebted to former Dean Andrew Cordier of the School of International Affairs, Columbia University, and to the Kellogg Foundation for the original support which made these papers and conference discussions possible. The Ford Foundation contributed to the costs of editing and publishing this volume, and the Rockefeller Foundation's Bellagio Study and Conference Center and its Resident Director, William C. Olson, provided superior arrangements for completing the editorial task. Stuart Fagan, William T. R. Fox, Stanley Heginbotham, Joseph LaPalombara, and M. Rashiduzzaman reviewed specific chapters. To Vincent Whitney go special thanks for early good counsel in preparing the conference in the first place. We wish to acknowledge the editorial assistance of Glenda Adams and the research assistance of Frank Ceo and Viraj Yipintsoi. We also extend our thanks to Linda Diorio, Mary Flower, and Melinda Legge for their patience and energy in typing successive drafts of the material.

Contents

Population, Politics, and the Future of Southern Asia

Chapter 1

Demographic Change and Politics: An Introduction *

W. Howard Wriggins and James F. Guyot

South and Southeast Asia encompass populations totaling more than 1 billion, about one-fourth of humanity.* The dozen states of the area range in size from India with over 500 million and Indonesia with 125 million, to the island city of Singapore with its 2 million inhabitants. India alone contains more people than all of Latin America and Africa combined. Southeast Asia has a larger population than either North or South America. Reasonable projections of current growth rates in Southern Asia suggest a doubling of total population by the end of the century. Huge migrations are also under way, principally to the urban areas and especially to a few "primate cities." A third salient characteristic is the advance of a large youth cohort, the leading edge of the postwar baby boom.

While there are some ambiguities in the data and considerable variation from place to place, there is no denying that these changes will add to the burdens political leaders must cope with in all countries of the area. Without doubt, these trends complicate the task of providing minimum maintenance requirements and services. Whatever additional burdens are imposed will depend very much on non-demographic phenomena—the nature of the political system, the style and skill of leaders, the expectations of large numbers of people regarding their participation in public life, the effectiveness of political and administrative insti-

* In this volume, *South Asia* includes India, Pakistan, Bangladesh, Sri Lanka (Ceylon), and Nepal, unless otherwise specified; *Southeast Asia* refers to Burma, Thailand, Malaysia, Indonesia, the states of Indo-China, Singapore, and the Philippines. Together they constitute *Southern Asia*. (Ed. footnote)

tutions, the level of economic resources and the translation of these resources into needed goods and services available to the leaders and populace. Except in the most dire circumstances, perceptions and subjective standards of what is locally appropriate will carry more weight in defining the minimum acceptable level of resources and services than any simple measure of what is required to preserve life itself. There are, then, numerous intervening variables linking demographic changes, maintenance requirements, and politics.

This chapter first considers major demographic trends in the area and identifies in a preliminary way more obvious interactions between demographic and political phenomena. It characterizes political tendencies we consider particularly important in the light of projected demographic changes and then discusses qualities of leadership, administrative strengths, and economic capabilities that can be brought to bear, noting some of the ways in which these variables interact. The chapter concludes with a brief consideration of problems of prediction and policy-making.

Major Demographic Trends

Our purpose here will not be to summarize the main points in the papers by Whitney and Jones, Goldstein, and Keyfitz. Together they supply a rich and detailed analysis of population characteristics of the area and of selected countries, and knowledgeable interpretations of causes and consequences deriving from the data presented. It will nevertheless be useful to identify a few of the salient population changes under way and set them alongside selected political trends that we believe to be of great importance for the future of the area.

In the first place, the magnitude of the population challenge is in part defined by the rates of population growth, which are generally high by world standards though less dramatic than those in South America. Table 1.1 shows the remarkable increase in the rate of population growth of the Third World regions over the past two decades.

Table 1.1 Rates of Population Growth by Region, 1950–60 and 1960–69

	1950–60	*1960–69*
South Asia	2.0	2.6
Southeast Asia	2.0	2.7
Africa	2.0	2.5
South America	2.3	3.0

Source: United Nations, *Statistical Yearbook, 1961,* Table 1a; *1970,* Table 2.

Table 1.2 reports the rate of growth for specific countries in South and Southeast Asia for 1953–60 and gives estimates for the period 1963–69.

Table 1.2 Annual Rates of Population Growth in Countries of South and Southeast Asia, 1953–60 and 1963–69

South Asia	*1953–60*	*1963–69*
Ceylon	2.7	2.4 [1]
India	1.9 [1]	2.5 [1]
Nepal	1.6	1.8 [1]
Pakistan	1.9	2.1 [1]
Southeast Asia		
Burma	1.0	2.2 [1]
Cambodia	—	2.2 [1]
Indonesia	2.2 [1]	2.5 [1]
Laos	3.2 [1]	2.4 [1]
Malaysia (West)	3.0	2.8
Philippines	3.2 [1]	3.5 [1]
Singapore	—	2.1
Thailand	4.3 [1]	3.1 [1]
North Vietnam	−0.2 [1]	3.1
South Vietnam	5.4 [1]	2.6

Source: United Nations, *Demographic Trends, 1961* and *1969* (New York: United Nations), Tables 1 and 2 respectively.
[1] Estimate.

Although in Singapore, Malaysia, Thailand, and possibly Ceylon the rate of growth is slowing down, in most other countries of the region growth is probably still accelerating. And peace in

Indo-China can be expected to bring a spurt of population growth there, too. In India, Pakistan, Bangladesh, and Indonesia the population base is so large that the actual numbers added each year are staggering. In India alone, 13 million more people have to be absorbed each year—more than the total population of any one of the 75 smaller members of the United Nations. South Asia now accommodates roughly 750 million. If present rates of growth continue, it is likely to have over 1.5 billion by the year 2000. Southeast Asia, now with 287 million, is projected to grow to 608 million. If these projections prove correct, each area will more than double its population in less than thirty years.

Secondly, internal migrations are of great significance. Quite apart from the huge migrations induced by warfare in Indo-China and the 1971–72 flow out of and back to Bangladesh, internal migrations to major cities are very large in many countries. Djakarta grew by 50 percent between 1961 and 1968, the influx swelling that sprawling "urban village" to over 4.5 million before its military mayor declared it a "closed city" and sought to stop the flow by setting up blockades at the city's margins. In Thailand, the magnetism of Bangkok, a truly primate city, pushed its population to 32 times that of the second city in the realm. Bangkok's population is expected to double by 1985 and, if present trends hold, treble by the year 2000. In less dramatic instances, the combination of increased growth from within cities and migration to them will mean a doubling of many urban centers within twenty to twenty-five years.

Thirdly, the age structure of populations is changing. Many more middle-aged people are living into old age than ever before. As more survive beyond the productive years, they add dependency burdens. Their longer lives give reality to the extended-family ideal at the very time when many young people are becoming less willing to live under the daily guidance of their elders, thus sharpening tensions between generations. More consequential to political life, a higher proportion of younger people are surviving beyond infancy than at any time in the history of that area. As Keyfitz argues, a 2.5 percent rate of overall growth may in fact conceal a 7 percent growth in younger age groups. They swell the ranks of student-aged youths who need to acquire useful skills and later to find jobs and appropriate places as adults. Indeed, roughly half the people alive today in South and Southeast Asia were born within the last twenty years. In Indonesia, following occupation, war, and the re-establishment of political order, there was a noticeable surge in the numbers in the youthful age groups. As this age bulge moves up the population pyramid, similar pressures will be experienced fifteen to twenty-five years from now when the offspring of these outsize cohorts in their turn seek entry into the adult world.

In other countries the surge of young people may not show up as discontinuities in the population pyramid. But the increase in sheer numbers and in the ratio of young people to adults poses complex political as well as social problems.

Population Change Affects Politics—and Vice Versa

The exact effects of these demographic changes will depend on the interaction among many other variables, to be discussed below. Nevertheless, it is helpful to note here in a preliminary way some of the more obvious and probable political consequences of rapid population growth, of migration, and of changes in the age composition of the population.

Merely to prevent a decline in the still very low standards of living in Southern Asia, the economy must at the very least grow as rapidly as the population. A population growing at the rate of 2.7 percent will double in twenty-five years. Government services will have to double simply to provide the same level of service to the same proportion of the population. This doubled maintenance and service obligation makes no allowance for the need to broaden the distribution of services to a larger proportion of the population. And an increasingly literate and politically mobilized populace is likely to demand more per individual in the future.

Centers of population will become more crowded, with the attendant increases in socio-political tensions produced by spatial crowding.[1] Man/land ratios will worsen, increasing competition in rural areas, altering socio-economic group relationships, and inducing migration to the cities unless there are compensatory technological or institutional changes in the countryside.

Migration may bring needed talents to areas where real opportunities are growing or where expectations attract the ambitious or the desperate. It may also be politically disruptive insofar as the arrival of migrants increases social tensions. These tensions in turn may take on a political character when anxious groups in "host" areas seek to block the arrival of newcomers and defend positions already gained, as Weiner's paper elaborates.[2]

A more youthful population obviously requires heavier outlays for simple maintenance and for training for the future. It has been argued that large youth cohorts have been sources of political instability in the past.[3] They tend to press for innovation, accelerating changes which may be long overdue. As Emmerson contends, they are likely to follow younger leaders who sense the future better than their elders, and may thrust aside older, more established figures.

In multi-ethnic societies, differences in growth rates and age structures among ethnic groups are likely to be perceived as affecting the distribution of political power for the future. Projected population trends may be thought to foretell changes in the political fortunes of competing ethnic groups decades hence. Accordingly, short-run demographic changes may loom large in the minds of competing political leaders of groups fearful of losing their positions. They may precipitate ethnic group conflict which a society composed of only one ethnic community would not have to deal with.

These population changes suggest that social, political, and economic conflict is likely to intensify. Traditional methods of conflict resolution may no longer be adequate, and improved modes of dealing with friction may have to be discovered.

While demographic changes shape political life, politics and policy decisions in turn influence the pace and direction of population change. Civil peace, a remarkable political accomplishment that is taken for granted unless it is disrupted, has been a requisite for rapid rates of population growth. During war, revolution, or protracted political disorders that increase personal insecurity, disrupt health measures, and separate families, birth rates normally decline. But civil peace in itself, though necessary, is not sufficient to promote rapid population growth. Direct government attempts to increase population, as in interwar France and contemporary Eastern Europe, paradoxically tend to fail, perhaps because the need to redirect social change is discovered only after glacial forces are well under way. Government attempts to constrain population growth have also had mixed results.

The major impact of public policy on population growth has been indirect, by way of the pursuit of two indubitable public goods—health and happiness, to say nothing of wealth. In deciding, for example, to apply resources to improving public health, thereby reducing mortality rates, political leaders and administrators have fostered an unintended demographic change —rapid population growth. Certain policy decisions, therefore, affect demographic phenomena as these, in turn, affect political life. But the particular form of the interplay of politics and population change in any one polity will be profoundly influenced by characteristic political trends and many other factors that are independent of demographic changes.

Major Political Trends

If growing populations were politically passive, asking for little beyond mere maintenance; if group relations were mainly collaborative and all energies were applied to using to full advantage available economic resources to successfully meet minimum maintenance requirements; if there were ample opportunities for young people and migrants were welcomed for their skills, then population growth, changing age structures, and migration would pose few political problems. Instead, a number of political and economic trends work in the opposite direction.

Each polity in Southern Asia differs significantly from the others; each has its own profile of capabilities and burdens, with the various elements of the political system interacting in unique ways. Nevertheless, we believe it is possible to suggest certain general political trends that will become increasingly apparent in most countries of the area during the next decade or two. Projected demographic trends are likely to aggravate the problems faced by each political system, but the specific manifestations of these complications will be deeply influenced by the following socio-political tendencies.

Political Mobilization. The political effects of population change will depend in part upon the type, direction, and scope of political mobilization. Political mobilization is a process that activates hitherto politically passive and disinterested subjects on behalf of political ends. It is encouraged by leaders who seek to arouse and channel the energies of the newly politicized in directions that will affect the distribution of political power or the direction of specific policies.

Where leaders are secure in their positions, as within ascriptive patron-client systems that can be taken for granted, they do not need to arouse defensive ethnic or other emotions to retain a following. If leaders are insecure, however, or are competing for power in open elections, their efforts to win supporters add to political mobilization. They may generate support by providing (or promising) more patronage. They may also mobilize by charismatic inspiration or by evoking a sense of danger from abroad, from some threatening internal agency or competing ethnic or socio-political group. In these processes, the level and scope of group demands made upon the political system will increase, and may become focused on mutually antagonistic, invidious claims.

Improved mass communications may also lead to political mobilization as more people receive information of political relevance of which they were previously ignorant. A population thus awakened is likely to believe it has some claim to participate in affairs of state or at least to regard their handling critically. A mobilized population is alert to grievances, more claimant of its rights, more jealous of competing groups. An unmobilized population will see public affairs as a drama performed far off, meting out pleasure or pain but beyond influence.

Political mobilization, then, tends to compound the burdens placed upon a political system by rapid population growth and changes in age composition. If the total load accumulates too rapidly and the political institutions prove insufficiently responsive and adaptable, the result may be a quick collapse, perhaps accompanied by the flourish of a military coup, and in any event resulting in a deflation of demands. An alternative course is a gradual but sure decline into lowered performance and eroded expectations.

If, however, a polity possesses a high initial level of economic resources or unusually imaginative and effective leadership, mobilization for mass participation may strengthen governance by tempering the institutions of participation and pressing the administrative engine to higher output.

Certain types of political mobilization may direct efforts mainly toward economic production in a command economy, as a number of Communist and "mobilizationist" regimes have attempted. It may even rally efforts to reduce fertility and reverse migration flows. For most countries in Southern Asia, however, political mobilization has contributed more to inflating demands than to increasing economic production or restraining population growth.

One consequence of political mobilization, then, is what might be called the participation explosion. The efforts of elites to recruit supporters, the extension of literacy, and the ideals promoted in schools, universities, and the mass media are altering conceptions of appropriate popular roles in politics. Larger numbers than ever before have come to believe that the divinely ordained order of things can be altered by human endeavor. No longer can a small elite assume that its ascriptive, inherited position entitles it to manage affairs for a passive, acquiescent populace. An aloof, all-knowing administration of "guardians" is no longer an acceptable administrative instrument. Greater popular participation in local, regional, and national life is changing the terms of rulership.

Occasionally, vigorous leaders may seek to constrain popular participation, as President Ayub attempted to do in Pakistan, Suharto in Indonesia, and Prime Minister Lee Kuan Yew in Singapore. These seem to be exceptions to the general trend toward increasingly active participation.

Traditional political structures are often weakened in this process. Formerly, patron-client dependency networks gave shape and restraint to, and defined leadership for, a large proportion of the politically active. Patron-client politics have often muted ethnic differences, or held caste or other antagonisms in check. As these lose their restraining character under the pressure of political mobilization, popular politics can sharpen invidious comparisons and aggravate group conflict, as has been seen in Ceylon and in the disintegration of Pakistan.[4]

Increased Demands. A second political development, operating even where population growth is slowing down but compounding the consequences of any growth in population, is the pressure of increasing demands. Population growth swells minimum maintenance requirements. But political mobilization and the participation explosion contribute still further to raising the level and extending the scope of political demands.

Educational systems must be expanded if rising numbers of young people are to be educated for the new and more complex world they will be entering. Ambitious parents, now more articulate and more claimant, press for more accessible school opportunities and at ever higher levels for their children. Most governments in Southern Asia are committed to broadening educational opportunities and cannot resist the pressures. Levels of literacy improve; more and more students learn the literary arts and skills of clerkship. Cora DuBois notes that all too often in Southern Asia, school systems induce unrealistic ambitions and divert young people from modest productive occupations, turning them into unemployables demanding nonexistent white-collar jobs. The papers by Keyfitz and by Jayewardene and Wriggins also stress this point.

Education and mass media may raise the level of expectations. Political mobilization transforms heightened expectations into politically relevant demands. Moreover, the contemporary preference in the area for shaping political purpose in socialist terminology and perspective casts government in the role of initiator, chief source of creative energy, and principal productive agency. In the Soviet Union, China, and North Vietnam, socialist ideology lays greater weight upon the duties of socialist man than upon his rights; and production, not consumption, is stressed. But in Southern Asia, the key role assigned to government means that the central government is expected to do what in other societies is done locally or privately, if at all.[5]

In consequence of these non-demographic developments, demand for government services and responsibilities is growing rapidly, quite apart from the increased burdens imposed by demographic change. At the same time, standards of performance are becoming more exigent. What would have been considered adequate service fifteen years ago is not likely to be considered good enough today. As Ted Gurr has pointed out, not unlike de Toqueville before him, what is politically relevant is the sense of *relative* (rather than *actual*) deprivation—deprivation relative to one's past, to one's expectations and ideas of what one deserves.[6]

Growing demands on bureaucracy are not necessarily to be deplored. Bureaucracies are notoriously prone to lethargy; the more detached and insulated a bureaucracy is from popular pressures, the less responsive it may become to real needs. Perhaps only intensified demands, experienced directly by the bureaucracy through political leaders or claimant social and political interest groups, will lead to better service for more people. Yet demands can become too intense; impatience can become too severe. Pressures for performance can lead to bureaucratic overload, compounding the difficulties of providing minimum services.

There is a circularity, not to say insatiability, about heightened expectations and increased demands. Unmobilized peasants make few demands on their government; they rightly expect little and take it for granted that government does not want to or cannot do anything for them. Once a government, such as Malaysia's or Ceylon's, shows some desire to improve peasant conditions and some capability to effect constructive change, expectations rise. And if a competitive political process enlarges expectations further, past accomplishment and future promise together perpetuate a rising level of demands. Accordingly, expectations, past demands, government performance, and political process combine to augment current demands well beyond minimum subsistence needs.

Growing Unemployment. Misery according to the Malthusian formula arises from the pressure of population growth on a food supply that is increasing at a slower rate. In the post-subsistence societies of Southern Asia the correspondingly dismal formula might be the unfavorable shift in the ratio of school leavers to jobs. While accurate statistical representation is difficult, since exact and comparable definitions of unemployment and underemployment for different countries and cultures simply do not exist, the growing magnitude of the problem is unarguable.

Although Java has long been a stark example of the excessive pressure of population on limited land with its attendant turmoil and miseries, most of the rest of Southeast Asia constitutes a food surplus area. And now other parts of the Southern Asian region have been given a perceptible, if transitory, relief from the pressure of people on food supply by the early fruits of the Green Revolution. It buys some time. But the simple advance of food production, or of its modern surrogate, Gross National Product, ahead of population growth does not suffice in a mobilizing polity where an urbanizing population transforms the disguised unemployment of the countryside into a manifest concern of the city. This problem is magnified by the increase in the size of youth cohorts coming onto the job market each year. The problem is multiplied once more by the increasing proportion of those in these large cohorts who claim some degree of higher education. As the paper dealing with Ceylon shows, in some countries the more education a person has, at least through high school, the more likely he is to be unemployed.

Educational credentials are translated into job claims based on a misreading of the career lines of a previous generation whose members participated in the independence dividend. In those days young nationalists took over the commanding political posts, and over several years the products of the expanded educational system were funneled into an enlarging civil service establishment. Old hopes were indulged, giving rise to new expectations. While it was relatively easy to expand the educational system, the capital investment and administrative costs of creating a corresponding array of appropriate jobs for the new graduates were more than the overstrained economies of most new states could bear. Small wonder then that those who came late to the table should feel relatively deprived.

A key factor in the development of relative deprivation is the reference group to which the subject group compares its standing. Since the demand for appropriate employment is a largely psychic phenomenon, it is more malleable as well as more inflatable than the need for food. Career expectations may be measured on a scale with an escalating zero point, as in the booming economies of Singapore or Malaysia. They may also be reduced by the reality of long-term job stagnation as in Burma during the last decade.

Intensified Competition and Conflict. These political trends are likely to compound a fourth tendency: intensified competition and group conflict. This is not to suggest that political competition was not already severe among groups that sought to improve their relative position through more traditional political processes. Inter-familial or factional politics were often very bitter in aristocratic or oligarchic systems. What is likely to change, however, are the scope and issues of competition and the size and number of the groups involved. In most polities in the area, with the possible exception of Thailand, political competition is no longer a game among a few well-placed elites but now engages much larger and more diverse groups. Rising levels of demand in situations of scarcity will intensify competition among political factions and social groups. Depending on whether there are political parties, contention may be shaped and channeled through party structures, or may more generally pervade the society.

Weiner shows how migrations impelled by economic development in India intensify group conflicts, provoking defensive political measures to impede or channel population movements. The migration to cities and the growth of urban populations from natural increase intensify simple space pressures, and these, in turn, press ethnic neighbors in upon each other. Scarcity of educational, health, and other services and threats to personal safety may aggravate group conflict, as Laquian's discussion of growing urban tensions illustrates.

Rapid population growth in rural areas where agricultural technology does not change will induce population movements. Burki argues that in the case of Pakistan it was actually economic growth that induced out-migration from the countryside. Whitney and Jones note that demographic change is forcing some of Thailand's mountain people to leave the valleys and move toward the plains, while plainsmen, increasingly crowded in their home territory, are penetrating the hills. As these peoples of different cultural, ethnic, and linguistic backgrounds now interpenetrate each other's territory, hostilities grow sharply.

The distribution of status-bearing jobs or real income often changes when economies modernize or grow. In consequence certain ethnic communities may find traditionally low-status groups rising well above them in income, political power, and social standing. Such disruptions of traditional patterns in ethnic- and status-conscious societies will be resisted or certainly resented, and political or more direct efforts to reverse the consequences can be expected. On the other hand, any conscious constraint of economic growth in the face of such dynamic forces as population growth, political mobilization, and larger demands will lead to further intensified stresses.

In the countryside, traditional modes of settling disputes between groups have sometimes been brought to bear by the allocation of village land or other traditional rural assets. Deteriorating man/land ratios resulting from rapid population growth in rural areas and changing land values resulting from new technologies tend to make traditional ways of settling conflicts unworkable. More formal legal or administrative methods, in many cases derived from foreign practices, are often unsatisfactory.[7]

Generational differences may produce sharp contention. The "independence generation" achieved its goal of breaking away from political dependence on the metropole. Emmerson's paper provides hard data to demonstrate that successor generations take that accomplishment for granted and press new challenges that the independence generation could not be expected to take very seriously. The rapid expansion of education separates rural and urban youth from their illiterate peasant and laboring parents. In the end children turn against parents who insisted on an education that was all too often futile and against schools and universities no longer able to care about the growth of individual students. The symptoms of these and related difficulties are only too evident in the ethnic violence of recent years in urban centers in Malaysia and the Philippines, analyzed by Laquian, and the generational and revolutionary violence in rural Ceylon, discussed by Jayewardene and Wriggins.

These and other unresolved conflicts usually precipitate new levels of individual, inter-family, or inter-class strife, often compounded by religious, communal, or ethnic group violence.[8]

Conditioning Circumstances

The complex of challenges thrown up by these demographic and political trends is conditioned by a variety of factors. The three most important conditioning circumstances in the Southern Asian context are probably the pattern of ethnic or group identifications, the general adaptive capacity of individuals and institutions within the particular societies, and the level of resources available.

Societies in Southern Asia are notably plural in composition with starkly particularistic identifications following ethnic, religious, linguistic, and regional fault lines. The sharpness of the different cleavages and the way in which some cleavages crosscut each other while others cumulate vary from the relatively simple two-part pluralism of Malaysia and post-independence Pakistan to the multi-layered fragmentation of India; from the fluidity of Thailand, where both the peripheral hill tribes and the urban Chinese are assimilated to the dominant majority culture, to the highly structured diversity of Indonesia. The pattern of pluralism is not a social constant since both the salience and the permeability of particular cleavages change under modernization pressures. Yet the root permanency of particular structures is indeed impressive, as with the transformed role of caste in India, the resurgence of ethnolinguistic politics in Ceylon, and the continuing centrality of Javanese political culture in Indonesia.

The simple phenomenon of differential population growth rates is translated into changing political potentials, with all the hopes and fears that they imply. Urbanization, which has often been hailed as a socio-cultural homogenizing force, is itself often channeled through these historically persistent identifications which structure the newcomer's introduction to urban life while at the same time shaping the forms of political mobilization and the scope and intensity of demands. The vitality of the youth cohort as an analytical category, or as a social force in its own right, depends in large part on the relative salience of several of the established ethnic, linguistic, or regional social segments.

Akin to the question of changing group identifications is the general capacity to adapt to changed circumstances by defining new roles, creating new institutions, and evolving new values. This ability varies extensively across the social groups of Southern Asia. An example of such variation which is close to the traditional concerns of students of population is the "demographic transition," or the fall in fertility rates following a fall in mortality rates, a causal sequence mediated by a host of social variables which required a span of some 150 years in Europe and over a century in Japan. It seems to have come into play more rapidly in the semi-Sinitic cultures of Taiwan, Singapore, and Malaysia, and beginnings may already be appearing in Thailand and Ceylon. The prospect elsewhere in the region is distant or uncertain. Responsiveness to the opportunities presented by urbanization and other migrations is strikingly differentiated within India itself, appearing particularly among the Marathas, Sikhs, Marwaris, and Tamils.

The easy availability of resources and the level of economic activity also affect the intensity of these challenges. Many countries and regions face persistent poverty, in large part simply because they are poor in resources. Often the key resource is arable land, as in Java. Here the interaction between conditioning factors becomes patent. Some countries such as Burma find themselves in straitened circumstances even with a favorable man/land ratio because of poor adaptive capacities, whereas Singapore presents the opposite picture. Overall, it cannot be denied that a comfortable economic surplus lubricates the friction of group conflict and can act as a cushion for policy mistakes.

Coping with Heavier Loads

Demographic changes and political trends intensify pressures on regimes and complicate the tasks of governance. Conditioning circumstances further complicate or ease these tasks. A regime's ability to deal with these difficulties depends on certain vital capabilities—the quality of leadership, administrative skill, and economic effectiveness.

The Quality of Political Leadership. It is not easy to identify those qualities which make for effective leadership without using clichés. Yet participants in public affairs or close observers know that the quality of political leadership makes an important—and sometimes critical—difference to the fortunes of a polity and to its ability to meet such challenges as population change and political trends impose.

Leaders who are self-indulgent, indecisive, venal, and shortsighted are easy to distinguish from those who are dedicated, decisive, and relatively free from the taint of corruption and whose actions are directed by a conception of how the future should be shaped.

Leadership in Southern Asia requires better-than-average qualities. To inspire loyalty and evoke support where religious, ethnic, linguistic, and social differences are so marked calls for political virtuosity of a high order. When resources are scarce, goals must be projected that will shape the direction of public policy and evoke effort without inflating popular demands unduly.

Typically, state structures lack authority and particularistic interests assiduously defend their privileges where there is political and administrative weakness, corruption, and ineptitude. By their powers of persuasion or of command, leaders seek to shape the direction of bureaucratic action. The ruler must inspire, cajole, or badger subordinates to do what he wants, while undermining the sense of legitimacy of entrenched opponents.

Administrative Capability. The ability of an elite to cope with growing requirements for minimum maintainence and additional demands will be fundamentally affected by the state's managerial capacity. Particularly where national political institutions such as political parties and legislatures lack legitimacy and organizational coherence, national bureaucracies may be all the more crucial to the effective functioning of the state.[9]

The bureaucracy may be the main armature that holds the polity together in time of crisis. It helps to sustain public order and constrains overt conflict. It is the framework for essential services—the agency of public safety, the main source of public health and medical care, of transportation and communications, and of training for the young. It becomes the instrument for implementing the ruler's policies as far beyond the capital as it can penetrate. Through taxes it acquires resources for most government programs. It must be able adroitly to change the sources of tax income as new sectors of the economy prosper and others are hard hit. It must discriminate between the goal of maximizing tax returns in the short run or prompting optimum development in the longer run, goals which may be incompatible. Ideally, the bureaucracy should be able to gather and analyze the best data available and project alternative futures if current social, economic, and political trends are left to play themselves out in the absence of official action. It should provide political leaders with proposals on alternative courses of government action designed to influence the future. It must distinguish between actions to be undertaken directly by government agencies and by those nongovernmental groups and organizations susceptible to encouragement by government incentives. Equally difficult, it must direct the activities of numerous and all-too-human public servants so that policies desired by political leaders can be implented in a timely and publicly acceptable way.

Typically, bureaucracies in Southern Asia are more than instruments for implementing government policy. They also provide principal career goals for educated youth and for their parents. Assured entry into the source of secure and high-status positions and prompt promotions become principal stakes in political contention. Disputes over language policy may in reality be over who shall have automatic advantage in public service examinations. In order to promote public peace and loyalty to government, positions must be apportioned to represent the multiple diversity of Southern Asian plural societies. Undue responsiveness to such social diversity can render bureaucracies incompetent, but insufficient attention to the representational function of bureaucratic job opportunities can bring national disintegration, as with the recent secession of Bangladesh.

Marshaling available resources to enhance economic productivity requires capable administration; this in turn can improve the chances of meeting minimum maintenance requirements. The administration itself can help to resolve individual and group conflicts. By providing medical attention and making family planning and abortion facilities available, an efficient administration can contribute directly to slowing the pace of population growth.

Economic Effectiveness. A country's resource base, economic effectiveness, and pattern of economic distribution underlie its ability to provide minimum maintenance requirements to a growing and increasingly exigent population. This is a question of the level of economic activity, its rate of growth, and how its fruits are distributed. It is obvious that the more rapidly an economy grows, the greater its chance of keeping up with or exceeding the rate of population growth. It also seems to be true for a number of countries in the area that a low current level of economic activity foredooms them to a laggard rate of future growth.

Where natural resources are relatively plentiful, where rapid industrialization or intensification of agriculture is creating new jobs in abundance and producing what people need, population problems will not be acute. Where foreign exchange earnings are readily available through the presence of exploitable primary resources or the production of high-demand crops or processed industrial goods, imports can ease local shortages. Where the populace turns its skills and energies in new directions in response to opportunities and does not yet set high consumption demands in return, larger numbers can be accommodated, new groups can press forward, and new demands can be met without depriving others. Plenty and ingenuity ease the task of answering demands and maintaining domestic peace, just as scarcity and lack of imagination make it more difficult.

Such fortunate conditions are rare. Far more common is the case of crowded land, where harsh limits to agricultural expansion are set by water scarcity, where there are few resources as yet untapped, where foreign markets no longer absorb formerly coveted tropical products, and where a higher level of managerial capability and skilled effort is required to generate resources to meet the needs of more people.

Economic development policies designed to stress labor-intensive activities call for approaches radically different from those of Western experience. Technological innovation must be tailored to the particular needs of diverse economies. This is not the place to elaborate the requisites for providing remunerative and productive work opportunities for a growing population in capital-poor countries. It is clear, however, that development policies differ in their ability to provide jobs to a rapidly growing population. Perhaps in Java and in Bangladesh, the limits of labor-intensive opportunities are being more nearly reached than elsewhere in Southern Asia.[10]

The approach to development policy, quite as much as demographic growth, will determine when and if such a limit will be reached in any particular instance. Hong Kong and Singapore show that rapid increases in population can be handled under densely crowded conditions, with no local natural resources. It requires an energetic and hard-working people, dynamic economic entrepreneurship and some capital, and a government capable of clear decisions and able to discriminate between what it should do itself and what it can encourage private citizens and foreigners to do. Larger agricultural surpluses produced in certain areas of India, Thailand, and Ceylon demonstrate what can be done in rural areas with policies appropriate to local natural, social, and economic circumstances. Far more effort, policy care, and organizational support will be required, however, where populations are becoming increasingly dense and resources are limited. If exponential population growth persists, the urban and rural successes so far achieved may prove to be only temporary.

Here the international economic system must be brought into consideration. Since the end of the Korean War boom in 1952, the terms of trade have been generally working against primary producers in Southern Asia.[11] Inflation in developed countries has raised the prices of the industrial products that primary producers must purchase abroad, while lessened worldwide demand for tropical products together with increased competition among producers has meant declining earnings for larger amounts of exports, and calls for greater export efforts to acquire equivalent imports. Yet, typically, import requirements have been rising as populations expand and economies become more complex. Accordingly, more regional resources have had to be directed toward obtaining indispensable imports, leaving that much less for coping with the effects of rapid population growth and providing economic development investment. To a significant degree, therefore, the effects of the world economic system as it presently operates intensify the population problem in Southern Asia.

The quality and emphasis of the educational system are important variables, as a number of the papers in this volume bring out. Where the educational system grows in phase with expanding job opportunities and provides to the many the skills the economy needs today rather than the white-collar training the colonial regime provided for the few in the past, job frustration will be less severe. Schools and universities, by promoting integrative values that lead to mutual collaboration among communities, regions, and generations rather than parochial, exclusive identifications, can encourage common endeavor and reduce group conflict, thereby easing the pressures of demographic change. More often, however, at present they compound the difficulties.

Problems of Prediction and Policy-Making

We stated at the outset that population changes and political trends now under way would confront policy-makers in Southern Asia with a number of major challenges. These are often framed as implicit goals such as a more humane quality to public life; an acceptable, if not improving, level of material well-being; the civic management of conflict; and, for the public decision-makers themselves, at least, political survival. The analysis we have presented of the probable complex of challenges by no means prescribes appropriate policy responses. Any such prescription would require an explicit specification and ranking of goals, which is beyond the scope of the present effort. It would also require a calculation of the probable consequences of pursuing alternative strategies toward these goals, which is beyond the capacity of our present knowledge of both population trends and the interaction of these trends with political developments. We can, however, at this point delineate the main limitations on our capacity for prediction and consequently for prescription.

The first caution to the construction of generalized demographic predictions for Southern Asia as a whole, brought out by our demographer participants, is the great variety among the national units of the region—variety in population size, density, rate of growth, and direction of change in the rate of growth. The population dynamics of a polity the size and diversity of India are bound to differ in a number of ways from those of a Singapore with its 3,500 people per square kilometer or a Laos where a total of about 3 million are spread out at an average of

12 to the square kilometer. While the rate of population growth for the region stands below that for Latin America, a few Southeast Asian countries matched the South American average of 3 percent during the 1960s. This group difference between regions should not obscure differences within Southern Asia, ranging from Nepal's low estimated rate of growth of 1.8 percent a year to the Philippines' explosive 3.5 percent. What is even more important for understanding the complexity of the region's future is the difference between what appear to be declining real rates of growth in Ceylon and in three of the more heavily Chinese countries of the area—Singapore, West Malaysia, and Thailand—and the generally rising rates of the other countries.

A second caution the demographers voiced concerning attempts to project demographic patterns into the future arises from the character of population data in that part of the world. Despite the apparent reliability of data in international compilations, there are large areas of inaccuracy. The last complete census of Burma, for example, was taken in 1931. Current figures are projections from that base adjusted by means of incomplete remains of the 1941 census and a partial census taken in the early 1950s. The full 1963 census on Ceylon is not yet available although a report on a 10 percent sample has been issued. In our discussions, one specialist estimated that for a number of major countries encompassing over half the population of the region we have no reliable estimates of life expectancy, which may range from 35 to 50 years even though official sources specify a single year with apparent confidence.

Numerous refinements that would endow the bare data with heightened analytical potential are just not available. For instance, we know that cities are expanding in population, the rate at which they are expanding, and to what extent migration rather than natural increase is contributing to that expansion. But we know little about who the migrants are—for example, what proportion in Bangkok are Thai and what proportion Chinese. The Burki paper looks at this problem in some detail in

Pakistan. Then there are questions of the inferences that can be made from partial data to provide full-fledged descriptions. Does the notch between 11 and 20 in the age distribution of the 1961 Indonesian census indicate a scarcity of births in the 1940s and a bulge of births in the 1950s coming up through the population pyramid in subsequent years? Or is this pattern an artifact of census-taking procedures? The Keyfitz paper examines this matter.

To raise such questions is not to challenge all demographic projections. Some are by their nature more secure than others. Indeed, knowing how many children under 10 there are today in a particular country provides only a rough basis for estimating how many children under 10 there will be ten years from now. But with this knowledge we can be fairly sure, barring major catastrophes, of the number of 10–19-year-olds at the end of the decade, and this older age group may be more important than their juniors for understanding the politics of that time. Then again, the rough estimates of the baby crop over the next ten years will be more accurate than extrapolations over the next twenty or to the year 2000 (since error in this area grows like compound interest). Such short-run projections are of considerable value. Not only is ten years a reasonable horizon for prediction; it may also exhaust the span of attention for planning purposes that we can expect of political leadership in the developing world. For such gross population characteristics as total size, a longer time horizon is feasible since current changes in fertility rates often will not have a substantial effect for a reproductive generation, for some twenty to thirty years at least.[12]

The third problem is the very tangled one of how to relate demographic and political factors to each other. It is usually assumed that the population change is cause and politics consequence, enabling one to follow that careful strategy of approaching the relatively unknown by way of the relatively known. By comparison with political materials, demographic data appear solid, grounded in careful statistical evidence. Noses have been counted, classifications by sex, age, location, and other objective characteristics have been made, and trend lines charted. The analytical question then seems to be how to make the causal leap from changing fertility rates, shifting age cohorts, and the rate and direction of population flows to such ambiguous variables as intergroup competition, public demands, and administrative overload.

A second look suggests the importance of a sharpened definition of some of the intervening variables. Public demands for education are a joint function of the size of the school-aged population, the level of aspiration and expectations, and how these are organized to bring political pressures to bear. How can we find some measure of the size and political import of that level of expectaions in specific instances? And how can we predict more accurately effective political demands resulting from such a level of expectations?

The impact of intercultural migration on conflict over the allocation of jobs or other benefits is mediated by the character of group identifications and the availability of conflict-resolving institutions. How can these difficulties be more accurately foreseen? How can both migrants and "host" populations be better prepared for dealing with the inevitable frictions that will develop?

The size of the youth cohorts now coming forward is already determined. But their effects upon types of political participation and the demands they will make on the political system are in part a function of how they identify themselves. Will they pass through the usual socialization stages and adopt the locally conventional roles, or will they come to constitute a unique political generation that seeks to remake the rules of the political game? Or, more to the point, what combination of these possibilities will evolve? How can one assess such developments? How does the type of education young people obtain affect their aspirations and identifications? To what extent will economic stringency or affluence, and expectations about appropriate and remunerative opportunities, make a substantial difference to such patterns of identification? How can educational institutions, public service opportunities, and other institutional devices provide greater individual satisfaction without adding unmanageable burdens to fragile political and administrative institutions?

The quantity and quality of services that a public bureaucracy can deliver can be estimated only roughly from knowledge of the changing ratio of dependent to productive population groups. More important is the performance of the economy and the character of the educational system.

Perhaps the weightiest factor, if one can get a firm grasp of it, is the quality of political leadership. Yet political leaders have their own time and success imperatives; they are not likely to give high priority to policies designed to have a major impact on population growth rates. If the population implications of major policies are to be taken into account or explicit population programs are to be implemented, political leaders must be enlisted to shape and carry out their policies in the light of longer-run demographic calculations. But the primary goal of most leaders, on their own and their followers' behalf, may well be to stay in power.[13] And that often requires acute concern with very short-run, immediate tactics and activities. Few are likely to risk their present political position for the sake of long-run demographic considerations.

Under what circumstances will the short-run political survival of leaders be compatible with active population policies? Under what circumstances are they likely to be most incompatible? And if there is the political "will" to undertake policies to discourage population growth or manage migration, is there the administrative capacity and the political power to carry them out? Can population flows be controlled by existing types of regimes? How in fact can family size be influenced by different regimes with different administrative capabilities?

Another look at the array of relationships suggests certain reverse flows of causation which have influenced demographic characteristics. There is already evidence that Malaysia's relative success in promoting family planning depends significantly upon the government's general capacity to formulate and implement policies, as compared with the Philippines, where the movement from policy to program execution is much more difficult.[14]

The rate of rural-to-urban migration will be affected by the relative opportunities perceived in each environment, as the Goldstein and Burki papers bring out. This in turn will result in part from the direction of investment, the distribution of administrative and government authority and services, and the perceived liveliness of big city life. It can also be argued that centralizing an administration in a capital city conduces to urbanization; administratively less centralized polities tend to have slower rates of migration to the capital, as a comparison of India and Thailand, to take two examples, suggests. At what points can political choice and administrative action cut into these relationships?

Some connections turn into mutually re-enforcing tendencies, as when improved and extended public medical services induce or sustain a high rate of population growth, which in itself increases the demand for medical and other government services, as the Ceylon case illustrates so well.

The variety of possible interactions between political and population factors is sufficient to perplex any political leader attempting to comprehend the full range of challenges awaiting him and his people in the next decade. Yet, if these interactions are not better understood, if measures are not taken to affect the rate of population growth, to deal with its consequences, and to cope with other parallel and aggravating political tendencies, the peoples of Southern Asia will be beset by intensifying mutual antagonisms. Nearly overwhelmed by the multiplicity of heavier burdens, administrations will be less and less able to provide the maintenance and other services demanded by rapidly growing and increasingly claimant peoples. Political leaders will lose even more of their ability to shape events. Any institutions that may be developing a capacity to cope with these trends by reshaping practices and changing perceptions may nevertheless collapse as the pressures of sheer numbers, migration, ethnic and regional splits, and changing age structures, with their attendant demands, intensify.

It is no doubt naive to expect that even the most sophisticated interdisciplinary research will lead to precise and simple answers to these acutely human problems. The insight of the gifted political practitioner or party head; the determination of the local social, religious, family or clan leader; the innovative bent of the creative entrepreneur, the labor organizer, the well-trained student or modern publicist; and the managerial capacity of the administrator—all will be needed to carry the polities of Southern Asia through the complicated decades ahead.

But it is not too much to hope that concerted, patient, and energetic multi-disciplinary exploration of these interconnections will help illuminate what can be done. No one Western discipline can encompass the relevant pattern of interaction. That is why in this volume, which we consider a preliminary attack on a multifaceted problem, we bring together demographers, political scientists, sociologists, an anthropologist, and a general administrator.

In this introductory chapter we have signaled what we consider to be the more important interactions between demographic and political phenomena. The subsequent chapters carry forward these introductory themes and develop others from a number of disciplinary and geographical perspectives.

Part one
The Basic Demography

Chapter 2

Population Change and Development in Southern Asia: An Overview * *Vincent Heath Whitney and Gavin W. Jones*

EDITORS' NOTE: This paper provides basic data on the demographic dynamics of the area as a whole. It identifies the main trends in mortality, fertility, and migration, stressing the major changes of the past several decades, and considers probable future magnitudes. The authors assess the costs to the economy of "dependency" deriving from the large proportion of the population now under 20 and note how the urbanizing trend compounds the demands which this expanding segment of the population places upon public services. The paper concludes that growth rates are likely to remain high in most countries during the next decades. Where "modernization" has gone farthest, declines in population growth can be expected. However, in all countries, the labor force is growing at an unprecedented rate, and massive numbers of individuals must somehow be absorbed at a time when international migration is foreclosed and economic opportunities for export of locally produced products appear to be limited.

The authors emphasize the need for alternative patterns of economic and social development more appropriate to the Asian setting than the European- or American-type mass consumption society. Their demographic analysis provides data and perspectives central to the issues handled in subsequent chapters in this volume.

Some Perspectives on the Population Problem

The major trends of population growth in the world since the inception of the Industrial Revolution are well known. It is not necessary here to repeat the statistics—ranging from highly

* In this and chapter 3, generalizations for the region as a whole taken from United Nations tables include data drawn from Iran and Afghanistan in addition to the countries we have designated as "Southern Asia." (Eds. footnote)

accurate to imaginative—for the three components of population change: births, deaths, and migrations. Population growth in recent decades has come to the fore as one of the critical problems facing the world and demanding a solution within a limited time frame. There are, of course, those who see simple solutions in the Green Revolution or a new dam or even in space stations. Technological innovations may indeed offer breathing space in the short run but, so rapid is population advance at current rates and so strong its cumulative effect even at low rates of increase, that all such solutions are temporary.

Over the last two centuries, the balance between births and deaths has been drastically altered. The event of death has been extensively controlled and deferred. The event of birth remains uncontrolled or only partially controlled in large areas of the world. This imbalance between fertility and mortality violates the fundamental ecological tendency toward equilibrium. Few demographers would quarrel with the conclusion that the present disequilibrium must be resolved in one of two ways: by a decline in births or by an increase in deaths. The real question is how long the temporary imbalance can be maintained by the input of increased resources made possible by scientific discoveries and technological adaptations. Furthermore, is there enough time to achieve the more acceptable solution of low fertility and low mortality rather than the forced return to the prevailing situation of the past—the combination of high fertility with high mortality?

All solutions involving imbalance are temporary. But is "temporary" to be measured in years, decades, centuries, or millennia? It will depend on innovations that are not yet accomplishments, in many instances not yet even perceived. Optimism, then, is a matter of faith and does not rest on available evidence. It is difficult enough to assess the trends and consequences of population phenomena in the short run, even in the next decade. For many areas population statistics are defective or simply do not exist, despite recent notable gains in the quantity and quality of such data. Information gaps persist even for countries with generally good population statistics. Moreover, in looking ahead, we cannot depend on the projection of past trends since this is but a mathematical exercise that assumes the continuation of an existing direction and rate of change. Finally, it cannot be overemphasized that the complex interdependencies between population factors and other social, economic, and political variables make accurate prediction of population changes even more complicated.

Population trends for the world as a whole, or for the less developed nations in their entirety, or for large areas like Asia, which includes countries as different as Pakistan, Thailand, and the Philippines, are of limited use in describing population change and its impact on economic and social trends in specific countries. The effects of population trends will vary with the particular conditions that characterize a given area, at a particular period. This is equally true of subregions within a large and heterogeneous nation like India. Thus, attempts to describe recent population changes in Maharashtra State and predict the course of events there from a knowledge of trends for the entire country could produce inadequate or misleading results. In the same way attempts to describe the fertility attitudes and behavior of a nation's women on the basis of studies of women from particular classes, age groups, or places of residence can only produce errors. Only by rare chance will an individual case coincide with averages derived from a summation of such cases. Population changes and their effects in Indonesia or in West Java, for example, are best understood not by generalizing from data for Asia or Southeast Asia, but by studying Indonesia or West Java itself.

Nevertheless, the broad subject of this paper makes it necessary to generalize and therefore to keep in mind that each area mentioned will to some degree exhibit deviations from the average levels or rates or trends for the larger region of which it is a part. The mean density of population in Southeast Asia, for example, was 64 persons per square kilometer in 1969, but the range was from 12 in Laos to 134 in North Vietnam.[1]

Recent Population Growth. The rate of growth of the world's population in 1970 was estimated at 2.1 percent annually. This is the highest rate ever recorded in the long upward curve of growth that has accompanied the Industrial Revolution. Before that time population growth was ordinarily well under one-half of one percent a year.

When the world today is divided roughly into developed and less developed regions, a sharp and consistent difference in rates of population increase appears. In the developed countries annual average rates of growth in the period 1963–69 ranged from −0.1 to 2.0. By contrast, for the same period in the less developed nations they ranged from a low of around 2.0 to a high of about 3.6.[2]

Nearly all of the countries in Latin America, Africa, and Asia are classified as "less developed." In Asia only Japan and Israel, at opposite geographical extremes, are exceptions. All the countries of South Asia and Southeast Asia [3] except Nepal showed rates of population growth of 2 percent or higher annually as recently as 1963–69, as shown in Table 2.1. The growth rate in several countries reached or exceeded 3.0 percent in this period. It was 3.0 in Iran; 3.1 in Malaysia, Thailand, and North Vietnam; 3.5 in the Philippines; and 3.6 in Brunei. At a rate of 2 percent, population will double in thirty-five years, at 3 percent in twenty-three years, and at 3.5 percent in twenty years. A continuation of present rates would mean that the number of people in the Philippines would jump from some 37 million in 1969 to 74 million by 1989. India's 1969 population of 537 million would exceed one billion before the end of this century.[4]

Recent Mortality Trends. Rapid population growth is not a consequence of high fertility alone. Rather, it reflects the combination of high fertility and low mortality. In many cities and some larger areas it also results from a new balance of inmigration. Low mortality was a gradual achievement in the West, tak-

Table 2.1 Rates of Population Growth for Countries of South Asia and Southeast Asia, 1953–60 and 1963–69

Region and Country	*Annual Rate of Population Increase*	
	1953–60	*1963–69*
South Asia		
Afghanistan	n.d.	2.1 [1]
Ceylon	2.7	2.4 [1]
India	1.9 [1]	2.5 [1]
Iran	2.1 [1]	3.0 [1]
Nepal	1.6	1.8 [1]
Pakistan	1.9	2.1 [1]
Southeast Asia		
Burma	1.0 [1]	2.2 [1]
Cambodia	n.d.	2.2 [1]
Indonesia	2.2 [1]	2.5 [1]
Laos	3.2 [1]	2.4 [1]
Malaya, Federation of	3.0	n.d.
Malaysia (East)	n.d.	3.3 [1]
Malaysia (West)	n.d.	2.8
Philippines	3.2 [1]	3.5 [1]
Singapore	n.d.	2.1
Thailand	4.3 [1]	3.1 [1]
North Vietnam	−0.2 [1]	3.1 [1]
South Vietnam	5.4 [1]	2.6 [1]

Source: Demographic Yearbook, 1961 and *1969* (New York: United Nations, 1961 and 1970), Tables 1 and 2 respectively.
[1] Estimate identified by the United Nations as "of questionable reliability."

ing a century or two and based on resources provided by development and modernization. By contrast, in Latin America, Africa, and Asia death rates as low as, or lower than, those in Europe and advanced countries elsewhere have occurred in decades rather than centuries.

The most pronounced gains have been made since the mid-1940s, with several Asian countries cutting their death rates by half or more. Ceylon is often cited for having reduced mortality in a single year by an amount that in Scandinavia took a hundred years. As in the West, such gains reflect sharply increased control over communicable diseases. This has been made possible by the borrowing of public health and medical technology,

Table 2.2 Death Rates for South Asia, Southeast Asia, and Other Selected Countries, c. 1960 and c. 1970

Region and Country	*Crude Death Rate*	
	c. 1960	*c. 1970*
Southeast Asia		
Brunei	10.9 (1960)	6.4 (1968)
Burma	35.0 (1955)	25.0
Cambodia	41.4 (1959)	25.0
Indonesia	20.0 (1954)	21.0
Laos	n.d.	22.0
Malaysia (East)	n.d.	5.0 (1969)
Malaysia (West)	9.5 (1960)	8.0
Philippines	n.d.	12.0–16.0
Singapore	5.9 (1961)	5.0
Thailand	20.0 (1956)	10.0–15.0
South Vietnam	n.d.	12.0–15.0
South Asia		
Ceylon	n.d.	8.0
India	19.2 (1958)	15.0–20.0
Iran	25.0 (1959)	19.0
Nepal	20.8 (1961)	n.d.
Pakistan	n.d.	15.0–20.0
Other Asia		
Israel [1]	5.7 (1961)	6.8 (1969)
Japan	7.4 (1961)	7.0
Oceania		
Australia	8.5 (1961)	9.0
New Zealand	9.0 (1961)	9.0
Europe		
France	11.0 (1961)	11.0
Italy	9.4 (1961)	10.0
Netherlands	7.6 (1961)	10.0
Sweden	9.8 (1961)	10.0
United Kingdom	12.0 (1961)	12.0
West Germany	10.9 (1961)	11.0
North America		
Canada	7.7 (1961)	7.0
United States	9.3 (1961)	10.0
USSR	7.1 (1960)	8.0

Source: Statistics for c. 1960 are from *Demographic Yearbook, 1961* (New York: United Nations, 1961), Table 3, pp. 121–25. Statistics for c. 1970 are from Dorothy Nortman, "Population and Family Planning Programs: A Fact-

available at low cost and often assisted by foreign funds. The current age structure of these populations, with a high proportion of young persons,[5] has contributed further to reducing death rates to as low as 5–8 per thousand annually in individual countries (Table 2.2). Most of these countries in South and Southeast Asia are currently characterized by death rates that are low to moderately low, reflecting in particular recent reductions in deaths among infants and children and a consequent substantial increase in the number of young adults.[6] What is open to question is whether such low levels of mortality can be maintained over any long period without either fairly sizable declines in fertility or increases in economic productivity or both, such as have occurred in the West.

There are pronounced differences in death rates at successive ages and also between males and females. Since significant variations in age and sex composition occur from area to area, crude death rates are a less reliable index of mortality conditions than is life expectancy. On average a baby may now expect to survive to approximately 50 years in both South and Southeast Asia. The highest expectancies are 63 years in Ceylon and 68 years in Singapore. The only ones reported as below 45 years are the 37.5 in Afghanistan and Portuguese Timor.[7] If continuing gains in life expectancy are made, the population at age 45 and over will gradually increase to proportions more in line with those in the developed countries. Presumably this will focus increasing attention on problems of the elderly, including the provision of services and perhaps the establishment of some form of social security for older persons beyond normal working years.[8]

Although mortality rates have dropped precipitously in many

---

book," *Reports on Population/Family Planning: 1971–72* (June 1971), Table 4, pp. 5–13, published by the Population Council, and with rates based on United Nations, *Population and Vital Statistics Report for January 1, 1970,* or on more recent country data—except that the source is the *Demographic Yearbook, 1969,* Table 3, where the rate is followed by a specific year.

[1] Jewish population only.

Asian nations, it is unlikely that morbidity rates have fallen as rapidly. Populations are living, but are they experiencing better health? Unfortunately, studies of health conditions among these populations have been sporadic and limited in scope. What evidence there is suggests that favorable factors, such as the existence of a widespread network of health stations, coupled with free or low-cost services, as in Ceylon, are far outweighed by the morbidity endemic to populations living under conditions of extreme poverty and without adequate food or medical care. In short, the prevention of death should not automatically be equated with improved health conditions.[9] What has occurred is that famine has been largely ended, communicable disease brought under control, and public health conditions improved to the extent that lives are maintained even in the face of continuing illness.

Recent Fertility Trends. The level of births in the less developed countries, both in Asia and other continents, is high compared with the more developed nations. In the latter, crude birth rates are consistently below 30 per thousand and usually between 15 and 25. The rates for the less developed countries generally exceed 30 per thousand, ranging between 35 and 50 for the most part.[10] Throughout South Asia births probably range even now from 43 to more than 50 per thousand each year except in Ceylon where the figure is 32. India has a rate in excess of 40 and possibly as high as 50.[11] Ceylon's present comparatively low fertility is related to late marriage. Average age at marriage for both men and women is the highest in Asia and thus invites comparisons with Ireland's position in Europe.

The picture in Southeast Asia, too, is one of continuing high fertility. Births appear to number more than 40 per thousand in all areas except West Malaysia, with an estimated 37 per thousand, and Singapore with 22. The crude birth rate for Burma, Cambodia, and Indonesia appears to be around 50, and it is as high or nearly as high in East Malaysia, Laos, the Philippines, and perhaps other countries.[12]

Table 2.3 Birth Rates for South Asia, Southeast Asia, and Other Selected Countries, 1959 and 1969

Region and Country	*Crude Birth Rate*	
	1959	*1969*
South Asia		
Afghanistan	50+ [1]	50+ [1]
Ceylon	37.0	31.8 (1968)
India	44+ [1]	43+ [1]
Iran	48+ [1]	45+ [1]
Nepal	47+ [1]	45+ [1]
Pakistan	50+ [1]	50+ [1]
Southeast Asia		
Brunei	52.5	43.9 (1968)
Burma	45+ [1]	48+ [1]
Cambodia	41.4	48+ [1]
Indonesia	50+ [1]	49+ [1]
Laos	45+ [1]	45+ [1]
Malaysia (East)	50+ [1]	48+ [1]
Malaysia (West)	42.2	37+ [1]
Philippines	50+ [1]	46+ [1]
Singapore	40.3	22.2
Thailand	50+ [1]	43+ [1]
South Vietnam	42+ [1]	40+ [1]
Other Asia		
Israel	26.8	26.1
Japan	17.6	18.3
Oceania		
Australia	22.6	20.0 (1968)
New Zealand	26.5	22.5
Europe		
France	18.3	16.7
Italy	18.3	17.6
Netherlands	21.4	19.2
Sweden	14.1	13.5
United Kingdom	16.9	16.6
West Germany	17.7	15.0
North America		
Canada	27.4	17.6
United States	24.1	17.7

Source: Birth rates not estimated by the authors are taken from the *Demographic Yearbook, 1969* (New York: United Nations, 1970), Table 12, pp. 256–75. Registration data are not considered reliable in the countries of South and Southeast Asia except for Brunei, Ceylon, West Malaysia, and Singapore. Most 1969 rates are provisional.

[1] Estimate by the authors. These are rough and are based upon country data, sample surveys and oral and written reports. They are not definitive but are to approximate the general levels of fertility for the year indicated.

Population Distribution: Migration and Urbanization. In less developed countries around the world migrants are continuously on the march into mushrooming cities, which represent, or appear to represent, opportunities for a better life. Asia is no exception as Table 2.4 indicates. Of the 20 largest metropolitan agglomerations in South and Southeast Asia in 1960, only the three Indian cities of Calcutta, Bombay, and Madras had more than a half million people in 1920. By 1930 the number of large cities had doubled with the addition of Manila, Djakarta, and Bangkok. By 1940 the number had nearly doubled again, reaching 12. By 1950 there were 21 large metropolitan cities [13] and by 1960, 25.[14] The comparable figure for 1970 is uncertain, but is perhaps 31.[15]

Rapid growth in cities of all sizes is a fact of considerable consequence for past and future development in Asia. Growth rates have tended to be particularly high in the larger urban places, which also contain a large share of the total urban population. Especially where the country is small in area, like Cambodia and Thailand, a single large city contains more than half the urban population (defined as population in places of 20,000 or more) and is responsible for over half the urban growth.[16]

The percentage of the total population of South and Southeast Asia estimated to live in urban areas (over 20,000), though rising, is still relatively small. In Southeast Asia the percentages, by year, are:

1920	4 %
1940	7
1960	13
1970	15
2000	27 (projected)

In South Asia the percentages are similar:

1920	5 %
1940	8
1960	13
1970	15
2000	25 (projected) [17]

Table 2.4 Population of Twenty Largest Metropolitan Cities, South Asia and Southeast Asia, 1920–69

Rank		*Estimated Total Population (in thousands)* [1]					
(1960)	*City*	*1920*	*1930*	*1940*	*1950*	*1960*	*1969*
1	Calcutta	1,820	2,055	3,400	4,490	5,810	6,900 [2]
2	Bombay	1,275	1,300	1,660	2,730	4,040	6,250 [2]
3	Djakarta	—	525	1,000	1,750	2,850	3,350 [2]
4	Delhi	—	—	640	1,310	2,270	2,874
5	Manila	—	600	900	1,475	2,150	3,450 [2]
6	Teheran	—	—	625	1,050	1,840	2,850 [2]
7	Karachi	—	—	—	990	1,830	3,060
8	Madras	525	640	765	1,355	1,700	2,700 [2]
9	Saigon-Cholon	—	—	—	1,200	1,400	1,900 [2]
10	Bangkok	—	500	625	750	1,325	2,900 [2]
11	Singapore	—	—	600	820	1,300	2,000 [2]
12	Lahore	—	—	—	650	1,250	1,823
13	Hyderabad	—	—	715	1,055	1,240	1,600 [2]
14	Bangalore	—	—	—	740	1,170	1,600 [2]
15	Ahmedabad	—	—	570	775	1,170	1,582
16	Surabaja	—	—	500	700	975	1,400 [2]
17	Kanpur	—	—	—	685	950	1,190 [2]
18	Bandung	—	—	—	575	925	1,200
19	Rangoon	—	—	—	675	900	1,150 [2]
20	Colombo	—	—	—	610	810	1,000 [2]

Source: Figures for 1920 through 1960 are estimates taken from United Nations, *Growth of The World's Urban and Rural Population, 1920–2000* (New York, United Nations, 1969), Table 46, pp. 11–12, except for the United Nations estimate of 1.025 million for Singapore in 1960, which appears to exclude the metropolitan population outside the city limits. (In Table 46, ordering differs from that given here.) Figures for 1969 are based on various sources, including United Nations, *Demographic Yearbook, 1969,* Table 7. (There may be a considerable margin of error in many of the figures cited, particularly for 1969.)

[1] By 1969 Hanoi and Dacca also probably had populations in excess of 1,000,000 and Poona and Nagpur were around 1,000,000.

[2] Rough estimate by the authors.

— Population below 500,000.

While documenting the reality of urban growth, these figures make it clear that the countries of South and Southeast Asia are overwhelmingly rural,[18] as Table 2.5 demonstrates. To be sure, except for the United States, the Soviet Union, and China, there are more persons living in urban areas in India than in any other country. But India is among the four most populous countries of the world. On a percentage basis, India has only some 18 percent of its population in centers defined as urban compared with 73.5 percent in the United States and over 50 percent in the Soviet Union.[19]

Table 2.5 Percent of Total Population "Rural," South and Southeast Asia, 1950 and 1960

	Percent "Rural"			
	By national definition		*By residence in places under 20,000*	
Country	*1950*	*1960*	*1950*	*1960*
Iran	80.0	66.5	78.4	73.0
India	82.8	82.1	88.4	86.3
Pakistan	89.9	86.6	92.1	90.4
Ceylon	84.7	85.0 [1]	88.6	88.0
Burma	85.3	83.8	91.2	89.7
Thailand	89.2 [2]	81.8	94.0	91.1
Malaysia (West)	68.8	53.0	81.2	75.8
Indonesia	87.3	85.5	91.0	89.2
Philippines	75.7	70.0	84.9	83.3

Source: Computations by the authors from data in United Nations, *Growth of the World's Urban and Rural Population, 1920–2000* (New York, 1969), Table 44, pp. 104–5.

[1] Increase probably attributable to definitional change.

[2] No official national definition of "urban." Data from Government of Thailand.

Another relevant dimension is the rate of urban growth. For the four decades between 1920 and 1960 rough estimates by the United Nations yield the following decennial percentage rates of increase for urban population.[20]

	1920–29	*1930–39*	*1940–49*	*1950–59*
World total	30%	30%	25%	42%
North America	33	11	29	35
Southern Asia [21]	26	46	52	51

The rates of urban growth vary but are substantial for all areas and periods except for the depression decade in Canada and the United States. The most rapid rate of growth was in the most recent decade shown, 1950–59, although high rates of growth for Southern Asia have been quite consistent since 1930. Rates as high, if not higher, have apparently occurred during the ten years from 1960 through 1969.[22]

By contrast, rates of growth for rural areas (places under 20,000) show much slower decennial growth rates:

	1920–29	*1930–39*	*1940–49*	*1950–59*
World total	8%	7%	6%	13%
North America	6	5	4	4
Southern Asia[23]	12	13	11	20

The upswing in rate of rural growth in 1960–69 for the world as a whole reflects comparatively high percentage increases in Latin America (19 percent), Africa (20 percent), and Southern Asia (20 percent). No other region showed a rate of growth as high as 10 percent.

From the statistics presented above, certain conclusions can now be drawn:

1. Most countries in South and Southeast Asia remain predominantly to overwhelmingly rural. They are low-income, subsistence-agricultural societies.
2. Rates of growth in rural areas are not inconsiderable, but they are well below those in urban areas. Nevertheless, because these rates are applied to a base that substantially exceeds that of the urban population, the absolute growth of the rural sector is much greater than that of all urban places combined.
3. Compared with Westernized areas, the *proportion* of the population that is urban is low, but the *rate* of urban growth is strikingly higher. There is nothing in Western experience (unless it is the 96 percent increase in urban population in the Soviet Union between 1930 and 1939) to match the growth of cities like Djakarta from half a million to nearly 3 million in thirty years, or Calcutta from under 2 million to nearly 6 million in forty years.

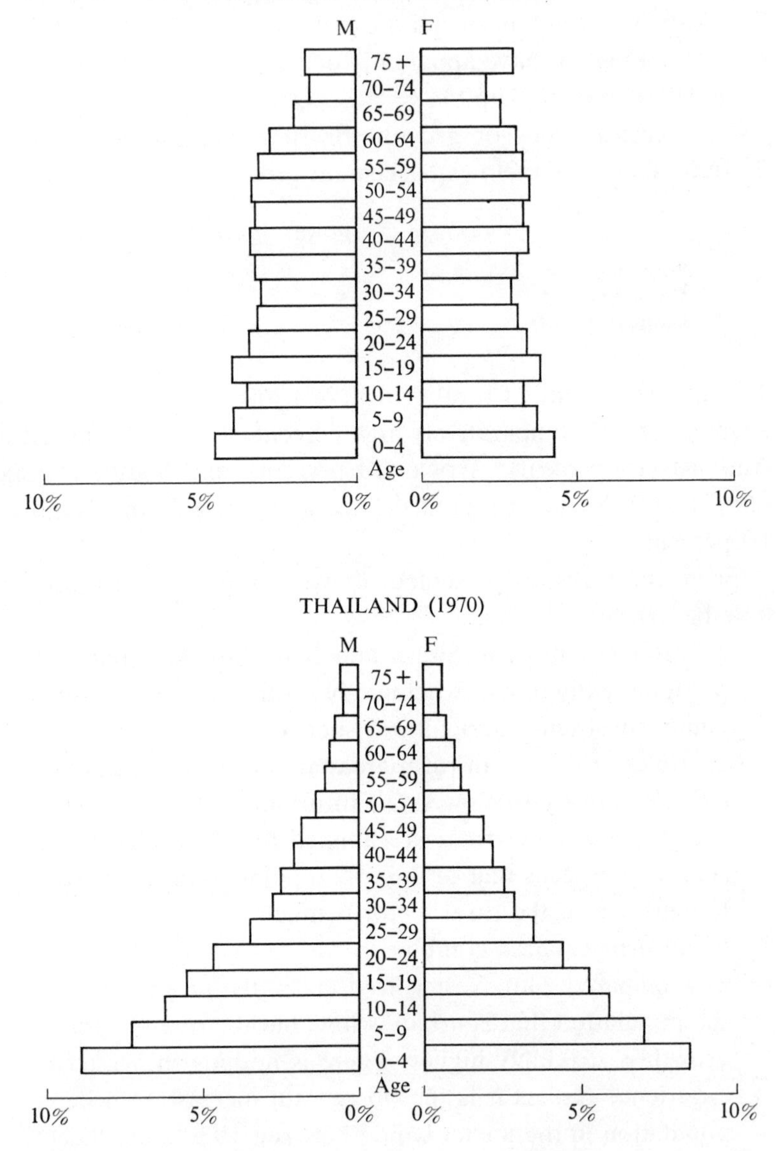

Figure 2.1 Population by Age and Sex, England and Wales (1966) and Thailand (1970)

4. Vigorous urban growth is closely related to the rapid expansion of total populations. Annual rates of growth of 2 to 3 percent in the countries of South and Southeast Asia are dwarfed by rates of increase of 4 to 6 percent and even higher for their urban parts. This results primarily from the addition of thousands of cityward migrants each year to the existing high levels of natural increase characteristic of both cities and countryside throughout the region.[24]

Trends in Age Structure. Populations with a history of high birth rates, like those in all countries of South and Southeast Asia, have a much higher proportion of children and a lower proportion of old people than do populations with a history of low birth rates. As Coale succinctly puts it: "The high-fertility population has a larger proportion of children relative to adults of parental age as a direct consequence of the greater frequency of births. Moreover, by virtue of high fertility a generation ago, today's parents are numerous relative to their parents, and hence the proportion of old people is small." [25] Figure 2.1, which compares the age structure of England and Wales with that of Thailand, illustrates the point: 23 percent of the population in England and Wales is under 15, compared with 44 percent in Thailand. Little more than a third of the population of South Asia is older than 25. Half of the people alive today in the region have been born since 1953.

The age composition of the Southern Asian countries has not changed markedly over the past decade, with the exception of those where birth rates have declined, as in Singapore and to a lesser extent in Ceylon and Malaysia, or where age composition has been somewhat distorted by the effects of war and revolution as in Indonesia. In countries with declining birth rates the proportion of young people in the total population is lessening. In Indonesia, new entrants to the labor force have been increasing rapidly, with the replacement of a relatively small cohort, itself the result of lower birth rates during the Japanese occupation and the struggle for independence, by a much larger one.[26]

In the other countries of Southern Asia there has been a tendency for the share of population in the younger age groups to increase somewhat with declining mortality (which saves the lives of more infants and children than adults) and possibly slight increases in fertility. As a result of these trends there is also a tendency toward a more youthful labor force, although in countries where education is expanding rapidly, this may be offset by entry into the labor force at increasingly older ages. In any event the number of potential young workers is growing rapidly as the teen-age population continues to expand. In India, for example, the group aged 15–19 numbered 55 million in 1970, compared with 42 million ten years earlier. Southeast Asia will experience a particularly rapid increase in the 15–24 age group during the 1970s, amounting to almost 40 percent by the end of the decade.

Dependency, as measured by the proportion of the non-working population to the working force, is considerably higher in Southern Asia than in the developed countries and has been increasing. Dependency ratios will remain high until there is a substantial decline in the birth rate. Although from the point of view of dependency, the labor force has grown too slowly, from the point of view of finding opportunities for productive employment, it has grown too quickly. This paradox of a labor force that is growing at once too slowly and too quickly can, of course, be resolved. The rate of growth of the labor force is too slow only in relation to the rate of growth of the total population. A lowering of birth rates would slow the increase in the number of children, and in time the more slowly growing labor force would constitute an increasing share of the total population.

Interrelations of Population Growth with Social and Economic Trends

It is impossible here to cover the voluminous literature dealing with the effects of rapid population growth on development. Only a brief review of some of the key issues in the relationships between population and economic development will be attempted.[27]

A number of economic growth models have been constructed pointing to the linkages between population dynamics and key economic variables such as personal savings rates, the structure of government spending, and the size and quality of the labor force.[28] By feeding alternative population projections into such models, the interaction of the population variables with the other variables can be traced out. These models are typically expressed as a set of equations with known or assumed coefficients of interrelationship and timing, which can be tested by fitting them to a period in the past and are used to project the growth of the economy in the future. Such models unfailingly indicate that a fall in the birth rate in the high-fertility countries will lead to higher per capita incomes and that as fertility drops, youth dependency falls, but that the labor force and presumably total output are as large as they would be in the absence of a fertility decline. Since total output is to be distributed among a smaller number of persons, income per head will be larger than it would have been had no fertility decline taken place. Over the longer run, the main reason for the continued lower per capita incomes in the high-fertility case is the lower capital-to-labor ratio and the consequent decline in the marginal productivity of labor. This holds true whatever the savings rate, the rate of technical change, and the rate of natural resource exploitation.

The argument between those economists who accept the general results of these models and those who remain doubtful about the long-run adverse effects of population change hinges on the importance of autonomous technical change, which is usually ignored or given a minor role in the models. Those who minimize the importance of the demographic obstacle to economic development argue that increasing population pressure in *itself* is likely to trigger offsetting changes in productivity and economic organization. Those who take the demographic problem more seriously argue that there are sharp limits to the output changes that such adjustments can bring about. Their query (and it is most serious) is: can we rely on technological progress to offset the classical law of diminishing returns in a densely populated Southern Asian country where population will increase five- or sixfold in sixty years if current rates of population growth continue?

Other social scientists may perhaps be excused for wondering at the sterility of some of the economists' model-building and theorizing. As Gunnar Myrdal has pointed out, the growth models that are taken so seriously are "mechanical" rather than "behaviorist." What the discussions of the effect of population trends on economic development typically ignore are the effects of population trends on unemployment, quality of administration, social conditions in urban areas, social, racial, and political tensions, and so forth. These may be serious omissions as the following two examples suggest. First, by requiring a doubling of government services and facilities in twenty-five years or less merely to maintain base-year levels, rapid population growth imposes tremendous strains on the normally fragile administrative capacity of a developing country. If the administrative apparatus is not equal to the task, the potential for unrest and violence, with their attendant effects on investment and economic growth generally, will no doubt be heightened.

Second, rapid population growth can exacerbate communal tensions in rural areas by altering a settled pattern of community relationships. For example, in parts of northern Thailand, population pressure is forcing lowland Thais to move to higher areas in search of new land at the same time that it is forcing hill-tribe agriculturalists to move down from their upland valleys, also in search of new land. The juxtaposition of these two different cultural groups in such a way is potentially explosive. Similarly, the Muslim-Christian clashes in parts of Mindanao are certainly not unrelated to rapid population growth in that area.

Although it is true that many of these effects are difficult to predict or measure, it is also true that they have a bearing on the long-term economic viability of the countries concerned. To ignore them is to leave a rather wide "credibility gap" between the economic theorists and their audience. We would argue that most of the neglected variables, if taken into account, would reinforce the conclusion that a decline in fertility rates facilitates more rapid economic development; but this is not a closed issue.

What, then, has been the effect of rapid population growth on the social and economic development of the countries of South and Southeast Asia during the last decade? We can say with confidence that during the 1960s economic growth, expansion of education and health systems, and probably increases in most of the other usual indicators of social and economic development proceeded at a faster rate than population growth in most of these countries. By 1970 their position had improved in terms of per capita GDP (gross domestic product), percentage of children attending school, ratio of health facilities to population, electricity generated per head, radio and television sets per head, and so forth.

Table 2.6 presents data on average annual growth rates in real gross domestic product, population, and GDP per capita from 1950–60 and 1960–68 for the developing countries of Southern Asia. For the region as a whole, growth of GDP in 1960–68 by 4.4 percent per annum, related to a population growth rate of 2.5 percent each year, yielded a growth rate in GDP per capita of 1.9 percent per annum. Therefore, it is fair to say that the rapid growth of population neutralized a good part (more than half) of the increase in gross domestic product. Moreover, the acceleration in population growth rates in the 1960s held the growth rate of per capita GDP constant at the level of the 1950s, despite the increase in the growth rate of GDP in the

1960s. It did not, however, prevent growth in per capita GDP except in Burma and Indonesia, in both of which mismanagement of the economy should probably be seen as the main culprit. The countries whose economies performed most poorly during the decade—India, Indonesia, and Burma—were not those with the highest rates of population growth. These facts tell us little, if anything, about the effect of population growth on economic development, but they should serve to deter us from overemphasizing rapid population growth as the key deterrent to economic development, to the exclusion of other deterrents.

It is worth noting that the per capita economic growth rate of the Southern Asian countries as a whole is around the middle of the range of growth rates achieved by the presently developed countries in the early stages of their growth. Of course, the latter did not face a "population explosion" like the one the Southern Asian countries are presently experiencing. Maintenance of this modest growth rate of 2 percent annually over a period of time would mean a quadrupling of per capita income in seventy years. But would this be fast enough? Translating as it does during the early 1970s into a rise of about $2 a year over the average Southern Asian per capita income of slightly more than U.S. $100, the increase seems modest. Indeed, a key dilemma of our times is that, despite the frequent expression of pious hopes to the contrary, the gap between per capita income in the Southern Asian countries and in the Western countries will inevitably grow wider during the remainder of this century.[29]

In many respects concern with per capita GNP or GDP as the yardstick by which development progress is measured is misleading. It tells us nothing about changes in the pattern of income distribution and qualitative changes in levels of living of different groups within a country's population. It tells us nothing about environmental conditions, extent of social security, unemployment problems, recreational facilities, human freedoms, or, most important, the progress in any or all of these fields *relative to expectations*. Inflation of expectations is fueled by improved

Table 2.6 Annual Growth Rates of Real Gross Domestic Product, Population, and Gross Domestic Product per Capita in Southern Asian Countries, 1950–68

		Annual Compound Growth: Percent		
Country	*Years*	*Gross domestic product* [1]	*Population*	*Gross domestic product per capita*
Burma	1950–60	6.3	1.9	4.3
	1960–67	1.3	2.1	−0.7
Ceylon	1950–60	3.0	2.5	0.5
	1960–68	4.8	2.4	2.4
India	1950–60	3.5 [2]	1.9	1.6
	1960–68	3.3 [2]	2.5	0.8
Indonesia	1951–60	3.3	2.1	1.2
	1960–68	2.6	2.4	0.2
Iran	1960–68	8.0	2.9	4.9
Malaysia (West)	1955–60	4.0	3.1	0.9
	1960–66	5.9	3.1	2.7
Pakistan	1950–60	2.5 [2]	2.1	0.4
	1960–68	5.6 [2]	2.1	3.4
Philippines	1950–60	6.9	3.1	3.7
	1960–68	4.6	3.5	1.1
Thailand	1951–60	6.4	3.8	2.5
	1960–68	7.8	3.1	4.6
Developing ECAFE countries [3]	1950–60	4.0	2.1	1.9
	1960–68	4.4	2.5	1.9

Source: ECAFE, *Economic Survey of Asia and the Far East, 1970, part two: Current Economic Developments,* February 22, 1971. Limited distribution.
[1] Gross domestic product at market prices.
[2] Net domestic product at factor cost.
[3] Includes South Korea and Taiwan as well as the countries of South and Southeast Asia.

communications and, in some cases, by the rhetoric of political leaders, and can very easily outstrip the $2 a year increase in income per head that is the reasonable prognosis for the next decade.

It is very difficult to get an adequate picture of trends in "social welfare," broadly defined, during the past decade. Income distribution is very uneven in most Asian countries, and although evidence on trends is scanty, ECAFE reports that inequality has probably increased in most countries in recent years.[30]

It is sometimes argued that widening inequality of income is not only inevitable in the early stages of economic development but also conducive to a faster rate of growth.[31] Certainly there is evidence that income inequality tends to widen in the earlier phases of growth,[32] though present trends in such inequality in Asian countries are not clearly in view. Of course, if total output is increasing fast enough, widening income inequalities may nevertheless be consistent with increases in the real income of the poorer classes. Social and political stability, however, may depend upon the nature of income distribution as much as, or even more than, upon average income. Oshima and others argue that if inequalities were to widen, this, "together with the rapid rate of growth of population, labor force and urbanization within the context of the flimsy social fabric and the shaky political consensus . . . [in so many Asian countries] . . . makes the prospects for rapid development in the seventies dim." [33] However, Oshima finds that widening income inequalities are not inevitable given the appropriate development strategy, with less emphasis on modern industrialization and more on achieving fuller employment than has been typical during the past decade. In any event, the Green Revolution has great potential for widening inequalities in the rural areas unless appropriate steps are taken to enable small farmers and those in less-favored areas to share the benefits of high-yielding crop varieties.

Food supplies per capita probably increased in most Asian countries over the decade, particularly as a result of a rapid rise in agricultural output in the late 1960s. Nevertheless, in 1965–66 the protein intake per head was even lower than in prewar years.[34] The Food and Agriculture Organization (FAO) has calculated that in the developing countries as a whole, because of increasing populations and incomes, demand for food will rise by more than 140 percent during the period 1962 to

1985. Population growth will be the dominant factor. "Changes in the composition and quality of the diet in developing regions will be relatively slow so long as a large part of the additional income has to be spread over a rapidly increasing population." [35]

Educational progress, in quantitative terms, has been dramatic in the Southern Asian countries, as the trends in educational enrollment rates in Table 2.7 show. The "educational imperative" —the notion that education, like malaria control, is a basic human right to which each person is entitled—is widely accepted by governments in the region, and the proportion of budgets devoted to education has been steadily rising. Yet it is only too clear that educational changes are often largely unrelated to the

Table 2.7 School Enrollment Rates for the First and Second Levels of Education, Southern Asian Countries, 1960 and 1967

		Enrollment Rate [1]	
Country	*Age Range*	*1960*	*1967*
Afghanistan	7–18	5	12 (1968)
Burma	5–15	31	n.a.
Cambodia	6–18	43 (1965)	48
Ceylon [2]	5–16	76	73
India	6–17	31	41 (1965)
Indonesia [2]	7–18	33 (1959)	44
Iran	6–17	27	43 (1968)
Laos	6–18	15	25 (1968)
Malaysia (West)	6–18	52 [3]	61
Pakistan	6–15	26	32
Philippines	7–16	68	87
Singapore	6–17	78	84
Thailand [4]	7–18	53	54
South Vietnam	6–17	21	60 (1968)

Source: Draft of table prepared for *UNESCO Statistical Yearbook, 1970* (Table 2.5).

[1] Enrollment rates refer to numbers enrolled in primary and secondary education as a percentage of numbers in the official age range for these levels of education.

[2] Rates reported here are different from those in chapters 8 and 10, which use different sources and definitions.

[3] Approximate.

[4] Estimates by the authors.

development needs of the country and are bringing into existence frustrated groups of educated unemployed who endanger the stability of the social and political system that so heedlessly produced them. Moreover, rapid population growth has put a brake on both the expansion of coverage and the improvement in the quality of education. If the number of children in Asia had not increased since 1950, the massive increases in enrollments between 1950 and 1967 would have been enough to provide school places for 81 percent of children of primary school age by 1967, but because of the rapid increase in the number of school-age children, only 51 percent were in school.[36]

Social conditions in Southern Asian cities remain desperately bad for at least the poorest third of the population, and conditions may have deteriorated during the past decade in many cities as they expanded. But it is easier to claim deterioration than to prove it. Seltzer's observation about the dialogue on population and environmental problems is appropriate here: "Free from the restraints of relevant data, the issues are 'resolved' on the basis of piecemeal statistics or trivia, anecdotes and speculations of doom or utopia." [37] We will simply note here some of the evidence for continuing appalling conditions and point out also that many urban residents *think* the situation is deteriorating.

The slum population of Calcutta and of metropolitan Manila is reported to account for one-half and one-quarter respectively of the population of these two cities.[38] Provision of low-income housing fell far short of requirements in all major cities of the region except Singapore and perhaps Kuala Lumpur. Bangkok-Thonburi, for example, has built one unit of public housing for every 20 constructed in Singapore, a city two-thirds its size. Pollution is unquestionably worsening as the cities grow larger and only minimal controls are exercised. Sanitation remains poor. Crime is widely believed to have increased in many cities, but it is not clear whether crime *rates* have increased.

Support Costs of Education, Health and Social Services. Table 2.8, which draws on the rather inadequate data available, shows the distribution of social expenditures in a number of Southern Asian countries. In most countries government expenditures in the social field constitute a very important share of the total budget, though the range is very wide: from a low of about 10 percent of all government expenditures in Pakistan to a high of about 35–40 percent in Singapore, Ceylon, and the Philippines.[39] Education typically accounts for more than half of such expenditures, and social services other than education and health (which include subsidized housing for the poor) form a very small proportion of total GDP in most of these countries. During the past decade spending on education has increased as a proportion of both GDP and government budgets in most countries and now equals half the expenditure on defense, but there has been little tendency for the share of other social expenditures to rise.

Rapid population growth and the costs of social services are clearly related. Governments normally aim at least to preserve existing per capita levels of such services. Because of population growth, this means an initial expansion of 2½ or 3 percent annually. In education Asian countries have adopted the goal of a universal primary education of six or seven years. In countries such as Singapore, where this target has already been achieved, future trends in primary school enrollments will be determined solely by population trends if targets are not raised further. In the countries that are still far from achieving their targets, enrollment increases will be the combined products of demographic trends and trends in the proportion of children at various ages who attend school. In a country with a youth population of one million increasing at 3 percent annually, a rise in the enrollment rate from 50 percent to 75 percent in ten years means an increase in enrollments, not of 250,000 as it would if population were not increasing, but of 508,000—more than twice as many.[40]

The aim of merely maintaining present levels of education, health, and other social services implies a fairly rapid expansion.

Table 2.8 Percentage Distribution of Government Expenditure by Functional Classification

		Social Services [1]						
	Year	*Total*	*Educa-tion*	*Health*	*Social security and special welfare*	*Other*	*Other Gov't Services*	*Total Gov't Services*
All government [2]								
India	1954	17.7	7.9	4.0	4.9	0.9	82.3	100
	1965	n.d.	8.7 [3]	3.8 [4]	n.d.	n.d.	n.d.	100
Malaysia, West	1960	17.3	10.1	4.5	1.5	1.2	82.7	100
	1965	20.8	13.4	5.0	0.4	2.0	79.2	100
Pakistan [5]	1956	9.7	6.4	n.d.	0.2	3.1	n.d.	100
	1966	9.6	5.7	n.d.	0.2	3.7	n.d.	100
Singapore	1956	37.4	18.3	11.9	3.9	3.3	62.6	100
	1966	35.6	19.1	9.8	1.7	5.0	64.4	100
Central government								
Ceylon	1956	35.4	14.3	9.4	— 11.7	—	64.6	100
	1966	37.9	15.1	7.1	— 15.7	—	62.1	100
India	1966	6.5	1.9	1.3	— 3.3	—	93.5	100
Malaysia, West	1960	17.7	10.8	4.8	1.4	0.7	82.3	100
	1965	21.2	15.1	5.5	0.4	0.2	78.8	100

Philippines	1956	31.7	23.9	6.1	—	1.7	—	68.3	100
	1966	39.2	32.0	5.8	—	1.4	—	60.8	100
Thailand	1959	26.4	19.5	2.9	3.2		0.8	73.6	100
	1966	27.3	16.5	3.6	3.8		3.4	72.7	100

Source: United Nations, *The Planning and Financing of Social Development in the ECAFE Region,* ECAFE Social Development Series No. 1, 1969.

[1] The definition of "social services" given in the United Nations, *Manual for Economic and Functional Classification of Government Transactions* (New York, 1958) was offered as a model for the preparation of replies, but could not be followed sufficiently closely to permit full comparability of the resulting analysis.

[2] Includes expenditures of state and local governments as well as of central governments. The ratio of central government expenditures to all government expenditures in the field of social services varies widely, from about 45 percent in India to 100 percent in Singapore.

[3] Capital expenditures are not included.

[4] Capital expenditures are partially included.

[5] Development expenditures only. Social services total does not include expenditures on health.

But even this is an unrealistically low target because it does not take into account the effects of migration from the countryside to the city, where health and education services are normally far more developed. In Thailand more than half the doctors are in Bangkok. In education it is not unusual to find a primary school enrollment rate of 90 percent in the capital city and of 30 percent in the rural areas of the same country. Therefore, educational planning predicated on the maintenance of the base-year enrollment rate, with predictable trends in costs, may be drastically upset by high rates of migration into the cities.

For example, consider a country with a million school-age children, 20 percent of whom live in the towns and 80 percent in the rural areas. The school enrollment rate is 80 percent in the towns and 20 percent in the rural areas. There are 160,000 students in each area, 320,000 altogether, and an enrollment rate for the country as a whole of 32 percent. A decade or so later the school-age population has increased 40 percent to 1.4 million. But because of rapid urbanization the school-age population living in the towns has more than doubled to 400,000 whereas the rural population has increased far more slowly to one million. If the educational authorities aim to maintain the base-year enrollment rate of 32 percent for the country as a whole, enrollments must rise to 448,000. If, however, they aim to maintain the base-year enrollment rates in urban and rural areas, total enrollments must rise to 520,000. *Instead of a rise of 40 percent, the required increase is 62 percent*. Even without any attempt to raise the low enrollment rates in the rural areas, total enrollments will have to grow much faster than the school-age population.

Therefore, aiming merely to maintain the base-year per capita level of social services is not likely to be politically acceptable since it will lead to a deterioration in the services available to much of the population, and especially to urban dwellers. The aim of maintaining the level separately in rural and urban areas is more realistic, though much more difficult to accomplish if the urban areas are growing faster than the rural. But even this goal, implying continuing wide disparities between rural and urban areas, can hardly be considered ambitious. Most countries give at least lip service to the aim of narrowing disparities in the availability of services between rural and urban areas. One reason for doing so, apart from egalitarian sentiments, is that lack of such services in rural areas may be a powerful stimulus to urbanward migration, thus accentuating problems of the cities. Narrowing the disparities implies, at the least, a rise in the coverage of the rural population while the urban ratio is held constant. And not only must coverage be improved but also quality. Farmers are not fools, and in both Ceylon and Thailand, and no doubt in other countries of the region, there is a tendency for rural health centers to be underutilized because the rural people prefer either to use the traditional ayurvedic physician or to make the extra effort to go to the hospital or larger health center in the town, where they know they can receive more expert attention.

In summary, it can be said that: (1) simply keeping social services in pace with population growth, though it will require an expansion of 2 or 3 percent a year in the next decade, is probably an unrealistically conservative aim; (2) keeping services in line with population growth separately in rural and urban areas is a more realistic minimum aim and may well require an expansion of 50 or 60 percent during the decade in some countries; and (3) any attempt to narrow the gap between rural and urban areas in the availability of these services will require still more rapid expansion.

While a substantial share of government budgets goes to social services in the countries of Southern Asia, most of this money is spent on running to keep in the same place. This will continue to be so through the 1970s because in the all-important field of education even a rapid decline in birth rates, beginning now, would have little effect on numbers in the school-age groups before 1980.

Nevertheless, over time, the savings on education, health, and social service expenditures resulting from a fall in the birth rate become substantial, whether the aim is to hold constant or to expand the coverage of the eligible population. A recent study for Thailand [41] revealed that, given the government's targets for expansion of educational coverage, educational expenditures must rise from 3.8 percent of the GNP in 1970 to 4.9 percent in the year 2000 if fertility declines only slowly, but will actually fall slightly to 3.7 percent of the GNP in the year 2000 if fertility declines rapidly. The costs will therefore be 32 percent higher if fertility declines only slowly. The total savings in the period 1970–2000 would equal 22 times the total expenditure on education in 1970 and 3½ times the total expenditure in the year 2000 in the low population projection.

Similar results have been obtained in studies for other countries and in studies of the effect of population trends on health costs.[42] A decline in the birth rate, then, enables any given target for coverage of the eligible population to be achieved at less cost, thereby opening a number of favorable alternatives for government: (1) to achieve its coverage targets more rapidly; (2) to improve the quality of the services more rapidly than it could otherwise have done; or (3) to leave the social services targets unchanged but to spend more in other developmental fields.

Such findings have been influential in reinforcing the commitment of governments in the region to the goal of lowering population growth rates.

Efforts to Reduce Growth Rates. Several Asian countries have adopted specific population policies to reduce rates of population growth through national family planning programs. It is presumed that such programs will lower fertility and effect reductions in the average size of families.[43] India in 1952 was the first country in the region to do so, but the actual program was limited in scope until the mid-1960s. Next to follow was Pakistan in 1960. Between 1965 and 1970 Indonesia, Iran, Malaysia, Nepal, the Philippines, Singapore, and Thailand instituted programs. Ceylon's status is ambiguous. The government provided limited aid to private family planning activities every year beginning in 1954, and then in 1965 adopted an official policy setting targets for lower future rates of population growth. At that time the government began to take over the private Ceylon Family Planning Association. Under the new government, elected in 1970, the earlier policy of reducing the country's rate of population increase shifted to one of providing family planning services as part of the government's regular maternal and child health programs. All formal population goals were dropped. Further changes seem possible.

There are various ways to measure the degree of success of these family planning programs. One, which tends to yield optimistic estimates of success, and which, not surprisingly, is often favored by program administrators and others with a stake in achieving program goals, involves a compilation of statistics on the number of clinics operating, doctors and nurses trained, clients accepting services, contraceptives distributed or intrauterine devices inserted. Data of this kind are necessary for program operation and useful in securing funds from legislative bodies and foreign organizations. But they are at best an indirect and partial index of the ultimate goal of fertility decline and reduction in the rate at which a particular population is growing. Only accurate vital statistics can measure success in reducing fertility and, ultimately, growth rates.[44]

It is useful to call attention to the distinction between family planning and population planning. The former is correctly viewed as a type of preventive medicine, and its proper goals are the improvement of the health and welfare of mothers and children. The latter is a part of economic planning, and its goals include a decline in the rate of population growth that will maximize the nation's ability to achieve its development planning targets. The voluntary fulfillment of individual wishes for a particular number of children will not usually produce the average number per family needed to reach the national development targets. It is worth noting that the initiative for national programs and policy statements designed to reduce rates of population growth has come especially from the economists and planners in every Asian country with family planning services.

Perhaps development officers themselves have been led to take far too simplistic a view of the achievements to be expected from a family planning program. The distinction between family planning and population planning often has not been observed. Instead, with growth reduction goals already set, the Ministry of Health or its equivalent has been given the assignment of establishing and operating a nationwide voluntary family planning program. Usually there has been inadequate inquiry into the ministry's understanding of national planning aims or of its readiness to carry out a program that would even approximate the planner's goals. But still more fundamental, it is assumed that a program of contraceptive services will result in a rapid reduction of fertility. Only recently has it been recognized that family planning, essential as it is, cannot alone solve national economic and social problems. But family planning, together with many other changes in the economy and society, can be a useful component in population planning. Its importance as a public health and social welfare measure is independent of its achievements in reducing national fertility levels.

What has happened to birth rates in the countries in South Asia and Southeast Asia with national family planning programs? The sharpest drop has occurred in Singapore with a steady decline from 45.8 births per thousand in 1953 to 22.2 per thousand in 1970. Singapore is, of course, largely urban with a considerable degree of modernization and development.[45] Further, it is in the ring of Chinese culture, and the people within this cultural sphere—the Taiwanese, the Koreans, the Japanese, the citizens of Hong Kong—have shown far greater receptivity to the use of family planning techniques than have the indigenous peoples of other parts of Asia.[46] A decline in the fertility of the Chinese in West Malaysia accounts for a major part of the drop in the birth rate there from 46.7 per thousand in 1956 to about 37 per thousand in 1970.

In Indonesia an official population policy was adopted in 1968, but the National Family Planning Institute, charged with carrying out the program to implement the policy, was not established in its present form until 1970. Fertility is high in Indonesia, probably between 45 and 50 births per thousand per year. With a 1970 population already around 120,000,000, a continuing rapid decline in mortality without a reduction in fertility would produce a population of 227,000,000 by 1991.[47]

India's family planning efforts have been substantial, but the enormity and intractability of India's economic and social problems have made demographic progress difficult. Crude birth rates for the country as a whole remain above 40 as against a current target of 32 by 1974.

The area now split into Pakistan and Bangladesh presents similar problems, compounded by the generally low status of women and the disruptions associated with the separation of the two wings. It appears that the birth rate has not yet dropped below 50 in Bangladesh and continues above 40 in Pakistan, providing slight hope of meeting the target of 33 set for 1975 for the country before partition.

In Iran, Nepal, Thailand, Malaysia, Indonesia, and the Philippines, the remaining countries in South and Southeast Asia with government family planning policies, there has been little change in fertility levels since the inception of their programs. But it would be highly optimistic to expect such effects since these programs began operation under official government policies only between 1966 and 1970, and all have been initiated on a limited basis. It can be argued that even in India and Pakistan the programs have not been under way long enough to induce changes of sufficient magnitude to be reflected in fertility declines. It has been suggested that the programs have an educational effect and are preparing the way for future reductions in fertility. Such reasoning clearly can be neither substantiated nor disproved except over time. Even then it will be difficult to separate the effects of a family planning program from that of other simultaneous changes such as urbanization, increased education, rising levels of living, and so on.[48]

It seems clear that in the less developed nations the family planning programs ordinarily judged most successful are operating in a context of rapid modernization and similarly rapid increases in gross national product and other economic indicators. There is as yet no convincing evidence that family planning activities will produce major reductions in fertility levels and rates of population growth except in association with the other consequential changes in an economy and society included in the term "modernization." [49] Where such changes are taking place, family planning can be highly useful as a means of implementing new values that favor smaller families.[50]

Looking Toward the Future

Asia at the beginning of the 1970s is the home of more than half the people now alive. Two of its countries, China and India, have the largest populations on earth. Together they hold probably a little more than one-third of all human beings. Japan and Indonesia are among the population giants, each with more than 100 million inhabitants. South and Southeast Asia together contain more than one-fourth of the world's people. Southeast Asia alone is larger in population than either North or South America and nearly as populous as all of Africa.

Any projections of present trends are by no means accurate predictions for the future. This is because the factors affecting the components of population growth are subject to short-run changes that are difficult or impossible to foresee accurately. At the moment this is particularly true of fertility. In the short run the level of mortality ought to remain low in countries where current death rates are already low and drop further in those countries where only moderate declines have so far taken place. The latter countries include India, Pakistan, Bangladesh, and Indonesia. International migration is limited everywhere and is not likely to be an important factor in population growth except temporarily where political events create one-sided population exchanges. Internal migration is a different story, with the city-ward flow of rural people accounting for a sizable part of urban growth.

Between now and the end of the century the population of every country in South and Southeast Asia will grow. It would grow even if the number of births remained constant, simply as a result of improvements in life expectancy. But for the *number* of births to remain constant, a fairly rapid decline in birth *rates* would be required. Whether any significant decline will occur depends upon an array of complex social, economic, political, and psychological factors. According to one estimate by the United Nations, the population of South Asia will grow from a little over 750 million people in 1970 to more than one and a half billion by the end of the century. In the same thirty years, the number of Southeast Asians will swell from 287 million to 608 million.[51] Such estimates—one of 105 percent and the other of 112 percent—may well be too low. All estimates of future levels of growth depend on assumptions. It must be assumed either that present trends will continue, an assumption which historical data have continually shown to be contrary to fact except for the briefest periods, or that they will change. If we assume change, we must assume specific degrees of change and justify these as reasonable responses to complex changes in the economy and society, which are themselves difficult to predict. Consequently, we can view the UN estimates, or others substantially higher or lower, as reasonable without holding them to be accurate predictions in any detailed sense.

The probabilities are strong that growth rates in the region will continue at high levels through the 1970s, a prediction that rests on the assumptions that (1) the social and economic context for a rapid reduction in fertility does not yet exist in the region as a whole and that (2) further modest declines in fertility during the period will be largely offset by additional declines in mortality. If we were asked to predict the changes in rates of population growth in the 1980s and 1990s, we would do our best to beg off. If we were not allowed to do so, we would ask those who insist we predict to specify the economic and social conditions of the period as a guide to some plausible demographic trends. The problem is only made more difficult by the range of possible occurrences in the many countries of the region with their heterogeneity in peoples, cultures, resources, economic activities, political organization, family structures, stage of modernization, and other relevant characteristics.

Definitions of the social and economic context for a rapid reduction in fertility vary widely. A few optimists consider modern contraceptives and a well-developed network of suppliers to be sufficient to induce a sweeping reduction in birth rates. A more generally accepted view, however, is that there is some as yet unspecified level of development at which fertility begins to decline as a consequence of societal changes that alter social structures and thereby modify traditional values.[52] It is often claimed, for example, that such changes as increased urban living, longer periods of compulsory education, child labor restrictions, and a sharp decline in infant and child mortality all combine to reduce the utility of large numbers of children and thereby alter values about ideal family size and lead to lower fertility levels.[53]

At the risk of great oversimplification, let us sum up the conditions necessary for substantial fertility decline in the term "modernization." [54] In every country in the world that has undergone modernization, fertility is comparatively low. In countries that have not, fertility is comparatively high although it may be at low levels in enclaves of development within such countries. Finally, in all those countries clearly undergoing modernization on a national scale, fertility has shown, or is showing, a steady decline.

No specific threshold has been established for the degree of modernization necessary to induce "take-off" for fertility decline to low levels. Nor is it certain that low fertility accompanies modernization in all cases or that low fertility cannot occur without some minimum level of development. Finally, although rapid population growth clearly hampers economic growth in densely populated, low-income, subsistence-agricultural countries, some economists minimize its significance in the short run as we have seen.

These general considerations lead to the question: What countries in South and Southeast Asia are modernized and what are their fertility prospects? So far as we can see, only Singapore qualifies,[55] and its birth rates have been more than halved in twenty years as has already been shown. An argument could be made that West Malaysia is modernized. Our own inclination is rather to stress that modernization is occurring and to note that birth rates there are dropping more than in most countries of the region.

It would be rash indeed to predict that fertility declines will not begin or accelerate in other countries in the region. Various logical preconditions for such declines exist to a greater or lesser extent in several of them. Such preconditions include national family planning services, organized and informal channels for the spread of information on means for limiting births,[56] and the widespread expressed desire for families of moderate size.[57] Control over the number of children born is already being practiced among some groups, particularly in urban areas. Deaths among children have been sharply reduced, ending the necessity of two births to assure one survivor.

In Thailand, where such conditions prevail, the birth rate appears to have begun to decline within the last two or three years. The rising number of contraceptives distributed through the national family planning services and through commercial channels provides indirect evidence that increasing numbers of Thai women are controlling births. According to our calculations, by mid-1971, 7 percent of all married women aged 15–44 in Thailand had accepted contraceptives in the national program and were using these to limit their fertility. By mid-1972 that figure was expected to increase to 11 percent.

Changes in structural factors have also been cited as conducive to lowered fertility. An increase in the proportion of the population living in urban areas is one frequently cited element. The presumption is that in urban centers traditional values are no longer appropriate and are replaced by others more rational in the new environment. The high fertility appropriate to the village is replaced by low fertility appropriate to the city. Clearly, this reasoning is based on many assumptions that may or may not be valid, one of which is the notion that urbanization in Asia is occurring for the same reasons, and will have the same consequences, as urbanization in the already developed countries.[58] Another is that a sizable part of the migrants to expanding Asian cities will live under conditions that will induce changes in their beliefs and actions and will in turn result in the two- or three-child family.

Clearly, population variables do not operate in a vacuum, independent of the social and economic setting. Conversely, social and economic activity, including development, is inevitably influenced by the existing demographic situations.[59] Whether and how rapidly individual countries in South and Southeast Asia achieve modernization and development depends on many factors, of which population is a significant one.

It is difficult to assess future changes in birth rates in the region. As we have seen, there are both optimistic and pessimistic views about the extent to which fertility will decline in different countries in the next decade or two. No country in any part of the world has yet made the transfer from high to low birth rates in the absence of social and economic development. Nor does any fully developed country have continuing high fertility. Still, we do not as yet have a final answer to the question: Can a country organize its limited resources to reduce birth rates to low levels in the absence of active economic growth and modernization? We doubt that it can, but we would be happy to be proved wrong.

In our view Asia will be faced with continuing rapid growth to the end of the century and beyond. In all probability India will have more than a billion people by that time, Indonesia may well be beyond 250 million, and smaller countries like the Philippines and Thailand could easily have between 75 and 100 million inhabitants. Whatever the exact numbers, the task of raising living standards will be made more difficult by high growth rates, given the enormous size of current populations in relation to land and other resources. Multiplying numbers are already piling up in rural areas. High fertility and the substantial spillover from the reservoir of rural growth are creating unprecedented rates of increase in urban areas and pushing big cities to multi-million levels which are difficult to comprehend, much less to control. High fertility and low mortality have created a high ratio of children to adults and a heavy dependency burden. Past births are responsible for unusually large numbers of new entrants into the labor force throughout the region and for intensifying problems of providing employment, particularly at rewarding work.

The notion that steadily increasing requirements for food, housing, jobs, education, and other services will be met without limit as they occur and that personal incomes will show a steady rise at the same time must be an article of faith. It is not based on any evidence we know. The much-heralded Green Revolution, for example, is no more a solution to *continuing* population growth than is the migration of population from densely settled to thinly settled islands of Indonesia or the Mahaveli migration and resettlement scheme in Ceylon. To the extent that each is successful, it buys time and may, of course, have direct benefits quite aside from contributing to any long-run solution to the problem of continuing population growth.[60] But this cannot obscure the fact that high rates of population increase must be lowered before they operate as permanent checks on modernization and development efforts. How long a period of leeway exists is unknown to any of us, but it is clear enough that the negative effects of rapid growth need to be dealt with now, not when they have become still greater handicaps to economic and social achievement.

All this applies equally to the growth of cities. In the 1970s and probably beyond, urban growth is likely to continue at a rate about double that of total population growth in most countries of South and Southeast Asia. Urban fertility is at least moderately high in countries with high rural fertility. It is kept so in part by the influx of migrants from rural areas, most of whom are young and in peak fertility years. They add not only their own numbers but also their offspring after arrival to the city's total increase. Moreover, despite crowding and squalor in many cities, death rates are lower than in rural areas. The result is a rate of natural increase that may be as high in cities as in the country. Still higher rates of growth, especially for the larger cities, appear likely on the basis of current trends. A steady rise in the proportion of the population that is urban seems certain.

The recent increased awareness of the special problems of large cities reflects in part the greater number of such places and also the extremely rapid expansion of individual cities. More attention has been focused on such evident urban problems as poverty, crowding, crime and delinquency, incompatible land uses, and inadequate public services. Cities have found it difficult or impossible to cope with such stubborn problems. It was perhaps not wholly in jest that a consultant proposed bulldozing as the ultimate solution for one Asian metropolis.

The role of cities in development has become the subject of growing debate and study.[61] In Asia there is serious question whether the historical function of Western cities as focal points for successful development will be repeated. In particular, the growth of most Asian cities is not based on an industrial growth similar to that which led the cities of Europe to flourish at an earlier period. The more traditional commercial and administrative functions predominate in Asia and are a questionable base for support of a large, continuing rural influx. The few efforts made to stop the flow of rural migrants to cities have had little success. Greater interest in improving the rural sectors of the economy and society has been shown recently by economists and planning officials in some countries, but it is unlikely that increases in rural levels of living will be great enough to provide any noticeable lessening of the migration to cities during the decade. Future successful distribution of population into large, medium, and small cities and into rural areas appears to require both careful planning based on more knowledge of effects than we have today and vastly increased productivity.

The problems of employment and of income distribution in Southern Asia in the 1970s will be closely linked, and it is hard to view rapid population growth other than as a factor aggravating already serious problems. The agricultural labor force will grow substantially during the coming decades, because the urban employment base is too limited to absorb more than a relatively small part of the massive increase in the rural labor force, even with the most optimistic assumptions about the pace of industrialization. Little additional arable land is available for settlement in the region. One estimate is that 85 percent of available land is already in use. Some countries, like the Philippines, that traditionally have had an agricultural frontier have it no longer. Others, like Ceylon and Thailand, still have some unused arable land, but the supply is dwindling and it tends naturally enough to be of poorer quality than land already occupied. Therefore, pressure on the land (as measured by rural population per cultivated hectare) will increase, and this will encourage the splitting-up of farms, increasing tenancy, and the settlement of poorer-quality land. All these developments will tend to hold down increases in output per man and hence in the welfare of rural populations.[62] They may also widen inequalities in the rural areas as will the tendency for the larger and wealthier farmers and those living in irrigable areas to benefit most from the Green Revolution.

Low farm incomes, rising education levels and expectations, and the relatively high wages earned by those fortunate enough to obtain employment in the modern sector in the cities will encourage rural-urban migration and the perpetuation of a large surplus labor pool in the cities.[63] Rapid growth of the urban workforce will tend to depress wages, and attempts to counter this through enforcing minimum wage legislation may backfire by encouraging the adoption of more capital-intensive production methods, resulting in higher levels of unemployment. For a variety of political and only quasi-economic reasons, workers in the modern industrial sector will tend to benefit from rising real wages.[64] But this relatively high-wage, capital-intensive sector is most unlikely to expand rapidly enough to deplete the pool of unemployed, which will be constantly refilled by new migrants from the rural areas.

As long as the labor surplus situation remains, the prospects for significant improvements in the real income of the masses remain dismal. At the same time the inadequate efforts to cope with the massive expansion of metropolitan areas—the wretched housing conditions, poor water supply, sanitation and public transport services, increasing inadequacy of recreational facilities, and so on—hurt the poor much more than they do the rich, who can afford good housing in better neighborhoods, private water purification systems, and chauffeur-driven cars and who can escape on weekends to the golf course or the beach. Similarly, it is the poor who suffer most from the delays in achieving universal education and improved coverage of health services resulting from rapid population growth. The rich do not have to rely on government-sponsored clinics or on government-provided free primary education.

Though it is difficult to measure trends in unemployment and underemployment, the situation remained serious in Southern Asian countries at the beginning of the 1970s,[65] with rates of unemployment running as high as 10 or 12 percent in Ceylon, 12 or 13 percent in urban areas of Malaysia and the Philippines, and perhaps even higher in East Pakistan. During the 1970s 176 million people will be added to Southern Asia's labor force age groups,[66] compared with 122 million during the 1960s. Open unemployment tends to be most severe among the young, and in particular among the relatively well-educated young entrants to the labor market. Estimates of underemployment (normally based on the number of people working fewer than 40 hours per week who say that they want to work more hours) are not as high in most Southern Asian surveys as is generally thought. A third or more of the rural work force in countries such as India, the Philippines, and Indonesia work less than 40 hours per week, but substantial numbers within this group do not want more work. However, these approaches to measuring the severity of unemployment problems are subject to many limitations. Unemployment is in a sense a luxury that the desperately poor cannot afford. They are willing to sit for long hours on the sidewalk (i.e., to be fully employed) in order to sell a few shoelaces. Seen in this light, the unemployment problem and the poverty problem are inextricably intertwined and difficult to measure in neat percentage terms. They are problems that will not "go away" in the 1970s.

The Population Dilemma and the Ultimate Aims of Development

At the beginning of the 1970s the paramount demographic problem in Southern Asia is the control of rapid population growth. It is a formidable problem. Compared with the expansion of Europe following the Industrial Revolution, the population base is enormously greater, the rate of population growth applied to this base is considerably higher in most cases, and the result is that absolute numbers of individuals far beyond anything known earlier must somehow be absorbed. All this is occurring at a time when free migration to open lands is no longer available to lessen temporary population pressures at home. Nor is there anything comparable to the rapid increase in manufacturing resources and markets that European traders found abroad.

So far in South and Southeast Asia the instruments for the reduction of population growth have been of limited effectiveness. The current type of family planning programs is probably inadequate to cope with the enormity of the problem. Broader social changes are difficult to effect even if we assume that there is agreement on their nature. How does one change the status of women in a nation, for example, except in relation to broad development programs? How does a nation with limited resources build the expensive infrastructure for development?

It would appear, paradoxically, that development is both the goal and the means to achieve that goal. But clearly, development in any Western sense for each country in Asia is an impossible short-time goal and a highly unlikely one over a longer period of time. For these reasons, there must be inventive new programs initiated in the 1970s to foster a development program better suited to the conditions in Asian nations.

So far we have assumed that development policies in the countries of Southern Asia are directed toward the rather traditional ends of raising output and per capita income, shifting the economic center of gravity from agriculture to industry, improving social services, and raising the welfare of the people. We have viewed their growth as similar to that of other countries which experienced their economic "take-off" a century or so earlier. It is generally taken for granted that the ultimate aim, for example, of the Indian government is to become another U.S.A., with a similar level of industrial development—measured in terms of concrete freeways per head of population, and all the rest.[67] But such assumptions raise serious issues. Success in achieving this aim could well impose intolerable strains on the world's supply of industrial metals and sources of energy and on the means of waste disposal and pollution control. Certainly, the strains of economic success would be even more intolerable if India's population reaches one billion by the end of the century as some projections indicate. An India of one billion people would have to produce and consume roughly 86 times more than it does at the moment to achieve present U.S. living standards. Even to reach present average European standards, it would have to produce and consume about 35 times more than it does now.

The point to be stressed is that the population in Southern Asia is already too large to permit the traditional pattern of growth toward the nirvana of the mass-consumption society, and that the massive population increases expected before the end of the century will only push that nirvana further into realms of fantasy. Some of the smaller and wealthier countries—Malaysia, Singapore, perhaps Thailand—could conceivably reach Western mass-consumption patterns, but for the masses of Southern Asia this just is not feasible. Development goals must be reformulated and development strategy reoriented accordingly. But there is little evidence that development planners in the Southern Asian countries, or in the international agencies, have faced this unwelcome fact.

Part two
Problems of Urbanization

Chapter 3

The Demography of Bangkok: The Case of a Primate City * *Sidney Goldstein*

EDITORS' NOTE: The opening paper on urbanization focuses on Bangkok, an exaggerated example of a prepondentant, primate city —one which in size alone overshadows its nearest urban rivals. In this and many other respects, it bears substantial resemblance to Djakarta and Manila, and to Bombay, Calcutta, and Madras in relation to their respective hinterlands. A number of the perspectives Sidney Goldstein uses in this first comprehensive analysis of the demographic characteristics of Bangkok were also utilized by the other writers concerned with problems of urbanization.

Beginning with an overview of urbanization in Asia, he then presents a detailed examination of the pattern of urbanization in Thailand, particularly the changing demographic characteristics of Bangkok and an evaluation of the city's central role in the economic and social development of the country. He discusses in- and out-migration, fertility differentials, and the contemporary importance of natural increase in swelling the city's size. His data, like Weiner's and Burki's, confirm that in-migrants are drawn to the city by expectations of income advantages, and their selective return suggests an ability to discern the comparative advantages of different locations over time.

* As in chapter 2, where generalizations about the entire area are taken from United Nations tables, they include data drawn from Iran and Afghanistan in addition to the countries included in "Southern Asia" as defined in this volume. (Eds. footnote)

AUTHOR'S NOTE: The project of which this study is a part was initiated while the author served, under sponsorship of the Population Council, as Demographic Adviser to the Institute of Population Studies at Chulalongkorn University, Bangkok. The cooperation of the National Statistical Office in Bangkok in making unpublished data available is gratefully acknowledged. This paper was completed pursuant to Contract No. NIH-70-2190 with the National Institutes of Health, Department of Health, Education and Welfare. The full text, including statistical tables, on which this report is based appears in Sidney Goldstein, *The Demography of Bangkok,* Research Report No. 7 (Bangkok: Institute of Population Studies, Chulalongkorn University, 1972).

The author presents considerable evidence bearing on the size and substance of the urban-rural gap. He compares Bangkok and rural residents in their educational opportunities, and their health, housing, and consumption patterns. Employment and growing unemployment are also considered. While administrative and political analyses of Thailand tend to emphasize the functional cleavage between Bangkok and the rest of the country, demographic analysis, at least, suggests that the rural-urban gap may be exaggerated.

Goldstein warns of the social consequences of Bangkok's present rapid rate of growth and speculates on policies which might help the city to deal with a threatened trebling of the population within the next twenty-five years.

Introduction

The rapid growth of urban agglomerations in developing countries constitutes a problem second only to the high rate of population growth. Indeed, the former may well be a function of the latter. At mid-twentieth century, just over one-fourth of the world's 2.5 billion people were living in urban places; but latest United Nations estimates indicate that by the end of the century over half of the world's 6.5 billion people will inhabit urban places.[1] This marked shift in rural-urban population distribution is made even more dramatic by the fact that so much of the world's urban growth has been concentrated in big cities of 500,000 and over.[2] In 1920 such cities contained 37.9 percent of the total urban population. By 1960 the big-city share had increased to 46.7 percent. And United Nations estimates for 1980 indicate a further increase to 53.3 percent.

Many of these big cities, particularly the increasing number in the developing world, dominate both the urban structure and the economic, social, and political life in their respective countries.[3] Many have grown as a result of population pressures in rural areas rather than industrial expansion. Most are characterized by inadequate housing, public utilities, job opportunities, educational facilities, and transport facilities.

Despite the many generalizations about urbanization that appear in the literature, much of our evaluation of levels and rates of urbanization in the developing world, of the components of urban growth, and of the composition of urban and especially big-city populations is based on scanty data. The United Nations and research organizations like the Institute of International Studies at the University of California have provided increasingly comprehensive and high-quality core data for regions and countries of the world and, to a lesser extent, for big cities.[4] These permit valuable comparative analyses and provide important insights into future trends. But their very comprehensiveness limits their value by precluding intensive examination of the process of urbanization. For such purposes in-depth studies are needed in a number of countries at different stages of development, in different regions of the world, and with different combinations of unique situations ranging from the city-state character of Hong Kong and Singapore to the highly rural character of countries like Nepal and Afghanistan.

Thailand is a developing country in which urbanization is assuming increasing importance. Moreover, in virtually all discussions of the role of big cities in urban and economic development, Bangkok is cited as a leading example of a primate city.[5] Bangkok also illustrates clearly the fact that big-city growth is disproportionate to urbanization and may be significantly out of line with economic development.

This paper examines, as far as the still limited available data permit, the patterns of urbanization in Thailand, with particular attention to the growth of Bangkok and to the characteristics of its population. The emphasis here, by intent, is on the demographic features of the city, which serve as the first step in the subsequent fuller evaluation of the city's role in the economic and social development of Thailand. Focusing on Thailand and Bangkok does not mean that their experiences typify all developing countries and big cities. The country and the city are both typical as well as unique, and thus we need both the global comparative approach exemplified by the United Nations data and the more intensive investigations of the type undertaken here.

Urbanization in Asia: An Overview

Although still one of the least urbanized regions of the world, Asia has begun to experience rapid urban growth. At the same time, however, the rural population of Asia also continues to increase. But because past and future patterns of change are not uniform throughout the region, a distinction is made here between East Asia and Southern Asia, and within the latter, brief attention is given to Southeast Asia, of which Thailand forms a part.[6]

At mid-twentieth century, East Asia contained 48 percent of the 1.35 billion persons of the continent, and Southern Asia 52 percent; and in each 15.9 percent of the population lived in urban places. But this close similarity soon ceased. By 1970 only 45 percent of the continent's 2.1 billion persons lived in East Asia and 55 percent in Southern Asia, with Southern Asia's urbanization level reaching only 21.2 percent compared with 28.6 percent for East Asia. Projections indicate that these differential trends will continue to the end of the century, when, according to United Nations estimates, East Asia's urban population will number half of its total population whereas that of Southern Asia will amount to only one-third. In sheer numbers this means a sevenfold increase in fifty years, from just over 100 million persons in urban places in each region in 1950 to 722 million in urban places in East Asia and 793 million in Southern Asia by 2000. Faster initial urban growth in East Asia will be mitigated by slower growth toward the end of the century, whereas in Southern Asia slower initial growth will be compensated by higher rates in succeeding decades.

In the meantime, the growth rate of the rural population in East Asia, which in 1950–60 was already below the world average and considerably below the average of less developed regions, will continue to decrease. The projections suggest that by the last decade of the century, East Asia's rural population will actually decline. By contrast, Southern Asia's population growth rate, already relatively high during the 1950–60 decade, will increase through the 1970–80 decade, after which it is expected to fall off. Yet, by the year 2000, the average growth rate of 1.4 a year will still be almost twice that of the world as a whole and 40 percent above that of the less developed regions of the world.

By the year 2000, East Asia's rural population will be only 24 percent greater than it was in 1950 and only 6 percent greater than in 1970, while Southern Asia's rural population will be three times greater than in 1950 and twice the estimated 1970 population. Yet, even more significant, the estimates indicate that between 1970 and 2000, 673 million persons will be added to the rural population of Southern Asia compared with an absolute increase of 555 million in the urban population. These changes will have significant implications for the quality of life in the rural places and possibly for the tempo of urbanization owing to pressures created by the crowded rural areas.

The problem is intensified by the rapid growth in the larger cities.[7] Before 1950 Asia had only 15 cities with populations of more than 500,000. By 1960 there were 79 cities of this size, nine of them with more than 2.5 million inhabitants. Asia's big cities in 1960 contained 40 percent of the total urban population, compared with just over one-fourth in 1920, and projections point to even greater proportions of the total urban population living in big cities in the next several decades.

Approximately one-fourth of Southern Asia's 1950 population was located in Southeast Asia, where the pace of urban concentration closely parallels that of South Asia as a whole. In 1950, 15 percent of Southeast Asia's population lived in urban places. This increased to 21.1 percent by 1970 and is estimated to rise to 33.4 percent by 2000. This means an increase from 26 million to 60 million between 1950 and 1970 and to 203 million by 2000. Although growing at a slower rate, the rural population will undergo an even greater absolute increase, rising from 147 million in 1950 to 227 million in 1970 and to an estimated 405 million by 2000.

The above figures all lend weight to the argument that levels and rates of urbanization are a vital part of the larger problem of rapid population growth.

Thailand: Historical Perspectives

Thailand's population, only about 6 million in 1900, numbered 26.3 million in 1960 and is estimated at about 35 million in 1970. This sixfold increase in seventy years reflects an average annual growth rate of about 2 percent for the thirty years following World War I, and, most significant, an annual increase to 3.2 percent between 1947 and 1960, and the same or a slightly higher rate since then.

Thailand's growth rate is among the highest in the world. It stems from a sharp drop in mortality coupled with a continuing high fertility rate,[8] averaging 45 per thousand as late as 1960–65. Although considerable interest is being evinced in family planning and the use of birth control is increasing, these attitudes and practices are not yet sufficiently widespread nor of long enough duration to have affected the birth rate significantly.[9]

Judged by both the residence and the economic activity of the population, Thailand remains largely a rural, agricultural country with over 80 percent of the economically active population employed in farming in 1960. But the significant increase in population density in the twentieth century has reduced arable land from 2.7 acres per person in 1930 to 0.9 in 1970; and a reduction to only 0.5 by 1990 is projected, thereby markedly increasing the pressure on rural resources.[10]

In Thailand, the level of urbanization is not only considerably lower than that of the developed world but also far below that of the rest of Southeast Asia. In 1960, 12.5 percent of the population lived in urban places compared with 22.9 percent for the developing world as a whole and 17.8 percent for Southeast Asia. Because the rural growth rate in Thailand is considerably higher than that of the rest of the world, the speed of urbanization is not as marked. Yet, although the projected level of urbanization continues to remain low, Thailand's urban growth rate is high, averaging about 5 percent a year.

The rapid increase of Greater Bangkok warrants particular attention. The capital city area, consisting of the twin cities of Bangkok and Thonburi, numbered 1.8 million persons in 1960; by 1967 the population had reached 2.6 million, and is estimated in 1970 at about 3 million. Containing over half of all of Thailand's urban population, Greater Bangkok accounted for almost two-thirds of all urban population growth in the country; its 1967 population was 32 times that of Thailand's next largest city, making its urban primacy the most striking in the world. Although urban development has begun to permeate all regions of Thailand and has become an important factor in the complex process of national, social, and economic development, the continuing primacy of Greater Bangkok requires that any study of urbanization in Thailand give particular attention to the dynamics underlying its growth and to the ways in which its population resembles or differs from the rest of the kingdom.

Bangkok is a relatively young city, having first been established as Thailand's capital in 1782. After the conclusion of a treaty with Britain in the mid-nineteenth century opened the way to trade with the West, the dual character of Bangkok as a preindustrial city and a rapidly growing commercial center emerged. The establishment of shipping houses and wharves at the end of the nineteenth century transformed it from a floating village into a modern metropolis with a population of almost one-third of a million by the end of the century.

Built on an alluvial silt delta of the Chao Phraya River, Bangkok was accessible to ocean-going ships and was at the same time intimately tied to the hinterland through a large and effective network of rivers and canals crisscrossing the central plain, "the rice bowl" of Southeast Asia.

Today Greater Bangkok is still the link between Thailand and the rest of the world and remains the integrating center for the country's political, economic, social, and intellectual life.[11] Concentrated within Bangkok are the major universities, a disproportionate number of the health services, the major industrial and commercial organizations, the important newspapers and other communications media, and the social and political elite. In all respects, Bangkok illustrates most aptly Mark Jefferson's belief that regardless of why one city might originally exceed its neighbors in size, once it did "this mere fact gives it an impetus to grow that cannot affect any other city and it draws away from all of them in character as well as size." [12]

Urbanization Patterns

In the absence of official statistical definitions of "urban," it is impossible to ascertain long-run trends in the development of Thailand's urban population.[13] But a number of approaches can be used to assess the pace and scope of urbanization.

Shorter-run patterns of urbanization can be analyzed by using the municipal area as the equivalent of urban population and relying upon a combination of census and registration materials.[14] The level of urbanization in Thailand increased from 9.9 percent in 1947 to 13.1 percent in 1960 [15] and had risen further to 14.4 percent by the end of 1967. Between 1947 and 1960, the urban population grew at an average annual rate of 5.0 percent, compared with an annual growth rate of 3.0 percent for the rural population. Between 1960 and 1967, this significant differential narrowed only slightly. Using the total population in municipal areas, however, may give misleading results because of the problems of definition. If, for comparative purposes, the analysis is restricted to those municipalities having 20,000 or more persons, the percentage of the Thai population classified as urban increased from 5.2 in 1947 to 11.7 in 1967. During these twenty years, the average annual rate of urban population growth was 7.0 percent compared with 3.0 percent for the other parts of Thailand. Using this definition of urban, therefore, produces an even higher rate of urbanization.

Changing levels of urbanization can also be assessed by comparing the number of places of given size and the distribution of population among them. Of the 116 places designated as municipal areas in 1947, counting Bangkok and Thonburi as a single unit, almost three-fourths had fewer than 10,000 persons and 95 percent were under 20,000. Judged by size of place, therefore, urbanization, with the notable exception of Bangkok, was at a very low level. By 1967, the profile had changed significantly. Of the 119 places, the number with fewer than 10,000 persons was reduced to just over one-third, the number of places with 10,000–20,000 inhabitants remained at one-third, but the number with 20,000–50,000 increased from 4.4 to 27.8 percent. Thus a considerable shift had taken place from small-sized to moderate-sized places.

In 1967, as in 1947, Bangkok-Thonburi remained unchallenged as Thailand's primate city and by then had become even more preponderant. The city's population, which in 1947 was 21 times greater than that of Chiengmai, the next largest place in Thailand 543 miles to the north, was 32 times greater in 1967.

The statistics on changing distribution of urban places by population size represent only the net changes. Ascertaining the actual shifts in size-categories for particular places permits a more accurate evaluation of urban development patterns. Of the total of 116 municipal areas in 1947, 81 had changed size category by 1960, and all but 2 moved up. Furthermore, although at least half of all places in every size category in 1947 had changed category by 1960, the smaller size groups showed proportionately less growth than the larger. Between 1960 and 1967 just under half of the municipal areas changed size category, all upward, with the smaller size groups again showing the greatest stability. Thus the superficial stability indicated between 1960 and 1967 for places with populations between 10,000 and 20,000 masks a considerable shift out of this size range balanced by an equally large shift into it from among the many places with populations below 10,000.

Changing urbanization level can also be judged by population distribution among size categories. At each successive enumeration, proportionately more persons were living in larger urban places. Almost one-half of the urban population lived in places under 20,000 in 1947, one-fourth did so in 1960, and just under one-fifth did so in 1967. The proportion living in places of 20,000–50,000 increased from 7.3 percent in 1947 to 22.0 percent in 1967. There were no cities of 50,000–100,000 in 1947, but this category accounted for 3.4 percent in 1967. Yet, completely dominating the scene is the primacy of Greater Bangkok with 45.1 percent of the 1947 urban population, 53.2 percent in 1960, and 55.9 percent in 1967.

Larger places clearly occupy a more important role in the overall growth of Thailand's urban population. Of the total urban increase between 1947 and 1960 of 1,648,526 persons, 68 percent is attributable to the largest 10 of the total of 116 urban places, with Greater Bangkok alone accounting for 61 percent of the increase. Between 1960 and 1967 the same pattern persisted. The few largest of 119 urban places accounted for 71 percent of the urban increase with Greater Bangkok alone accounting for 63 percent.

In each of Thailand's four regions, the proportion of persons living in urban places was higher in 1967 than in 1947, showing that despite the continuing dominance of Bangkok-Thonburi in the Central region, overall urban development had begun to permeate the country and had become an important factor in the complex process of national, social, and economic development.

On the other hand, the existence of primate cities such as Bangkok-Thonburi encourages more industrial, commercial, and service activities to locate within them. This in turn attracts potential migrants to the primate city and detracts from the growth potential of other cities and from the positive effects that even greater decentralized urban growth might have on economic and social development in other regions.

Components of Urban Growth

Natural Increase. Urban population growth results from the net impact of several processes: (1) natural increase or decrease, reflecting the balance between births and deaths; (2) net migration, resulting from the balance between the total movement into and out of the urban areas; (3) increases due to changes in urban boundaries, usually through annexation of adjoining areas; (4) designation of new areas as urban places as they meet the official criteria. In Thailand urban growth in recent decades has been only minimally affected by the designation of new urban areas. Increases in the urban population therefore result mainly from the interaction of the first three processes. Yet because of deficiencies in available statistics it is difficult, if not impossible, to identify the separate components of urban growth. Data from a Survey of Population Change, which was conducted in the mid-1960s and encompassed the entire country except Bangkok-Thonburi,[16] suggest that urbanization contributes significantly to reductions in fertility levels, for regardless of the fertility measure used, the level of births in municipal areas was far below that in non-municipal areas.

The data on mortality indicate that the standardized death rate for municipal areas is approaching half that of the non-municipal areas and that the infant mortality rate is only three-quarters as high. Thus, despite the poor conditions often associated with urban life in developing countries, the net effect on health, as measured by mortality levels, is favorable. The exclusion of Bangkok-Thonburi from the survey precludes direct comparison with smaller urban and rural places.

The most recent data for Bangkok, from its own registry, show a death rate fairly consistent with that noted by the Survey of Population Change for municipal areas. Bangkok's birth rate is considerably above that of other municipal areas and even above the crude birth rate of the non-municipal areas, as reported in the Survey. However, since the city's death and birth rates are uncorrected for underenumeration and are unstandardized, they must be used with caution.

The 1960 Thai census ascertained the number of children ever born to all ever married women in Thailand; and these data have been used to evaluate urban-rural differentials in fertility level.[17] Urban-rural residence is related to fertility, with a clear decline in the level of fertility from the most rural to the most urban category.[18] Bangkok's level, 25 percent below that of the most rural parts of Thailand, corroborates the significant impact of the urban metropolis on fertility.

Research not reported here suggests that factors such as selective migration to the metropolitan area and the selective effect of factors such as age at marriage, percent married, and participation in the labor force contribute to these rural-urban differentials. But regardless of specific reasons, the association of higher urbanization levels with lower fertility suggests that increased urbanization may become an important factor in reducing the overall levels of fertility in Thailand.

Rural to Urban Migration. The rapid pace of urbanization and its significance for social and economic conditions in the developing world emphasize the need for consideration of the role of migration in the urbanization process and its relation to social, economic, and demographic development.[19] Research on the potential for social change inherent in migration is particularly needed. Migration may well have a strong impact not only on the large metropolis and on smaller urban places to which migrants move but also on the small, isolated villages that the migrants leave and to which a number of them return. Movement in both directions may serve as a catalyst speeding up modernization and economic development in the extensive rural segments of the developing world while heavy migration may at the same time exacerbate the problems in urban places.

Data from the 1960 Thai census give some insights into the relation between migration and urban growth.[20] Two sets of internal migrants can be identified: (1) persons who were living in a different province from that in which they were born, known as lifetime migrants; and (2) persons living in a province different from that in which they resided five years before the census, known as five-year migrants. Both sets of data have all the defects inherent in these types of migration statistics, compounded by the problems associated with census-taking in a developing country.[21] Although they give no definitive answers to the role of migration in urban growth, they clearly point to the importance of migration to urbanization.

The data on lifetime migrants indicate that over one-third of all persons living in Bangkok were born in a different province; this percentage declined consistently to less than 10 percent for those living in rural, agricultural places. The place-of-birth statistics also show that for all age groups the percentage of lifetime migrants is higher for Bangkok than for any of the other categories, urban or rural, with the differentials between Bangkok and the most rural category most marked. The magnitude of Bangkok's levels, reaching 60 percent or higher in the age group 35–39 and over, is consistent with Bangkok's high rate of growth. Clearly such growth could only have resulted from heavy movement into the metropolitan area. However, the significantly higher proportions of older persons who are lifetime inmigrants suggest that an increasing proportion of the city's growth in recent decades may be attributable to natural increase, representing births occurring both to native residents of the city and to migrants. At the other extreme of the urban-rural continuum, data suggest that a high degree of stability characterizes the population still living in rural places in 1960. Any upsurge in movement on the part of this large rural population reservoir, especially to urban places and to Bangkok, could have significant implications.

Using the five-year residence criterion, the overall level of migration is considerably lower, but again Bangkok shows the highest in-migration, taking males and females together. The five-year data demonstrate the selective nature of migration: rising levels characterize the young, peaking at ages 20–24 for males and 20–29 for females, followed thereafter by fairly continuous decline with increasing age. These age differentials clearly characterize each of the urban-rural categories, but tend to be particularly accentuated in Bangkok where one out of every five males between 20 and 24 in 1960 had moved into the city during the previous five years. Except for the two youngest age groups, where there is close correspondence between males and females, the rates for females are consistently below those for males. Urban places outside of Bangkok also experienced heavy in-movement, indicating that in recent years moderate-sized urban places in Thailand have begun to undergo rapid growth.

In Thailand, as in many countries of the world, migration is not a one-way process,[22] and out-migration from highly urban areas is an inherent part of the urbanization process. Almost 10 percent of the capital's native-born population had moved to other parts of Thailand by 1960. Furthermore, while 127,500 migrants moved into the provinces containing the Bangkok metropolitan area between 1955 and 1960, there was a corresponding movement of half this number from the capital provinces to the rest of the country.

The importance for the developing country of this substantial out-migration from the primate city must not be overlooked. The Thai data indicate that a considerable portion of the out-migrants from Bangkok go to smaller urban places. These may be people who have not found work in Bangkok or who seek to take advantage of new opportunities in the growing, moderate-sized urban places in the other regions. As an ILO survey of migrants in Bangkok found, the primary reason for coming to the city was economic.[23] Most of the migrants had no definite plans to return home unless they could not find employment and the economic outlook proved unfavorable. These data suggest that Sovani may be correct in his conclusion that rural-urban migration is not such a blind phenomenon resulting in over-migration to urban areas because of the rural push. The migrants seem to be cautious and discerning, and the migration process is reversible. But the fact that the out-migration from Bangkok includes a substantial number of persons born in the capital area also suggests that out-movement is not restricted to return migration.

These census statistics are generally superficial and give no insight into the dynamics underlying the migration process itself, the effects such movements have on the migrants or on the places of destination and origin. The magnitude of the movement does suggest that internal migration may be a major instrument of change both in the industrialization and economic development of the country by attracting persons to urban places and in the spreading of urban values and patterns of behavior through the movement of significant numbers from the large metropolis to rural places or smaller urban locations. But to the extent that the manpower needs and economic conditions in the metropolis may not justify such large numbers of newcomers, migration may also exacerbate the problems faced by Greater Bangkok and contribute to the maladjustment of the migrants themselves.

Interrelations of Migration and Fertility. The fertility differentials characterizing the migrant and non-migrant segments of the population illustrate in part the role of migration in inducing social change.[24] The fertility levels of the five-year migrants are lower than those of non-migrants in all urban-rural categories, but especially in Bangkok. They are also well below the levels of the non-migrants in the rural, agricultural category from which most of the migrants probably came. The data do not permit full determination of whether migration operated as cause or effect of lower fertility. Yet this clear association of migration with lower fertility level, coupled with the fact that the fertility level, regardless of migration status, is considerably lower for residents of urban places than rural places, attests to the important role of both migration and urbanization in affecting fertility levels. In Bangkok, the age-standardized fertility of migrant women is 2,982 children ever born per 1,000 ever married women, compared with 3,427 for the non-migrant women. But even more significant, in the rural, agricultural category, fertility averaged 4,468 children ever born per 1,000 ever married women. These differentials by both migration status and urbanization level suggest that movement to urban places, while compounding some of the problems associated with rapid urbanization, may have the positive by-product of reducing fertility levels for migrant women. At the same time, a considerable movement out of the large cities to other parts of Thailand may affect fertility levels in the smaller places through the ideas and patterns of behavior the migrants bring with them after exposure to life in the metropolis.

Some insights into the relative importance of migration and natural increase in Greater Bangkok's growth can be obtained from the data available for Thailand.[25] The place-of-birth data indicate that a large majority of persons 25 years old and over were born outside Bangkok, suggesting that in earlier decades migration provided the major source of population growth. Two sets of data indicate, however, that in recent years natural increase accounts for more of the growth than migration: (1) a significant majority of the inhabitants of Bangkok under age 25 were born within the city and its province; (2) more directly, estimates based on registration data show that between January 1, 1961, and December 31, 1967, natural increase accounted for between 60 and 67 percent (depending on the completeness of vital statistics) of the total population increase of the metropolitan area.[26]

Both sets of data therefore support Davis' claim that, contrary to popular opinion, the main factor in the rapid inflation of city populations is not rural-urban migration but sheer biological increase at an unprecedented rate.[27] In supporting the validity of such a conclusion for Bangkok, it is important to recognize (1) that a considerable portion of the natural increase in recent years is attributable to the fertility of the migrants who had moved into Bangkok earlier; and (2) that in the overall growth of Bangkok, the reduced level of migration in recent years still contributes significantly to total growth, particularly since it reflects the effect of net migration only. In pointing to the importance of natural increase in Bangkok's growth, these data stress that even if migration were to slow down, the city would continue to grow at a considerable rate because of the large excess of births over deaths. This underscores the pressing need for greater success in efforts to reduce fertility levels in the metropolitan area as well as in Thailand as a whole.

Family Planning Activities. In general, studies of the knowledge, attitudes, and practices (KAP) of the population regarding family planning have shown a high level of interest and motivation among Thai women, but with knowledge and practice varying according to levels of education, urbanization, and modernization.[28] Where family information services are available, acceptance is higher than in most Asian countries, although not attaining levels equal to the interest shown in survey results. Until 1970 Thailand did not have an official policy favoring birth control, although a number of programs had been undertaken to make birth control information available to women seeking it. Most family planning activity has taken place in Greater Bangkok where the major hospitals and clinics are concentrated and where the population is more amenable to practicing family planning.

According to the official statistics prepared by the Ministry of Public Health,[29] as of April 1971 almost 700,000 women in Thailand had accepted some form of contraceptives through clinics operated by the Department of Medical Services and other programs. Of this number, 28 percent lived in Bangkok, far above what one would expect on the basis of Bangkok's 7 percent share of Thailand's total population. With the development of a national program and the diffusion of facilities and trained personnel throughout the country, this concentration of family planning activities in Greater Bangkok can be expected to diminish in proportion to activities in the rest of the country over the next decade.

In fact, such a trend is already evident in data on acceptors of contraception obtained from a national reporting system begun in 1969. Whereas Bangkok initially accounted for one-fourth of the monthly number of acceptors in Thailand, by 1971 the number had diminished to 10 percent. This change could begin to have a significant impact on the rate of population growth and, in turn, reduce the pressures fostering the rural exodus to Bangkok and other urban places. At the same time, the continuing development of the family planning program within Bangkok and the greater availability there of contraceptives sold commercially or through private prescription provide some hope that the city's rate of natural increase and population growth may decline.

Until the results of comparative surveys in urban and rural parts of the country become available, comprehensive evaluation of rural-urban differentials in knowledge and practice of family planning must remain speculative, although available evidence, including a lower birth rate, points to Bangkok as the major center for family planning activity. On this basis, its role as an initiator of social change in this important demographic sphere may be indicative of the role that the metropolis occupies as a diffusion center in the urban hierarchy as well as in relation to the large rural hinterland.[30]

Intra-Urban Distribution and Mobility

Using registration data, Sternstein analyzed population growth patterns in the Greater Bangkok Metropolitan Area between 1956 and 1960, paying particular attention to intra-urban population distribution.[31] He found that the residential densities declined regularly from 100,000 per square kilometer in the center of the city to a lobed periphery of little more than 5,000 per square kilometer. Four-fifths of the twin cities' populations lived in density areas of fewer than 50,000 per square kilometer and half of them in areas with fewer than 20,000 to the square kilometer.

Comparison of the 1960 distribution patterns with those of 1950 indicate that

> the less densely settled outer portion of the built-up area and adjacent wards, as well as those where roads traverse the surrounding cultivated lands, gain population through movement while the more densely settled inner portion of the built-up area and the greater part of the agricultural environs lost population through movement. The net effect was that in wards which were already thickly settled, density lessened but gently for the most part whereas in wards less closely settled, densities generally increased, but usually not markedly.

Consistent with our findings, Sternstein concludes that "the major part of the great growth of population in Greater Bangkok Metropolitan Area during the period 1956–1960 is attributable to a notable rate of natural increase, though a substantial in-migration contributed handsomely." [32]

By contrast, changes in the distribution of the population within the city reflect largely the effects of internal movement, compounding the instability that may already characterize the metropolitan area as a result of relatively large in- and out-movements. Although nine wards had an excess of out-movements, no ward experienced an absolute loss of population because natural increase was sufficiently high to compensate for net losses due to out-migration. Above all, Sternstein emphasizes that the data suggest a general "transientness." Evidently, many provincials find employment in the city for short periods of time and then leave. Moreover, neighborhood relocations are considerable. Sternstein concludes that much of the vigorous extension of the built-up area between 1956 and 1960 appears attributable to a domestic movement from the center to the periphery, with migrants from elsewhere replacing losses from the inner area and augmenting gains to the outer area. Such a pattern may represent the beginning of suburbanization.

Population Composition

Concern with the sheer numbers involved in city growth in the developing world should not supersede examination of the social and economic differences between urban and rural populations.[33] The kinds of problems that cities face, the role of the urban metropolis in the overall modernization process, and the adjustment of the population to urban life may all be influenced by the differential composition of the urban population. Special tabulations from the 1960 Thai census provide one of the first opportunities to compare comprehensively the characteristics of the Bangkok population with those of inhabitants in smaller urban places in Thailand and in the rural segments of the country. The discussion here will focus largely on Bangkok. In all comparisons, age is controlled by direct standardization.[34]

Age-Sex Composition. As is typical of most developing countries, and reflecting its very high birth rate, both Thailand as a whole and Bangkok are characterized by a very young population. Despite the selective migration characteristic of movement to Bangkok and the differential patterns of fertility and mortality, the age composition of its population is similar to that of the total kingdom and to each of the four other categories—urban, agricultural; urban, non-agricultural; rural, agricultural; and rural, non-agricultural. More than half of the Thai population are under 20 years of age, and only 3 percent are 65 and over. Almost 40 percent are under 13 years of age, suggesting the enormous challenge that the country as a whole and the urban metropolis in particular face in the task of education and eventually in providing adequate employment opportunities.

The effects of migration show up more with respect to sex composition. Because migration to Bangkok has been more heavily male, Bangkok has a higher sex ratio, 103 males per 100 females, than does the total kingdom. But these differentials do not operate uniformly throughout the age structure. Reflecting the combined effects of differentials in sex ratio at birth, which favor males, the higher sex ratio of migrants, the higher mortality rates of males, and undoubtedly, errors in census reporting, the sex ratio tends to be irregular among different age groups.[35] However, the dominant male migration to Bangkok is clearly evidenced in the excess of males over females between the ages of 25 and 40. By contrast, with only one exception, the sex ratio favors the females in older age groups, where women outnumber men by almost two to one. In a society that has not yet developed a comprehensive system of social security and medical care, such a distorted sex ratio among the aged may contribute significantly to urban problems, particularly as the aged group grows.

Marital status. Both fertility levels and the overall stability of life in the urban metropolis may be affected by the marital status of the population.[36] A number of studies have suggested that the unmarried outnumber the married in the movement to the city. Limited information on the marital status of migrants supports such a conclusion. The marital composition of Bangkok's population also shows significant differences from that of rural areas and the kingdom as a whole.

In the total kingdom 38 percent of all adult males (aged 13 and over) were single and 57 percent were married; the remaining small proportion were widowed or divorced. By contrast, in Bangkok 45 percent of all males were single and 48 percent married; 5.3 percent were widowed or divorced. A combination of a higher proportion of both single persons and those widowed or divorced suggests that the city attracts in particular those without immediate family ties, or at least that it is easier for such individuals to leave the rural areas for the city. Moreover, within the married group, Bangkok contains a disproportionate number of persons living without their spouse, almost one-fourth of all married males, in contrast to virtually none in rural, agricultural households.

The basic pattern is similar for females, including a large proportion with spouse absent. It may be that in a number of cases the absent spouse was actually resident in Bangkok but the nature of the employment required separate residence. Some women working as domestic servants, for example, may live in and thus be counted as married with spouse absent. On the other hand, a number of married persons may leave their families in the village until they become established economically in the urban metropolis, or as suggested by the volume of return migration, until they can leave the city. Whatever the reason, with about 40 percent of Bangkok's total adult population married and reported living with spouse, there remain large numbers of unattached individuals in the city, many of whom are probably recent migrants and a considerable proportion of whom may be either unemployed or underemployed. Meeting the social, psychological, and economic needs of these individuals presents a major challenge.

The differential in marital composition reflects in part a differential in age at marriage, which in Bangkok is later than in the rural parts of Thailand. For males in Bangkok the age at which 50 percent are married is 26.7, more than two years higher than the 24.3 average characterizing rural, agricultural areas. The differential is not as great for females, but it is also higher for Bangkok, 22.7 compared with 21.3. Such later age at marriage may contribute to, but also not entirely account for, the lower fertility of the Bangkok population. The later age at marriage, however, does contribute to a much higher proportion of single, unattached persons in age groups under 30.

In his study of Southeast Asian cities, McGee questions the contention that the traditional ties of family life are breaking down under the impact of urban life.[37] Census data in themselves are inadequate to test whether the traditional network of social relations continues even though the members of the nuclear family are separated. More information is needed on the extent to which such individuals rely on kinship ties, associating with and often living with kin in the city, as well as the extent to which they maintain ties with kin in the village.[38]

Labor Force and Occupation. Both the volume and direction of migration have been influenced by a complex series of factors that have frequently been subsumed under the concepts of "push" and "pull." [39] Among those factors classified as "push," most prominent are the high rate of rural population growth and the stagnant rural economy, with the consequent increase in population density and the pressure on limited land resources. This situation is aggravated in many places by the low level of agricultural industrialization resulting in low efficiency and productivity. In a number of villages the lack of non-agricultural occupations to absorb the surplus labor and the stagnation of handicraft industries contribute further incentives for exodus to towns and cities. At the other extreme, classified as the "pull" factors, are many aspects of the urban way of life such as better employment and educational opportunities, better housing and social facilities, the chance for social mobility, and the excitement of urban life itself. But increasingly, studies have emphasized that it is an extreme oversimplification to attempt to isolate "push" and "pull" factors.[40] Not only are the factors affecting movement complex; the decision to move may often be a function of the individual's perception of the comparative situations rather than of real differentials. The high levels of turnover and return migration support such a conclusion.

Yet, overriding all the other factors cited as cause of "push" or "pull" are economic considerations and particularly the differential in employment and income-earning potentials, at least as this differential is perceived by migrants.[41] But to the extent that the opportunities available in the still underdeveloped industrial sector of the urban metropolis do not match either the numbers of migrants moving in or the educational and occupational skills of the migrants, the urban population and particularly the big-city population may be subject to considerable unemployment, underemployment, or concentration in occupations, especially in the service sector, that require minimum skill and minimum economic resources.

Reflecting the close similarity in age structure between Bangkok and the rest of Thailand, minimal differences exist in the proportion of persons of working age in the metropolis compared with rural areas and the kingdom as a whole. Yet there are significant differentials in the proportion of individuals who are economically active, particularly among females. Among males aged 11 and over, just under 70 percent in Bangkok were in the labor force in contrast to 88 percent of males in rural, agricultural households. This differential stems mainly from the earlier entrance of the rural males into the labor force and their tendency to remain economically active for a longer time. In Bangkok, a large proportion of the males under age 20 were still students, and after age 50 there is a greater tendency for men to withdraw from the labor force.

The female labor force shows even sharper differences between Bangkok and rural Thailand. Only 34 percent of Bangkok's women aged 11 and over were in the labor force in contrast to 87 percent of the women in rural, agricultural households. This high labor force participation rate for women —one of the highest in the world—is, in part, a statistical artifact, since all women engaged in farming are counted as members of the labor force even though they are unpaid family workers. This practice has resulted in virtually all older women in rural, agricultural households being counted as members of the labor force. The differential between Bangkok and rural, agricultural Thailand is even more marked for particular age groups. Whereas in rural Thailand labor force participation reaches 97 percent among women 20–24 and remains at this level through the 45–49 age group, dropping only to 70 percent for those 50 and over, in Bangkok labor force participation reaches a peak of only 48 percent in the 35–39 age group and is considerably lower for both younger and older women.

These data strongly suggest that the close interrelation between economic life and domestic life for rural women has been broken for many Bangkok women. Other research has suggested that this has great significance for fertility levels; [42] the data for Thailand support such a conclusion insofar as labor force participation in rural Thailand does not seem to affect the number of children born, whereas participation in the labor force in the city contributes to lowered fertility.

If a considerable portion of urban population growth due to migration does not reflect an actual economic need for additional workers, then Bangkok should have a considerably higher level of unemployment than the rural, agricultural category. The 3.4 percent reported as unemployed in Bangkok contrasts with the less than 1 percent unemployed in the rural, agricultural group. Yet Bangkok's level is not especially high.

This disproportionate concentration of unemployment in Bangkok is also evidenced by data from the 1967 Labor Force Survey.[43] Whereas Bangkok's labor force of one million constituted almost 7 percent of Thailand's total labor force, the city accounted for almost one-third of all of Thailand's 64,000 individuals reported as unemployed. Furthermore, over two-thirds of the unemployed were under 25 years of age, and the great majority of these had never worked, indicating the growing problem for the urban metropolis in providing employment opportunities both to those moving in from rural areas and to the increasing numbers of young persons born in the city and now reaching working age. Recent estimates indicate that Bangkok needs to create 150,000 jobs annually during the 1970–80 decade to meet these combined needs.[44]

Even though the levels of unemployment are relatively low, underemployment may constitute a more serious problem. Some insight into the extent of such underemployment is provided by information on the occupational composition of the labor force. Because of Thailand's highly rural character, the contrasts in occupational patterns between Bangkok and both the total kingdom and the rural, agricultural areas are very sharp. Craftsmen account for the largest single group in the male labor force of Bangkok, over one-third of the total, followed by sales workers with just over 20 percent. Vying for third place are service workers and clerical workers with about 10 percent each. For women the single largest employment category is sales work, followed by craftsmen and service workers. Clerical work accounts for only 5 percent of female employment in Bangkok. The proportion of the labor force engaged in tertiary industry is not as high in Bangkok as in several other cities in developing countries, suggesting possibly that the movement to Bangkok to date has been more "efficient." This, in turn, may be related to the generally lower level of urbanization that still characterizes Thailand and may afford the urban metropolis an opportunity to anticipate future movement and incorporate appropriate programs in its development plans. It may thereby avoid increased unemployment and underemployment by diverting some of the future movement to smaller urban places, encouraging individuals to remain in rural places, and developing industrial employment opportunities in Bangkok itself.

Literacy and Education. Any effort to modernize a developing country must include provision for reducing the rate of illiteracy and raising the level of education. Compared with other developing countries, Thailand's population is highly literate. Defining as literate anyone 10 years of age or over who is able to read and write in any language, the 1960 Thai census showed that four out of every five men and three out of every five women qualified as literate. But for both men and women, these levels were higher in urban places than in rural. Bangkok's level of literacy was substantially higher than that of the rural, agricultural places for both males and females, yet the literacy levels of the other urban, non-agricultural and urban, agricultural places exceeded Bangkok's. The somewhat lower level of literacy in Bangkok may reflect the impact of migration. Migrants are normally more educated than those remaining in the village but find themselves less educated than the urban population they join.[45] The lower education of migrants may also affect their chances for jobs in the urban job market.

Reflecting the significant extension of education throughout Thailand, literacy level varies inversely with age for the country as a whole and for Bangkok and the rural sectors. It is encouraging to note that even in the rural areas as many as 90 percent of the males between 13 and 24 are literate, and in Bangkok this is true of the groups between ages 10 and 30. For females in Bangkok peak literacy is at ages 13–19, reaching 88 percent, and in all age groups under 35 at least three-fourths of the members are classified as literate.

Literacy is only a crude measure of population quality; enrollment in school and education completed give a more accurate picture. Thailand has recognized the importance of education in achieving its development objectives. The country entered the 1960s with an educational system that for coverage of eligible population was among the best in Asia. Nonetheless, rapid population growth has imposed a heavy burden on both physical facilities and trained personnel, although both have improved and increased, and has significantly hampered the achievement of educational goals. As a result of the population increase, a somewhat smaller proportion of Thai children have been enrolled in school in recent years than in 1960.

In Thailand, four years of primary education are compulsory and the educational system at this level has largely achieved its goal. However, the educational pyramid narrows sharply thereafter with enrollment in Bangkok considerably higher than in the rural, agricultural places, particularly for the 13–19-year age group.

Educational differentials can be evaluated better by examining the number of years of school completed by persons 20 years of age and over. These point to a similar pattern. Among males, the percentage of individuals without any schooling is similar for Bangkok and the rural, agricultural extreme. The significant differential appears in the numbers who have attended school for only the compulsory four years and those who have gone on to more schooling. In the rural, agricultural category 62 percent of all males had no more than a primary school education, and in Bangkok 33 percent. Thus, taking account of those without any schooling, one-third of the Bangkok population had an education beyond four years compared with only 5 percent of rural, agricultural males. Moreover, whereas virtually all of the rural males who went beyond four years restricted their additional education to secondary school, in Bangkok almost half of this group continued on to pre-university education.

For females, somewhat more rural, agricultural women had not had any schooling compared with those in Bangkok. Yet from the primary level on, the educational profiles of women in Bangkok and in rural, agricultural areas are much more similar than was true of males, reflecting a cultural pattern that puts much less stress on formal education for women. For the rural, agricultural areas, 99 percent of all women aged 20 and over had four years or less of schooling, and for Bangkok 80 percent, well above the two-thirds level characterizing men.

While confirming that Thailand as a whole and Bangkok in particular rate well with respect to literacy levels and percentage of students obtaining some education, these data indicate that the overall quality of education, as measured by numbers of years of school completed, is still comparatively low. Considerable effort must be made in this direction if education is to play a crucial role in the development and modernization process. In particular, education must provide the kinds of skills needed both in the urban metropolis and in rural areas. Given the continuing rapid population growth and the strain that this growth will add to educational facilities, vocational education becomes all the more important, particularly in rural areas where education can either better train the youth for work in agriculture and thereby encourage them to remain in the villages or give youth the skills that better qualify them for work in the urban labor force.

Ethnicity and Religion. Reflecting the metropolitan and primate character of Bangkok, its population is quite cosmopolitan. Not only have more Thais migrated here from other parts of the country; it also has greater ethnic and religious diversity than the rest of the country. The Chinese community of Bangkok predates the founding of the capital and still forms a substantial part of the population. During the first decades of the twentieth century, as many as 40,000 Chinese a year entered Thailand, accounting for as much as one-third of all population growth in the country. Most of these settled in Bangkok, and it has been estimated that in 1828 three-fourths of Bangkok's population was Chinese and half of the balance was at least partially of Chinese descent.[46] Beginning in 1927–28, a series of immigration acts led to increased restriction on Chinese immigration, and since 1950 the number of Chinese entering the country has not exceeded several hundred a year. Yet as late as the 1950s ethnic Chinese made up nearly half the population of the city.[47]

Any effort to estimate the number of Chinese in Thailand or in Bangkok today is frustrated by the quality of the statistics available and the definitions used. The only official data on ethnicity refer to citizenship. The 1960 census showed that 13 percent of Bangkok's population were Chinese citizens. In 1966 a total of 368,000 aliens were registered in Thailand of whom 345,000 were Chinese, and of this total just over half were living in the two provinces containing Bangkok and Thonburi.[48] Yet, by the definitions used in everyday life, both Thais and Chinese regard the Chinese as being much more numerous than indicated by official statistics. The number of Chinese ethnics is generally estimated at 3 million to 3.5 million for the country as a whole, with a high proportion concentrated in Bangkok.[49] In three Bangkok districts—Sampeng, Bangrak, and Bomtrad—over two-thirds of the population are Chinese. These areas display typical patterns of Chinese urban residence: row houses two or three stories high, with the ground floor used as the place of work and the family living above. The pattern produces a high population density, in sharp contrast with the lower densities of the Thai sections of Bangkok.[50] The role of Chinese ethnics in the commercial life of Greater Bangkok is best evidenced by the fact that in 1966, 36 percent of all business establishments in the twin cities were owned by Chinese, compared with one-fourth of those in smaller towns and only 10 percent of those in rural places.[51]

Further evidence of the concentration of Chinese in the capital city area is provided by the census statistics on religion, which distinguish among Buddhists, Moslems, Confucians, and others. Virtually all of the Confucians are Chinese ethnics, although this does not encompass the entire Chinese population, since many Chinese are Buddhists. Confucians constitute only 2 percent of Thailand's population. But in Bangkok almost one out of every five persons was so classified. The impact of the earlier waves of immigration on the concentration of Chinese in Bangkok is indicated by the fact that among those aged 50 and over one out of every four persons was classified as Confucian. This decreases to only 15 percent of those between ages 13 and 24, suggesting that as the older persons die and as greater assimilation takes place through education, intermarriage, and residential integration, the Chinese community within the metropolitan area will become increasingly smaller and less cohesive as a social force.

Income and Expenditure Patterns. Some insight into the comparative economic status of the Bangkok population is provided by information collected in the 1962–63 Household Expenditure Survey.[52] The results of that survey were tabulated separately for the Bangkok-Thonburi municipal area, all other municipal areas in Thailand, and all villages. A marked dissimilarity is revealed in the income distribution of families within these three types of places, ranging on the average from a monthly income of only 480 baht ($24) in villages to 1,519 baht ($76) for Bangkok. This sharp differential supports the assumption that economic considerations and the differential in employment and income-earning potentials are significant in accounting for population movement from rural to urban places.

The marked differential in income becomes even more meaningful when viewed within the context of the differentials between Bangkok and rural Thailand in the proportion of families with more than one employed member. In Bangkok half of the families have only one employed member or even none working, whereas among the villages surveyed this was true of only one in five family units. At the other extreme only one in five families in the capital city area, compared with 43 percent of family units in the villages, had three or more members employed. This variation may partly reflect urban-rural differences in size of family and in residence patterns; but even so, it emphasizes the significant change produced by urbanization in the relation between domestic life and economic activity at several stages of the life cycle.

It is noteworthy that the average income per family in relation to number of earners shows a different pattern for Bangkok than for the villages. In the metropolis the average income increases from just over 1,000 baht per month for families with one or no earners to almost 25,000 baht for those with four or more. In the villages the average also shows a positive relation to number of earners, but the differential is minimal between families with one earner and those with four or more. These data therefore suggest that, in contrast to the villages, Bangkok provides an opportunity for family income to increase considerably if more persons in a family become earners. This opportunity may be an important stimulus for movement to the city.

Finally, for patterns of consumption, the material from the Household Survey shows that virtually identical proportional allocations for food, housing (including furnishing and household operations), medical and personal care account for about two-thirds of the total budgets of both Bangkok and village families.[53] The only noteworthy differentials occur with respect to clothing, a category that consumes over twice as much of the limited total expenditures of villagers compared with the larger total expenditures of Bangkok families. By contrast, both recreation and transportation account for almost twice as much proportionately of the total expenditures of Bangkok households. Such a pattern reflects both the greater separation of work and home and the greater opportunities for recreation and education in the urban metropolis. But the overriding similarities in the distribution suggest that the life style of the Bangkok population, as judged by expenditure patterns, may not be too different from that of the rural population.

Housing and Urban Conditions

Among the most serious environmental problems faced by Asia's cities are the housing shortage and the poor condition of so many of the existing units.[54] Such deterioration is particularly characteristic of the large urban areas where rapid population growth has led to increases in the cost of land. The high cost of land, the rapid movement of rural population into the cities and the difficulty of migrants in obtaining adequate jobs and income, and the housing shortage itself all have combined to produce spontaneous, unplanned urban settlement in the form of shanty towns occupied by squatters. A disproportionate number of these squatters are migrants.[55]

Bangkok's housing shortage is severe. Since 1940 a total of only 7,000 low-income housing units have been constructed while the city's population has grown from about half a million to approximately three million. It has been estimated that approximately 100,000 Bangkok families are without proper housing, and this number is increasing at the rate of 20,000 annually. The situation will become more serious as migrants continue to arrive and the cost of land and rent steadily rise. In this respect, Bangkok's experience resembles that of several other Asian cities.[56]

As of 1970, 25,000 families consisting of some 162,000 persons were reported living in 39 distinct slum areas. A general lack of funds represents the single most important barrier to remedying this situation. A recent estimate put the need for additional construction of all types of dwelling units at 42,000 per year over the next ten years. The cost of constructing the low-income units alone would amount to 35 times the present yearly government expenditure of approximately 20 million baht ($1 million). Since such a goal is unrealistic, acceptance of the squatter settlements as a natural response to the dilemma confronting low-income earners and efforts to help the slum residents organize into more viable communities are now being considered.[57]

For many, shanty towns serve as a bridge between village and city. For example, a survey of the residents of Klong Toey, Bangkok's largest squatter community, found that many inhabitants saw living there as a solution to a number of problems encountered in a metropolitan area.[58] Despite overcrowding and lack of public utilities and services, they felt pride in their homes and a strong attachment to the community. More than half considered that security, health, and living conditions for children were acceptable or good, and only 7 percent said they would prefer to rent an apartment in a public housing project.

Perhaps the most significant finding was that 75 percent of Klong Toey's inhabitants had lived there for five years or more, half for ten years or more, and only 6 percent had arrived during the previous year. Data are not available on the numbers that have moved out, but the overriding impression given by the statistics is one of great stability.

The attitude of these Thai squatters points to one of the positive functions of such a community. In the absence of any general improvement in their economic situation, it may be inconsistent to change their housing environment. Unless housing is made a part of the larger development program in which migrants and others living in squatter communities are fully integrated into the total community, greater maladjustment may result from relocating them into better housing.[59]

The growth pattern of the Bangkok metropolitan area has been described as natural, unplanned, and uncontrolled.[60] Although serious attempts in city planning began during the 1960s, extreme difficulties on the technical, organizational, and legal levels continue.[61] Several city plans have been commissioned, but as of 1970 legal power to enforce such plans was lacking. Most control acts have dealt only with safety and structural strength but not with the location, type, or use of buildings, or zoning in general. Expansion in Bangkok and in smaller urban centers generally takes the form of strip development extending into the rural environments along highways and canals. Within Bangkok itself, the lack of zoning regulations and construction control has permitted creation of a varied mass of buildings and development of many squatter communities and slums. Along the *soi* (lanes) branching off from the main arterial roads, modern high-rise buildings, both business and residential, crowd next to run-down shacks.

Complicating Bangkok's general land use and planning problems are the difficulties arising from rapid population growth and increasing economic prosperity of some segments of the population. As one Thai put it, "Bangkok is choking on its own prosperity." The city had 80,000 registered vehicles in 1962 and 280,000 in 1970. But road mileage increased by only 10 percent in the interval. Designed originally for canal and river traffic, the city has had to fill in a considerable portion of its waterways to make roads. But the network, while suitable for canal boats, is not adapted to automobile traffic; and the resulting congestion, complicated by large numbers of bicycles, motorcycles, and three-wheeled taxis (*samlor*), makes for one of the worst traffic situations in the world.

The great numbers of vehicles on an inadequate road network have caused a serious rise in air pollution. Because of the elimination of so many canals and the destruction of so many trees to make way for asphalt roads and concrete buildings, the city has become hotter than ever. A report by the Acting Chief of the Sanitary Engineering Division in the Department of Health has found that the air and water pollution are beginning to affect people's health and working efficiency.[62] Among other serious problems plaguing the city might be included the following items: poor drainage facilities result in considerable flooding during the rainy season; sections of the city experience water shortages, especially in the dry season; garbage removal and sewage disposal systems are inadequate; bars, night clubs, massage parlors, and brothels have mushroomed and contribute to criminal behavior and venereal disease; and telephone lines are in short supply.

Future Growth

Estimates of the future population of Bangkok and of other urban places in Thailand are almost as numerous and varied as the experts concerned with the topic. The most recent reliable projections come from the National Economic Development Board (NEDB).[63] Defining municipal areas with populations above 20,000 as urban, three different methods of projection are used, based on different assumptions about the pace of urbanization and the relation of Bangkok's population to the total urban population of Thailand. These varied estimates demonstrate that, regardless of method and despite conservative assumptions, during the remaining decades of the twentieth century the increase in Thailand's urban population and that of Bangkok will be spectacular. Even according to the low projection, the 1970 urban population will double by 1985 to 8.6 million.

This rapid urban growth will occur at the same time that Thailand experiences a continuous and substantial rural growth. During the same 15-year interval, the rural population is estimated to increase by at least 12 million persons. Although this represents a growth of only 39 percent, the absolute numbers far exceed the estimated increase of 4.3 million in the urban population. In the remaining years of the twentieth century, the same basic trend is likely to continue. The low projection estimates that Thailand's urban population will reach 15 million by the year 2000, 3.5 times greater than the 1970 population. During the same thirty years, the rural population, according to this estimate, will have grown by three-fourths to 55.6 million. These growth rates mean that by the turn of the century one out of every five Thais will be living in urban places of 20,000 and over in contrast to 12 percent estimated for 1970.

Difficult though it may be to estimate the urban population of a country, it is even more difficult and daring to project that of a city such as Bangkok. As the NEDB report points out,[64] development of an improved transportation network bypassing Bangkok or of an international airport in the north of Thailand, deliberate efforts to develop industries in smaller towns, or a number of other possible steps could all affect the rate of Bangkok's growth and its share of Thailand's total urban population. The conclusion reached by the NEDB that Bangkok's share of the population is not likely to rise much higher seems fully justified in view of the city's present extreme primacy. If Bangkok maintains its current share of the total urban population, estimates indicate that the metropolitan population would probably be between 10.5 and 11.5 million by the year 2000, assuming that in the meantime a substantial decline in the birth rate occurs. Otherwise, a metropolitan population as high as 12 million is possible. In any event, Bangkok's 1970 population of 3 million will about double by 1985, and by 2000 it will be more than three times greater than its 1970 population.

This growth poses enormous problems. Increasing attention is being given to the possibility of slowing the growth rate of the city's population and holding it at a level of 4 to 5 million by 1990 in the hope that present health and living levels can be maintained and the costs of social services kept within reason. The programs suggested for achieving this goal are geared to encouraging urban growth elsewhere in Thailand on the assumption that this will both create a stronger national economy and enhance the attractiveness of other cities to rural persons who might otherwise migrate to Bangkok. More specifically, some of the programs put forward include the following: inducements to industry to locate in smaller towns; the creation of industrial estates; improved transportation systems; establishment of new towns; creation of "service centers" providing a group of villages with processing industries and various social, cultural, economic, recreational, and administrative services, thereby giving the population access to a number of amenities that are associated with urban life; decentralization of government to the greatest extent possible; decentralization of educational, medical, and other services; electrification of rural areas, even before extension of such programs in Bangkok itself; and development of port facilities south of Bangkok and restricted use of the Bangkok facilities.[65]

A number of policies focus directly on agriculture. These include land reform, irrigation, improved soil fertility, payment for agricultural work, increased public investment in rural education and rural social development in general, greater reliance on new cereal varieties, and differential systems of taxation. At the same time, emphasis is also being given to the need for alleviating the serious problems within the metropolitan area, including better land utilization, amelioration of transportation problems, more emphasis on economic growth, relocation of industry on the outskirts of the city near ring roads and superhighways, and creation of new business centers. The possibility of expanding the metropolitan area to encompass at least two of the nearby provinces, Nonthaburi and Samutprakan, is already generally accepted and envisages a total area of 730 square kilometers, which may be able to accommodate as many as 6.5 million people and enable industrial sites to locate far from the center of present-day Bangkok. As a first step in the development of the Metropolitan area, as of January 1972 the twin cities of Bangkok and Thanburi were merged to form a single municipal area.

Despite the multiplicity of problems associated with urbanization and with the growth of big cities such as Bangkok, there is general agreement that the overall urbanization process should not be stopped or reversed but rather so directed that it contributes to economic and social development. In part, this rests on the assumption that social change and modernization are desirable and that they are highly correlated with urbanization. But any development program must recognize the close interrelationship between city and village, both because the urban way of life is increasingly impinging on rural areas and because many migrants are bringing the rural way of life to urban places and maintaining it there for a considerable time. In Thailand as in most developing countries, a considerable portion of urban population growth, especially in the primate city, probably does not entirely reflect an actual need for large urban population concentration.[66] Rather, it results from the movement of large numbers of rural out-migrants who believe that cities are places where most new job opportunities exist. For some they do; for many these hopes are not realized.

Even if a number of the programs for decentralizing urban and industrial development were implemented, it seems unreasonable to assume that such developments could prevent the growth of the metropolis. At best, they would reduce its growth rate and relieve some of the congestion. Rather, decentralization would probably make its greatest contribution through the stimulus to the development of local natural resources, the modernization of agriculture,[67] and the development of modern skills among the local resident population.

The greater occupational diversification and mobility that usually accompany urbanization, the greater willingness to accept change, and the positive influences resulting from increased contacts with the outside should contribute to rising levels of living in these smaller cities and to that extent reduce somewhat the motivation for movement to the capital itself. The differentials between the inhabitants of Bangkok and those living in smaller urban places and rural areas suggest that within Thailand, as elsewhere, urbanization may be linked to modernization and general economic advancement. However, the empirical interrelationships among the different variables are undoubtedly complex and do not operate uniformly throughout the population living in the big cities.

Indeed, if population movement to Greater Bangkok and even smaller urban places is generated by the externally induced declines in mortality and the consequent increase in rates of rural population growth and in pressure on limited resources, both the migration itself and the resulting urbanization may not be directly linked to modernization and economic development. The degree to which they are will be determined by the socio-demographic characteristics of the migrants, their motives for moving, and the extent to which their traditional social structures and values persist after migration. Earlier comparison of a number of the demographic characteristics of the Bangkok population with those of persons in other parts of Thailand also suggest that in many respects the demographic differentials are minimal. This in turn may indicate that there still persists within the confines of the big city a fairly strong perpetuation of rural ways of life.[68] Urbanization that is too rapid may impede the general development process, particularly through the strains it imposes on urban economic, educational, social and health facilities. Yet the very condition of primacy, despite all its tribulations, may offer a definite advantage to Bangkok as an instrument of social, economic, and political change.

To a very great extent, the data examined in this review of Bangkok's growth and composition are much too limited to permit testing the full implications of population change. Because they represent the first reasonably comprehensive set of data available for Greater Bangkok and for other urban places in Thailand, trend analysis is precluded. Their greatest value lies in providing bench marks against which future change can be evaluated. More immediately, the data highlight the challenge that Bangkok faces as a result of the rapid growth it has already experienced, the particular socio-economic profile of its population, and the continuing growth likely to occur.

Chapter 4

Urban Tensions in Southeast Asia in the 1970s

Aprodicio A. Laquian

EDITORS' NOTE: This paper looks at urbanization from a political and administrative point of view. Professor Laquian's study considers the growing tension, open conflict, and manifest violence which are accompanying urbanization in most countries in South and Southeast Asia. He emphasizes the interactive processes which link rural and urban phenomena to each other. Discussing the effects of creeping urbanism as urban influences penetrate the countryside, he also explores the ruralization of Asian cities as large migrations bring to the great urban centers a rural populace with its own attitudes and life styles. He also discusses the administrative problem of providing improved services to rapidly growing cities, a task complicated by sharpened ethnic conflicts and growing political awareness. Contrary to the optimistic wisdom of some years back, Laquian finds little evidence that urban centers are producing a melting pot effect, diminishing ethnic, linguistic, or other group divisions.

But the author is not entirely pessimistic. Governments and many private groups are seeking ways to deal with these difficulties. He notes numerous innovations combining traditional and modern institutional forms for attacking important problems of contemporary urban life.

Malay and Chinese rioters killed each other in the streets of Kuala Lumpur in 1969. Alleged Communists were massacred all over Java in 1965 and 1966. Christians and Muslims are shooting it out in Cotabato, Southern Philippines. Urban terror erupted at random in the streets of Saigon. And in Manila's Plaza Miranda, two hand grenades ripped through the speakers' platform at a political rally in August 1971, nearly wiping out the leadership of the opposition Liberal Party.

These events are only some of the outbursts that have hit the headlines, datelined Southeast Asia. For most Westerners such outbursts seem to confirm that the region is rife with tensions and troubles. But few people are likely to label them urban problems although some of these events have happened in the region's largest cities, for Asia does not evoke images of urban life.

Yet Southeast Asia is one of the most rapidly urbanizing regions in the world. Urban growth is occurring not only in the very large cities but also in towns and intermediate cities. Some have questioned whether the concentration of people in Southeast Asian cities is true urbanization, and such terms as "pseudo-urbanization," "overurbanization," "subsistence urbanization," and "premature urbanization" have been substituted.[1] It cannot be denied, however, that significant numbers of people are leaving the countryside for the towns and large cities. Their concentration in urban places in high densities is producing economic, social, and political tensions, and the institutions designed to manage governmental affairs are inadequate to cope with the resulting problems.

Tension can be seen as the essence of urban life. City life is more hectic. Time is short and valuable, leaving little chance for human relationships to develop or personal differences to heal. Rituals and institutions to ease the life of the urban dweller have not been developed. Moreover, there are the harsher realities of unemployment in a monetized economy where survival depends on a regular source of income. Poverty is widespread, even as the privileged few engage in conspicuous consumption and create cynicism, apathy, or an outraged sense of social justice among the poor. Demands on kinship ties become stronger even as the increasing impersonality of life weakens them. The need for urban services becomes greater while the capacity of urban governments to pay for these services suffers from the inability or refusal of urban residents to pay taxes, and from administrative inefficiencies, corruption, and the dominance of central government needs over local ones. Finally, there is the widespread belief that the major problems of Southeast Asian nations are rural problems, and that any urban problems are found only in the capital.

Urban tensions create conflicts, and conflict is the essence of politics. Asia's urban centers are both the focus of national political developments and the source of political influence over the countryside. The tensions created by urbanization and urbanism can be seen as either disruptive or constructive. The basic question, therefore, is whether urban tensions can be likened to a cinder that irritates and blinds or to a grain of sand that induces a pearl from an oyster.

It is well to keep in mind that conditions in different Southeast Asian countries vary although, to be sure, certain common processes are at work in each. There is, first of all, the process of *dualism* wherein a segment of the people live in large urban centers while another segment continues to live in tradition-bound villages that have hardly changed in centuries. There is, also, the process of what has been called *creeping urbanism* in which the dual societies are brought closer together by the spread of urban values and practices to rural areas. Finally, there is the process of *ruralization* whereby rural values and practices spread to urban places through rural-urban migration, nationalistic appeals, or the persistence of "urban villages." [2] To be more precise, then, one should talk of rural-urban processes in Southeast Asian countries, creating tensions that can explode or remain subtle and evolutionary.

Dualism: Tensions in City and Country

Two distinct life styles, rural and urban, exist in most countries of Southeast Asia and generate tensions as they interact. A large part of the city-dwelling population is usually concentrated in one or two major cities. The great majority of the population are scattered in small towns or villages across the countryside. This condition appears in its most extreme form in Thailand, where at most 12.5 percent (or one-eighth) of the population can be considered urbanites, and over half of them are in Bangkok.

These primate cities are the centers of economic, political, and administrative power. As such they generate distinctive problems of their own. There are also problems arising from tensions between center and periphery that affect not only urban but national development as well.

Internal City Problems. The inundation of Southeast Asian cities with migrants from the countryside, combined with the relatively high natural growth rates in urban places, creates problems that inevitably result in personal, social, economic, and political tensions. A cursory examination of the statistics on housing, unemployment, crime, education, social welfare, transportation, health and sanitation, and the prevalence of natural and man-made calamities in Southeast Asian cities reveals a pathetic situation. Standards of urban services become meaningless in the face of shortages. The incapacity of urban governments to plan and effectively deliver needed services breeds extra-legal or illegal processes resulting from desperation: squatting, invasions, looting, and riots. Failures in the city's economic system spawn "marginal" economic callings (peddling, hawking, pedicab driving) that keep body and soul together but do not efficiently contribute to general economic growth.

Typical of internal city problems faced by Southeast Asian cities is the situation in the combined cities of Bangkok and Thonburi. In 1967 Bangkok's labor force made up 7 percent of Thailand's total labor force, yet its working-age population accounted for almost one-third of all of Thailand's 64,000 individuals reported as unemployed. About 100,000 Bangkok families were without proper housing, and this number has increased at a rate of 20,000 annually. Only 7,000 low-income housing units have been constructed in Bangkok since 1940, while the city's population has grown from half a million to about 3 million in the same period. About 25,000 families (roughly 162,000 persons) were reported living in thirty-nine slum areas. In 1962, Bangkok had 80,000 registered vehicles. These increased to 280,000 in 1970, but road mileage increased by only 10 percent within the period. These serious problems can only become worse as the city increases its population to an estimated 8.6 million by 1985.[3]

Conditions are not much better in Djakarta where it is estimated that while some 40,000 new households are added each year, only about 2,000 to 3,000 new permanent housing units are approved annually. Of course, slum and squatter housing is not included in the units approved, but this only points to another much larger problem: It is estimated that only 20 percent of the housing units in Djakarta are permanent. Services are critically inadequate. Only 8 percent of permanent dwellings use both electricity and municipal water. As a result, industries and firms resort to expensive private electricity-generating systems, which produce 50 percent as much power as the entire Djakarta system. The transport system depends heavily on about 200,000 *betjaks* (tricycle taxis) which provide employment for some 400,000 drivers who will be thrown out of work if the system is rationalized. The *betjaks* are usually blamed for the sluggish traffic, which is already bad enough because nearly 40 percent of all motor cars and 20 percent of all trucks and buses in Indonesia are concentrated in Djakarta.[4]

Urban service problems are bad in large metropolitan areas like Bangkok and Djakarta, but they can be worse in intermediate cities that have fewer resources than capital cities. In a survey of five intermediate cities in the Philippines made by this writer in 1971, the service situation was found to be deplorable.[5] In each of these cities, a typical slum or squatter community was intensively studied and yielded the results shown in Table 4.1.

Conditions in a slum area in the City of Manila studied as part of this survey were only slightly better. In the Manila community, 40.3 percent of the households did not have a toilet, 76.8 percent had no regular garbage collection, and 89.1 percent of the interviewees said there was no children's playground in the vicinity.[6]

To a greater or lesser degree, the main metropolitan areas in

Table 4.1 Urban Services Lacking in Selected Slum Communities in Five Intermediate Philippine Cities, 1971

Service Condition	*Baguio*	*Cebu*	*Davao*	*Iligan*	*Iloilo*
No electricity in household	19.3%	56.0%	10.0%	56.2%	51.5%
No water system, water bought from vendors	0.0	0.2	14.3	3.6	57.7
No toilet	4.1	93.2	3.4	56.0	41.5
No regular garbage collection	32.0	87.9	67.4	98.0	85.0
No children's playground	96.5	91.1	99.3	99.2	96.0
Number of households surveyed	512	570	470	500	499

Southeast Asia share the internal city problems of Bangkok, Djakarta, and Manila. It is true that in most cases population increases in large cities are due to in-migration of former rural dwellers who find conditions even in the poorest of urban slum areas better than in their rural places of origin. Still, the increasing gap between needs and available services and the "revolution of rising expectations" generated by urban living sooner or later create personal and social tensions.

Ironically, problems may arise even as conditions improve. The provision of services to an increasing number of urbanites tends to heighten tensions created by the gap between needs and resources. To most rural-urban migrants, initial lack of services calls for palliatives and creative substitutes. As government and private enterprise provide services, however, people get used to them and become dependent on them. Thus, the disruption in services that has come to be taken for granted is more likely to create anxieties and tensions, sometimes erupting into violence. Thus, transport strikes in Manila have resulted in riots and killings. Electric blackouts have increased the incidence of theft and robbery. Typhoons and floods have paralyzed urban places. As urban service mechanisms have become more complex and interrelated, they seem to have become more vulnerable to disruptive influences. As Goldstein has said of Bangkok, "Bangkok is choking on its own prosperity." [7]

Center-Periphery Tensions. The conditions responsible for many internal city difficulties can often be found outside the boundaries of the city itself. Many studies have pointed to the creative and innovative role of the city and to the process of urbanization as a source of hope in national development. Since much of the hope for modernization and economic and social progress in developing countries is pinned on the extension of urban benefits to the countryside, tensions arising from center-periphery relations and their resolution are thus of paramount importance.

Experience with urbanization in the West has shown the liberating effect of cities. With functional specialization and the growing complexity of life in urban areas, it is often argued, affective loyalties to family, clan, local community, caste, or other primary grouping are eroded and replaced by wider identifications. Eroding these ties paves the way for loyalty to the nation-state. The more rapidly urban influences spread to rural areas, therefore, the sooner can nation-building be achieved.

The cleavage between urban "modernizing elites" and rural "traditional folk" obviously works against this approach to nation-building. Appeals to national identity made by the urban elites sound suspiciously like justification for economic and social dominance by the center over the periphery. Demands for recognition by the rural folk are branded as particularistic and divisive by power holders at the center, and are often seen as threats or portents of separatism. In extreme cases, the center's response may be punitive and violent, thus further widening the gap between center and periphery.

In some Southeast Asian countries (the Philippines, Malaysia, and to a lesser extent Indonesia and Pakistan), nation-building has been attempted through interest-mobilization with the use of movements and political parties. Movements for independence and freedom from colonial rule have been exceptionally successful in welding national sentiment. When the excitement of fighting for freedom gives way to the day-to-day administration of the country's affairs after independence, however, enthusiasm turns to bitter frustration. Political parties, confronted with policy options, conflicting interests, and particularistic pressures, fail to function properly. Generally, parties become urban-based, mouthing modern slogans to cope with age-old ills, and combining personal followings and machines in an effort to aggregate a shaky political following. To the rural folk, whose life is barely touched by these political activities, hope turns to cynicism and later to resignation and apathy. Politics becomes a city slickers' game. Nation-building turns to meaningless squabbles among power blocks greedy for the spoils of power.

It is at this time of disillusionment that the split between city and periphery tends to take place along ideological lines. Communist ideologists have spelled it out clearly. Colonialism is just an extension of capitalism according to Lenin. Central cities and the central governments they symbolize are extensions of a colonial past. The countryside is exploited by the city in the same way that the mother country exploited the colonies and that capitalists continue to exploit the workers and peasants. The urban power elite, abetted by foreign capitalists, is holding the country in bondage. What is needed, therefore, is a "war of national liberation," to be achieved by encirclement of the city, wresting the power from its leaders, and returning power to the poor people of the countryside. Fanned by hatred of rich urbanites who wield economic and political power and enjoy social status and prestige, such reasoning is persuasive among the people.

Rural insurgencies in Southeast Asia have had mixed results, however. In Malaysia, the Philippines, and Indonesia, they have been put down at least once. In Vietnam, Laos, Cambodia, and Thailand they are still in progress. In all cases, the Establishment's control over the army and police and the support given these so-called "monopolies over violence" by foreign powers have meant the difference between success and failure for the insurgents. In some countries, it is the military that provides the only means for maintaining a semblance of unity in the nation-state.

Aware that a long struggle can sap the strength of an insurgency, some rebels have resorted to urban action characterized by selective terror, bombings, robberies, assassinations, kidnappings, disruption of urban services, riots, general strikes, etc.[8] This strategy, which borrows heavily from Latin American revolutions (success in Cuba, failure in Venezuela), is on the increase in Southeast Asia. Saigon has experienced urban terror for years. The rash of bombings, kidnappings, and assassinations in Manila may herald a shift to urban insurgency by the "New People's Army," the younger but more fervently ideological successors to the Huks.

Ironically, as previously mentioned, further improvement in urban services in Southeast Asian cities may make them more vulnerable. Disruption of urban services may create panic and riots. Systems of services become more closely integrated and interdependent as they improve—disruption of one may paralyze others. Urban insurgents may infiltrate vital services such as communications and police. And in the city they also have easier access to guns, explosives, money, and trained people.

By its very nature, however, an urban uprising has to be a quick, decisive, and bold lunge at complete victory. If power is not seized in a short time, the authorities may be able to regroup their forces and win. As such, urban insurgency is a more risky gamble than a protracted rural rebellion, and Southeast Asian rebels may use it to cap a rural insurgency rather than to start one.

Creeping Urbanism: City Problems in Village and Town

The concept of creeping urbanism has been advanced by Guyot, who cited the example of Malaysian efforts to improve conditions in the countryside as having both intended and unintended effects in spreading urbanism.[9] Nation-building in Southeast Asia often takes the form of conscious attempts to transform rural-traditional values and practices into more "modern" ones. Programs to improve agricultural productivity (agricultural extension, rural credit, infrastructure projects) are all agents of creeping urbanism. They introduce new ideas, new ways, new gadgets, and new words, which slowly but surely transform rural folk into urbanites.

In some countries the very success of rural development programs is responsible for worsening urban problems. One result of increased crop production may be rising expectations, dissatisfaction with rural life, and migration to cities. As some have said of the "rice and roads" program in the Philippines, the more rice a farmer has, the more money he gets; and the more roads the government builds, the easier it is for the farmer to leave the farm and go to the city. With the cities already facing severe problems, the influx of people with high expectations can only mean more trouble.

To cope with urban congestion, some Asian governments have tried back-to-the-land schemes. Notable among these are the Federal Land Development Authority (FLDA) program in Malaysia and the National Resettlement and Rehabilitation Administration (NARRA) scheme in the Philippines. On a different scale and of a different type were the *xia fang* and *hui-fang* movements in China where urban cadres were "sent down" to work in villages and people who were not needed in the cities were returned to their native villages.

With dwindling virgin lands in most Southeast Asian countries, however, stress on resettlement has lessened. At present, regional development schemes revolving around "growth poles" are starting to be favored. Regional development authorities have been set up in the Philippines. Burma is pursuing a policy of decentralization that seeks alternatives to Rangoon. Malaysia is adding a spatial component to its comprehensive plans. All these moves are based on the hope that migration to large cities can be slowed down by enhancing growth in other places that may hold the migrant.

The above schemes, while rational, have encountered various problems. In most Southeast Asian countries linguistic and ethnic lines separate local units. The influx of new people into a "growth pole" area disturbs the "ethnic balance," creating tensions and violence.

The Muslim-Christian war now raging in Mindanao in the Philippines may be explained in these terms. Between 1903 and 1960 the Philippine government encouraged migration to Mindanao as the "land of promise" with the result that within this period the proportion of Muslims to the Mindanao population dropped from 31 to 20 percent.[10] Between 1948 and 1960 about two million people were added to Mindanao's population. The total cultivated area in the region increased from 2 million acres to more than 4.2 million. At this rate, it is estimated that all available farm land in Mindanao will have been occupied by 1972. Perhaps more people can be accommodated in Mindanao after that by decreasing average farm holdings from the current 10 acres per family. By the end of the 1970s, however, Mindanao will cease to be the frontier area for absorbing excess population growth.[11]

In the 1960s a trend toward migration to Mindanao's cities was observed. These cities have been growing rapidly not only because of migration from Luzon and Visayas but also because of migration from Mindanao rural areas and towns. This trend is already creating urban pressures. Thus, Jolo and Marawi (the remaining cities dominated by Muslims) have the worst squatter and slum conditions in Mindanao. Cities like Davao, Cotabato, and Iligan are growing extremely fast, with no planning and no provisions for needed services. Most important, urban life will bring Muslim and Christians more closely together, but instead of producing cooperation and understanding, violence may erupt.

Aside from ethnic tensions that may be created by the clash of dualistic cultures, development of the countryside by planned "growth poles" may also entail problems for the country as a whole. Social justice and nation-building arguments have been advanced in favor of balancing growth between urban and rural sectors in a country. However, telling economic arguments have also been put forward in favor of concentrating productive resources in a few areas to take advantage of external economies, agglomeration economies, and economies of scale. The productive capacities of developing countries, it is argued, are often extremely limited and dispersing them all over the country entails high costs. The urban areas of most developing countries will not be subject to the diseconomies arising from urban overconcentration (pollution, congestion, noise, loss of privacy) for some time. What they need, at this point, is an optimal exploitation of their meager resources, a policy that calls for concentration rather than dispersal.

The "growth pole" approach, which underlies so many of the policies designed to promote creeping urbanism, envisions a small number of "leading industries" whose high growth rates are expected to generate enough development to benefit other sectors. Generally, this means an emphasis on industrialization or at least efficient manufacturing, which is, in turn, heavily dependent on efficient markets and final consumption demand. The dispersal of public or private investments from centers of economic and social activity, therefore, tends to promote the uneconomic use of precious resources. Furthermore, the hinterland is most often endowed with agricultural or natural resources, hardly a good base for leading industries. The additional costs imposed by extending to the undeveloped countryside infrastructures such as transportation and services for managers and technicians who have to be attracted there may price the industries located in growth poles out of the market and result in much higher total national costs of development and diseconomies for the whole country.

Ruralization: Village Problems in Asian Cities

It is hardly necessary to belabor the point that urbanization in Southeast Asia is primarily due to the massive movement of rural people to urban areas. The percentage of urban dwellers not born in the city is high throughout Southeast Asia—74 percent in Djakarta, 46.9 in the Philippines, 47.7 percent in Cambodia, and 26.6 percent in Thailand. Many reasons have been proposed for this exodus—insecurity of life in the countryside, pressures on the land, perceived differences in opportunities between rural and urban life, and so on. An extensive literature is available on this subject, and the main findings of internal migration studies need not be mentioned here.[12]

The most dramatic impact of this rural-urban migration has been the transplantation of essentially rural and traditional beliefs and practices to many Southeast Asian cities. While many of these beliefs and practices have had beneficial results on city life, some of them have created conflicts and tensions that make urban administration and management of services very difficult. Among the areas of tension and conflict are kinship relations, ethnic and racial interactions, and administration of urban services.

Kinship Relations. Kinship in the traditional Southeast Asian village, in the jargon of anthropologists, is patrilineal, patrilocal, and operates on many levels of segmentation. In the case of the Toba Batak of Sumatra, for example, it has been stated that "Every Batak, living and dead, has a place on the tribal genealogy and persons in different descent lines are always able to determine their proper relationship to one another by tracing their social distance from a common male ancestor." [13] These relationships are carried by Bataks wherever they go. When Bataks who have migrated to Medan meet each other for the first time, for example, "the parties involved almost invariably determine their respective positions in the kinship grid before any extended interaction . . . the Batak frequently prolong these preliminary discussions about kinship since they find many satisfactions in the process. . . . Once established, the kinship relationship structures all subsequent interaction; the individuals involved relate to one another as kinsmen." [14]

Life in the city is vastly more complicated, however, and kinship relations that governed rural life effectively may prove dysfunctional in the urban setting. Such relationships are invariably hierarchical; for example, parentage places one in either a superior or a subordinate position in relation to other relatives. In the city, factors such as wealth, education, occupation, and political position enter into a man's superior-subordinate relation to others. These factors may create tensions in the interaction of people who were formerly linked together mainly by kinship. An urban man with wealth and power who finds himself in a subservient position to a poor relative is put in a predicament, for example.[15]

> Our wealthy Batak urbanite wants to preserve his capital and he must guard against excessive demands on his time, but he dares not offend his poor relative . . . because this could lead to widespread criticism that he fears; he realizes that if his situation changes in the future, he may need the support of his kin group. He is also aware that any flagrant violation of the Batak social and ceremonial system may lead to severe economic, political or social sanction.

So the wealthy Batak urbanite bends to the demands of kinship and tries to please his relative, even if this creates undesirable burdens for him.

In a similar study in Taegu, Korea's third largest city, it was observed that kinship ties seemed to be declining. This phenomenon was traced to "status conflict" arising between rich and poor relatives. Younger people seem to be more critical of traditional customs that make helping relatives obligatory. This rebellion against traditional ties, however, does not seem to be due to growing individualism but to a greater concern for family. Loyalty of the younger generation is to the nuclear not to the extended family. "Young couples do not give much consideration to their relatives, ancestors or even their parents. They want to provide their children with all the available resources and opportunities, at any cost." [16]

In another study of urban families conducted by this author in Manila in 1963 there were suggestions that wives resented the influence of the extended family on their own lives more than did husbands. This finding was interesting in the light of the more traditional orientation of the Filipino woman. More respondent wives, however, admitted that the family tensions created were mainly economic. As the Filipino wife is the financial manager in the family, demands of relatives for a share of the husband's earnings usually pose problems for her.[17]

In the Taegu study, additional tensions were raised by the need for some wives to work for a living. An independent income not only undermined the position of the husband but also widened the wife's sphere of influence and increased familial conflicts.[18]

Conflicts and tensions involving family and kinship relations tend to become worse when they enter the realm of politics and administration. As kinship ties remain strong even in the city, they are used to extract favors from those in power. Demands for favors from relatives confront the Malay politician, Filipino civil servant, Thai military official, or Burmese bureaucrat.

Kinship demands (expanded enormously by appeals to common village of origin, common language, *compadrazgo* or ritual kinship, common religion, etc.) come in direct conflict with the performance of the official's duties. Whether he gives in to those demands or resists them, there are benefits and consequences. He is torn, therefore, between ideals of particularism and universalism which arise from the mixture of rural and urban characteristics in the Southeast Asian city. Much of what is regarded as "corruption," "nepotism," and "anomalies" in Southeast Asia today may be traced to contradictions created by kinship.

Even as rural-traditional influences create urban problems, however, many practices and institutions that recently rural folk bring with them to the city also provide a stabilizing influence so necessary in urban environments undergoing rapid economic and social changes. As observed in a study of a slum-squatter area made by this author in the Philippines, traditional influences tend to be perpetuated in small communities that are made up of "urban villagers." In such communities, many traditional practices survive, especially those that are rooted in indigenous institutions like the family. In some instances, new social forms may also arise.

In response to the demands of the more complex urban environment, some kinship groups, such as those of the Toba Batak, have created new forms of social organization not previously found in rural society. The urban Batak, according to Bruner, form clan associations (*dongan samarga*) which are simultaneously residence groups, descent groups, and voluntary associations. The clan associations establish scholarships, provide loan funds, and take care of financing life-crisis rites such as births, weddings, and funerals.[19] These new social forms clearly benefit the urban Batak because they provide services that cannot be obtained from the government or other sources. At the same time, as particularistic groups that may demand and obtain special concessions and favors from the government, they may contribute to "corruption."

Similar "peasant voluntary urban associations" have been observed by Hart in Manila, although here, common place of origin rather than kinship alone forms the basis of organization. Tracing the whereabouts of rural folk who left his village of study and moved to Manila, Hart found that [20]

> Most residents from Borongan, the capital of Eastern Samar Province, who live in Manila belong to NOBITCOM (Natives of Borongan in the City of Manila). Similar associations are organized among Samarans working in Manila who came from barrios in this province. The Lalawigan Circle had about 100 members in 1956 . . . the Circle has a written constitution and was run by elected officers. . . . Members paid monthly dues of 20 centavos—unless they were jobless.

The voluntary associations generally had two major functions —to celebrate the barrio fiesta in Manila, and to aid members in time of need. Contributions were collected on behalf of members who were sick or bereaved. Help was given to fellow members looking for jobs and to those who, having had no luck in the city, desired to return to their village of origin. These associations help ease the adjustment problems of new migrants to Manila and to this extent they help lessen tensions.

New social forms of a beneficial nature may be created by rural people who move to cities, but in some instances traditional forms may also deteriorate in a manner that creates conflict and tension. To some extent, this is what is happening to the institution of *compadrazgo* (ritual kinship) in the Philippines. Originally, it was an honor to be named *compadre* (feminine, *comadre*) to a child and entrusted with the child's religious training and education. A ritual bond was established between parent and godparent that took on more than religious significance. In the city, however, *compadrazgo* has become, to many people, a means of acquiring power and influence. Ambitious parents use the ceremony to ingratiate themselves with power holders; and highly placed officials, politicians, administrators or other members of the urban elite are usually in great demand as *compadres*. In some churches, in fact, a rule limiting the number of *compadres* and *comadres* to two has been enforced. *Compadrazgo* is becoming a form of dyadic relationship or a political patron-client linkage based on reciprocity and particularistic mutual advantage.

The examples cited above reveal forms of social adaptation on the part of rural people who move to urban settings. The kinship association of the Bataks, as pointed out by Bruner, are remarkably similar to the clan associations of overseas Chinese, the urban tribal associations of West Africa, the *zaibatsu* of industrial Japan, or the clan associations of the Caribbean. To the extent that they make the adjustment of rural-urban migrants to the city less traumatic, they play an important role in easing urban tensions.

Ethnic and Racial Tensions. The high densities of urban life frequently magnify ethnic and racial differences. While proximity may result in closer interactions that bring about tolerance and understanding, familiarity may, indeed, breed contempt. Asia, with its varied ethnic and linguistic groups, has seen both cooperation and conflict in its cities. Chinese and Malays in Malaysia, Muslims and Christians in the Philippines, Hindus and Muslims in India and Pakistan, Burmese and Karens in Burma, Cambodians and Vietnamese in Pnom Penh, Chinese and Indonesians in Djakarta—at one time or other, blood has been mutually shed by these groups in open conflict.

It has been hoped that urbanization—the great leveler, the force that undermines primary group loyalties and replaces them with functional identifications, the air that makes man free—will bring about a lessening of ethnic and racial tensions. While urbanization has encouraged nation-building, it has also created substantial problems. The Malaysian dream involves a racially mixed Kuala Lumpur where Malay, Chinese, Indians, and other Malaysians would live in harmony. These hopes were shaken by the riots of 1969. It was hoped that the high-rise apartments and dwellings on Jalan Pekeliling would bring Chinese and Malays together. However, experience has shown that [21]

> Mixing Chinese and Malays within the crowded tenements . . . heightens tensions and frictions that may remain latent without the phenomenon of proximity. The life styles of Chinese and Malays clash in some instances within the confines of the crowded flats. The smell of Chinese cooking, reeking heavily of pork, is irritating to many Malays. So are the many Chinese celebrations such as wakes, characterized by feasting and gambling. Little things like these become magnified because of propinquity.

Nor is rivalry and conflict primarily due to subtle differences in life style alone. Economic and political conflict makes ethnic tensions in Kuala Lumpur especially volatile. The June 1957 census in Malaysia found that Chinese made up 62.0 percent of the population of Kuala Lumpur, against only 15.0 percent Malays, 16.9 percent Indians, and 5.9 percent others. This proportion is not exactly an easy thing to swallow in a city which is the federal capital of Malaysia. The proportion of Chinese to other groups in Kuala Lumpur has been declining since 1957 as more and more Malays join the civil service or enroll in the educational institutions there. However, the Chinese influence over the economic activities in the city shows little sign of waning. In 1969, Chinese accounted for 67.7 percent of property holdings in the capital. When annual values of such holdings are analyzed, Chinese account for 71.7 percent.[22]

In other countries in Southeast Asia, the presence of the *Nanyang* or Chinese living abroad has been a source of tension. In some degree, the misunderstandings may be due to the tendency of Chinese to stay in urban enclaves—the ubiquitous Chinatowns of practically every large city in the world. In the Philippines, Thailand, Indonesia, and other countries where the Chinese play a dominant role in trade and commerce, they are often justly or unjustly accused of manipulating economic activities for their own advantage.

Characteristically, the influence of the Chinese in Southeast Asian countries where they form a minority is often greatly exaggerated. This is shown by the situation in Bangkok where the 1960 census reported that only 13 percent of the city population were Chinese citizens; yet "by the definitions used in everyday life both Thais and Chinese regard the latter as being much more numerous than indicated by the official statistics. Estimates of Chinese ethnics generally run as high as three to three and a half million persons for the country." (In 1966, 368,000 aliens were registered in Thailand, of whom 345,000 were Chinese.)[23]

Communist China, whose presence is felt throughout Southeast Asia, may be one reason why local Chinese populations are suspected of working against their host countries. The Indonesians expelled many Chinese after Sukarno's overthrow and the abortive uprising of the PKI (Indonesian Communist Party). In the Philippines, President Ferdinand Marcos blames the rash of violence in the country on "Maoist groups aided and abetted by a foreign power." Blaming the Chinese is not new in the Philippines. A historian once wryly observed that every revolt or revolution in the country's history always started with a massacre of local Chinese—whether the uprising was against the Spaniards, the British, the Americans, or the ruling Filipino elite.

More subtle reprisals are often taken against the Chinese for economic reasons. It is a fact, or at least a widely held belief, that Chinese control the trade and commerce in Southeast Asian countries far in excess of their actual numbers. This dominance is most obvious in urban areas. Thus in 1966, 36 percent of all business establishments in the twin cities of Bangkok and Thonburi were owned by Chinese, compared with one-fourth of those in smaller towns and only 10 percent of those in rural places.[24]

Fear of Chinese control usually brings about nationalization. The Philippine government nationalized retail trade, followed closely by nationalization of rice, corn, and timber concessions. The influence of the Chinese in Burma also has been drastically reduced by nationalization. In no other country are conflicts between Chinese and native populations more apparent, however, than in Malaysia.

Ethnic tensions in Malaysia may be traced to the fact that the Chinese are more dominant in trade and commerce, which are mainly urban endeavors, while Malays are concentrated in agriculture, government, and educational establishments which tend to be more rural and traditionally oriented. Malaysia's leaders have put forward the concept of *bumiputra* (sons of the soil) allegedly to further the development of Malays, but this goal has also meant discrimination against the Chinese. Malays are favored in entrance to crucial sectors of the civil service and in educational institutions. They are given advantages in entrepreneurial activities and exploitation of natural resources. It is no surprise, therefore, that racial tensions have remained high in Malaysia, in spite of the country's relative prosperity.

Goodman, in a provocative paper, has proposed the "fragment hypothesis," wherein he expressed pessimism about the developmental role played by urbanization in Southeast Asia because of the conflict between the "migrant Chinese fragment" and a "folk" or native fragment. According to Goodman, urban Southeast Asia is heavily influenced by the Chinese fragment, which in turn has resulted in the creation of a native fragment hostile to Chinese interests. Being only a fragment, the Chinese are not motivated or encouraged to use their resources for national development. The folk fragment, on the other hand, brings particularistic values and practices to the urban situation also. The small modernizing elite spends most of its time trying to maintain power by bargains with the folk fragment and by blaming the Chinese. Under these conditions, according to Goodman, political orthodoxy persists and development is severely hampered.[25]

Even in racially homogeneous countries in Southeast Asia, however, ethnic tensions along linguistic or regionalistic lines persist. An interesting manifestation of this are the criminal gangs found in most Philippine cities (particularly in Manila). Manila's papers frequently report violent killings, slum riots, prison riots, and other events in the long feud between the criminal gangs. Prominent among these gangs were the *Oxo* and the *Sigue Sigue,* although the *Bahala na Gang* and others have also figured in some of the clashes.

Reliable reports trace the origin of these gangs to the prisons, especially the National Penitentiary in Muntinglupa just outside metropolitan Manila. The gangs grew along language lines, with people from the Visayas (speaking Cebuano, Waray, or Ilongo) filling up the *Oxo* ranks while Tagalogs, Ilocanos, Pampangos, and other persons speaking Luzon dialects formed the *Sigue Sigue.* Initiation into the gangs occurred in the harsh confines of the prison. A new inmate was promptly recruited by the gangs, and since survival usually depended on membership, no special efforts were needed to gather new members. Members bore distinctive tattoos, learned identification symbols, and became blindly loyal to the gangs. Adherence to the gang continued after release or escape from prison. An *Oxo* or *Sigue Sigue* gang member draws, shoots, or stabs on sight or upon recognition. Hence urban territories have been carved out by each gang, if only to cut down on casualties. Outbreaks occur primarily when new areas are contested or when personal vendettas are carried out. There are some rumors that gangs have joined political parties and factions as bodyguards and private armies, but so far, these have not been confirmed.

In sum, the hope that urbanization will have a leveling or "melting-pot" effect on multi-racial or multi-ethnic societies in Southeast Asia has not been fulfilled. To observers of life in Southeast Asia's teeming cities, the reasons for this failure are obvious. Prior to their trek to the city, most residents of Southeast Asian cities lived in cohesive villages separated from each other by considerable distances. The identity of people from the same village was clear; the bonds that held them together were strong. These centrifugal forces persist in the city, and resist influences to undermine them.

Concentration of people in space, which is the main characteristic of city life, fosters not only basic instincts of identity and cohesiveness but also feelings of being threatened. People from other groups interfere with the migrant's life. They compete with him for jobs and services. Their life styles challenge his. People who were poor, lacked status, or were thought of as not good enough in the village suddenly become successful. Worse, such people cannot be ignored, for others keep making comparisons.

Perhaps, in time, after several generations, primary group identifications and traditional beliefs will give way to a more tolerant if not a more homogeneous society. In the meantime, differences among ethnic groups are likely to persist, rendered more serious by propinquity and competition.

Urban Services. The sheer numbers of rural people migrating to cities strain urban services. Squatter shanties and slum areas reveal the housing shortage, and traffic jams point up the problems of transportation. There are also electricity blackouts, water shortages, periodic epidemics, and lack of toilets and garbage disposal.

While these conditions are bad enough, migrants also bring with them to the city certain habits and practices that make urban administration a nightmare. For example, Southeast Asian cities are hard to keep clean because people are used to disposing trash on the spot instead of looking for waste disposal containers. The open markets are filthy, smelly, and noisy, but housewives prefer to go there instead of to the cleaner but higher-priced supermarket. Food is preferred fresh, increasing the danger of contamination, though freezing and other ways of preserving it are available. Traffic jams occur because of slow-moving funeral processions or the refusal of people to use sidewalks or clearly marked crossing areas. All these, somehow, can be traced to survival of practices and modes of behavior that were learned in rural areas but still persist in the cities.

When urban services deteriorate, many city dwellers in Southeast Asia revert to old forms and practices. Food shortages make them till backyard gardens, blackouts bring out oil and kerosene lamps, inadequate police protection results in the creation of community patrols, lack of housing is solved with self-built shanties. The pace of urbanization, however, is running far ahead of these traditional responses. Large numbers of people require services that can only be offered by complex structures featuring specialization and coordination. These structures take time to create, and it is not easy to train people to run them.

Once again, however, the ability of urban dwellers in Southeast Asia to revert to old forms or come up with new ones to cope with basic service needs may provide the bases for some creative rather than destructive tension. It is easy to spot service inadequacies in Southeast Asian cities, especially when "minimum standards" and other measures based on essentially Western demands are used. In view of the peculiar nature of Southeast Asian urbanization, however, some more hopeful trends may be pointed out.

The service frequently cited as most critical in Southeast Asian cities is housing.[26] Shortages are usually stated in terms of the rate of household formation compared with the rate of housing units provided. Statistical proof is often supplemented by colorful descriptions of life in slum and squatter areas, for these communities have symbolized the Asian city to most Westerners for years.

And yet, how accurate are statements of housing needs based on standards and norms that most Southeast Asians do not subscribe to? The person who lives in a slum or squatter shanty in Manila, Bangkok, or Djakarta may believe that his housing is perfectly adequate for his present economic and social status. If the fact does not bother him and does not prevent him from creating a better life for himself in the future, is the society justified in condemning him? More realistically, should the meager capital resources of the nation be used for more "satisfactory" housing that would far outpace the capacity of the urban dweller to pay and force him to devote a much greater percentage of his income to this service?

Perhaps, for lasting benefit to the city and the poor city dweller, other more critical services should be provided. Water, for example, is essential to life—not only for drinking, washing, and cooking, which are basic needs, but for sanitation and firefighting as well. Similarly, medical and health facilities have to be provided, for their absence or lack poses direct threats to urban life. Employment-generating enterprises should be preferred to capital-intensive or highly technological undertakings. And transport is necessary for economic health.

For the fact must be faced that cities in Southeast Asia lack resources because the products they generate are used not only to solve their local problems but also to cope with problems in rural and peripheral areas. To the extent that urban needs can be dealt with through the use of local resources (which include traditional institutions and practices commonly classified as rural) the tensions created by rapid urbanization may be reduced and their disruptive effects overcome. Then, perhaps, precious resources can be optimally used for developmental activities, and the cities can play their rightful role in national development.

Conclusions

Many of the urban tensions in Southeast Asia arise from the peculiar nature of the urbanization process occurring there—a process that packs people close together within a small space and allows little time for the evolution of new ways of managing urban affairs. Faced with the bewildering complexity of urban life, many traditional Southeast Asians have shown great creativity in adapting new to old ways or vice versa. But creating, borrowing, or adapting has proven to be insufficient in the face of changing times, and anxieties and tensions have sometimes broken out in urban disturbances and violence.

In the 1960s most governments in Southeast Asia recognized the dangers from rapid urbanization, and their urban policies and programs have reflected their concern. In Malaysia official policy is committed to balanced urban growth. The growth rate of Kuala Lumpur, the federal capital, has been high, but growth has also been encouraged in other places so that a condition of primacy has not arisen. In the Philippines President Marcos included an urban policy statement in his State of the Nation Address in 1965, and again in 1969. A legislative resolution on the protection of the environment has been passed. Unfortunately, more pressing problems (e.g., the imposition of martial law allegedly because of dangers from a rural- and urban-type insurgency) require more immediate attention from the authorities, and prospects are dim for a comprehensive approach to solving urban problems in the immediate future.

Thailand has had little success in channeling growth away from Bangkok, and her problems have also been made more difficult by rural unrest, especially in the Northeast. Promises for urban reform, however, may be seen in the combining of Bangkok and Thonburi under a single government. The Burmese government is valiantly trying to decentralize responsibility for urban problems to local government units, but economic problems have frustrated most of these attempts. Pakistan had been engulfed in a tragic civil war, which created urban problems not only within her borders but in India as well. In the Southeast Asian countries involved in the Indo-China war, of course, virtually nothing has been done to cope with rapid urbanization and the problems that it creates.

It has been suggested that in the 1970s the Green Revolution will enable villages and towns to hold on to more people and migration to the cities may slow down. This suggestion is coupled with the hope that, because conditions in Southeast Asian cities are so bad, perceived opportunities for betterment will increase for the countryside. Based on what has happened in the past, however, these suggestions may be too optimistic, at least in the short run. Improvements in the countryside may keep successful persons there, but the less successful may still move to the cities. These people, seeing no future in the countryside, will not be deterred by bad urban conditions. On the contrary, bad conditions create slums and squatter areas which are their natural habitat, and decay may encourage them to move to these places.

Recognizing that rapid urban growth is due not only to migration but also to overall rates of population growth, almost all Southeast Asian countries have launched stronger programs for family planning and birth control. The impact of such programs, however, which are only being introduced now, will not be felt until late in the 1970s. Hence it is too early to even guess the effect of these family planning programs on urbanization, especially since they have created serious tensions and conflicts of their own, ranging from religious opposition to suspicion that stronger nations are attempting to use family planning to undermine the growth potentials of the weak ones.

There is some hope that urban development policies for regional and "growth pole" development will reap some success in Southeast Asia in the 1970s. Research and planning are continually focusing on this subject and official policies on this matter have been adopted in some countries. However, there are still many problems to be solved in this area. The countries of Southeast Asia, with the exception of Singapore, are predominantly agricultural, and they naturally tend to devote more resources to agriculture. It is hoped that there is a reserve of goodwill in the cities that can tolerate more tension and deterioration while problems are solved in the countryside. But it is becoming increasingly clear that this may not be the case. The threat of urban disruptions and even insurgency seems to be just as serious as rural unrest. For the time being, therefore, in spite of native resources and good intentions, the prospects for peaceful and constructive urbanization in Southeast Asia are likely to become worse in the 1970s before they get better.

Chapter 5

Migration, Urbanization, and Politics in Pakistan *Shahid Javed Burki*

EDITORS' NOTE: Shahid Javed Burki's paper, which forms part of his larger effort, *Social Groups and Development: A Case Study of Pakistan,* rounds out our consideration of urbanization by analyzing in some depth several distinct types of urbanization in one country, Pakistan, and their possible political meaning. The author examines different explanations for the unusually rapid rate of urbanization in Pakistan. He uses a variety of data to demonstrate the mobility of Pakistan's rural population, contradicting the common impression of the static countryside. The data suggest that it is not stagnation in the agricultural sector which leads to migration to the towns and cities, but rather economic dynamism. Burki also considers why some migrants go to towns and others to cities.

He seeks to link demographic change and politics through political group analysis, and speculates on how migration, population growth, and politics interact in different political sectors. The substantial migration from rural areas to towns is of particular interest and, according to Burki, helps provide some explanation for his finding that the anti-Ayub movement began there rather than in the cities.

Introduction

Pakistan's urban society played a significant role in the struggle for independence. Once independence was achieved, it continued to determine to a very large extent the direction of the country's political, social, and economic development. However, the urban population in 1947 or at any time after that was not homogeneous. It was made up of a number of diverse elements, each one determined to play its own part. Since these were by no means always consistent with one another nor with the politically influential elements outside the cities, political conflict ensued.

In this essay, I will explore aspects of urbanization in Pakistan with a number of questions in mind.* What have been the major contrasting types of urbanization and the principal sources of differing patterns of rural-to-urban migration? Has the socio-political group composition of different segments of the population and of migration flows affected the political positions taken by different cities and towns? Are there plausible connections between these and related demographic phenomena and the demise of the Ayub regime?

Urbanization here is understood as a phenomenon that leads to the growth of a "continuous collection of houses inhabited by not less than 5000." [1] In Pakistan, urbanization proceeded far more rapidly than it did in India and Ceylon. Between 1910 and 1961 the urban population of India more than tripled, from 25.7 million to 78.8 million.[2] The experience of Ceylon was somewhat similar to that of India.[3] By contrast, Pakistan's urban population grew more than sixfold during the same period (Table 5.1). Partly because of rapid rural-to-urban migration but particularly because of the inflow of 7 million refugees from India (2 million more than fled the country) most of whom settled in her towns and cities, Pakistan's urbanization was not only "more rapid than that which occurred earlier in the areas of north-west European culture," [4] but proceeded at a faster rate than in most developing countries.

Kingsley Davis has argued that in most developing countries the contribution of rural-urban migration to the growth of urban centers is not as important today as it was for the industrializing countries of the eighteenth and nineteenth centuries, since mortality in the cities then was substantially higher than in the countryside and fertility was significantly lower, while today, improved public health and medical services have sharply lowered urban mortality rates and fertility has increased.[5] In the case of

* The main focus of this discussion is the territory of contemporary Pakistan, formerly known as West Pakistan.

Pakistan, however, immigration has continued to play a very significant role in the urbanization process.

Table 5.1 Urbanization in Pakistan, 1901–61

Census Year	*Total Population (millions)*	*Percent Variations (per decade)*	*Urban Population (millions)*	*Percent Variation (per decade)*	*Percent of Urban Population*
1901	16.6		1.6		9.8
1911	19.4	+16.9	1.7	+ 4.3	8.7
1921	21.1	+ 8.9	2.1	+21.9	9.8
1931	23.5	+11.5	2.8	+34.6	11.8
1941	28.3	+20.1	4.0	+45.0	14.2
1951	33.8	+19.4	6.0	+49.9	17.8
1961	42.9	+26.9	9.7	+60.4	22.5

Source: Computed from Government of Pakistan, *Population of Pakistan,* Vol. I, II, and III (Karachi: Ministry of Home and Kashmir Affairs, 1961).

Pakistan's urbanization differs from that of other developing countries in at least two respects. During the past half-century the rate of urbanization in Pakistan has been greater than in most other Asian countries. And in recent years, significant additions to the urban population have come from in-migration rather than from natural growth.

Urbanization is a more complex process than indicated by the above simple definition. It should be viewed as the end product of economic, social, and political forces that induce people to move from the countryside to a relatively large, dense, and permanent settlement of socially heterogeneous individuals. How can one gain a better understanding of the forces that induce people to move to the towns and cities?

According to one sociologist, the rate of urbanization in the developing world and the size of the major cities are "more expressions of lack of economic development than the result of it." [6] The main argument in favor of this hypothesis is that the low level of rural development in these countries makes it extremely difficult for their agricultural sectors to absorb all the members of the new labor force produced by the very high rates of population growth. Therefore, cities with overcrowded agricultural hinterlands are swamped with the migrants rendered surplus by the slow rate of growth of the rural economy.[7]

The opposite phenomenon, however—the pull factor—can also play an important role in urbanization, and rapid urbanization can sometimes be a symptom of economic development. Industrialization can provide jobs for only a small fraction of the unemployed; for a larger fraction it holds the promise of employment in some distant future. Even a small increase in industrial development can have a strong magnetic effect on the unemployed or semi-employed labor force in the countryside. Accordingly, a high rate of industrial development can produce disproportionate urban growth, as Karachi well illustrates. With no overcrowded agricultural hinterland of its own, Karachi attracted people from the cities, towns, and villages hundreds of miles away. Even East Pakistan, separated geographically from West Pakistan by 1,000 miles of Indian territory, made some contribution to Karachi's labor force. The migrants to Karachi came in the thousands, pulled toward the great city not by the jobs that were waiting to be filled but by the promise held out by industrial growth that jobs would eventually become available.

It has been suggested that the pull factor produces a greater impact on the economies of towns than of cities. For instance, a United Nations study showed that the increment in employment resulting from the location of a factory in a small town may be accompanied by an actual increase in the overall level of unemployment,[8] since more people are attracted to the town than can possibly be accommodated by the otherwise primitive economy. But in Pakistan, the government made only a few half-hearted attempts to effect some dispersal of industry. The few existing cities, "with their social equipment for the support functions (transport, communications, mechanical power sources, etc.)" [9] attracted the bulk of industrial investment. According to Gustav Papanek's survey, 97.3 per cent of the total industrial investment

Table 5.2 Population of Urban Areas in 1951 and 1961 According to Size of Towns

Size	*Number*		*Population (millions)*		*Percent of Total*	
	1951	*1961*	*1951*	*1961*	*1951*	*1961*
Over 100,000	9	12	3.206	5.685	54.1	58.8
50,000 to 99,999	7	10	0.483	0.702	8.2	7.3
25,000 to 49,999	22	30	0.789	1.100	13.3	11.4
10,000 to 24,999	53	78	0.759	1.150	12.8	11.9
5,000 to 9,999	74	106	0.545	0.778	9.2	8.1
Under 5,000	41	79	0.145	0.239	2.4	2.5
Total	206	315	5.927	9.655	100.0	100.0

Source: See Table 5.1.

in Pakistan between 1948 and 1958 went into six large cities.[10] The concentration of industrial wealth in a few large cities is no doubt responsible for the concentration of Pakistan's urban population in a few urban centers. According to the 1961 census, twelve cities in Pakistan with populations of more than 100,000 accounted for 58.8 percent of the total urban population (Table 5.2). In India, cities of similar size had only 44.5 percent of the total urban population.[11]

Three Types of Urbanism and Their Political Roles

While we know that the politics of developing countries is often dominated by their major urban centers, we still know very little about the interests being served, the direction public policy will take, or the probable direction and shape of political change in the near future.

A political analysis could begin by considering the many distinguishable socio-political groups whose competition and collaboration define the character and direction of urban and national politics. I have sketched elsewhere in detail the changing roles of such long-standing socio-political groups as the landed aristocracy, the lawyers, the students and *ulema* (religious leaders) who were already active in pre-partition components of Pakistan. Refugees from India, Muslim merchant-industrialists, and industrial and commercial labor were new socio-political groups. Together with the civil and military bureaucracies, these groups form the principal actors in Pakistan's polity.[12] The political role of Pakistan's cities will be seen to depend substantially upon the activities of these different groups in particular cities and in the wider, national political arena. The character and distribution of social power, we believe, will provide a useful explantory line of analysis.

In discussing Calcutta, Nirmal Bose observes that this is "the scene of a major confrontation between the enduring institutions of old India—her caste communities and diversity of ethnic heritages—and the pressures and values arising from the urbanization that presages India's industrial revolution." [13] This confrontation is also taking place in other cities of the developing world. Its outcome will shape the course of political development in these countries.

But the pattern of urbanization is more complex than that, and Pakistan illustrates these contrasts. It will be helpful first to draw a distinction between traditional and modern cities. Traditional cities are those that have grown gradually around a nucleus that originally served the countryside. As the needs of the surrounding countryside increased, the urban nucleus expanded. The growth of the urban nucleus, in turn, increased its own urban demands; their fulfillment further increased the size of the city. This process of expansion around a nucleus left the city with a strong inward orientation. No matter how far the periphery of the city stretched, the nucleus continued to exercise its political, social, and economic influence on the entire population.

Modern cities, by contrast, are those that emerged suddenly, sometimes because of the establishment of a new industrial enterprise, or because of the creation of a new administrative center, or for other reasons. Having been organized around some modern form of activity, the city continued to expand. The modern city may have developed with or without a nucleus; if there was one, it was dominated by some such modern activity as industry, commerce, or government.

Then there are the mixed cities that are the by-product of traditional as well as modern paths of growth, for example the traditional cities to which some form of modern activity has been added at a point in time. It is important to ask how these mixed types are to be classified, for many of the cities of the developing world belong to this category. They can best be characterized in terms of the interplay between the various social forces that dominate the political and economic life of the city. As the traditional city comes under some modern influences—industrial, commercial, administrative, educational, etc.—the old social groups have to compete with the new interest groups for political, social, and economic control of the city. If the population remains attached to the old social groups, the city can be described as traditional. If, on the other hand, the population comes under the political and economic control of the new interest groups, the city can be classified as modern.

What factors influence the transformation of a traditional city into a modern one? Or, conversely, what factors keep a city traditional even when it is subjected to modern influences? It is possible to identify several static factors, focusing especially upon spatial distribution of the urban population, its composition, size, and density. It is also possible to lend a dynamic character to the analysis by emphasizing phenomena such as the pattern of population movements into the urban area as well as within it. These movements, of course, influence over time the distribution, size, composition, and density of the city population.

The present study is focused primarily on the spatial distribution of population and its socio-political group composition, my hypothesis being that these two factors are the principal determinants of the political attitude manifested by the population of a city. In order to lend support to this hypothesis, I shall briefly examine the ecological structure of three different types of urban community: the traditional city of Lahore; the more modern city of Rawalpindi; and a typical town, Gojra, in Lyallpur District of the Punjab.

Lahore. The ecological structure of Lahore, the capital city of the Punjab, demonstrates the continuity of traditional arrangements. As the second largest city of Pakistan, Lahore has well over a million inhabitants. In recent years its growth has been rapid; during the 1950–60 decade the population increased by over 50 percent.[14]

Lahore's history can be divided into a number of periods, each leaving its distinct ecological mark on the city. During the Hindu period (up to 1036) Lahore grew from a large village into a middle-sized town serving the rich agricultural country between the Ravi and the Beas. In the Pathan period (1036–1526) Lahore acquired the status of a garrison town, protected on three sides by a sturdy brick wall with seven gates and by the Ravi on the fourth. With the advent of the Moghuls (1526–1721), the city acquired its multi-nuclear character.[15] The arrival of the British (1846–1947) brought the usual paraphernalia of government buildings, civil lines, district courts, cantonments, race clubs, colleges, universities, and the like.

During all these vicissitudes, however, one thing survived: the group of powerful notables who took part in managing the administration and economy of the political hinterland of Lahore. These notables had one thing in common—they possessed large landed estates bestowed upon them by their political masters in recognition of their service to the state. Because of their interest in the land, they developed strong ties with the Muslim peasantry in the surrounding countryside. As the notables protected the broad interests of their dependent peasantry, the peasantry in turn rendered service on the land or in their patrons' homes, thus developing a reciprocal network of patron-client relationships. By helping the rulers of the Punjab maintain the general tranquility of the surrounding area, the notables further increased their power. Accordingly, while the city of Lahore experienced ups and downs in its political and economic strength, the influence of its nobility over the countryside increased almost continuously.

This process continued even under British rule. The government's recuitment policy in the Punjab, however, did not create the kind of impact that the British system produced in some other parts of India. A large number of posts were filled by individuals who had strong ties of kinship, caste, clan, or tribe with the city's notables. Some of them owned large tracts of land in the villages that once had been outside the periphery of Lahore city but became part of the metropolis at the beginning of the twentieth century. Thus British patronage extended to the landlords of Baghbanpura, Moghulpura, and Mianmir consolidated their social and political position even as their land gradually became more urbanized. At the same time they profited economically from urbanization, which continued to increase the value of their properties, and by selling their land they were able to invest their money in commercial and industrial activities.

An analysis of the members elected in the second election to Basic Democrat local councils, for example, gives a good indication of the influence wielded by the old Arian families of Baghbanpura in the political life of Lahore (Table 5.3). In 1964, the people of Baghbanpura returned 68 councillors. While nearly two-thirds were businessmen, only one-third indicated business as their principal source of income. Over half identified land as the single most important source of their earnings. We infer that a sinificant proportion of businessmen were also landlords, underlining the landed background of Baghbanpura's political elite. An analysis of Mozang, another of Lahore's several traditional nuclei, gives a similar result: the political elite was chosen from among the classes that exercised economic and social power when Mozang was rural and its population depended upon land for sustenance.

Old Civil Lines and the Cantonment areas, by contrast, owe their existence to the British *raj*. While the old landed-cum-busi-

Table 5.3 Background of Basic Democrats Elected in Lahore in 1964

	Baghbanpura *N=68*	*Mozang* *N=84*	*Old Civil Lines* *N=54*	*Cantonment* *N=43*
Occupation				
Business	62%	64%	3%	1%
Lawyers	2	2	52	46
Retired officials	2	—	22	36
Landlords	2	5	7	3
Other	30	29	16	14
Principal Source of Income				
Business	34%	38%	16%	11%
Legal practice	2	2	42	41
Land	51	27	25	27
Government pension	0	—	2	3
Urban property rent	10	2	12	9
Other	3	41	3	9
Average Yearly Income	Rs 7,800	Rs 6,700	Rs 4,200	Rs 3,800
Average Age	48 years	51 years	42 years	41 years
Percent Re-elected	72	67	41	22
Community				
Sheikh	12%	29%	9%	7%
Arian	33	11	12	12
Kashmiri	15	13	11	14
Pathan	7	5	12	10
Kake Zai	11	18	10	13
Other	22	24	46	44

Source: Lahore Municipal Corporation (unpublished records).
Note: Not all percentages add to 100 because of rounding.

ness families dominated local councils in the traditional centers, these newer centers were controlled by members of the legal profession. In both the Old Civil Lines area and the Cantonment, 44 percent of the Basic Democrats cited the legal profession and government pensions as their principal source of income. The Basic Democrats representing the older centers were older, wealthier, and more politically secure than those elected from the new centers. There was also some difference in the community affiliation of the local councillors, with one community dominating each of the traditional centers while all the important communities were sharing power in the new centers.

The social groups that dominate areas like Baghbanpura and Mozang have played an exceedingly important role in the political life of the city of Lahore. Their political influence has given a conservative cast to Lahore's politics to this day. In the post-partition history of Lahore, the anti-Ahmadya movement was the only occasion when the people of Lahore actively opposed the policies followed by the government of the day.[16] At other times, as in 1965 (Pakistan's first presidential election), in 1966 (Anti-Tashkent Declaration movement), and in 1967–69 (the anti–Ayub Khan movement), Lahore showed little taste for opposition politics.[17]

Rawalpindi. Rawalpindi is a city that developed under the impact of more modern institutions. Before the advent of the British, Rawalpindi was a large *pind* (village) strategically located on the roads linking the Khyber Pass and the Kashmir Valley with the cities of Lahore and Delhi. Rawalpindi began to develop into a major urban area at the end of the nineteenth century after the northern command of the British army moved there for strategic reasons. Moreover, the river Rawal provided a good source of water in an otherwise arid region. The city's population crossed the 100,000 mark between 1911 and 1921. By the time of the partition of the Indian subcontinent, it had a population of more than 200,000 (Table 5.4). The same reasons that commended it to the British also convinced the new government of Pakistan to make Rawalpindi the country's military capital. Ayub Khan's decision to shift the political capital of the country to Islamabad, a new city built expressly for this purpose in the foothills of the Himalayas, only ten miles from Rawalpindi, stimulated a new surge in the city's growth.

There was, however, an important difference between the changes brought to Rawalpindi by the British army in the 1870s

Table 5.4 Decennial Changes in the Population of Lahore and Rawalpindi Cities, Gojra Town of West Pakistan

	Lahore		*Rawalpindi*		*Gojra*	
Year	*Population*	*Percent change*	*Population*	*Percent change*	*Population*	*Percent change*
1880	149,369		52.975			
1890	176,854	18.4	73,795	39.3		
1900	202,964	14.8	85,278	15.6	2,589	
1910	228,687	12.7	86,483	—1.4	5,417	109.2
1920	281,781	23.2	101,142	17.0	7,622	40.5
1930	429,747	52.5	119,284	17.9	9,799	28.3
1940	671,659	56.3	185,042	55.1	12,964	32.6
1950	849,333	26.5	236,877	28.0	20,407	57.4
1960	1,296,477	52.6	340,175	43.6	29,665	45.4

Sources: For *1880* see Government of India, *Statistical Abstract Relating to British India, 1876/77 to 1885/86,* No. 21 (London: Her Majesty's Stationary Office, 1887), Table 24, p. 50; for *1890* see Government of India, *Statistical Abstract Relating to British India 1889/90 to 1898/99,* No. 24 (London: Her Majesty's Stationary Office, 1900), Table 22, p. 38; for *1900* to *1960* see Government of Pakistan, *Census of Pakistan, 1961, Vol. 3, West Pakistan* (Karachi: Ministry of Home Affairs, 1961), II, 116–21.

and by the Pakistan army in the 1940s and the changes brought by the civilian government apparatus in the 1960s. In the first two instances, both British administrators and, after independence, the Pakistan army recruited skilled professionals and others with specific administrative and military skills making for a carefully selected population. The social, political, and economic changes produced by the arrival of the British in Rawalpindi, therefore, were totally different from those produced by them in Calcutta, Bombay, and Delhi. The arrival of the Pakistan army quickened the pace but not the direction of change. Right up to 1958, Rawalpindi remained a city steeped in the traditions of conservative politics.

The arrival of the central government thereafter brought more active politics to the city. In less than a decade, Rawalpindi began to share many characteristics with the great modern cities of India. The ratio of students to total population, of university students to non-university, of unemployed to employed, of migrants to native-born, of non-government to government employees, all increased substantially. These changes produced a politically and economically restive society within the city.

Gojra Town. A third type of urban area has played a very important role in determining the direction of Pakistan's political, economic, and social development. Towns of 10,000–100,000 account for roughly one-third of the country's urban population. There were 119 of these in 1951 with a population of 3.1 million, constituting 32 percent of the total urban population. In 1961, their number increased to 161 and their population to 4.2 million or 34 percent of the urban population.

Gojra Town in Lyallpur District of West Pakistan illustrates the peculiar place of these towns in the social, political, and economic history of the country. According to the Imperial Gazeteer of India, published in 1908, "Gojra was an important grain market on the Wazirabad-Khanewal branch of the North-Western Railway." [18] In 1901 it had a population of 2,589; by 1961 it was nearly 30,000, a twelvefold increase in sixty years. Even in recent years, towns like Gojra have been growing more rapidly than the cities. Thus, between 1941 and 1961, the population of Gojra Town increased by 129.3 percent. In the same period the populations of the cities of Lahore and Rawalpindi increased by 93 and 84 percent respectively (Table 5.4).

This rapid rate of population growth in towns like Gojra results mainly from in-migration from rural areas. Projecting from a survey I made in 1970 of 13 randomly selected towns in the provinces of the North-West Frontier, the Punjab, and Sind, based on union council and town clerk *(patwari)* records, it can be concluded that over one-third of the population of West Pakistani towns moved in from the rural areas from 1961 to 1969.[19] (See Table 5.5.) However, there is considerable range in the proportion of the rural migrants into specific towns included in the survey, from Pasrur in Sialkot district with only 11 percent contrasted with Kamoki town in Gujranwala district, where nearly 37 percent had moved in from the countryside from 1961 to

Table 5.5 Growth of Survey Towns and Proportion of Migrants in Their Populations, 1951–69

		Population			*Rate of Growth*		*Migrants*	
Town	*District*	*1951*	*1961*	*1969* [1]	*1951–61*	*1961–69*	*Number*	*Percent of population*
Haripur	Hazara	7,979	10,217	12,200	28.0	19.2	3,420	28.0
Charsadda	Peshawar	27,048	37,396	49,300	38.3	31.7	6,730	13.7
Gujarkhan	Rawalpindi	8,496	11,529	15,700	35.7	35.8	4,890	31.1
Gojra	Lyallpur	20,409	29,665	43,200	45.4	45.7	10,100	23.4
Jaranwala	Lyallpur	17,969	26,953	39,600	50.0	46.8	11,300	28.5
Kot Radha Krishna	Lahore	8,657	10,536	12,100	21.7	14.8	1,730	14.3
Kamoki	Gujran-wala	5,588	25,124	40,300	61.5	60.4	14,800	36.7
Sangla Hill	Sheikhu-pura	9,379	13,738	19,200	46.5	39.4	3,890	20.3
Daska	Daska	15,375	20,406	27,600	32.7	35.3	7,420	26.9
Pasrur	Sialkot	9,403	10,836	12,000	15.2	10.8	1,280	10.7
Burewala	Multan	15,372	34,237	61,800	122.7	80.4	17,800	28.8
Rohri	Sukkur	13,243	19,072	24,200	44.0	27.0	6,800	28.1
Larkana	Larkana	33,248	48,008	63,900	44.4	33.2	13,300	20.8
Total		202,166	297,772	421,100	47.3	41.4	103,460	24.6

Sources: Government of Pakistan, *Census of Pakistan, Vol. 3, West Pakistan* (Karachi: Ministry of Home Affairs, 1961), pp. II-112 to II-128.

[1] Estimates made from Survey II data.

1969. That more than a third of a town's population may be composed of rural migrants engenders a political, social, and economic environment totally different from that of the large cities.

In contrast, we find from studies of Pakistan cities that the proportion of the total population coming from rural areas is far smaller than that shown in my survey of towns. Thus, according to a 1959 survey of Karachi, 17.5 percent of the total population was classified as in-migrants—persons whose original place of residence in Pakistan was not Karachi.[20] According to a 1960 socio-economic survey of Rawalpindi, 23 percent of the city's population had come from rural areas.[21]

We should perhaps stress here the obvious fact that cities and towns are part of the social system in which they are located. As such, they are part of the structure of economic, political, and social power. "Cities tend to dominate a political system; the pattern of cities in a country may tell us something about the dispersion of power in that political system." [22] Given the three types of urban communities described above, it is inaccurate to speak of one urban Pakistan. The response of people in the three types of urban areas to economic and political problems can be very different. Moreover, urban societies made up of a large number of cities and towns display political characteristics quite different from those in which the society is dominated by one or a few large cities. In the former there is sufficient competition between the urban centers to prevent any particular political life style from dominating the society—unless, of course, all the cities and towns belong to the same type. In the latter, however, there prevails a condition of political oligopoly in which a few urban centers can dominate the political society. Thailand, as discussed in Goldstein's paper in this volume, is an example of a near-monopoly based on Bangkok. By contrast, India is a type of society not influenced by any one urban center. Between these two are countries like Pakistan, in which a seesaw condition prevails. In these societies political, economic, and social factors can make one type of urban center dominate the scene for a while until a new set of events brings another type of urban community into prominence. The social, economic, and political history of Pakistan, therefore, can be seen as a continuous interplay between these different urban forces.

For Pakistan, three political periods can be identified with a fair degree of accuracy. First, 1947–58, the eleven-year period in which the refugees from India dominated the political and economic society of the country. The cities and towns that had a large proportion of the refugee population played an important part in this period, particularly the city of Karachi. Secondly, 1958–65, the seven-year period in which Ayub Khan's conservative economic and political program activated some of the traditional social groups. In this period the cities where these groups dominated played an important role. Thirdly, during 1965–69, a series of economic factors transformed the towns into foci of political and economic unrest. In this period the towns that grew rapidly as a result of large-scale rural-to-urban migration played a very significant part. Two of these periods, the first and the third, are connected with patterns of migration and therefore deserve to be discussed here. Why urban growth takes place, and how it does so, are always economically and politically significant questions. They may also provide some clue to understanding the social, political, and economic history of Pakistan.

Refugees from India and Urbanization, 1947–58

The bulk of the migration caused by the partition of the Indian subcontinent occurred in the four months between August and November 1947. It is estimated that in this period some 6 million refugees moved into Pakistan. The flight of refugees continued up to 1951, though at a considerably reduced rate. According to the 1951 census, in a population of 73.8 million nearly 10 percent described themselves as *muhajirs*—displaced persons who had to move into Pakistan as "a result of partition or fear of disturbances connected therewith." [23] Out of these, 6.5 million or 90 percent of the total came into West Pakistan, while the remainder went to the eastern wing of the country. More than 80 percent of the *muhajirs* who entered West Pakistan came from the districts of East Punjab and Delhi, the capital city of India. Although the bulk of the refugees entering West Pakistan were Punjabis, they were very different from the inhabitants of that part of the Punjab included within Pakistan.

It is probably true of all minorities that they tend to congregate in urban areas. In the case of the Muslim minority in East Punjab and the Hindu and Sikh minorities in West Punjab before partition, a higher proportion of them lived in urban areas where each was a minority rather than a majority of the population. Moreover, the urban population, largely because of the greater communal disturbances in the cities and towns, showed a greater propensity to migrate than did the more isolated rural population. In the population movement of 1947–51, therefore, the proportion of urbanites among both Muslim and non-Muslim streams was far greater than in the population at large. This urban bias had a profound impact on Pakistan's political and economic development.

According to the census of 1951, nearly 40 percent of the urban population was made up of refugees from India, many of them replacing non-Muslims who evacuated to India. The bulk of the migrants tended to go to the large cities, with the result

Table 5.6 Refugees in Pakistan's Urban Population, 1951

	Urban Population (millions)		*Refugees as Percent of Urban Population*	
	Total	*Refugees*		
Cities	3.202	1.574	55.5	49.2
Towns				
25,000 to 100,000	1.230	0.481	21.2	39.2
10,000 to 25,000	0.789	0.360	13.6	45.6
5,000 to 10,000	0.572	0.177	9.8	31.0

Source: Government of Pakistan, *Census of Pakistan, 1951*, p. 22.

that nearly 50 percent of their population was made up of *muhajirs*. The proportion of the refugees in the total population declined as the urban center decreased in size (Table 5.6). It is interesting to note also that the largest concentrations of the *muhajir* population were found in 1951 in the cities that did not have powerful traditional social groups, i.e., those cities which I defined in the above analysis as modern. In Karachi, Hyderabad, Lyallpur, and Sargodah over 60 percent of the 1951 population was made up of refugees. The traditional cities—e.g., Lahore (43 percent), Multan (49 percent), Sialkot (26 percent)—had proportionately fewer refugees. This suggests that in its quest for a permanent habitation the *muhajir* community not only was looking for the places with good economic opportunities but also was seeking out those with good social and political prospects, i.e., those not dominated by powerful traditional forces.

Thus Karachi in the 1950s became a city dominated politically, economically, and socially by the Urdu-speaking Muslims of Delhi and the United Provinces (the present-day Uttar Pradesh). On the other hand, Lyallpur became a city dominated by the small-business communities of East Punjab. The political alliance that Ayub Khan forged in the 1960s and his transfer of the capital from Karachi to Islamabad displaced the Urdu-speaking *muhajir* community as a strong political force and weakened their early unique economic advantages. Accordingly, in the elections of 1965 Karachi voted overwhelmingly against Ayub Khan. His administration's sympathetic treatment of the East Punjab refugees provided him with the political support that kept cities like Lyallpur, Sargodah, and Multan relatively calm during the period of political turbulence that started in the spring of 1967.

The refugees who moved to Pakistan tended to concentrate in a few areas. "Many towns beyond the River Jhelum in the Punjab and in the interior of Sind and the N.W.F.P. were practically deserted," while Karachi and some Punjabi cities were made to bear an almost intolerable burden.[24] Whereas Karachi and Hyderabad in Sind received refugees mostly from Delhi, the United and Central Provinces and Rajputana, the cities of West Punjab absorbed refugees from East Punjab.

Before partition, tthe 1941 census estimated that there were some 500,000 Hindus and Sikhs living in cities in what was to become Pakistan, while Muslims in what was to become Indian Punjab numbered 420,000. According to the 1951 census, some 750,000 refugees were then in the cities of Pakistan's Punjab. This means that partition touched off a process that saw a number of small-town people move to the cities. Not all of them stayed in the cities. Many later took advantage of the government's permanent rehabilitation measures to move from cities to the towns of Pakistan Punjab, for they were hard pressed by what Gerald Breese has called "subsistence urbanization." This is urbanization of a very high density; of individuals living under conditions that may even be worse than the rural (or semi-urban) areas from which they have come; or of not having available the kinds of work or the means of support which will permit them to do more than merely survive.[25]

Evidence of the city-to-town migration of refugees is to be found in my survey of 13 towns. In these towns, the refugees eventually constituted nearly 25 percent of the total population. That they did not all come immediately after partition is also clear from the data. Only 14 percent settled in these towns in the period 1947–50. The largest proportion, 43 percent, came between 1950 and 1955; another 40 percent settled between 1955 and 1960; and the remaining 3 percent arrived between 1960 and 1969. Therefore, for 86 percent of the refugee population outside the cities, settling down was a two-stage migratory process—from India to the cities and from the cities to the towns. Perhaps 2 percent of the refugees went to the towns after initially settling in the countryside whereas 84 percent moved in from the cities.

Two questions need to be answered at this point. Who were the people who moved out of the cities and settled in the towns?

And for what reasons did they leave the cities? In answering the first we also partially answer the second. The 1951 census shows that 1.3 million or 55 percent of the self-supporting *muhajirs* aged 12 years and over were agriculturists.[26] Since the bulk of the non-agriculturists settled in the cities, the census data can be interpreted to represent the city refugee population. Among the non-agriculturists roughly 21 percent were unskilled laborers, 28 percent were skilled operators, 21 percent were sales workers (mostly small shopkeepers and their workers), 15 percent were service workers (mostly domestic servants), 10 percent belonged to the technical and professional classes, and 2 percent belonged to the administrative and managerial classes. These occupational categories used for the 1951 census were also employed to analyze the occupational background of the non-agriculturist refugees who are now settled in the 13 towns surveyed for the larger study, of which this is a part. From a comparison of the census with the survey data it is clear that a higher proportion of the professional middle and upper classes—the clerical and office workers, administrative and managerial personnel, and technicians and professionals—settled in the city than in the towns (15 percent and 8 percent of the refugees respectively). In 1951 the refugees represented 42 percent of the city population, but by 1969 only 33 percent of the city population were refugees. To be sure, the city population had grown in the meantime. But taking all the evidence into account, we conclude that the urban professional classes from among the refugees found it easier to settle down in the cities while much skilled and unskilled refugee labor had to leave the cities and settle in the towns.

The census and survey data also explain the power wielded by the refugees in the economic, political, and social life of the cities. In 1951 the Muslim urban professionals who migrated from India constituted only 7 percent of the city population, but they made up a startling 70 percent of the entire urban professional class.[27] The urban professionals in the pre-Ayub era wielded tremendous political and economic power. As such, the prominent role played by the refugees during the first years of independence when the capital was located in their greatest area of concentration becomes somewhat easier to explain.

Rural-Urban Migration and Urbanization

Urbanization is said to take place when the proportion of total population residing in places defined as urban is rising, or when the urban population is growing at a faster rate than the average rate of growth for the country.[28] Growth in urban population is composed of three components: (1) natural increase, which means the excess of births over deaths; (2) net rural-to-urban migration, and (3) net international migration. The last component has not played any part in the building up of Pakistan's urban population after 1951, the year in which the migration of Muslims from India decreased to an insignificant trickle.[29]

Since the overall growth of Pakistan's population in the decade 1951–61 was 26.9 percent while the growth of the urban population was 60.4 percent, a significant portion of urban growth must have come from rural-urban migration. The 1951 or 1961 population census of Pakistan does not provide any direct evidence for the growth of the urban population as a result of rural-to-urban migration. All that we have from the 1961 census is the assertion that "the growth of urban population during the period 1951–1961 indicates that there has been an acceleration in the trend towards urbanization during the last 10 years." [30] However, a careful examination of a variety of other data provides some suggestive observations.[31]

In Karachi, in 1959 some 83 percent of the population were immigrants—refugees from India accounting for 65 percent and in-migrants, i.e., those born in other parts of Pakistan, accounting for 18 percent of the city's population.[32] The bulk of the immigrants from India (some 60 percent) came from the cities while the bulk of the in-migrants came from the towns and villages. An analysis of their socio-economic characteristics strongly suggests that the in-migrants were considerably more impoverished, less skilled and educated, and less "urbanized" than the rest of Pakistan's population. The picture of in-migrants therefore corresponds to that of the urban marginals in other major cities of the developing world.[33]

Is this also true for migrants to other urban areas of Pakistan? Detailed demographic studies of other principal cities of Pakistan are not available. However, drawing on the results of my 1970 survey of 13 towns in West Pakistan, we see that in 1969, 24.6 percent of the population of these 13 towns were in-migrants (Table 5.5). There were, however, considerable differences among the towns themselves. The proportion of in-migrants ranged from 11 percent for Pasrur in Sialkot District to 37 percent for Kamoki in Gujranwala District. Despite this, the proportion in 10 of the 13 towns was more than for Karachi city. Of the total in-migrant population of 103,460 estimated for 1969, roughly 17 percent arrived before 1951. The remaining 86,000 moved into the towns in the eighteen-year period between 1951 and 1969. This means that in-migration to these towns accounted for 39.5 percent of the increase in their total population. The remaining 61.5 percent can be attributed to natural increases among both the indigenous and the migrating populations.

Can we learn anything about the differences between the in-migrants living in the cities and towns from the data available from the Karachi survey of 1959 and the 1970 survey of 13 West Pakistan towns? There are, of course, some dangers in comparing the results of two surveys conducted ten years apart. One should be cautious in generalizing to other Pakistani cities from the Karachi survey, for Karachi is by no means a typical metropolitan city either in Pakistan or in the developing world. There are also some difficulties in comparing the data from the surveys that did not always use the same questions for obtaining information from the respondents. However, several surveys of Indian cities show that there are remarkable similarities between the socio-economic characteristics of their migrants and those of Karachi. We may therefore use, with some reservation to be sure, the

Karachi survey to represent the status of in-migrants into Pakistani cities more generally.

A comparison of the two types of data show that the migrants to Karachi traveled further than those going to the towns; [34] that they are younger (92 percent under 40 compared with 83 percent); and that a much smaller proportion (41 percent) of the city migrant males are married than are those who migrate to the towns (71 percent). Undoubtedly a large number of migrants must have moved to the cities after having first tried their luck in the towns, as step-wise migration is indeed fairly prevalent in the developing world.[35]

There are also some significant differences between the occupational background of the two types of migrants. In the cities more than half of the migrants are unskilled laborers, while one-fourth are white-collar workers. The proportions are almost reversed for the migrants living in the towns. The survey of the towns also indicates that two-thirds of the migrants were either landless laborers or peasants before leaving the countryside. This perhaps suggests that nearly one-half of the people belonging to this class, on reaching the towns, can find occupations that are not regarded as unskilled. A large proportion of the rural-town migrants—more than one-third—described their previous occupation as "landlords." This gives one explanation for the difference in the earnings of the migrants in the towns and in the cities. Whereas 60 percent of the city migrants earned less than Rs 100 per month, almost the same proportion among the migrants in the towns earned more than Rs 100 per month.

From this comparison we see the rural migrant living in the town as older and more prosperous and with a more stable family background than his counterpart in the cities. There can be two explanations for this. First, the socio-economic difference between the rural-town and rural-city migrants may be produced by the process of two-step migration. The poorer of the rural-town migrants, not finding in the towns the kind of economic opportunities they seek, move on to the cities. This makes the migrant population that remains behind seem to belong to a different class than the city migrants. Second, there may be important differences between the social and economic backgrounds of the village people who choose to migrate to the towns and those who go directly to the cities. We will argue below, with the help of some more survey data, that the second of these two propositions has greater validity.

In 1970 I carried out a socio-economic survey of 27 villages in Pakistan. The survey used both records maintained by the *patwaris* and pre-tested questionnaires administered to a randomly selected section of the population. The basic results from this survey have been included in my larger study, already referred to. This source provides some interesting information for understanding the phenomenon of migration in urbanization. Migrants to and from the survey villages fall into three categories: those who move between the villages, those who move from the villages to the towns, and those who move from the villages directly to the cities. The survey also distinguishes between different types of migrants: landlords, tenants, and landless laborers.

Analysis of the data showed there was a large turnover of the village population in the decade 1959–69 (Table 5.7). In 1961 the 27 survey villages had a population of 53,000. In the decade for which data on migration was collected, 9,400 males moved out of the villages while 2,800 males came in from the outside. These statistics give a turnover of 23 percent of the population! The turnover coefficient would be somewhat higher if the data on migration also included the movement of the female population. These figures strongly contradict the picture of static village life that has been painted so often in anthropological writings on the villages of India and Pakistan.[36]

Yearly data for migration are available for 8 of the 27 villages. From this we learn that 3 percent of the out-migration took place between 1964 and 1969. This bunching of migration nearer the end of the period is confirmed by data on in-migrants

Table 5.7 Turnover in the Populations of 27 Surveyed Villages, 1959–69

	Number of Males Migrating					
Type of Migrant	*Out*	*Percent*	*In*	*Percent*	*Net*	*Percent*
Landlords	1,675	17.7	189	6.8	1,486	22.3
Tenants	3,382	35.8	822	29.5	2,560	38.4
Landless laborers	4,389	46.5	1,773	63.7	2,616	59.3
Total	9,446	100.0	2,784	100.0	6,662	100.0

Source: Calculated from Survey of 27 Villages in West Pakistan.
Note: Total 1961 population of the 27 villages was 53,332.

now living in the towns and cities. We believe it had a political significance.

The expectation that the bulk of the population that migrates from the rural areas goes to the large cities is fulfilled for West Pakistan as well. Tables 5.8 and 5.9 summarize movements of landlords, tenants, and landless laborers. Out of some 9,400 out-migrants, 4,400 moved to the cities. In other words, the cities claimed 47 percent of the migration from the countryside. The share of the towns and villages was 35 percent and 18 percent respectively. In regard to those who return to their villages, the proportion of the migrants returning from the towns to the villages is higher than those returning from the cities—44 percent in the case of the former and 42 percent in the case of the latter. The village-to-village movement contributes only 14 percent to the stream of back migration.

There are significant differences in the socio-economic composition of the streams of out- and in-migrants. Among the out-migrants 46 percent were landless laborers, 35 percent were tenants, and only 18 percent were landlords. The in-migrants were weighted even more heavily in favor of the landless laborers. Among the returning migrants, 64 percent had been tenants and only 7 percent landlords. The simple conclusion to be drawn from these figures is that for the landlords migration was more in

Table 5.8 Out-Migration from 27 Surveyed Villages to Cities, Towns, and Other Villages, 1959–69

	Landlords		*Tenants*		*Landless Laborers*		
	Number	*Percent*	*Number*	*Percent*	*Number*	*Percent*	*Total*
Destination							
Cities	399	23.8	1,476	43.6	2,558	58.4	4,433
Towns	1,210	72.2	798	23.6	1,326	30.2	3,334
Villages	66	3.9	1,108	32.7	505	11.5	1,679
Total	1,675		3,382		4,389		9,446

Source: Compiled from data obtained from the *patwari* and union council records.

the nature of a permanent move from the countryside to the urban areas than was the case for the other social and economic groups.

There is a significant difference in the destination of out-migrants belonging to the three socio-economic classes we are considering. The bulk of the landlords went to the towns while one-fourth moved to the cities. The landless laborers showed a clear preference for the cities, three-fifths going there and less than one-third to the towns. By contrast, the tenants showed fewer marked preferences, less than half going to the cities and less than a third to other villages.

Table 5.9 In-Migration to 27 Surveyed Villages, 1959–69

	Landlords		*Tenants*		*Landless Laborers*			
	Number	*Percent*	*Number*	*Percent*	*Number*	*Percent*	*Total*	*Percent*
Destination								
Cities	72	38.1	214	26.0	890	50.2	1,176	42.2
Towns	96	50.7	268	32.6	863	48.6	1,227	44.0
Villages	21	11.1	340	41.4	20	1.1	381	13.7
Total	189		822		1,773		2,784	

Source: Compiled from data obtained from the *patwari* and union council records.

Among the landlords who returned to the survey villages, one-half came back from the towns, 31 percent from the cities, and 11 percent from other villages. Among the returning tenants, 41 percent migrated back from other villages, 33 percent from the towns, and 26 percent from the cities. Finally, among the old landless laborers who returned to the survey area, 50 percent came from the cities, 49 percent from the towns, and only 1 percent from other villages.

Out-migration / in-migration ratios for the migrants by destination and socio-economic characteristics were also calculated. These ratios provide a measure of the capability of a certain type of migrant to integrate himself in the society into which he moves. They suggest a picture of the town society in a tremendous state of flux. The towns received a large number of migrant landlords who were accepted economically and socially in their foster societies. At the same time the towns received a large number of landless laborers who were not so readily accepted. Therefore, in this period the political, social, and economic societies of numerous small towns must have gone through a period of great change, trying to absorb one section of the in-migrants while rejecting another. It will be argued below that the serious political and economic consequences resulting from this phenomenon contributed to the fall of the Ayub regime.

Our survey provides another set of interesting statistics on out-migration from the rural areas. These data pertain to the ownership of land by the landlords who migrated out of the villages during the period covered by the survey. It is significant that 87 percent of the landlords who migrated to the towns owned less than 25 acres of land, while only 12 percent owned between 25 and 50 acres. A few landlords who migrated retained title to their land and rented it out, but the bulk of the land of migrating landlords was purchased by the middle peasantry owning between 50 and 100 acres.

A politically important point derives from the bunching of these movements from the land to the towns at the end of the

1959–69 decade: 73 percent of the landlords who left during this period did so during the second half of the decade. This was a time of substantial innovation in Pakistan's agriculture, and in some areas productivity increased sharply. The agricultural revolution in West Pakistan began some years before the Green Revolution. These innovations were made possible by the political and economic emancipation of the middle peasant from the conservative and unproductive dominance of the landed aristocracy, a change affected in the early years of the Ayub regime. The regime also provided easy credit so that middle-level farmers could sink tube wells, thus obtaining a sufficient and controllable supply of water. And seeds and fertilizers were made more accessible to those who had the capability to move them from the towns to their farms.

In the 1965–67 period, the subcontinent was beset by two years of severe drought. This brought economic recession in the hardest-hit agricultural areas, where systematic or individual irrigation was not available, adversely affecting the incomes of landless laborers, small landowners, and those town professionals and businessmen who made their living providing services to the rural population. Despite the drought, output continued to improve in much of the Punjab where large-scale irrigation or individual tube wells brought regular water. It is significant that it was precisely during such a period in irrigated areas that numbers of small-holder landlords sold out and went to the towns.

Another point of interest is that the rural poor account for 96 percent of the inter-village migration. This means that when the poor decide to leave a village they do not necessarily head for the urban areas. In fact, a large number of them move to other villages, often not very far away. We find that 21 percent of the migrating tenants and landless laborers went from the survey villages to other villages. Ownership of landed property seems to be an important variable determining the selection of the destination for those out-migrants who choose to leave the countryside for the urban areas. Thus 91 percent of the city-bound migrants belong to the unpropertied class as against 64 percent of the migrants bound for the towns.

The survey of Karachi, results from which have been used in this analysis, looks at the in-migrants as members of an urban population. A survey conducted in the fall of 1969 in five villages of Haripur *tehsil* in North-West Frontier Province of West Pakistan gives some useful information about the out-migrants from those villages to Karachi and some other cities of West Pakistan.[37] With the help of the data of this survey we can look at the migrants to the cities as being parts of a village population.

There was substantial out-migration from the survey villages to the cities in the period 1961–68. Of the 1,035 males who migrated to five cities of West Pakistan, 362 or one-third returned to their villages of origin. In the net migration from these villages, the city of Karachi, which was at the greatest distance from the *tehsil* of Haripur, claimed the highest proportion. It is significant that Karachi had a higher out-migration / net-migration ratio than other cities of West Pakistan which received some migrants from the survey villages. Put another way, Karachi proved less able to absorb in-migrants than the other major cities. If we use the traditional-modern dichotomy developed earlier in this essay, the differences between modern and traditional cities in the capacity to absorb become evident. According to the definition adopted above, Karachi and the twin cities of Rawalpindi and Islamabad are modern, whereas Peshawar, Lahore, Hyderabad, and Sukkur are traditional in character. The out-migration / net-migration ratios for the migrants to these two different types of cities is 159 and 122 respectively. Migrants are more easily absorbed through the patron-client mechanism, which commands the distribution of resources in the traditional cities, than through the market mechanism that characterizes the modern cities.

Examining the data on the migrants returning home after having spent some time in the city of Karachi, we find that in the eight-year period 1961–68, 24 percent of returning migrants had spent less than a year in Karachi. As many as 30 percent returned after spending between one and two years in the city. This means that more than one-half of the back-migrants into the villages of Haripur had spent less than two years in the city of Karachi.

Some Causes of Rural-Urban Conflict

We have already seen that there is some statistical evidence that the rate of rural-urban migration increased in Pakistan over time. The survey data from the 27 villages in the Punjab and the five villages from Haripur show a definite increase in the second half of the decade of the 1960s. What caused this increase?

The usual assumption is that the main reason for the movement of a large number of people out of the countryside is a combination of (1) the stagnation of the agricultural sector and (2) an increase of the population on the land.[38] For this hypothesis to be valid, there should be statistically significant relationships between migration on the one hand and agricultural output and population pressure on the land on the other. We should, in fact, expect a negative correlation between rural out-migration and growth of the agricultural sector and a positive correlation between out-migration and pressure on the land.

The statistics from the survey of the villages of the Punjab contradict the first proposition but lend support to the second. In fact, we discover that there is a high positive correlation over the years between the rate of out-migration, in-migration, and net migration on one hand and the rate of growth of crop production on the other. In other words, there is a direct correspondence between the turnover in the village population and the rate of growth of agricultural production. There is a positive but statistically insignificant relationship between out-migration and population density. However, if we adopt a different index of the pressure of population, that of the number of males per household, we find that the relationship becomes statistically significant, with a large positive coefficient.

What do we learn from this simple statistical analysis of the causative factors involved in rural-urban migration? First, we can conclude that it is economic dynamism in the agricultural sector that produces dynamism on the demographic front as well. Our analysis elsewhere of the development of agriculture in West Pakistan during the period following Ayub Khan's coming to power particularly in the early 1960s, shows that expanded output coincided with a genuine loss of political power by the aristocratic landed group, coupled with the regime's substantial attention to the middle peasants who worked between 25 and 100 acres.[39] They were ready to take maximum advantage of Ayub's policy innovations. The more dynamic and efficient of the middle-level landlords improved their relative position. Output analysis confirms that those holding 25 to 50 acres did better than those with smaller holdings, and those with 50 to 100 acres showed even more marked output and therefore income advances. With newly earned assets they began to add to their holdings if they could. Where they could not enlarge their holdings by acquisition from the larger landlords, who often had no immediate desire to sell any except their less productive acres, they sought to purchase land from their less successful smaller neighbors. The landed aristocracy may have been hard on their tenants. But the dynamic middle-level landlord was hard on his smaller competitors. It is therefore not coincidental that most of the landlords who migrated to the towns were those holding 25 acres or less, that the 50–100-acre farmer acquired more land than any other group, while both the large landholders and those with under 25 acres lost land.

Accordingly the rate of growth of crop production was linked positively with the numerical presence of the middle-class landlords in the villages. We can now proceed a step further: the larger the proportion of land held by the middle farmers, the higher the rate of growth of agricultural production, and the higher the level of out-migration. To this net of causation we must add another population variable. The critical variable here is not the density of population but the density of male population in the households. Regression analysis has shown that 68 percent of the variance in the level of out-migration is explained by the combined effect of the variables of rate of growth and density of male population.

So far we have confined ourselves to the factors that induce a section of the rural population to leave the countryside. In the introduction to this chapter it was stated that the "pull" factor also played a significant part in the phenomenon of rural-urban migration. It will now become apparent that the really significant part that "pull' plays in rural-urban migration is in helping the migrant decide on his place of future residence. One hypothesis is as follows: A combination of economic and demographic factors operating on the countryside displaces a section of the rural population. A combination of economic, social, and political factors that determine the nature of life in the city influences the displaced rural inhabitants to find for themselves some place within the entire spectrum of urban life. This spectrum is represented by traditional cities at one extreme and modern cities at the other, with numerous towns in between.

The fact that the process of industrialization generates an inevitable pull on the surplus or potential surplus labor in the agricultural sector, as well as on the labor in the traditional sector of the urban economy, does not need any elaboration. What needs to be emphasized here is the difference between the kinds of "pulls" exercised on the rural population by the urban economy. To understand this, the preceding discussion about the differences between traditional and modern cities, as well as the differences between the destinations selected by different socio-economic out-migrants from the rural sector, will prove useful.

The social, economic, and political structures of traditional cities are built up on patron-client relationships. As these cities grow economically, the size of the resources that can be distributed by the patron-client mechanism also expands. However, the distribution of these resources and hence the absorption of new entrants into the urban economy and society are confined to the persons who can get themselves accommodated in this social framework. These are the erstwhile clients or potential clients of the city patrons. Erstwhile clients are those who lost their patrons at some previous stage to the urban economy. Potential clients are those who can make use of their caste, tribe, or family associations to find themselves accommodated in the patron-client network. Absentee landlords (for example, the *Arian* families of Baghbanpura) providing employment to their tenants illustrates the first kind of process; landlords turned businessmen (for example, the Sheikhs of Mozang) finding jobs for their fellow tribesmen or kinsmen is an illustration of the second process. Rural-urban migration involving the tenants and landless laborers from the countryside and influential patrons in the traditional cities is fairly stable. Pathan businessmen, for example, were able to accommodate the labor and tenants who left the villages of Haripur for the traditional cities of Lahore, Peshawar, Sukkur, and Multan. The stability of this kind of out-migration was greater than in modern cities such as Karachi.

In deciding to move to the modern cities, however, the rural poor are guided only by the similarly poor migrants who have already gone from their villages and settled in the urban areas. These old migrants can provide little more than short-term security to their kinsmen and fellow villagemen who join them in the cities. The new migrants, like those who moved to the cities before them, have to depend upon the market mechanism for their absorption into the city economy. That such absorption is not always easy was illustrated by the pattern of Haripur-Karachi migration.

There is a third type of migrant who has received a great deal of attention in this analysis. He is the small landlord, displaced by the newly found dynamism in the agricultural sector. Among rural-urban migrants he occupies a peculiar place. He is not pulled to the traditional city for he is not a part of the patron-client network that attracts some of his fellow migrants. He is not pulled to the modern city, for he either cannot provide or is not willing to provide the kind of labor that is needed by this type of urban economy. Accordingly, he moved to the towns that occupy a place somewhere in between the traditional-modern spectrum that has already been described for the cities. The town of his choice is usually close to the village of his previous residence, explaining the very high proportion of short-distance migration to the 13 towns surveyed for the purpose of this study. He usually moved with his family, which accounts for the low male-female ratio for migrants to the towns. He usually finds himself a place in the business sector of the town economy, which explains the high level of middle-class migrants in the town. Finally, for him it is usually a one-direction process of migration, a fact that explains the very small proportion of landlords among back-migrants.

Summary of the Urbanization Process

Our understanding of the social, political, and economic processes at work in Pakistan is enlarged if we can clearly perceive the complex process of urbanization. Two factors contributed to a rate of growth of the urban population that was greater than that for many countries at the same stage of their development. The cross-migration of population after partition of the subcontinent brought a heavy in-flow to Pakistan's urban communities. The educated and skilled among the refugees remained in the cities while most of those who moved to the towns or the countryside were either unskilled or had rudimentary skills. The professional and commercial elites within the refugee community tended to go to the modern cities like Karachi or Lyallpur, where the modernized social groups could expect to wield greater political and economic power than would have been likely in the more traditional cities such as Lahore. And because the new state was very short on people with such talents, the refugees acquired a remarkable degree of political power, dominating political and economic affairs until the regime of President

Ayub deliberately sought to reduce their power. Moving the capital to Islamabad was but a step toward this goal.

The industrialization promoted by import substitution policies served as one internal stimulus to rapid urbanization, drawing the unskilled and the landless of West Pakistan to the larger cities. The agricultural innovations pressed by the Ayub regime also stimulated rapid urbanization. A major demographic by-product of these changes was a remarkably high turnover among the population in the countryside. Indeed, it was the areas of greatest increase in agricultural productivity which showed the most emigration to the towns and cities. Displaced smaller landlords tended to move to the towns and to remain there. Landless labor and other unskilled workers tried their luck in the cities or towns but in many cases returned to their villages or migrated between villages in search of employment. Pakistan's towns showed substantial population movement. Rural Pakistan does not conform to the image of the stagnant countryside so often depicted in anthropological literature.

Some Political Implications

In the absence of regular elections or detailed periodic opinion polls, it is difficult to identify shifting popular or elite judgments about a regime's legitimacy or performance. But a political crisis, such as brought down the Ayub regime, can provide a useful point of focus for analyzing the political implications of these demographic and socio-economic developments. Certain demographic changes appear to have played a role in these events.

Many explanations of Ayub's downfall have been put forward by knowledgeable observers. Some argue that the decline was precipitated by the military failure to oust the Indians from Kashmir in 1965 and the subsequent Tashkent agreement, which did so much to alienate the army.[40] Others, mainly economists, have argued that the exuberant claims of the regime associated with the 1967 celebrations of the Decade of Development only sharpened people's awareness of persisting and even intensified inequities, such as inflation coupled with stable wage levels in the face of claims of dramatic economic success.[41] Illness sapped Ayub's strength, seriously weakening a regime so dependent upon the decisions and energies of one man.[42] Corruption of his family and the civil bureaucracy [43] and an overconcentration of policy-making authority in the hands of an unrepresentative and unresponsive public service have also been blamed.[44] Some have held that the political agitation of Zulfiqar Ali Bhutto was responsible as he swung from covert to vehement opposition, a move to which West Pakistan's students responded with such enthusiasm.[45]

There is no doubt some truth in all these explanations. The sense of grievance aroused by these factors and the weakening authority of a tired and anxious regime both contributed to Ayub's downfall. But it is possible to find more fundamental causal linkages, tying the beginnings of the anti-Ayub movement to the underlying socio-political forces we have been discussing.

An analysis of data on arrests will help to pinpoint the beginning and location of serious unrest. Since independence the government of Pakistan has maintained statistics on acts of violence. The regime used Section 144 of the Criminal Procedure Code and various provisions of the Defense of Pakistan Rules to regulate public political behavior. Unwillingness on the part of the public to follow government-established rules of conduct usually brought on arrests. Any such defiance leading to arrest was interpreted as a "riot." These data, along with those reflecting other types of violence, are regularly aggregated and reported in the *Year Book of Pakistan*.

To be sure, data on arrests are themselves difficult to interpret. Fluctuations may represent changes in government control policy or the increased or decreased eagerness of local officials as much as changes in genuine levels of unrest. However, since official policy in response to "riots" remained reasonably consistent and it would be difficult to demonstrate a correlation between personnel changes and the changes in frequency of recorded riots in the areas of our concern, we believe the data do provide a useful basis for analysis.

If the figures on arrests per thousand of urban population are disaggregated for the ten quarters between October 1966 and March 1969, a significant time series can be assembled, as indicated in Table 5.10.

Table 5.10 Number of Arrests per Thousand of the Urban Population in Cities and Towns Made Under Various Preventive Detention Ordinances, 1966–69

	1966 (quarter)	*1967 (quarter)*				*1968 (quarter)*				*1969 (quarter)*
	4th	*1st*	*2d*	*3d*	*4th*	*1st*	*2d*	*3d*	*4th*	*1st*
Pakistan	0.15	0.14	0.21	0.24	0.22	0.25	0.41	0.49	0.48	0.38
Punjab	0.14	0.13	0.18	0.18	0.19	0.26	0.43	0.49	0.53	0.40
Punjab cities	0.15	0.14	0.14	0.14	0.14	0.14	0.42	0.54	0.62	0.45
Punjab towns	0.12	0.12	0.23	0.24	0.28	0.42	0.39	0.41	0.41	0.32

Source: Author's Survey.
Note: A city is defined as an urban center with a population of more than 100,000 and a town as an urban center with a population of between 10,000 and 100,000.

The time series for the number of arrests per thousand of urban population shows two discontinuities, one in the second quarter of 1967 and the other in the second quarter of 1968. The index shows an increase of 50 percent between the first and second quarters of 1967 and 64 percent between the first and second quarters of 1968. It then becomes clear that the anti-Ayub movement did not start in the fall of 1968 but substantially earlier, in the spring of 1967 before it became publicly apparent. Can this kind of data be linked with the socio-economic factors that contributed to the anti-Ayub movement?

Table 5.10 also enables us to locate more precisely the geographical areas of maximum and initiatory violence. While the data for the cities shows very little change right up to the second quarter of 1968, it is in the towns of the Punjab that the sharpest differences are recorded. In effect, the 38 percent increase in the level of political unrest in the Punjab is almost wholly accounted for by the towns. Therefore, if the anti-Ayub movement is to be given a time and a place for its birth, we can say with some confidence that it started in the spring of 1967 in the towns of the Punjab.

In an effort to seek correlation between social unrest and other socio-economic variables, the number of arrests per thousand of the urban population were compared for 45 districts from the four provinces of Pakistan.[46] Causal relationships between arrests per thousand and important social and economic indices are represented in Table 5.11. We find that the regions within the country that have achieved higher degrees of urbanization, literacy, social heterogeneity, and industrialization exhibited somewhat less predilection toward political violence. We also find a negative correlation between arrests and the rate of growth of industrial production. This unexpected finding is underlined when we look at the industrial product per head as well as the rate of industrialization. It was in areas which were newly industrializing and where industrialization had not yet gone very far that the most marked negative correlation between

Table 5.11 Correlation Between Number of Arrests Per Thousand Urban Population (NATP) and Certain Social and Economic Variables in 45 Districts in Pakistan

N=45	
Growth rate of urban population	−.43 [1]
Proportion of literate in population	−.48 [1]
Proportion of persons born outside of district	−.51 [2]
Proportion of refugees in total population (1951–61)	−.29 [3]
Proportion of refugees in urban population (1951–61)	−.33 [3]
Per Capita industrial product (1967–68)	−.55 [2]
Growth rate of industrial production	−.31 [3]
Proportion of farmers owning more than 50 acres	+.30 [3]

[1] Statistically significant at .01 level.
[2] Statistically significant at .001 level.
[3] Statistically significant at .05 level.

Table 5.12 Correlation Between Number of Arrests per Thousand of Urban Population and Certain Socio-Economic Variables for Cities and towns in 19 Districts of the Punjab

	Punjab [1]	
Variable	*Cities*	*Towns*
Proportion of principal city population to total district population	−.31	−.41 [2]
Growth rate of urban population	−.87 [3]	+.49 [2]
Per capita industrial product	−.24	−.78 [2]
Proportion of literate in population	−.48	+.42 [2]
Proportion of persons born outside district	−.49	+.27 [3]
Proportion of refugees in urban population	+.27	+.55 [2]

[1] Number of observations: cities, 8; towns, 44.
[2] Statistically significant at .01 level.
[3] Statistically significant at .05 level.

rate of industrialization and violence was found. At the same time, the larger industrial centers, such as Karachi, also showed a notably low per capita rate of violence.

Further analysis of socio-economic variables possibly associated with this unrest reveals little that is significant, if the data for cities and towns are dealt with together. But if the data for cities and towns are handled separately, the number of significant relationships between the level of political violence and various socio-economic indicators increases, especially in the Punjab.

As Table 5.12 indicates, the three variables which show a positive correlation with the level of violence in the case of the towns are the growth rate of their populations, the proportion of literates in their population, and the proportion of refugees.

There are two significant differences in the relationships between violence and socio-economic factors for the cities and towns of the Punjab. We see from Table 5.12 that whereas the rate of growth of the city population appears as a politically stabilizing factor, it is destabilizing for the towns. The same applies to the level of literacy: in the cities the higher the proportion of literate population, the lower the level of violence; for the towns the opposite holds. We can thus conclude that for the cities in the Punjab growth contributes to political stability, but in the towns it breeds political discontent and frustration great enough to have resulted in violence.

If these propositions have validity, it is obvious that the size of the "urban" community is significant. We hypothesize that small urban units are less able to cope with or absorb the effects of urbanization. An influx of laborers from the countryside, we have seen, brings highly mobile persons, apparently unable to find a firm niche in the towns. Numerous migrants are harder to absorb in towns than in cities—they stand out as a group and their mutual self-help measures more visibly impinge on the fortunes of indigenous townsmen. If they have access to government compensation, as occurred in the Punjab, they may have capital which can permit them to vault into money lender or other roles which are notorious sources of tension in smaller communities. Two-step migration to the cities, i.e., from countryside to town and then either back to the countryside or, for the successful, on to the city, may mean that those migrants who at any one time are in the towns are closer to rural ways, have not yet accommodated to "urban" life, and are therefore more acutely alienated than those who have "settled" for city life. City dwellers may have been more impressed with the effectiveness of city police or with the futility of political protest during the Ayub era than the townsmen, who would have been less aware of state authority than those who lived in the cities.

Moreover, the high literacy in towns with marked unrest suggests a significant middle class, capable of playing upon and inducing overt discontent if they themselves were alienated from the regime. Indeed, small-town lawyers and professionals found themselves in the vanguard of opponents of the regime, along with local students who were home for the holidays, as indicated in Table 5.13. A post-agitation survey of students' assessments of their prospects showed that college students from the towns were

Table 5.13 Students and Lawyers Arrested in Nine Punjab Towns under Preventive Detention Ordinances During Second Quarter of 1967

Town	*Number of Arrests* [1]	*Students*		*Lawyers*	
		Number	*Percent*	*Number*	*Percent*
Gujar Kahn	13	7		4	
Gojra	17	8		5	
Jaranwala	28	15		11	
Kot Radha Krishan	6	2		1	
Kamoki	24	11		7	
Sangla Hill	6	2			
Daska	11	4		4	
Pasrur	6	3		1	
Burewala	19	11		8	
Total	130	63	48.4	41	31.5

Source: Survey II.
[1] Includes multiple arrests, i.e., one person arrested more than once.

much more pessimistic than students from the cities. City students better understood the white-collar job market than the boys from the towns and they possessed a network of family contacts able to help them search for urban jobs that the town students could not match. The latter would have it borne in upon them with particular force how few jobs there would be in the towns, where simple administrative structures and service sectors did not require the services of the highly educated.

Nearly one-third of the persons arrested in the first phase of the anti-Ayub movement were lawyers. Town lawyers were often those educated in the main law schools but who could not—or did not—"make it" in the city. Many took up town practices as a second-best profession and were therefore incipiently disgruntled. The post-agitation survey showed that they, too, were more pessimistic than their city colleagues about their future prospects. Ayub's reforms of tenure and other rural practices, limited as they were, nevertheless had undercut some of their traditional and often lucrative practice, and a sharp decline in incomes of certain peasants and middle farmers brought about by the severe drought in 1965 and 1966 affected their own incomes very promptly. Articulate and alert, with the special flexibility of their profession, they were an important source of effective organized resistance to the regime in West Pakistan's towns.

We have already noted that the small landowners who had sold their land and gone to the towns had found a modest economic niche for themselves. But they were not satisfied with their new circumstances. In the absence of detailed data on their attitudes, we can only speculate. They had expected greater improvement in their condition than had actually occurred when they moved to the town. Before, they may have been hard pressed by rapacious money lenders or an unpredictable agricultural market, but at least they were in control of the choices they made, apart from what nature imposed through drought or blight. Transposed to the towns, they now lacked the standing they had possessed as landowners in the countryside. And if they had retained some direct economic links to agriculture when they turned their land over to others, their incomes, too, declined with the drought-induced agricultural depression. In addition, the small-town *ulema* had resented the modernizing reforms of the Ayub regime, and the mosque had become a center for the disenchanted.

Accordingly, demographic changes, including patterns of migration, economic depression in rural areas, and the negative by-products of progressive reforms combined to place the middle-class professionals in the towns in the forefront of opposition to Ayub. They lacked legitimated channels for articulating and aggregating their demands. The steps they took to express their grievances led to their arrest by a regime unable to accommodate their aspirations and no longer ready or able to deter the public demonstration of their disenchantment.

By contrast, the migrants to the city, the bulk of whom came from among the displaced landless laborers from the agricultural sector, did not go through the same kinds of social and political changes as the landholders migrating to the towns. This was for two reasons. First, a section of the migrating labor moved to the modern cities where they became part of the politically passive society that Joan Nelson has described for urban marginals.[47] For them the movement from the village to the city constituted a pure economic trade-off. If the ratio of the expectation of earnings was greater than unity, they moved to the city. If, having once moved to the city, the ratio of expected income in the village was greater than the actual earnings in the city, they moved back to the village. Secondly, for a large number of those who moved to the traditional cities, migration involved little social and economic change. On moving to the cities, they became part of the patron-client network of which they either had once been a part or were its potential components because of their tribal links.

To argue that the towns were politically more restive than the cities seems to go against conventional wisdom, yet our evidence strongly suggests that it is the towns which become the centers of social, political, and economic turmoil in a changing society.

We see from this that the process of urbanization produced in Pakistan the kind of social restiveness for which the political system developed by President Ayub provided no legitimate channel for expression or correction. Nor could the political or coercive systems contain it within bounds. A dramatic change in leadership and in political institutions inevitably followed.

Chapter 6

Socio-Political Consequences of Interstate Migration in India *Myron Weiner*

EDITORS' NOTE: This essay on migration in India considers the social sources and the political consequences of movement not only to such large urban centers as Bombay and to new industrial towns like Bhubaneshwar but also to rural areas such as Assam. It analyzes the distribution and sources of social and nativist political opposition to migrants from alien linguistic and cultural areas. Weiner notes the simultaneous trends of increasing migration of Indians to areas of economic opportunity while long-term residents turn to political action to resist the job competition and cultural dilution represented by the newcomers. Similar responses were dramatized by anti-Bihari movements in urban and rural Bangladesh.

Weiner critically examines available census and other sources of data, describes the patterns of movement, identifies the principal types of migrants, and assesses why they move. It is not so much migration itself which provokes difficulties as migration of large numbers of one cultural group into the territory of another, where different appearance, language, and life styles make for visibility and friction. Middle-class and skilled migrants, not laborers and the unskilled, turn out to be principal targets of nativist agitation. He sets out the political manipulations of these nativist movements, identifies governmental responses to them, and assesses the results.

Economic development and an open society call for substantial

AUTHOR'S NOTE: The research on which this paper is based was made possible by a grant from the Behavioral Sciences Research Branch of the National Institute of Mental Health. I wish to convey my appreciation to Professors P. N. Dhar, A. M. Khusru, Ashish Bose, and other members of the staff of the Institute of Economic Growth in New Delhi, where I worked as a visiting research scholar in 1970–71, for the generous hospitality which they accorded me, and to the Registrar General and Census Commissioner, Mr. A. Chandra Sekhar and members of his staff for the continuous assistance they provided. I am also grateful to the Indian Council of Social Science Research for supporting my request to the Government of India for a visa to conduct research in India on the socio-political consequences of internal migration.

migration flows and socio-cultural intermixing. How can India—and other multi-ethnic countries in Southern Asia—reduce the conflicts likely to become more pronounced as political awareness increases in polities where representative practices give local authorities greater power to resist the types of migration he reports?

Modernization, Integration, and Mobility

The growth of interstate migration in India has created a new tension in the complex relationship that exists between modernization and integration. So long as the sense of regional identity was not well articulated, Indians were generally disposed to be tolerant toward or, more often, indifferent to those individuals speaking other languages and subscribing to other cultural traditions who entered their state to work and settle. The cultural encapsulation of minorities within a social order based upon cultural pluralism, social hierarchy, and group solidarity was the framework within which interstate migrants settled in the past. Prior to independence the numbers of such migrants was, moreover, small, and the oft-repeated statements that Indians, like most pre-industrial people, were attached to their land seemed valid. In 1931 only a little over 8 million persons, or about 2.3 percent of the population in all of what is now India, Pakistan, and Bangladesh, lived in states other than the one in which they were born.

In recent years, however, there has been a growing nativist reaction to migrants and the descendants of migrants who have moved from other cultural-linguistic regions. Moreover, the number of migrants has substantially increased since independence. By 1961 some 23.7 million persons in India alone, about 5.4 percent of the population, had come from other states or from across international borders.[1] But more important than the change in numbers is the change in attitudes of people in each cultural-linguistic region toward themselves and toward "outsiders." In recent years there has been growing opposition to the unrestricted right of Indians to move and to maintain their own regional traditions after they move. Many Indians now believe that the local population, speaking the local regional language, ought to have a prior claim to employment and housing; that "outsiders" are not loyal to the culture and traditions of the region; that all too often they tend to "exploit" local people and are "clannish"; and that if they or their children remain, they must be assimilated to the local language and culture and identify themselves with the region in which they now live.

These nativist sentiments have intensified since independence with the establishment of linguistic states, the mushrooming of regional nationalism, and an increase in popular political participation. Regional languages are now growing in usage with an expansion of regional networks of communication and of a middle class more deeply rooted in the local culture and economy. To an extent unknown a generation ago, the people within each region are becoming increasingly aware of their own regional identity.

As a result, in state after state, especially in places like Assam and Maharashtra where the proportion of migrants is high, there are demands for ordinances and legislation to restrict the opportunities and cultural position of the migrant: domicile regulations in employment and housing; domicile rules for admission into universities, medical schools, and engineering colleges; language or residence requirements for employment in the universities and in state bureaucracies; restrictions on the use of other regional languages as the medium of instruction in schools to which migrant children are sent; and limitations on the granting of licenses to "alien" entrepreneurs.

But while some features of the development process increase regional identities and engender nativist antagonisms toward out-of-state migrants, still other features of the development process encourage greater migrations. Economic development in India has been accompanied by (one might even say, partially caused by) increased internal migration. The industries of Bombay, Calcutta, Delhi, Madras, Hyderabad, and Bangalore were started by entrepreneurs from all over India; and their laborers, office, and technical personnel were often widely recruited. The tea and coffee plantations started by the British recruited their labor force from across linguistic regions—tribal laborers from Bihar to Assam, Nepalis to Darjeeling and Jalpaiguri, and Kerala labor to Mysore. And there has been national recruitment for India's most modern institutions, her industrial enterprises, the national civil service, the military, universities, research institutions, and the courts. Indeed, historically, the migration of skilled people in India—bureaucrats, educators, professionals, entrepreneurs, and technical personnel—has played an important role in India's modernization. And as the country continues to modernize and social mobility increases, we can expect skilled people, as in other modern societies, to seek opportunities wherever they are available. The expansion of the professions, the requirements of modern industry, the growth of a national market, the establishment of national educational institutions, all contribute toward the making of a society in which there is mobility of persons not simply from rural to urban areas but from one part of India to another. The accompanying map identifies districts and cities which have been receiving substantial numbers of migrants from different cultural areas.

The right to migrate within India is, moreover, guaranteed by the Indian constitution, which specifies that all citizens "shall have the right to move freely throughout the territory of India" and "to reside and settle in any part of the territory of India." [2] The constitution also provides that those who move can retain their regional identity by permitting their children to attend schools conducted in their own regional language.[3]

There are thus two sets of principles in growing opposition to one another, each supported by different sets of people, each strengthened by different elements of the modernization process. One principle builds on the notion of a common Indian citizenship made up of diverse cultures whose members freely intermingle; the other assumes more autonomous regional cultures and a

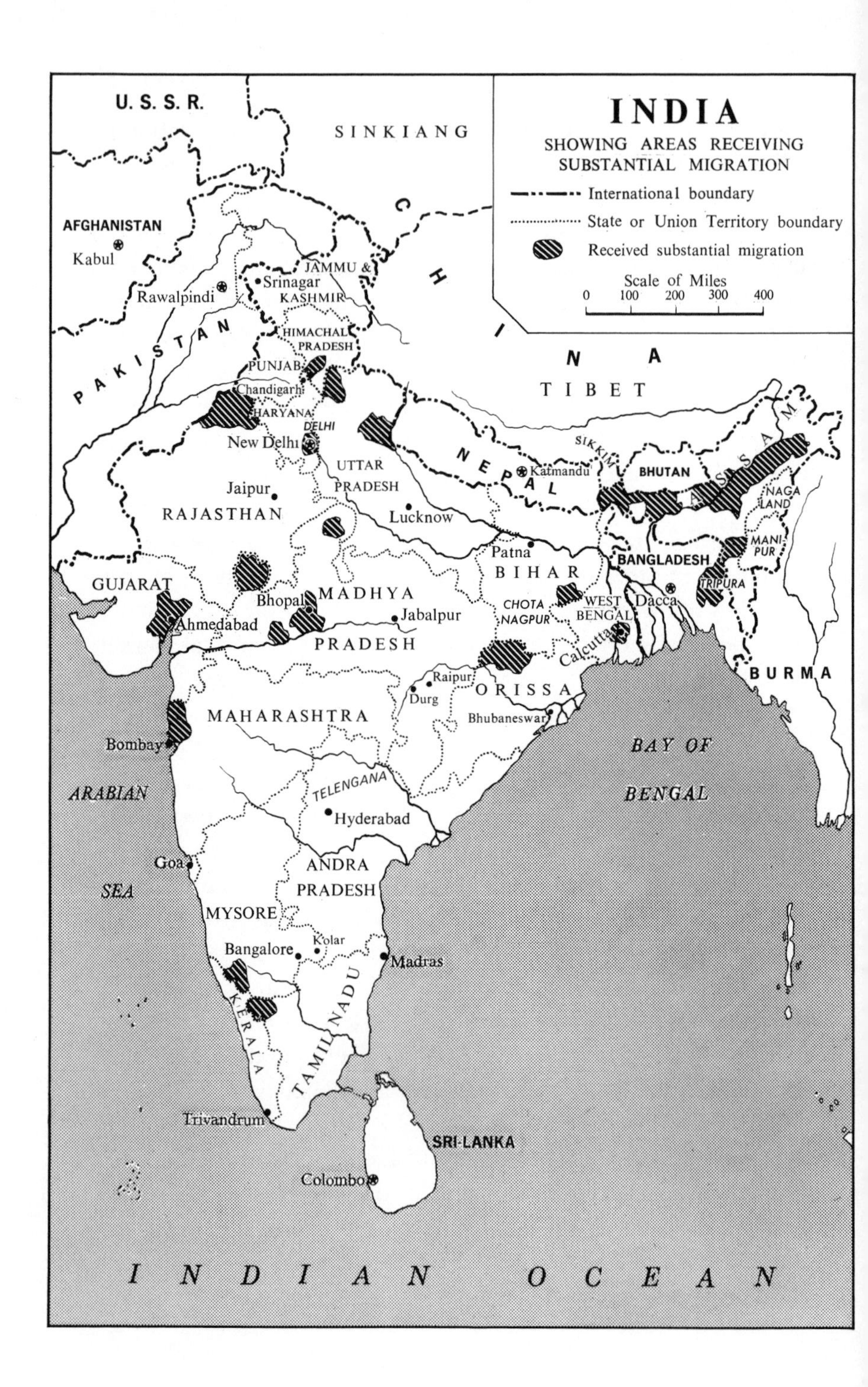
INDIA
SHOWING AREAS RECEIVING SUBSTANTIAL MIGRATION
International boundary
State or Union Territory boundary
Received substantial migration
Scale of Miles
0 100 200 300 400
U. S. S. R.
SINKIANG
CHINA
AFGHANISTAN
Kabul
Rawalpindi
PAKISTAN
Srinagar
JAMMU & KASHMIR
HIMACHAL PRADESH
PUNJAB
Chandigarh
HARYANA
DELHI
New Delhi
TIBET
NEPAL
Katmandu
SIKKIM
BHUTAN
ASSAM
NAGA LAND
MANI-PUR
TRIPURA
BANGLADESH
Dacca
BURMA
UTTAR PRADESH
Lucknow
Jaipur
RAJASTHAN
Patna
BIHAR
CHOTA NAGPUR
WEST BENGAL
Calcutta
GUJARAT
Ahmedabad
Bhopal
MADHYA PRADESH
Jabalpur
Raipur
Durg
ORISSA
Bhubaneswar
MAHARASHTRA
Bombay
TELENGANA
Hyderabad
BAY OF BENGAL
ARABIAN SEA
Goa
ANDRA PRADESH
MYSORE
Kolar
Bangalore
Madras
KERALA
TAMIL NADU
Trivandrum
SRI LANKA
Colombo
INDIAN OCEAN

national political system based not only on dual identities but even on dual citizenship with special rights and privileges accruing to citizens within each state.

In a multi-ethnic society internal migration has both an integrative and a disintegrative potential. It can lead to a sense of national awareness and of the benefits of a larger national polity and economy; or it can lead to civil strife as it did in Nigeria and Malaysia. In this paper we shall explore several dimensions of this tension in India—by looking first at the magnitude of interstate migration, then examining some of the effects of migration on the people who reside in the areas in which migrants settle, and finally, reporting on some of the political and governmental responses to interstate migration.

Magnitude and Distribution of Interstate Migration

According to the 1961 census 23.6 million persons were reported as having been born outside of the state in which they resided.[4] Of these, 14.6 million came from other Indian states, 8.3 million from Pakistan, another half million from Nepal, and the remainder came from other countries. 94.6 percent of the Indian population lived in the state in which they were born, and 5.4 percent came from outside the state. A considerably larger number of Indians, 92 million, moved within their own district and another 29 million moved across district lines within their own states. In all, one-third of the Indian population, about 145 million, were born outside the place of enumeration.

The provisional 1971 census estimates that 170 million Indians live outside their place of birth, of whom 19.4 million come from other states, 8.1 million are from Pakistan or Bangladesh and a half million come from Nepal. A slightly smaller proportion of the population in 1971 was born outside the state—5.2 percent—as compared with 5.4 percent in 1961, but this decline reflects a decrease in migrants from Pakistan, Bangladesh, and Nepal. Interstate migration actually increased slightly from 3.3 percent to 3.5 percent of the population. (The 1971 census estimates are based upon 1 percent sample data.)

In some respects these figures of interstate and intrastate migration overestimate and in other respects underestimate the extent and importance of migration. For one thing, much of the migration in India consists of marriage migration, that is, brides leaving their parents' house and their parental village.[5] Of the 120 million who have moved within their state, 86 million are women and of these 75 million live in rural areas. Among interstate migrants the proportions change sharply, with males outnumbering females. But no matter how great the distance, the proportion of females to males among migrants is always greater in rural than in urban areas.

The magnitude of migration is also overestimated because of birth migration. Children born outside the place of enumeration because their mother returned to her parental residence to give birth may be reported as migrants. Thus, the large number of migrant brides may also lead indirectly to an overreporting of male migration.

There may, however, also be some underestimation of migration since the Indian census only reports lifetime migration. Census enumerators ask three questions of direct relevance to the study of migration: Where were you born? Where do you now live? How long have you lived in your present residence? Persons who have moved and then returned to their place of birth are not, therefore, reported as migrants. The 1961 census, for example, reports that slightly more than 2 million persons had migrated across state boundaries within the previous year, but there were 4 million persons who had been migrants from one to five years. Had all the first-year migrants continued to remain away from home, the number of persons who had been migrants would be twice the number, suggesting that about half of the first-year migrants had again moved. Similarly, the number of interstate migrants in residence for six to ten years was 2.6 million, about a third fewer than would be expected if all the migrants who were in residence from one to five years continued in residence. We can roughly estimate that 1 million of the first year's migrants move,

1.5 million move after five years, and .5 million move after ten years, a total of 3 million.[6] How many of these 3 million persons returned home and how many migrated to still another location is not known.

We should also note that a considerable number of people who are seasonal migrants are in their place of residence when the census enumerators conduct their investigations. This number may be high since the census is conducted in February and March when seasonal labor migration, especially of agricultural laborers and pickers for tea and coffee plantations, is small.

A still more fundamental limitation in the use of census data for the measurement of inter-state migration has been the frequent redrawing of state boundaries in the last twenty-five years. Persons who migrated from one district to another when the districts were within the same state are now classified as interstate migrants when the district in which they were born or to which they moved has been transferred to another state. Similarly, individuals who moved from one state to another will not be classified as interstate migrants if the districts concerned are now located in the same state.

There have been four major redrawings of state boundaries since 1947. There was partition itself which divided Bengal and the Punjab. Migrants who moved within these states prior to partition are now classified as international migrants, and there is no precise way of knowing whether migrants from Pakistan came specifically from Bengal, Punjab, or other states of Pakistan.[7] Shortly after independence, the princely states were combined to form larger political units, or merged with the former states of British India. In 1956 there was another reorganization of states largely along linguistic lines; Madras, Andhra, and Mysore were the states most affected. Since 1956 a number of states have been divided into smaller units including Bombay into Maharashtra and Gujarat; the Punjab into the Punjab and Haryana; and Assam into Assam, Meghalaya, and Nagaland.

Where do interstate migrants come from and where do they

move to? The largest "exporting" states in 1961 were Uttar Pradesh (2.58 million), Bihar (2.04 million), Punjab (1.31 million), Rajasthan (1.13 million), and Madras (1.09 million). However, there may be as many as 2 or 2.5 million Punjabis and Bengalis from Pakistan in states other than West Bengal and the Punjab, and perhaps another .5 million or more Sindhi migrants from Pakistan. In percentage of population of each state found in other states, Delhi is first (with 7 percent), followed by the Punjab (6.5 percent), Rajasthan (5.6 percent), Bihar (4.5 percent), and Kerala, Mysore, Uttar Pradesh, and Madras (all with 3.4 or 3.5 percent). West Bengal is below the national average of 3.3 percent (with only 1.5 percent of its residents outside); but if East Bengal migrants to India are included (e.g., the 775,000 East Bengalis in Assam and the 395,000 Bengalis in Tripura), then in both absolute numbers and in percentage the Bengalis also appear high on a list of migrant communities in India.

To what states do migrants move? In the 1951–61 decade the major flows were to West Bengal (especially the industrial belts in the Hooghly and Damodar Valley regions), Maharashtra (Greater Bombay and Poona), Punjab (the industrial towns along the railway between Amritsar and Delhi), Assam (the tea plantations), Mysore (the industrial complex around Bangalore and the gold fields at Kolar), and Madhya Pradesh (with the heavy electrical industries at Bhopal).[8]

In proportion of immigrants to total population, West Bengal and Punjab with 15.7 percent and 14.2 percent respectively are foremost, though the centrally administered areas of Delhi (with 56.4 percent) and Tripura (with 37.2 percent) have an even higher proportion. Assam comes next with migrants composing 11.4 percent of its population, followed by Maharashtra with 7.3 percent and the hill state of Himachal with 6.6 percent.

There are twenty-six districts (see Table 6.1) or centrally administered areas (out of nearly 400 districts in the entire country) in which more than 10 percent of the male population are migrants from other states, or from Pakistan or Nepal (excluding

Table 6.1 Migrant Districts, 1961

	Percent of Male Migrants			
Migrant District	*From other states*	*From Pakistan*	*From Nepal*	*Total*
Ganganagar, Rajasthan	18.3	11.0		29.3
Sundargarh, Orissa	9.4	1.7		11.1
Nainital, Uttar Pradesh	5.8	6.4	3.4	15.6
Dehradun, Uttar Pradesh	8.9	6.4	2.9	19.2
Coorg, Mysore	16.5			16.5
Bombay, Maharashtra	34.1	2.7		36.8
Thana, Maharashtra	7.2	4.1		11.3
Niligiris, Madras	15.1			15.1
Gwalior, Madhya Pradesh	10.2	2.4		12.8
Mandsaur, Madhya Pradesh	10.8			10.8
Indore, Madhya Pradesh	13.0	2.5		15.5
Sehore, Madhya Pradesh	8.3	2.4		10.7
Ahmedabad, Gujarat	8.6	1.8		10.4
Dhanbad, Bihar	11.7			11.7
Darjeeling, West Bengal	10.7		6.6	17.3
Jalpaiguri, West Bengal	11.7		2.8	14.5
Calcutta, West Bengal	23.2			23.2
Howrah, West Bengal	10.2			10.2
Delhi	36.6	19.1		55.7
Tripura	1.8	34.6		36.4
Goalpara, Assam	3.3	9.5		12.8
Darrang, Assam	7.1	6.9	1.5	15.5
Lakhimpur, Assam	9.0	4.2	1.6	14.6
Nowgong, Assam	3.5	11.3		14.8
Cachar, Assam	1.6	9.7		11.3
Simla, Himachal	22.0			22.0

Source: Derived from part III-C of the state census volumes of the census of India, 1961.

Bengali and Punjabi immigrants from Pakistan to West Bengal and Punjab). These include five districts of Assam, with large numbers of East Bengali immigrants; the centrally administered area of Delhi, where more than a third of the population comes from other states and nearly a fourth from Pakistan; and twenty other districts.

A majority of interstate migrants move to urban areas. Of the 14.6 million interstate migrants, 8.6 million live in urban areas and 6 million in rural areas. Among the migrants from Pakistan slightly more are living in urban than in rural areas—4.3 million against 4.0 million. Only the Nepalis are more rural than urban —359,000 in villages as against 140,000 in cities and towns. About 38 percent of the interstate migrant urban dwellers, or approximately 3.3 million, live in the cities of Bombay, Calcutta, Delhi, Madras, Ahmedabad, and Bangalore where they constitute roughly one-fourth of the combined populations of these cities. Of India's 107 cities with populations exceeding 100,000, thirty have interstate migrants exceeding 10 percent of the population.

To put the figures still another way: there are migrant concentrations (10 percent or more of the population) in 26 districts of which 7 (Bombay, Calcutta, Delhi, Howrah, Ahmedabad, Gwalior, and Indore) have cities with large (i.e., more than 10 percent) migrant populations. In addition there are twenty-three other cities with large interstate migrant populations. Of India's 14.6 million interstate migrants, about 6.2 million live in these 26 districts and 23 cities. In other words, though there are districts and towns with substantial numbers of interstate migrants (i.e., more than 10 percent of the population), there are still millions of migrants scattered throughout India. There is hardly a district or town in India without some interstate migrants. It is rare to find a town where the proportion of out-of-state immigrants is less than 2 percent, or a district with less than 10,000 migrants or 1 percent of the population.

Determinants of Interstate Migration

Who are the migrants who move across state boundaries, what do they do, and why have they migrated? Why have millions of people moved, sometimes over long distances, and often to states in which alien languages are spoken?

1. Many of the immigrants have not moved long distances at all, but to neighboring districts which happen to be located across the state boundary. Large numbers of Punjabis, for example, have migrated to the nearby districts of Nainital and Dehra-

dun in Uttar Pradesh and Ganganagar in Rajasthan where they have occupied newly irrigated lands. Similarly, Bengali agriculturalists in many of the densely populated districts of East Bengal (especially Mymensingh) have moved across the border to the lowland valley areas of Assam. In some instances, the border district is already occupied by people who speak the language of the neighboring state so that crossing the state boundary does not involve moving into an "alien" cultural area. Thus, Kolar district of Mysore (with its gold mines) is 53 percent Telugu-speaking; Tripura, 63 percent Bengali; Cacher district in Assam, 79 percent Bengali; Ganganagar district in Rajasthan, nearly 28 percent Punjabi; Bangalore district in Mysore, 17 percent Telugu and 16 percent Tamil; Greater Bombay, 19 percent Gujarati; Niligiris district in Madras, 31 percent Kannada and another 20 percent Malayalam; and Coimbatore, 20 percent Telugu-speaking.

2. Many interstate migrants are brides marrying men whose families had previously settled in a neighboring state. Thus, female migrants from Bengal exceed male migrants since the eastern districts of Bihar have large numbers of Bengalis whose families settled there in the nineteenth and early twentieth centuries. For the same reason there is an "excess" of female migrants to Orissa and of Tamils from Madras to some neighboring districts of Andhra and of Mysore.

3. There are well-established migration streams from one state to another and often from one district of a state to a district or city of another state. For several decades there was a movement of Munda, Oraon, and Ho tribesmen (and women) from districts of Chota Nagpur in Bihar and districts of northern Orissa to tea plantations in the hill areas of Assam, a stream of migrants from western Andhra to the Kolar mines in Mysore, and a stream of Malayalees from northern Kerala to the coffee plantations of Coorg. Some districts of northern Bihar regularly "export" their surplus agricultural laborers to the factories of Calcutta and Howrah; and Nepalis from the hill districts of

eastern Nepal have regularly moved to Darjeeling and Jalpaiguri districts in West Bengal to work in the tea gardens. Bombay and Bangalore have always had a small stream of educated migrants from Madras taking jobs as clerks, typists, stenographers, and administrators in business houses. In many towns and villages from which migrants come, it is quite common for one or more sons in a family to join a relative who had previously migrated. These patterns of migration, so familiar to many other developing societies, are well established in India.

4. There are some industries which depend upon a migratory labor force since the laborers are used seasonally or for short duration. Many of India's dams, irrigation schemes, office buildings, and roads are built by migrant laborers from Andhra and Rajasthan. Day laborers are often organized into work gangs that move from one labor-intensive project to another. Members of agricultural labor families are often organized in this fashion. Some work in the fields during the harvest season and move off to construction projects for the remainder of the year while others move to nearby urban centers seeking daily work. There are Biharis plying rickshaws in Gauhati, Rajasthan construction laborers in Hyderabad, and Telugu laborers in Bangalore.

5. There are certain skills for which there is a limited labor market, and those who have these skills seek employment anywhere in the country where jobs are available. When an aluminum factory is opened in Belgaum, or a new steel mill opens in Roorkela, metallurgists throughout the country will be considered for the new jobs. Members of the modern professions—engineers, professional managers, computer experts, scientists, economists, etc.—tend to be occupation-oriented rather than place-oriented and are often willing to change their residence if they can improve their status, income, or work satisfaction. Thus, if one walks into the offices of the Heavy Engineer Corporation in Ranchi, the Atomic Energy Laboratories in Bombay, or Hindustan Aeronautics in Bangalore, one finds a mixture of professional personnel from all over India.

6. Indian entrepreneurs have availed themselves of the opportunity created by a common national government and a common market to move and invest freely throughout the country. India's largest single entrepreneurial community, the Marwaris, can be found in every state and in virtually every town: 460,000 or 7.4 percent of all Marwari-speaking individuals are found outside their home state of Rajasthan. Though they are concentrated in the nearby Hindi-speaking states, they can be found as far off as Assam where there are 21,000 Marwaris in a few towns. Punjabis, especially Sikhs dominate the transport industry—taxis, trucks, automobile repair, petrol pumps, automotive parts, and more recently, tractors and related agricultural equipment—in many portions of the country. There are 200,000 Punjabis in Assam, Andhra, Bihar, Gujarat, Kerala, Madras, Maharashtra, Mysore, Orissa, and West Bengal—states that are a good distance from the Punjab. West Bengal alone has 54,000 Punjabis and Maharashtra 64,000.

In India's larger cities, the major industrial enterprises are almost all owned by "outsiders"—not Europeans but Marwaris from Rajasthan; Parsis from Bombay; Gujaratis, Punjabis, and Sindhis. It is a rare large city—Ahmedabad is one of the few—in which the major industries are owned by individuals who linguistically belong to the state.

7. There are cultivators who have moved across state boundaries in search of land. Though India has not had any large frontier, there are areas that have been opened by improved technology—waste lands made arable, dry lands that have been irrigated, and malarial areas reclaimed through the elimination of mosquitoes. Large hydroelectric dams and irrigation works have attracted migrants to Ganganagar in Rajasthan and to Nizamabad district in Andhra; malarial reduction and reclamation projects have opened districts in Uttar Pradesh along the terrai; and in Assam large-scale jumming or deforestation (often illegally) has made it possible for Bengalis and Nepalese to settle lands in the hills along the Brahmaputra Valley.

8. A small but important number of migrants moved into administrative positions in other states when those states were politically subordinate. In the bilingual presidencies of Bengal and Madras, Bengalis and Tamils were in a position to take posts in the state administration which then covered areas far beyond the Bengali- and Tamil-speaking regions. Bengalis migrated to Assam, Bihar, and Orissa throughout the nineteenth century when those provinces were under the administrative jurisdiction of Calcutta; and Bengali, along with English, became the administrative lingua franca throughout northeastern India. Similarly, Tamils migrated to Andhra and to portions of Mysore and Kerala governed from Madras. The control over state administration by Bengalis and Tamils in much of northeastern and southern India had spillover effects into the universities, into private businesses, and into central government administration. Moreover, since the Bengalis and Tamils were educationally more advanced than other linguistic groups within the Bengal and Madras presidencies, they were better able to pass the examinations for various administrative services. We continue to find Bengalis in the university at Cuttack manning the post offices and railways in Ranchi and working as clerks in the tea plantations of Assam, and we find Tamils at the universities in Andhra and in the state secretariat in Bangalore. Though changes in political boundaries and the growing education of communities previously governed from Calcutta and Madras have substantially diminished the proportion of Bengalis and Tamils in these professional and administrative positions, small migration streams still continue.

9. It is difficult to measure, and therefore easy to underestimate, the impact which many aspects of the development process have had in liberating individuals from an exclusive attachment to their place of birth. The monetization of land makes it possible for peasants to buy and sell land; the establishment of a cash nexus between peasants and artisans and between peasants and agricultural laborers makes it possible for those who do not own

land to move more freely to places where they can increase their income; the growth of non-agricultural occupations has opened new occupational possibilities for the children of those who work on the land; the growth of education and exposure to newspapers, radio, and the cinema have made individuals aware of new employment opportunities away from their home; and the improvement of transportation now makes it possible for individuals to go long distances and still be able to return home at a reasonable cost.

In short, while some of the factors which account for interstate migration in India may be the result of specific political and historical circumstances, there do appear to be many persistent elements in the modernization process that lead to a continuation if not an expansion of inter-state migration even when it involves the movement of individuals over considerable distances across cultural-linguistic regions.

Migration and Cultural Regions

Interstate migrations are not necessarily intercultural or interlinguistic; nor do intercultural migrations necessarily involve movement across state boundaries. Both these qualifications must be understood before we consider the political and social effects of interstate migrants in India.

The Hindi-speaking zone of northern India is crisscrossed by state boundaries so that persons moving across these boundaries do not necessarily move into another linguistic area. There are six states in which Hindi is recognized as an official language: Bihar, Madhya Pradesh, Punjab (now the Punjab and Haryana), Rajasthan, Uttar Pradesh, and Delhi. Within each of these states there is considerable linguistic heterogeneity. There are not only many variants of Hindi (e.g., Urdu, Awadhi, Baghelkhandi, Pahari, Chhattisgarhi, and Khariboli) and many languages akin to Hindi but considered by their speakers if not by linguists as distinct tongues (e.g., Bhojpuri, Maithili, Magadhi, Kumauni, Rajasthani, Punjabi, Marwari), but also languages quite alien to Hindi (e.g., the tribal languages of Santali, Bhili, Gondi, Munda, Ho, and Kurukh/Oraon).

There are substantial population movements across state lines within the Hindi-speaking states; a total of 4.3 million persons within these six states come from one of the other states.[9] Of these, slightly over one million come from Punjab (as of 1961), a large proportion of whom presumably are not Hindi-speaking but Punjabi-speaking. Many of the other migrants within the Hindi-speaking belt belong to non-Hindi-speaking communities, including Marwaris, Rajasthanis, and some of the tribal communities. It is common within the Hindi-speaking states to identify certain migrant communities by the state or region from which they come: "He is a Punjabi, a Bihari, a Rajasthani or a Marwari." But among Hindi-speaking migrants from Madhya Pradesh, Uttar Pradesh, Haryana (the Hindi-speaking districts of Punjab which now form a separate state), and Delhi, territorial terms for identity are not commonly used.

Previously we spoke as if intercultural migrations are synonymous with interstate migrations, but there are at least two reasons for not doing so. First, an interstate migrant does not, as we have noted, necessarily cross from one cultural or linguistic region to another. There are a number of cultural-linguistic groups that are divided by state boundaries so that the crossing of a state boundary by a migrant may be within what is to him a common cultural area.

There are three such patterns: (1) ethnic groups that are a majority in one state, but still cross a state boundary into a neighboring state in which they are a minority, e.g., the Marathi-speaking people in the northern districts of Mysore, the Hindi-speaking people in the eastern districts of Maharashtra, and the Telugu-speaking people of southern Orissa; (2) ethnic groups that are minorities in all the states in which they live, generally because one or more state boundaries cut through the territory they occupy, e.g., the Konkoni-speaking people who reside in Mysore, Maharashtra and Goa; the Santalis who live in Bihar and West Bengal; and the Ho, Oraon, and Munda tribes of Bihar and Orissa; (3) ethnic groups that are a majority in two or more states, e.g., the Hindi-speaking people of Uttar Pradesh, Madhya Pradesh, Haryana, and Bihar.

Secondly, the movement of people within a state may involve the movement across a cultural-linguistic zone. Even if we use language as our sole criterion for cultural differences (clearly too narrow a definition), virtually every state in India must be considered multi-cultural. In most states, at least 10 to 15 percent of the population speak a language other than the official language of the state. In Assam the proportion may be as high as 45 percent. In some instances the language may be considered "local" or "indigenous" to the state (e.g., Bodo in Assam) and in other instances as an alien language of another state (e.g., Bengali in Assam).

However, while those who speak the majority language may be prepared to consider minorities within the state as "local," the minority community may consider those who belong to the majority community as "outsiders." Thus, Biharis from the northern part of the state are prepared to incorporate the Ho, Oraon, Munda, and Santali-speaking people, but the tribal people are likely to refer to Biharis as "outsiders" or, in their local languages, as "dhikus." [10] As far as the tribal people of Chota Nagpur are concerned, the Biharis are as much "dhiku" as are the Bengalis, Marwaris, and other non-tribal communities, whether they are indigenous to the state or not. The anti-migrant sentiment among the tribals of Chota Nagpur is thus directed against the movement of all non-tribals into the area, irrespective of state or district boundaries.

A local community may also view immigrants as outsiders even if they speak the same language; for example, in the Telengana region those who were born or permanently resided in the former princely state of Hyderabad, which included portions of what is now Maharashtra, Mysore, and Andhra, were called "mulkis." Now the term has come to mean those who were born or permanently reside in the districts of Andhra which formerly belonged to Hyderabad, i.e., the districts now collectively known as Telengana, including the city of Hyderabad. Since the Telengana districts were merged with the Telugu-speaking districts of Madras to form the state of Andhra, there has been growing resentment against "Andhra" migrations into Telengana, and agitations for the creation of a separate Telengana state. In this instance the supporters of Telengana insist that the Telengana people are culturally distinct from the other Telugu-speaking people of the state though they share a common language. Outsiders may find these differences virtually imperceptible (the people of Telengana prefer tea to coffee, use more Urdu words in their vocabulary, celebrate some festivals more common to northern than to southern India, and give greater importance to certain polite mannerisms than do the Telugu-speaking people of the delta districts), but an awareness of these differences has grown in recent years and has become the basis for distinctive identities.[11]

These differences became even more intense after a ruling by the High Court in late 1972 reinstating the old Mulki Rules of the Hyderabad government which provided, in effect, that only residents of the Telengana region (mulkis) could be employed by the state government in Telengana, a decision which aroused feelings of second-class citizenship among the "non-mulkis" in the state. By 1973 there were substantial groups in both portions of the state advocating the division of Andhra into two separate states.

In any study of the relationship between migration and cultural regions in India we must stress the present fluidity of cultural identities. In recent years cultural groups that are part of a larger political identity have been asserting the autonomy of their own culture. There are now nascent movements for more cultural, and in some instances even political, autonomy among the Kumauni, Konkoni, Bhojpuri, and Maithili-speaking peoples, and among many tribes in north-eastern and central India. There are substantial sentiments not only within Andhra but within Maharashtra, Madhya Pradesh, Assam, and Bihar for the creation of smaller states based upon the cultural and historic affinities of people who live within regions of these states. The growth of such identities has an important bearing on whether migrants to a given city, district, or region are considered by local people to be "outsiders" or fellow members of a common cultural identity.

Sons of the Soil

The English phrase "sons of the soil" is now widely used throughout India to emphasize the rights of local people against migrants from "outside," but the phrase is neither as rich nor as complex as the many terms used by local people in their own language to refer either to themselves or to outsiders. In some instances the indigenous term is explicitly ethnic, while in other instances the term may be explicitly territorial. "Dhiku," for example, is an ethnic concept, while "mulki" and "non-mulki" are essentially territorial.

The English phrase "sons of the soil" ambiguously incorporates both concepts. It may refer to those who are born, raised, or permanently settled in a given territory, or it may refer to those who belong to, identify with, and are accepted as part of, a given cultural group without regard to their place of birth. This ambiguity is a major source of tension between those who belong to the dominant culture of a state or locality within the state and those who were born within the area but are considered by members of the dominant culture as outsiders because their parents or ancestors migrated into the area and therefore belong to a culture which has its roots elsewhere. Two examples may point up this conflict, one from Bihar and the other from Assam.

Nativism in Bihar. The Chota Nagpur plateau of southern Bihar, the homeland of the Santal, Munda, Ho, and Oraon tribes, has been the object of migration from the more densely populated districts of north Bihar and West Bengal for the past hundred years.[12] The result is that not a single one of the six districts in this region now has a tribal majority. Table 6.2 reveals the pattern:

Table 6.2 Linguistic Tabulations for Six Bihar Districts

	Language Spoken (percent speaking)		
District	*Hindi, Bihari, and Urdu*	*Bengali*	*Munda, Ho, Oraon, and Santali*
Santal Parganas	48.9	13.0	33.8
Palamau	92.5	—	5.8
Hazaribagh	89.2	1.3	7.6
Ranchi	53.5	1.1	39.5
Dhanbad	75.1	12.2	9.0
Singhbhum	14.0	20.8	39.6

Source: Census of India, 1961, Vol. IV, Bihar, Part II-C, Social and Cultural Tables.

Two factors account for the low proportion of tribals in Chota Nagpur. The first is that Biharis from the north and Bengalis from the east have been attracted to the employment opportunities resulting from the region's industrial development. Singhbhum district contains the city of Jamshedpur, historically India's major center for steel; and Dhanbad district is a major coal mining area. Ranchi city, the largest urban center in Chota Nagpur, is the site for the Heavy Engineering Corporation, contains the headquarters of Hindustan Steel, and is a growing industrial center. Dhanbad and Singhbhum continue to attract migrants from other states—13.3 percent of the male population of Dhanbad and 9.7 percent of the male population of Singhbhum are interstate migrants; and Dhanbad also attracts large numbers of migrants from other districts of the state—18.4 percent of the population are migrants from other parts of Bihar, more than twice that of any other district in the state.

The second factor accounting for the low proportion of tribals is that throughout the nineteenth century, even while others were entering the region, tribals were moving out in search of employment. Assam tea planters, unable to find plantation workers in Assam (since the state had almost no agricultural laborers), imported their labor force from the tribal areas of Chota Nagpur. Though by now most of the tribals have adopted Assamese as their mother tongue, the 1961 census still reports that in the six districts of the Brahmaputra Valley of Assam 182,000 persons list Santali, Oraon, and Munda as their mother tongue.

Though the tribal population is now statistically holding its own in the Chota Nagpur region, the tribals are clearly losing the race in the movement to the cities. A far smaller proportion of the tribal people live in the urban areas than do the Hindi- and Bengali-speaking people of the state: 3.7 percent of Bihar's rural population is Santali, but only 0.4 percent of the urban population is Santali. For Mundaris the percentages are 1.3 as against 0.5, and for the Oraon it is 1.2 as against 0.8. What this indicates is that industrialization, and the urbanization accompanying it, has had a greater impact on the non-tribals than on the tribals and that non-tribal migrants have been better able to avail themselves of the new opportunities created by industrialization and urbanization than the tribals who reside in Chota Nagpur.

One consequence of this differential response to industrialization and urbanization is that during the past century there have been a number of uprisings of the tribal peoples against the "dhikus" or non-tribal outsiders who have moved into Chota Nagpur. Though the Chota Nagpur Tenancy Act restricts the sale of tribal land to non-tribals and a number of rules have been established by the state and central government to facilitate the employment of tribals in government service and in government-run industries, none of these measures have equalized the economic position of the tribals and non-tribals or protected the tribals from the subordinate social and economic position they are now in.

Since the mid-1930s, the anti-dhiku sentiments have found a number of organized political outlets—through the Jharkhand

Party and most recently through the militant Birsa Seva Dal, an organization which appeals to tribal youth. While many of the older tribal leaders sought to protect their communities from the encroachment of outsiders into sectors of the economy such as agriculture and forests which were traditionally controlled by tribesmen, many of the younger leaders are more concerned with finding ways to increase their share of the modern sectors, by demanding reserved positions in public and private sector factories and by agitating for the creation of a separate tribal-dominated Chota Nagpur state government.

By now, however, a majority of the non-tribal population in Chota Nagpur have been born there and consider themselves domiciles of Chota Nagpur. Some Jharkhand and Birsa Seva Dal leaders now insist that they are not pressing for a tribal-dominated state, and recently the Birsa Seva Dal has raised the slogan "Chota Nagpur for the Chota Nagpuris"; but few non-tribals are persuaded that the tribal leaders are more concerned with regional development than they are with the interests of their own tribesmen.

Nativism in Assam. A somewhat similar but more violent situation exists in the northeastern state of Assam, which has over 2 million Bengali-speaking persons out of a total population (in 1961) of 11.9 million.[13] Of these Bengali-speakers, 61 percent were born in Assam, so that in terms of birthplace they are as much "sons of the soil" as are the Assamese. The large number of settled Bengalis is a consequence of migrations in the late nineteenth century and the first half of the twentieth. Between 1901 and 1971 Assam's population increased from 3.4 million to 14.9 million, an increase of 340 percent as against 129 percent for India as a whole, the difference accounted for by immigration. The largest migrations were from the adjoining districts of East Bengal, especially between 1911 and 1931 when Muslims migrated from the densely populated district of Mymensingh to the comparatively low-density areas of the Brahmaputra Valley in Assam. The 1931 census reported that 338,000 persons residing in Assam had been born in Mymensingh, and the census director of Assam that year estimated that over a half million persons in the state were migrants from Bengal. The 1951 census reported that there were 573,000 Bengali migrants in Assam, a half million of whom came from districts now in Bangladesh; and in 1961 the census director estimated that in the previous decade another 220,000 persons, mainly Muslims, had migrated from East Bengal.

There have been at least two types of clashes between Bengalis and Assamese. There have been religious conflicts between Assamese Hindus and Bengali Muslims encroaching upon land in the Brahmaputra Valley. Since Assam was governed by a Muslim League Ministry until 1946, the government reportedly permitted encroachments by immigrants on government lands, grazing and forest reserves. After major communal disturbances in 1950, the Indian parliament passed the Immigrants (Expulsion from Assam) Act aimed at the removal of post-independence Muslim immigrants, technically known as "infiltrators."

There have also been conflicts between Assamese and Bengali-speaking Hindus, with language rather than religion the focal point of the conflict. A major disturbance occurred throughout the valley in July 1960 in the midst of a statewide conflict over the government's decision to adopt Assamese as the official language. This outburst, known locally as the "Bengali kheda" ("kheda" or roundup is a term commonly used to refer to herding of elephants), represented an accumulated build-up of resentment by Assamese against the Bengali Hindu middle classes who occupied competitive positions in government and in the professions. Another violent outburst took place in late 1972 and early 1973 after the state government issued new rules concerning the medium of instruction and examinations in the colleges and universities in the state. Almost all the major towns in the Brahmaputra valley were affected. In this connection it should be noted that the Bengalis are more urbanized than the Assamese. Of the 913,000 persons living in urban areas, 350,000 were Bengali-speakers as against 304,000 Assamese. For Assam as a whole the percentage of urban population reporting Assamese as the mother tongue is only 33.4 percent as against 37.9 percent Bengali and 13 percent Hindi. In some districts of the valley the Bengali percentage of the urban population is higher: it is 44.5 percent in Nowgong, 42 percent in Goalpara, and 40 percent in Darrang.

Another major anti-immigrant outburst occurred in Assam in the late 1960s against the Marwari business community. In 1967 there was a major "Marwari kheda" in the city of Gauhati. The Marwari bazaar and residential quarter was set afire and looted by bands of young men who identified themselves as members of an underground movement known as the Latchit Sena, which seeks to eject non-Assamese from Assam.

While some Assamese have called for the expulsion of non-Assamese, and still others have demanded that at the least employment preferences should be given to "local," i.e., Assamese-speaking, people, many Marwaris and Bengalis point out that they too are Assamese though they speak a different language and belong to another culture. Most of the second- and third-generation migrants reject the argument that permanent residence in the state implies that they must adopt the majority language and culture of the state as a precondition to sharing in the rights and privileges of residence.

Urban Nativism

Both the Chota Nagpur and Assamese nativist movements command support in rural as well as in urban areas since in both instances the migrant population resides in the countryside as well as in the towns. India's other major nativist agitations are more exclusively urban, reflecting the fact that inter-state migrations are more largely to urban than to rural areas. India's best-known anti-migrant political party, the Shiv Sena, exists exclusively in Bombay where it has agitated against the city's Tamil population and pressed for domicile restrictions in employment. In Bangalore, another local party, again exclusively urban, known as the Kannada Chaluvalagars (or "agitators"), has won seats in city-wide elections on a campaign of restricting Tamil and Telugu migrations.

Even when nativism exists in rural areas, the initial impetus for the movement and much of its leadership has come from the urban areas. The anti-Bengali and anti-Marwari agitations in Assam have been most virulent in Gauhati and Lakhimpur; and the Jharkhand Party and the Birsa Seva Dal have been most active in the towns of Ranchi, Chaibasa, and Hazaribagh. In the western part of the state of Andhra a nativist party known as the Telengana Praja Samiti has succeeded in winning region-wide support for its demand for the creation of a separate state which could impose domicile restrictions on the employment of Telugu-speaking people from outside the Telengana region, but this party too had its initial base in the city of Hyderabad from which it spread.

The growth of nativist sentiment in many Indian cities is associated with three factors.

First, a very substantial proportion of many Indian cities consists of inter-state migrants: about a third of Bombay, nearly a fourth of Calcutta, a third of Jamshedpur, more than half of Delhi, and a very substantial proportion (exceeding 20 percent) in the cities of Gauhati, Bangalore, Kolar, Indore, Gwalior, Thana, Jabalpur, Bhopal, Durg, Raipur, and Howrah. Moreover, in many cities the migration influx has persisted for enough years so that the combined population of migrants and the descendants of migrants speaking non-local languages often exceeds the local population. In Bombay, for example, the Marathi-speaking population constitutes less than 50 percent of the city and, as we noted earlier, Bengalis outnumber Assamese speakers in most of the urban settlements of Assam.

Second, it is the middle-class youth in cities who have tended to articulate nativist sentiments. Strongest support for the Telengana agitation came from the schools and colleges in Hyderabad and from the lower levels of the state bureaucracy consisting substantially of graduates from local schools and colleges; in Assam, the attacks against Marwaris and Bengalis were led by students, and the Latchit Sena is primarily a force at the college in Gauhati; in Chota Nagpur, the Birsa Seva Dal is primarily a youth movement as is the Shiv Sena in Bombay. And in Bangalore, the Kannada Chaluvalagars uses as its election symbol the bicycle, which effectively identifies both the social class and the age group that gives it support.

Third, the target of nativist attacks tends to be middle-class not working-class migrants. Little opposition has been expressed toward factory and construction workers, rickshaw pullers, and other working-class migrants, but there is considerable opposition to "alien" businessmen, professionals, clerks, and other middle-class migrants. The working class in India appears to be neither a source of nativist sentiment nor its target, in contrast to the nativist configuration which formed an important element in American politics in the nineteenth and early twentieth centuries. There is, for example, no organized political opposition to the Hindi, Bihari, and Oriya migrants who constitute the overwhelming proportion of the labor force in the Calcutta industrial area, while the small Marwari business community is a constant target of Bengali political parties. Similarly, the Shiv Sena is not critical of the Hindi-speaking workers who reside in Bombay, but does attack the numerically smaller south India migrants who hold middle-class clerical and managerial positions.

Among the factors, then, which affect the growth of nativist movements in urban India are (1) the percentage of interstate migrants within the city; (2) the growth of an indigenous middle class under conditions of scarce resources, particularly employment opportunities; (3) an ethnically self-conscious and hence not easily assimilated migrant population, typically belonging to the middle class; and (4) the growth of a deep attachment to the regional culture by a politically articulate local middle-class population and the diffusion of such attachments to ever larger portions of the society.

The new ethnic configurations now emerging in urban India (and in parts of rural India) as a consequence of interstate migration not only involve larger numbers of people than previously but exist under wholly new political and cultural conditions—emerging regional identities, and expanding middle class, an educational explosion, rapid urban growth, new levels of political participation, and the emergence of political leaders searching for issues and popular sentiments on which to build mass political organizations.

Costs and Benefits

It is a commonplace observation that immigrants benefit from having migrated. People do not migrate unless there is a perceived disparity between the place in which they live and the place to which they choose to move. Most of the benefits are related to employment or safety. Refugees move across international borders to cholera-infested camps where there is inadequate shelter and food because they believe their lives are more seriously endangered by remaining where they are. And agricultural laborers may move to Calcutta or Bombay to sleep on pavements in order to earn a few rupees in the factories or as rickshawallas. A grim life, perhaps, but from their point of view a better one than remaining unemployed in their village. Unless there are some differentials in rewards, individuals are not likely to move.

While the migrant may gain, it does not follow that local people necessarily gain from an influx of immigrants. While some gain, others may lose. Let us first consider some of the gains.

Insofar as immigrants are willing and able to engage in occupations which local people choose not to enter, the immigrants have enlarged the total range of economic activities pursued in the area. By becoming construction laborers, workers on dams and irrigation schemes, laborers on roads and builders of railroads, immigrants have contributed to the development of a region's infrastructure and thereby made it possible for local people to engage in economic activities which they had previously been unable to do. These benefits would continue even if the immigrants remained to man railroads, hydroelectric and irrigation dams, postal and telegraph services, and road maintenance

It is often argued, however, that if industries started by immigrants mainly employ other immigrants, there is no economic gain to the local community. There are still, however, substantial benefits, though these are less apparent than if employment were given by the entrepreneur directly to local people. The local community may gain if the manufacturer is required to pay local taxes for the use of land, water, roads, and other facilities. Other local producers may gain if the manufacturer purchases local products and raw materials which are produced or sold by local people. Immigrant workers buy their consumer goods and food supplies locally and thereby provide income for both local producers and traders. Local farmers and merchants have larger markets for their goods. Finally, the goods produced by the immigrant manufacturer may be sold in the local market, and local people may now be able to buy goods at a lower price.

Thus, even if the manufacturer is an immigrant and a large portion of his labor force consists of immigrants, the economic activity generated by a new industry and the increased purchasing power created in the local market may indirectly increase employment for local people. But the more indirect these benefits are, the smaller they are likely to be and the fewer are those likely to be benefited. If the manufacturer is an immigrant, the labor force consists largely of immigrants, the shopkeepers are immigrants, and the tradesmen purchasing agricultural produce from local peasants are also immigrants, then the economic benefits to the local people will be substantially less than if any of these occupations are held or shared by local people.

Moreover, there are members of the local community who

may suffer an economic loss as a consequence of immigration. Marginal local producers and merchants may be eliminated by more efficient immigrant entrepreneurs and traders. Migrants may buy land from local peasants and, while the peasantry may initially gain from the higher price they earn for their land, they may not be able to find alternate employment. With an increase in the number of landless laborers, wages may decline. Moreover, ignorant local farmers may not know that the value of their land may subsequently rise because of irrigation works currently under construction.

If, moreover, we consider benefits and costs in terms of perceptions rather than in terms of income measures, then the costs to local people rise sharply. While the real income of local people may actually increase as a consequence of the economic activities of migrants, local people may find themselves in subordinate economic roles. If the larger, more prosperous farmers, and the owners, managers, and other personnel of factories and shops are all migrants, local people may suffer a lowered status which is not compensated by a rise in income. Even if the small producer or tradesman has gained an expanding market for his goods, he may now be economically subordinate to larger alien manufacturers and wholesalers. Moreover, while the local peasant may be able to buy goods that he could not previously afford, the immigrant laborers in the factories may be able to buy an even larger quantity of these goods. And if the manufacturer finds it is more profitable to employ migrants than local laborers, local people believe that they have lost employment opportunities they would have had were the manufacturer a local person who would have given preference to local job seekers.

Migrants may also create social and economic costs for the community as a whole. A large migrant influx imposes new demands upon the local water and sanitation system and upon health and education services. There may be shortages of drinking water, the sanitation system may be overloaded, and schools and hospitals may become overcrowded as a result of a population influx. As far as the local people are concerned, a large immigrant population may be responsible for growing environmental pollution and a diminution of their health and educational well-being.

Immigrants may also be psychologically threatening since their very success may imply a defect in character on the part of local people. Is the outsider more successful because he works harder, has more skills, is more education-minded, more punctual and efficient in his work, better attuned to the market requirements of the outside world? Or is he more successful because he engages in dishonest business practices, adulturates his goods, and gives employment preferences to his kinsmen? Whichever explanation the local person accepts, he must decide whether to emulate the migrant's behavior in order to compete. Can the small local merchant or manufacturer compete with an immigrant who has banking and trade connections outside the local community and greater knowledge of the larger market? Can the local middle-class person compete with a migrant who is willing to work harder in the office and go to school in the evening to improve his typing, stenographic, or accounting skills? Can the local farmer compete with the migrant who has brought in new seeds, is more experienced in the use of irrigation, and is experimenting with new crops?

Migrants often create a compulsion for change which local people do not welcome. The compulsion may arise because the local person does not wish to become subordinate in income and social status to the migrant, but the changes he needs to make to successfully compete may be ones he prefers not to make. For one thing, his cultural heritage may itself devalue competition; the very notion of changing oneself to compete may be anathema. For another, the specific qualities of the immigrant which he perceives as the reasons for success may be qualities the local person would prefer not to emulate: these may range, as we have noted, from dishonesty in the conduct of business to working hard for long hours.

Finally, local people may perceive immigrants as a political threat, particularly if they are so numerous or so wealthy as to become politically influential. The management of the political system by persons perceived as outsiders is typically viewed by local people as humiliating and threatening to their cultural survival. Insofar as the local community sees its cultural system interlocked with its political order, the loss of control over the political order or even the sharing of power is perceived as dangerous to the cultural system.

The linguistic and cultural norms of the migrant may be both hated and emulated simultaneously. The success of migrants in the world of business and administration may lead local youth to emulate their dress, their style of living, and their language; and as they emulate migrants they may simultaneously fear the loss of their own cultural identity.

For the migrant there is always a net gain in migrating. Were there no net advantage, he would not have moved or he would return home. But for the local person who has chosen to remain in his place of birth, the costs and benefits of having migrants in his midst are the consequences of someone else's actions, and if there is a net loss to him, he is not likely to see emigration for himself as a solution. If he believes that he has lost more than he has gained, then he is likely to take political steps to discourage further immigration and to encourage or even force those who have come to leave.

Government and Political Responses

There is a hardly a state in India which does not have a policy of giving some preferences to local people and therefore imposing some restrictions on migration from other states.

Firstly, there are restrictions on the admission of out-of-state residents to colleges and universities, especially to engineering and medical colleges. These are, however, hardly different from those imposed by state universities in the United States, though the quota for out-of-state persons in India is generally smaller than in American state universities. The shift to regional languages as the medium of instruction, especially in the arts colleges, has also served to discourage the migration of students across state lines. Compared with the United States, moreover, there are fewer educational institutions with open recruitment; these include several national universities such as Delhi University, Banaras Hindu University, and a number of national institutes of technology and medical schools.

In employment, virtually every state government is committed to giving preferences to "domiciles," generally defined as a person who was born in the state or has resided in the state for ten or fifteen years.[14] Preferences are given for employment in the state administration and in state-run public sector enterprises. State governments also urge private enterprises to follow the same system of preferences, at least with regard to unskilled and semi-skilled jobs and clerical positions at salaries of less than Rs. 600 per month.

Central government public sector enterprises are guided by similar employment practices. In the employment of unskilled workers they are to hire exclusively in the area in which the enterprise is located. In the employment of semi-skilled persons, including clerical personnel, preference is given to local persons, but "outsiders" may be employed if local people do not have adequate skills. And for the employment of persons at salaries above Rs. 600 and for all technical posts, recruitment is on an all-India basis.

Private employers are required by law to notify government-run employment exchanges of vacancies, but they remain free to recruit outside the exchanges. The district employment exchanges register only those persons who are residents of the district (not the state), but there are also state-wide employment exchanges for technical and professional personnel.

Few states have restrictions on the buying of land, but there are a number of notable exceptions. There are restrictions on the sale of land to non-domiciles in many of the border regions including NEFA, Nagaland, and Meghalaya; and non-Kashmiris cannot purchase land in Kashmir. The Indian Constitution also enumerates certain tribal areas as scheduled areas where the transfer of land from tribals to non-tribals is severely restricted.[15] There are substantial areas of Orissa, Madhya Pradesh, Assam, and Bihar where such restrictions exist.

Though the terms "local" or "domicile" generally refer to persons who are born or reside in the *state* for a specified period, there are many instances in which these terms have a more restricted meaning. "Domicile" may refer to a person living in a *district* or *region* of the state. In Andhra, for example, the Requirement as to Residence Act [16] specified that there shall be parity in the appointment of persons to the state government (including the appointment of schoolteachers) for the major regions of the state, a law aimed at providing preferences for the less developed Telengana region. Other states have imposed similar safeguards for their more backward regions. And as we have already indicated, the term "local" is understood by employment exchanges to mean those who reside in the district in which the employment exchange is located.

The extension of benefits to members of scheduled castes and tribes by state and central governments also involves territorial restrictions. The reservations of seats for admission into colleges and universities and reservations (or quotas) for appointments into state administration are only for scheduled castes and tribes who reside within the state. Each state thus has its own list of castes and tribes domiciled within the state who are entitled to benefits. A member of these castes and tribes seeking college admission or employment in another state may receive no such benefits. Similarly, as we have noted, members of certain scheduled tribes can only sell land to members of their own tribe if the land they own is within a scheduled area specified by the government.

In considering the effects of policies on migration we must consider not only government policies but political actions directed at discouraging migrants from entering an area. Local political groups may not only press government to impose restrictions on immigrants but may also attempt to persuade employers that preferences in employment should be given to local people. Their typical argument is that local people are there by birth, not choice, and that therefore they should not be relegated to inferior economic and political positions within their own homeland no matter how much more skillful outsiders may be. Moreover, inasmuch as a particular culture and language is associated with the land and the indigenous people who dwell there, outsiders should be required to adapt themselves to the customs of the land, and those who do not identify with the land and its culture should not be allowed to dwell within it. Almost every culture has the equivalent expression, voiced by one Tibetan, that "he who drinks the waters of the land must abide by its customs."

It follows that only those who speak the local language, adapt to local customs, identify with the land and its people, and treat local people and their culture with proper dignity ought to remain, and all others should be asked to leave. Thus, the migrant manufacturer and the migrant shopkeepers who do not employ local people have by their very acts betrayed the local community and demonstrated that they do not properly identify with the land and its people. From the point of view, therefore, of the local person who is hostile to migrants, the terms "domicile" and "sons of the soil" had best be left vague precisely because they assume a certain emotional identification with local people and certain standards of behavior which only local people can adequately define. The nativist political movement may be as concerned with encouraging the assimilation and identification of migrants to the local community as with pressuring employers and government to give preference to local people in employment.

From implied threats to explicit violence is a small step for many nativist political organizations. In Assam, Bombay, Chota

Nagpur, and Telengana there have been frequent agitations against migrants. There are many forms of what the British call "Pak Bashing." Marwari shops have been burned in Gauhati, Bengalis have been beaten in Lakhimpur, Tamil cars have been overturned in Bombay, and Andhra-owned shops and houses have been attacked in Hyderabad. Those who use violence have many objectives—to force immigrant businesses to employ local people, to humble "arrogant" immigrants, to encourage immigrants to leave, and to discourage others from coming. Moreover, the violence of young militants can be used by the established political leadership of the community as an argument for passing laws and ordinances to give preference to local people, and to put pressure on businesses to give preference to local people on the grounds that such measures are necessary if further violence is to be avoided.

The Effects of Nativist Policies

Until the migration tables for the 1971 census are published, it is premature to report the impact which restrictive policies and political agitations have had upon inter-state migration, but some preliminary estimates can nevertheless be made.

The efforts of state governments to give residents preference in government employment seem to have been the most successful of these policies. Indeed, there are many accusations that state governments have in practice extended these preferences to those who speak the regional language as their mother tongue and have avoided giving appointments to descendants of migrants. In Assam and Bihar, for example, there have been sharp decreases in the number of Bengalis employed in the state government, but the state government has argued that this is primarily a consequence of the growing educational accomplishments of the "local," that is, the Bihari- and Assamese-speaking, people.

No statistics are available on the migration of students across state boundaries, but in any event it would be difficult to ascertain whether any change in mobility was a result of the restrictions imposed by colleges and universities or by the shift to regional languages. Moreover, the growth of nationally run educational institutions may have compensated for some of the reduction in mobility to state-run institutions.

The impact of restrictions on employment in the private sector is equally difficult to ascertain. Many Indian businesses are under the same pressures as foreign firms are all over the world to employ local people, and they know that many restrictions can be imposed upon them if they do not take into account local political sentiment. There are a number of reasons, however, why in practice entrepreneurs find it difficult to change their recruitment patterns. For one thing, in the employment of technical and professional personnel, employers prefer to recruit more widely than from the local community. Consideration must often be given to the friends and relations of those who are already employed within the firm as well as to the skills of the candidates. Even in the employment of unskilled and semi-skilled workers, as we have noted, there are often well-established labor migration streams which work efficiently and which managers are reluctant to disrupt. Similarly, as we have observed earlier, there are well-organized work gangs that are regularly employed by contractors for the construction of buildings, roads, hydroelectric projects, and irrigation schemes. Finally, in the employment of office personnel such as typists, stenographers, accountants, and clerks many employers give preference to people from Kerala and Tamilnadu since it has been their experience that people from these states are often more reliable and efficient office workers than local people.

Nonetheless, there are reports that business firms in Bombay, Hyderabad, Gauhati, Bangalore, and other cities with large migrant populations are making an effort to hire local personnel, especially for clerical positions and for front-office jobs where employees deal with the public. While statistically the effects may be small, business managers often see such shifts in recruitment as essential to maintain good relations with the local community.

The provisional population totals for the 1971 census do not reveal any noticeable decline in migration in areas in which there have been anti-migrant agitations, though until the migration tables are published we cannot make any definitive statements. Nonetheless, the data do show that Assam, though it has been one of the most disturbed areas for immigrants, had a population growth of 34.4 percent between 1961 and 1971, substantially above the country's population growth of 24.6 percent. The additional 10 percent presumably consists of migrants from other states and from East Bengal. Neither the anti-Bengali and anti-Marwari agitations nor the system of preferences established by the Assamese government for the Assamese seems to have resulted in any substantial decline in migration over the previous decade when population growth (from 1951 to 1961) was 35.1 percent.

Greater Bombay, the site of the Shiv Sena agitations, had an accelerated growth from 1961 to 1971—42.9 percent as against 38.7 percent in the previous decade, an increase which was more than matched by the surrounding urbanized district of Thana where the population increased sharply from 28.9 percent to 37.7 percent. Conceivably, there may have been a decline in out-of-state immigration accompanied by a more than corresponding increase in migration from other districts of Maharashtra, but there does not appear to be any evidence thus far that the Shiv Sena agitations and Maharashtra's many domicile regulations have had any noticeable impact on out-of-state migration to Bombay.

Hyderabad, a major center for anti-Andhra agitations in the last few years, showed a phenomenal increase in population during the past decade, from 1,110,000 in 1961 to 1,800,000 in 1971, an increase of 63 percent. Much of this increase is reported to be migration from the delta districts, a factor in the conflict between the Andhra and Telengana districts. Since the anti-Andhra agitations were in the late 1960s, however, the census data are not likely to record any decline in migration that may now be occurring.

There is thus no evidence yet that either political agitations or government restrictions have had any noticeable effect on interstate migrations, though it seems likely that some areas of the country will be affected if they have not been so already. The trend in interstate migration has been consistently upward throughout the century,[17] and it will not be easy to arrest this trend. Indeed, the rise of nativist agitations and the growth of government restrictions on migration can be seen as the consequence of this growth. The pressures for mobility may be so substantial that agitations and restrictions may have far less effect than intended or expected. Few countries have had much success in regulating the internal movement of people. Moreover, the political issue in India is not merely one of slowing internal migration but rather of imposing an element of ethnic selectivity in migration, a particularly difficult objective to achieve.

Conclusion

At one level of society, interstate, intercultural migration is an integrating force which brings together men and women of diverse cultures and languages who share common occupations and common membership in modern institutions. At another level of society, such migration is economically and culturally threatening. The multi-ethnic society is thus confronted with a particularly painful dilemma. The process of development tends to stimulate spatial-mobility within the multi-ethnic society as elsewhere, but in such a society mobility is likely to result in interethnic conflict, nativistic reactions, and violent confrontations. To take no action to either protect local people or enhance their capacity to compete with migrants is to sit idly by as racial and linguistic conflicts grow. But to cope with the problem by attempting to prevent the migration of skilled and motivated persons will either fail or, to the extent that such measures do succeed, substantially slow the country's rate of economic growth while simultaneously destroying the many advantages of a common citizenship.

Part three
The Larger Youth Cohorts

Chapter 7

The Youth Cohort Revisited *Nathan Keyfitz*

EDITORS' NOTE: This chapter analyzes the problems posed and opportunities opened up by the successively larger youth cohorts, particularly in Indonesia's rural sector and its capital, Djakarta. In reviewing the Indonesian evidence, the author notes that an overall rate of growth of 2.5 percent may in fact conceal a 7 percent rate of growth in certain youthful age groups. Being the most dynamic and aspiring sectors of the population, they are potentially the most politically significant. Many of the young people are innovative and mobile so that the cohort requires a rate of job creation at least commensurate with the pace of its growth.

Keyfitz's analysis of Java's village economy emphasizes the rich texture of overlapping mutual obligations and shows that, despite the end of traditional land redistribution in each generation and great overcrowding, parents still believe it advantageous to their old age to have numerous children. No one can know when population growth rates will start to fall. This paper, like the others in Part III, stresses the importance of education in shaping values and focusing ambitions, thereby prompting the young to migrate to urban centers, and providing the minimum requisite for upward mobility in the cities. The author examines the attractions of urban life, which, in Indonesia, account for the flow to Djakarta.

With their newly awakened desire to participate in the national entity and being increasingly differentiated from their parents, can these larger youth cohorts be absorbed into economic and political life? This paper emphasizes the massive problem of youthful unemployment expected in the 1970s.

AUTHOR'S NOTE: I am indebted to Ansley Coale, Ronald Freedman, Charles Hirschman, Karl D. Jackson, Geoffrey NcNicoll, Robert Repetto, Gordon Temple, and especially to the late Everett D. Hawkins for discussions of Indonesia and of the problems taken up in this paper. The skill and cooperativeness of officers of the Central Bureau of Statistics in Djakarta were helpful at every step. No one mentioned is in any way responsible for the way I used his data or his suggestions. Most of the paper was written at the University of Wisconsin.

The size and character of the cohort of young people now coming of age in Indonesia will help determine the economic, political, and social development of that country in the decades ahead. To understand those developments we need data and inferential structures that will allow us to shape answers to four kinds of questions:

1. How many young men and women are entering adulthood each year? How has this number changed since the 1940s? How will it change during the 1970s? If the youth cohort were increasing at the same rate as the population as a whole, it would double in twenty-five years. The 1961 census suggests a doubling in a bare five years. How can we estimate its true size and rate of growth?

2. What sorts of people are the new entrants, at least in such demographically distinguishable characteristics as education and urbanization? What is their schooling as compared with that of their elders? In particular, has the school system been able to expand as fast as the increase in the population of school age? Most of the youth cohort was born and brought up in a village. How do these villagers see their future careers? For what fraction is the local prospect so dim that they are willing to try the big city? Aside from the search for a livelihood, to what extent do political and social motives draw them in the same cityward direction?

3. How does the young, urban, educated category differ in its attitudes toward development and in the strength of its mobility drives from the old, rural, illiterate segment of the population?

4. What are the objective possibilities for useful and remunerative employment in the city? How large are the capital needs of such employment? Can low-capital, labor-intensive employment be arranged for those who fail to make it into the new offices and factories, and at what wages? Can these adjustments be made to accord with intuitive notions of social justice, at least sufficiently so that the present stability is maintained?

These are ambitious questions, and in the present state of

knowledge they are hardly answerable. Even the apparently simple question of the size of the youth cohort is complicated because of the uncertainty of existing data. Though it is possible after considerable effort to estimate that the doubling time for young adults is fifteen years, this is only the first step in our argument. The combined force of increasing education and declining agricultural opportunities that has mobilized youth in a cityward direction must be studied in conjunction with economic and demographic analyses accompanied by attitudinal field research. How to deal with the consequent employment demands of the near future requires both analysis of the concept of social justice and an investigation of how different social groups enter the development process. Our main resource in confronting these difficulties will be aggregate data in the census categories of age, education, and rural-urban residence.

Age Distribution, 1961 and Present

The point of departure for our discussion is the age distribution reported in the 1961 census of Indonesia, which is shown in Table 7.1. A striking feature of this distribution is the sharp drop at about age 10. Under age 10 there are over 15 million in each five-year age group; from age 10 to 24, about 8 million. The level from 10 to 24 remains almost constant. The whole provides a surprising configuration.

The hollow in the age distribution after age 10 has struck many students of the census. The Japanese demographer Kozo Ueda, who spent some years working in the Indonesian Central Bureau of Statistics, concludes that the number of persons 10–19 is small because those born between November 1941 and October 1951 had to undergo the hard period of war and the struggle for independence.[1] Widjojo Nitisastro declares:

After taking due account of inaccuracies in age reporting, the age composition of the 1961 population shows certain features which can be traced to past changes in vital rates. Thus, the number of persons age 10–19 in 1961 was relatively small. These were survivors of the

Table 7.1 Population by Age and Sex, Indonesia, 1961

Age	*Males*	*Females*	*Total*	*Percent*
0–4	8,462,000	8,580,000	17,042,000	17.7
5–9	7,684,000	7,639,000	15,323,000	15.9
10–14	4,319,000	3,861,000	8,179,000	8.5
15–19	3,834,000	3,874,000	7,708,000	8.0
20–24	3,452,000	4,339,000	7,791,000	8.1
25–34	7,334,000	8,542,000	15,876,000	16.5
35–44	5,720,000	5,363,000	11,083,000	11.5
45–54	3,559,000	3,483,000	7,042,000	7.3
55–64	1,898,000	1,850,000	3,748,000	3.9
65–74	796,000	829,000	1,625,000	1.7
75–	378,000	407,000	784,000	0.8
Total	47,494,000	48,825,000	96,319,000 [1]	100.0

Source: Statistical Pocketbook of Indonesia, 1963.
[1] Excludes the estimated population of West Irian (700,000), but includes 117,000 persons of unstated age.

births between 1942 and 1951. On the other hand, the 0–9 year age group was very large in 1961. It consisted of the survivors of the births of 1952–61.[2]

The accuracy of the census, however, has been challenged by Van de Walle. He finds that the labor force questions asked of everyone 10 years of age and older, which were a nuisance for the enumerator, caused many individuals to be reported as under 10 when they were in fact over.[3] Ansley J. Coale (in correspondence with me), and Coale and Demeny come to the same conclusion. They point out that in these censuses age is estimated by the enumerator rather than reported by the respondent.[4] Further, the distribution by sex in Table 7.1 looks suspicious indeed. The notch at age 10 is greater for females than for males and 900,000 more women than men are reported as aged 20–24, and about 1,200,000 more at ages 25–34. It is almost as though the women in the youth groups were reported as older relative to men, enumerators perhaps estimating their ages from the fact that they had children in sight. These difficulties are largely in the rural population: the urban population shows both a smaller notch (the drop from the 5–9 to the 10–14 group is only 30 per cent as against 50 per cent in the rural) and there is less discrepancy between the sexes (Table 7.2). The Coale–Van de Walle argument is supported by studies of other countries of Asia and Africa, in whose 1960 censuses similar census-taking procedures were used and similar notches in age distribution appear.

Table 7.2 Rural and Urban Population by Age and Sex, Indonesia 1961

Age	Males	Females	Total	Percent
		RURAL		
0–4	7,259,000	7,404,000	14,663,000	17.9
5–9	6,676,000	6,649,000	13,325,000	16.3
10–14	3,619,000	3,177,000	6,795,000	8.3
15–19	3,098,000	3,164,000	6,262,000	7.6
20–24	2,738,000	3,607,000	6,345,000	7.7
25–34	6,185,000	7,299,000	13,484,000	16.5
35–44	4,889,000	4,600,000	9,489,000	11.6
45–54	3,104,000	3,039,000	6,143,000	7.5
55–64	1,658,000	1,603,000	3,261,000	4.0
65–74	702,000	713,000	1,415,000	1.7
75–	335,000	346,000	682,000	0.8
Total	40,311,000	41,649,000	81,960,000 [1]	100.0
		URBAN		
0–4	1,203,000	1,176,000	2,379,000	16.6
5–9	1,008,000	990,000	1,998,000	13.9
10–14	700,000	684,000	1,384,000	9.6
15–19	736,000	710,000	1,446,000	10.1
20–24	714,000	731,000	1,446,000	10.1
25–34	1,149,000	1,243,000	2,391,000	16.6
35–44	830,000	763,000	1,594,000	11.1
45–54	455,000	444,000	899,000	6.3
55–64	240,000	247,000	487,000	3.4
65–74	94,000	116,000	210,000	1.5
75–	42,000	60,000	103,000	0.7
Total	7,183,000	7,176,000	14,348,000 [1]	100.0

Source: Statistical Pocketbook of Indonesia, 1963.
[1] Excludes the estimated population of West Irian (700,000), but includes 117,000 persons of unstated age.

Comparison of Indonesia with Other Countries of Southeast Asia

Table 7.3, compiled by Everett D. Hawkins, shows notches in the age distributions of the Philippines, Thailand, Malaysia, and

Table 7.3 Percentage Distribution by Age, under age 35, in Five Asian Countries

Age	Indonesia 1961	Philippines 1960	Thailand 1960	Malaysia 1957	Singapore 1957	Singapore 1966
0–4	17.7	16.9	16.1	17.8	18.3	14.0
5–9	15.9	16.1	15.2	15.2	15.1	15.4
10–14	8.5	12.7	11.8	10.8	9.4	14.1
15–19	8.0	10.4	9.5	9.7	9.4	11.3
20–24	8.1	9.1	9.2	8.3	8.2	6.7
25–29	8.9	7.2	7.9	7.0	7.7	7.0
30–34	7.6	5.8	6.1	5.9	6.2	5.9

Source: Census data and the *1966 Singapore Sample Household Survey,* compi by Everett D. Hawkins.

Singapore similar to those for Indonesia. The 1957 Malaysia and Singapore data are compatible with the thesis that the notch was caused by the drop in infant mortality about ten years earlier, in 1947. The drop would not have occurred simultaneously in all countries, for the others entered their postwar period earlier than Indonesia, whose war continued through 1949. If the drop in infant mortality as a result of malaria control occurred about 1947 or 1948 in the Philippines and Thailand, their 1960 percentage for ages 10–14 would show an average of cohort sizes between pre- and post-malaria control and would be higher than that of Indonesia.

One feature of the table is the change in the percentages for Singapore between 1957 and 1966. The Singapore figures demonstrate that the 1957 notch in the age distribution above the 5–9 age group advanced during the nine-year period to a corresponding position just above the 15–19 age group. Clearly this could not have been an artifact of census-taking procedures. Also interesting is the decline in the proportion under 5 years of age, which reflects the large-scale birth control program Singapore initiated in the interval.

Evidence of the 1971 Census

How does the Indonesian notch hold up over time? The preliminary figures of the 1971 census presented in Table 7.4 show a drop from 11.4 million at ages 15–19 to 8.0 million at 20–24, a larger decrease than would be expected with a stable population increasing at Indonesia's 2.3 percent per year, but much less than if the 1961 distribution for ages 5–14 were correct. But the 1971 census also shows the number aged 5–9 at 18.9 million with a fall to 14.2 for those aged 10–14. Again, we have a substantial, though smaller, fall at the same point in the age distribution as in 1961, and this without the benefit of such a handy explanation as the cessation of turmoil a decade earlier. One can sum up Table 7.4 in gross fashion by saying that the notch both moved along from age 10 to age 20, which it ought to have done if it was real, *and* reappeared at age 10, which it would have done if it was an artifact of census-taking. The overall figures therefore tell us that there is some truth in both hypotheses.

One way to study the matter is to compare the projection from 1961 with the 1971 census (Table 7.5). The life table and birth rates used in the projection are confirmed by the fact that at least in total it reproduces the census as closely as could be expected—it gives 121.5 million against the census count of 119.2 million.[5]

Table 7.5 gives millions as projected from 1961, and as counted in 1971, for both sexes together for the whole of Indonesia. Agreement is by no means perfect at any of the ages, as it would be in a proper projection if both censuses were correct in their age distributions. There is evidently some error that is random in relation to either of the hypotheses between which we

Table 7.4 Population under Age 30 by Age and Sex, Indonesia, 1971 (*millions*)

Age	*Males*	*Females*	*Total*
0–4	9.7	9.5	19.2
5–9	9.6	9.3	18.9
10–14	7.3	6.9	14.2
15–19	5.6	5.7	11.4
20–24	3.6	4.4	8.0
25–29	4.0	5.0	9.0

Source: Central Bureau of Statistics, Djakarta.

Table 7.5 Population under Age 30 in Indonesia in 1971 As Projected from the 1961 Census and As Counted by the 1971 Census (*millions*)

Age	*1961 Projection*	*1971 Census*
0–4	18.5	19.2
5–9	16.5	18.9
10–14	15.5	14.2
15–19	14.7	11.4
20–24	7.8	8.0
25–29	7.3	9.0

Source: For projection, Keyfitz and Flieger, *Population: Facts and Methods of Demography* (1971), p. 393; for census, Central Bureau of Statistics.

would like to discriminate. But the biggest discrepancy is at ages 15–19, where fully 3.3 million more are shown in the projection than in the census. Evidently the 1961 census exaggerated the number of persons aged 5–9. But surprisingly in view of this, it did not greatly underestimate the number then aged 10–14 which, when projected to the 20–24-year-old group of 1971, totaled only 0.2 million lower than the census. This cohort could well be understated in both censuses.

Certainly the 1971 census spreads the notch over more ages than does the projection. Instead of a single drop of 6.9 million from age 15–19 to 20–24 shown in the projection, we have a drop of 3.4 million from 15–19 to 20–24, and another of 2.8 million from 10–14 to 15–19, and a third of 4.7 million between 5–9 and 10–14. The 1971 census is closer to the stable age distribution than is the 1961 census; and this greater smoothness, along with other evidence, suggests that it was more carefully enumerated.

A central question for our purpose is the number of new entrants into adult life during the five years subsequent to 1971. Let us take ages 20–24 as the time of entry into adult life, recognizing that this is arbitrary. The census counts the labor force from age 10; the typical age of marriage is older than this; voting age is 18 and so is the usual age of high school graduation;

the age for making contracts is still older. The calculations that follow would come out about the same with any other age, but the hump in the entry of the youth cohort of course occurs at a slightly different time depending on how the youth cohort is defined.

If the 1961 census and its projection were correct, we would have at ages 20–24 an increase from 7.8 million in 1971 to 14.7 million in 1976 (shown as 15–19 in 1971) less the mortality among the 14.7 that would bring it down to 14.3. The population in this age group 20–24 would be increasing at about 13 percent per year. The 1971 census tells us that this projected rate is too high.

Performing the same calculation with the 1971 census, we compare the 8.0 million counted at 20–24 with the survivors after five years from the 11.4 million counted at 15–19, which is 11.1 million. Now we have an increase of 3.1 million or 38 percent over the five years to 1976, which comes out to about 7 percent per year.

The 1961 census tells us that this important group is increasing at 13 percent per year; the 1971 preliminary figures tell us that it is increasing at 7 percent per year. We can apparently trust the latter more than the former. From a slightly different viewpoint the 1971 census is saying that the same increase will be spread over a longer period of time than was suggested by the notch at age 10 in 1961.

If the 1971 census is correct, the five years from 1976 to 1981 would show an increase in the number aged 20–24 from 11.1 to 13.6 million, or 23 percent; 1981–86 would show 32 percent. These are smaller than the 1971–76 increase, but they are greater than the present increase in the population as a whole, which is apparently about 15 percent per five-year period. Accepting the 1971 census tells us that over the next fifteen years the annual increase in the entrants into adult life would average about 5 percent per year.

The 7 percent per year for the increase over the next five

years in those aged 20–24 is not the same for the sexes taken separately, but according to the 1971 enumeration is much larger for males. For reasons that are not easily surmised the number of males was 20 percent less than the number of females in the 20–24 and the 25–29 age groups, with the sexes about equal at ages 15–19 in both 1961 and 1971. Whether this is due to the tendency to omit males, or the tendency to overstate or understate the ages of females, is not clear.

For males in 1971 we have 3.6 million at age 20–24 against 5.6 million at age 15–19. Allowing for mortality gives a prospective increase of 54 percent for the five years, or about 9 percent per year. For females we have 27 percent for the five years, or about 5 percent per year. Thus the 7 percent annual increase shown for both sexes is made up of an average of 9 percent for males and 5 percent for females.

The difference between males and females throws an element of uncertainty into the analysis that is not easily removed. Some questions will apparently have to await the 1981 census.

Date of Shift in Cohort Size

The 1971 census seems to tell us, as did the 1961 census, that a new high number of survivors is attained by recent cohorts. The two censuses agree that most of the rise occurred in respect of the cohorts born in the 1950s, but the 1971 census makes the rise more gradual. The near doubling from about 8 million to about 15 million that would have taken five years or so according to the 1961 census now seems, from the 1971 count, to have taken from ten to fifteen years. Instead of increasing at about five times the rate of growth of the population as a whole, the survivors in the cohorts now around age 20 seem to be increasing at only about twice the rate.

Thus the current evidence is that cohorts born in the 1960s are double the number born in the 1940s, but the shift was spread through the late 1940s and the whole of the 1950s instead of occurring about 1950. This is the main respect in

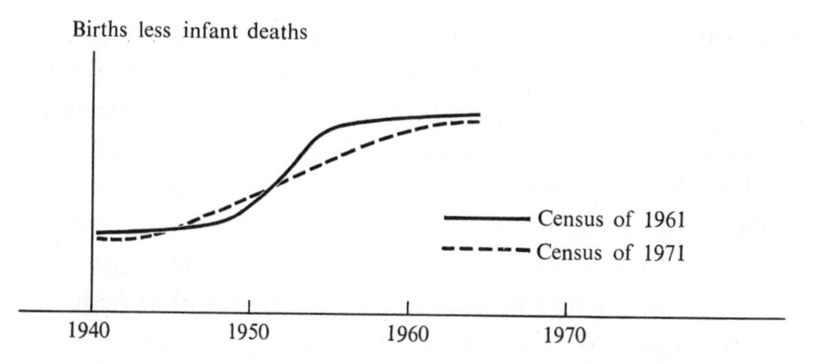

Figure 7.1 Hypothetical Curves of Survivors Among Cohorts Born from 1940–1970 As Suggested by 1961 and 1971 Censuses

which the 1971 census improves on and corrects that of 1961. Figure 7.1 shows the pattern of cohorts born in the three decades of interest, not in terms of total births which varied less, but in the net difference of births less infant deaths. A further step in the analysis will be possible with release of final 1971 data for Indonesia.

Effect of Differential Increase Among the Several Ages

If the 1961 census is even half right, as the 1971 census suggests, and the increase of the youth cohorts is more rapid than that of the population as a whole, the consequences are important. When promotion is according to seniority, those who are born ahead of an increase of births (or of births less infant deaths) are advantaged. The Indonesians who are now over 30 will be promoted rapidly, like those who are ahead of the postwar baby boom in the United States. In both cases the large number in the later cohorts push up the smaller number in the older cohorts: thus the demand for supervisors, teachers, and army officers is greater when there are more junior workers, students, and lower ranks of soldiers.

Conversely, the younger adults, members of the larger cohorts following, find their way blocked. Despite better education—for education has been improving—their access to leadership jobs is limited because there are so many of them competing, the leadership posts are already filled, and the economy is expanding at a pace that doubles output every fifteen years or so but has no similar effect on employment. That the situation constitutes a challenge to leadership was the theme of an earlier article.[6] The generation conflict of Western countries has no less rationale in Indonesia and would be accentuated by the rapid growth in the cohorts about 20 years of age. Contrasting sources of generational conflict are discussed in Donald Emmerson's paper in chapter 8 of this volume.

The number at the young adult ages is of special interest for the same reason—geographical mobility—that makes their enumeration difficult. Both internal and external migration in all countries consists in large part of those who have not yet settled on their careers and who are trying their fortunes in various occupations and places. In the Indonesian context the mobility of young adults is partly the result of their lessened integration in village society, but mobility in turn helps to make them psychologically less integrable in the villages. These points need closer examination. We will look first at the expansion of education.

Schooling

The expansion of formal education has been a main aim of the Republic of Indonesia since its inception, and however much other aims may have been neglected, this one has been pursued with vigor. Official statistics show the number of pupils at all levels to have gradually risen during the years before 1940, but they numbered only 2.4 million in that year.[7] By 1960–61, 9.9 million children were at school, a fourfold increase. According to the 1961 census well over half of the 10–14 cohort had some schooling, the fraction with schooling falling steadily with increasing age to about 7 percent of those 75 and over. Literacy declined correspondingly from 69.6 percent among those 10–14 to less than 10 percent for those 75 and over.

The colonial experience impressed on Indonesians that education was the key to upward social mobility in the city, and imposed a social ranking in terms of schooling, non-manual occupation, and income. This has been strengthened with independence. It coexists today with the quite different village scale that ranks families by their relation to the land. One cannot say that the two are entirely incommensurable, since a government employee can use some of his income to buy agricultural land and so put himself at the top of both the rural and the urban ladder.

The mass of those born and maturing since independence are aware of both the village and the city scale of social prestige. They have gone through the *sekolah rakjat* (primary school), have had contact with a teacher who knows something of the city, and have written copybook exercises about the wider national life in which one is not bound to his fellow men in such durable and intricate ways as the village imposes. The four-year course in the village school introduces a pupil to what we would call civics, the nation and its constitution, its politics and economy. By the time he graduates from the village school he has begun to think in terms of the 120 million inhabitants of Indonesia, not only of the 800 inhabitants of his village. Says a Middle School textbook of civics: "Kamu harus merasa bangga mendjadi anggota bangsa jang besar itu." [8] ("You must feel proud to be a member of so large a nation.")

The school is a means to upward mobility, and also helps to kindle the desire for mobility in strata that might otherwise be static. Complemented by reading to which a young person is introduced, the school makes him alert to the existence of the nation, to political parties within the nation, and to the values of consumption. Schools may be formally and officially justified as preparing citizens for their place in production; an observer in Indonesian classrooms, analyzing the material taught, finds that they prepare future citizens at least as much for consumption of both private and public goods.

Except for the Minangkabau and a few other areas of Sumatra, Indonesian schooling beyond the third grade is in a language not even distantly resembling common local speech. Instead of Javanese, Sundanese, or some other local language with its elaborate inflections oriented to social status, the pupil comes to speak Indonesian, in which everyone is addressed simply as fellow citizen. That the pupil's parents typically cannot speak Indonesian adds a component to the generation gap beyond that known in Western countries.

Given the population increase at youthful ages, it has often been asked whether the school system will be able to expand sufficiently so that the percentage attending remains at least constant. It seems not only to have kept up, but at some points to have shown, according to the 1971 census, a clear increase in the proportion at school (Table 7.6). The rise at age 9 from 56.7 percent to 66.7 percent must mean that the elementary school is retaining a larger number of its pupils for more years. Since the high dropout rate has been a main concern, this is encouraging. But we also note that the peak percentage attending school occurs at age 11, where it is 72 percent both in 1961 and in 1971: Indonesian pupils start school much later than American pupils.

Age Distribution and Educational Planning

Age distribution is changing in respects important for educational planning over the coming years. Up to now a very large fraction, 80 percent or so, of each cohort start elementary school, but only about 35 percent of the cohort finish. Cost per student is of the order of 5,000 to 6,000 rupiahs per year. About 20 percent of the cohort start secondary school, and there the cost is of the order of 25,000 to 30,000 rupiahs per student, so the total national expenditure for secondary schooling is about equal to that for elementary.

The improvement in primary schooling, along with the lowered fraction of dropouts indicated by the 1971 census, will stimulate a greater demand for secondary school training. This

Table 7.6 Number and Percent of Population Age 5 and Over at School, by Age and Sex, Indonesia, 1961 and 1971

	1961			*1971*		
Age	*Total population*	*At school*	*Percent*	*Total population*	*At school*	*Percent*
5	3,296,000	150,500	4.6	3,830,700	0	0.0
6	3,072,600	589,400	19.2	3,941,900	630,400	16.0
7	3,327,500	1,326,100	39.9	3,866,500	1,533,500	39.7
8	2,883,800	1,484,300	51.5	3,820,200	2,132,200	55.8
9	2,743,000	1,556,300	56.7	3,412,800	2,276,900	66.7
10	2,381,400	1,505,300	63.2	3,654,200	2,448,700	67.0
11	1,341,200	972,600	72.5	2,462,500	1,772,600	72.0
12	1,912,300	1,148,800	60.1	3,167,000	1,916,400	60.5
13	1,344,100	737,800	54.9	2,481,300	1,418,800	57.2
14	1,200,400	528,900	44.1	2,462,900	1,078,400	43.8
15	1,794,400	432,100	24.1	2,781,700	872,900	31.4
16	1,223,100	297,200	24.3	2,138,200	644,300	30.1
17	1,333,700	244,900	18.4	2,275,300	479,600	21.1
18	2,211,800	230,200	10.4	2,696,200	450,900	16.7
19	1,145,200	133,500	11.7	1,500,000	269,300	17.9
5–9	15,323,000	5,106,500	33.3	18,872,200	6,573,100	34.8
10–14	8,179,400	4,893,400	59.8	14,227,900	8,634,900	60.7
15–19	7,708,200	1,337,900	17.4	11,391,300	2,716,900	23.8
20–24	7,791,000	279,200	3.6	7,961,300	513,500	6.4
25+	40,158,300	212,800	0.5	46,838,000	201,700	0.4
N.S.	116,800	2,200	1.9	7,900	1,300	17.0
Total	79,276,600	11,832,000	14.9	99,298,600	18,641,400	18.8

Source: Central Bureau of Statistics.

will be reinforced by urbanization and other tendencies. As larger numbers of people get drawn into the modern sector, they will want their children to attend high school. Since each student in high school costs about five times as much as each one in elementary school, the national education bill—paid by government, private groups, or parents—will go up far more than in proportion to the total number of students in the combined elementary and secondary system. Promotion of the new Development Schools will further raise the requirements for funds, since they give better training than the run of secondary schools and are more expensive.

To these demands the age changes in population are bound to

add substantially. The 1971 census tells us that the primary schools have virtually passed the notch—that is to say, they are now at the higher level of the post-1950 cohorts, and their constituents are now only slowly increasing. The same would also be true of the secondary school on the basis of the 1961 census, but the 1971 figures modify this somewhat. They show the number aged 15–19 in 1971 to be 11.4 million. By 1976, this age group will encompass the survivors of the 14.2 million who were between 10 and 14 in 1971. By 1981, this age group will be comprised of the survivors of the 18.9 million who were between 5 and 9 in 1971. Thus the 15–19 group is bound to increase over the next ten years at a fairly steady rate of about 5 percent per year. After 1981 they will have arrived at a peak, and the rate will slow down to less than the increase of the population as a whole.

The Department of Basic Education reports student increases that accord with the census. Between 1960–61 and 1967 it shows an increase in pupils from 9.9 million to 14.3 million, a growth of 43 percent in the seven years.[9] This compares with a rise from 11.8 million in the 1961 census to 18.6 million in the 1971 census, or 57 percent for the ten years. The census figures are inclusive of private and religious schools, which are not always counted in the statistics of the Department of Education. At ages up to 15, proportions at school in rural areas increased somewhat, while those in urban areas declined. Above age 15 increases appear in both rural and urban areas, but were more marked in rural areas, where they now come up to some 25 percent at ages 15–19. The comparable proportion for urban youth is over 50 percent.

Urban Migration and Age Distributions

Table 7.2 shows decided differences between percentage age distribution of rural and urban populations. The urban is lower up to age 10, higher from then until age 35, after which it is lower again. The biggest excess of urban is in the two age groups 15–19 and 20–24. These are clearly the mobile ages.

The movement into Djakarta is slightly weighted toward males, and very heavily toward ages around 20. This was visible in the 1961 census, which showed about 4 percent more males than females in Djakarta, while Indonesia as a whole reported about 2 percent more females. In age the biggest difference was at 20–24, which contained 11.8 percent of the males of Djakarta and only 7.3 percent of the males of Indonesia. In 1971 the corresponding percentages were slightly closer together, at 9.4 for Djakarta and 6.1 for Indonesia.

The age of migrants and their children comes from projecting the 1961 population and seeing how this differs, in total as well as by age and sex, from the enumerated 1971 population. Our method projected a grand total for the whole of Indonesia in excess of the census by only about 2 percent. It gives for Djakarta in 1971 a total of 3.7 million as against the 4.6 million enumerated. Since the projection takes no account of migration, and the census takes full account of it, the difference of 892,000 for the decade, or 89,200 per year, is the effect of migration into Djakarta, somewhat below the annual net in-migration of 100,-000 per year frequently mentioned locally.

Table 7.7 comparing projection and census by age shows a remarkable concentration of the differences. Of the 892,000 due to migration for the decade, fully 472,000, over one-half were between ages 15 and 29. Some reverse flow is shown at ages 40 and over. The number under age 10 is evidently related to the number aged 15–29; immigrants between 15 and 29 either bring children with them or else have children shortly after coming to the city.

European students of the dynamics of migration have spoken of push—disagreeable conditions in the place of origin—and pull—favorable conditions in the place of destination. One hypothesis is that when people are poor and ignorant only a sharp push—no ac-

Table 7.7 Age Distribution in Djakarta: Census of 1971 Compared with Projection from 1961 (thousands)

Age	*1971 Census*	*1961 Projection*	*Difference*
0–4	773	571	202
5–9	650	514	136
10–14	539	463	76
15–19	512	384	128
20–24	449	245	204
25–29	412	272	140
30–34	340	323	17
35–39	283	281	2
40–44	210	215	− 5
45–49	136	158	−22
50–54	102	101	1
55–59	56	62	− 6
60–64	47	47	0
65–69	26	21	5
70–74	19	18	1
75+	15	9	6
n.s.	8		
Total	4,576	3,684	892

Source: For projection, Keyfitz and Flieger, p. 501; for census, Central Bureau of Statistics.

cess to land, the sheer threat of starvation—will cause them to leave their homes. When they are better off and better educated, they may be susceptible to a pull, the attraction of better possibilities somewhere else. Those who are better off are not in general the first to move; an exception is where primogeniture gives younger sons of propertied groups the push, and their education gives them the pull. But the dynamics of present-day Southern Asia are very different from those of nineteenth-century Europe, and we need more knowledge of self-selection in migration in Indonesia and other countries.

The Productive System of the Village

For many parts of rural Southern Asia push and pull act simultaneously on much of the youth cohort. Let us consider first the push, in a typical village in which the land is fully occupied and the generation coming of age sees no corner into which it can squeeze.

The sense in which Asian rural land is fully occupied is a concealed one, for over the centuries many kinds of claims to land have developed, among which the European and American ideal of outright ownership of a fixed acreage that the peasant tills himself is relatively rare. Much more common is sharecropping by which, for example, peasant A (or his wife and daughters) plant and weed a half hectare of the land of B, and in return are granted one quarter of crop. But A and his large family cannot live on this, so he has his wife and daughters go out at harvesttime and join in harvesting some of the land of C, D, and E, for which they obtain one-fifteenth of what they cut. In addition A may do odd jobs, and his wife may sell onions and spices in the marketplace.

The food security which a new entrant to village adulthood expects may be perceived in a number of ways. Income differences are reflected both in the style of eating and in purchases of non-food items. Rice is the favored food in Java; next comes corn; at the bottom is cassava. The relative positions of these foods are partly a recognition of their nutritional qualities but partly also a continuance of the traditional esteem in which they are held. One of the ways in which the peasant measures his welfare and social standing is by counting the number of months before the rice harvest that he has to eat corn. And another way is by whether he has a surplus of grain that can be exported to the cities in exchange for the non-agricultural goods that are part of life in the village—flashlights, kerosene, shoes, clothing, dyestuffs, pottery.

Indonesian economists speak of the shortage of money in the countryside and of the way life is managed with minimum recourse to money. Cash expenditures, cash wages and profits, and speculative gains have been less in evidence than mutual help and endless barter negotiations, with the use of local goods rather than money as the unit of value.

In the past few years some movement toward monetization of the countryside has been observed. The government makes cash grants to each village, and also to each *kabupaten* (regency), the money to be spent on local improvements according to the discretion of the local authorities, under the *lurah* (village head) and the *bupati* (regent) respectively. The amounts have not been large; in one instance the equivalent of 25 U.S. cents per inhabitant. But the success of the plan is such that they are to be increased in the future. The subsidy has the double objective of giving employment in the countryside, and of creating such public works as will make the countryside more productive and hence more attractive and so slow the movement to the cities.

Increasing monetization of the countryside also results from the changing style of agriculture. With new crop varieties and more fertilizer the peasant tends to become a farmer, the head of a business enterprise. He must borrow from a bank to buy the inputs, and has no option but to sell much of the output in order to repay the loan. He comes to think of his turnover in money terms, and is likely to have a paid servant rather than one who is compensated in kind. He could well be less hospitable to friends and relatives who in earlier times would have been welcome to share his home and board. This might drive some of the landless villagers to the cities, but no one yet knows just how population and increased agricultural productivity will interact. The effect of the set of changes known as the Green Revolution on the economy and society of the peasant and the village will stand close observation in the years ahead.

Effects on the Birth Rate

In its present circumstances Java would seem ripe for a sharp decline in its births. If there is no possibility of further land in his village, then each additional child is a future liability to the peasant. Emigration is difficult, and those who stay can only have the effect of further dividing the crop. At the individual peasant family level the land is already divided into postage-stamp plots. Would not parents wish to avoid more division by having as few children as possible?

In a regime of purely private property parents tend to ensure the unity of the family farm, and at the same time make the best possible provision for their old age, by having about two children who live to maturity. If they have many children and their land is already too small, their security in old age will be threatened. The demographic history of Europe suggests that this is the situation which leads to effective birth control once the death rate starts to fall. That stability requires birth rates about equal to death rates would seem to be conveyed to individual couples, so that they should want to average no more than two surviving children in a situation where private property in land effectively signals collective shortages down to the individual level.

But the Javanese village is not in theory based on private property. The majority of villagers are no longer landowners. Those who hold land do so in what is thought of as a trust, and in principle village lands are redivided among the charter families of the village in every generation. While in practice the redivision and rotation of ownership are no longer observed, yet the attitude persists that all land—especially the most valuable part low enough to be irrigated, on which rice is grown—is the property of the village as a whole, and the more children one has the more land will be allocated to one's family to work. I have found this expressed widely in Java, but since in fact rotation has ceased and ownership has become frozen, it is hard to know what weight to assign to such memory of the tradition.

A more enduring influence is wage labor. The sugar plantations of colonial times for more than half a century hired men, women, and children to plant and harvest the cane and to run the factories in which the cane was pressed. Where landed property is no part of a family's means of support, and it lives by the unskilled wage labor of its members, then indeed old-age security comes to depend on the number of children a couple have. In most parts of Western Europe wage labor had a smaller place than in colonial Java.

These two reasons seem to explain why old-age security in Europe was identified with having *few* children, while in Java at least it is identified with having *many*. In view of the fact that the land has ceased to rotate among the village families and that wage jobs are now scarce, all of what is said above is a matter of the effect of tradition on the birth rate rather than of a rational approach to the family's current real problems.

To urge the advantages of birth control in circumstances where people are really benefited by having more children is not very hopeful; but where they are acting merely in accord with tradition and against their current interests, education becomes important. If the situation is as I have described—that in fact the traditional redivision of the village lands in each generation has ceased to be operative, and wage jobs are scarce—and if these matters of current reality can be communicated to parents, then the birth rate can be expected to fall. But there is no statistical evidence that it has yet started to do so in the rural parts of Java. And if the Green Revolution is welcomed as a means of feeding larger families, then the birth rate could stay at present levels for a long time. The case for communicating the advantages of family planning is strong, and the government is advertising with billboards and other means the desirability of fewer children. To this effort to change people's interpretation of their situation is added a network of clinics, now 1,600 in number, that provide the means. Pending fundamental changes in population dynamics and agricultural practice in the countryside, the inexorable push of youth to the city continues.

The Attraction of the City

When the migrant arrives in the capital city, Djakarta, he finds visible confirmation of the dramatic new national entity that the village textbooks told him about. Wide boulevards and expressways, a department store, stadia, and parade grounds outdo the corresponding village structures as the nation itself outdoes the village. The migrant may not be able to see all 120 million Indonesians assembled in one place, but he can on occasion see a million, where the village would barely have been capable of assembling 500. And Sukarno's presidency was marked by especially frequent evocations of the nation.

Economic possibilities abound. Thousands upon thousands of people who have left the village just ahead of today's migrants have become ensconced in government jobs, civil or military, that carry the same degree of security as the outright ownership of hectares of land. It is true that housing is difficult to find, but with luck and skill one can arrange to be allocated a house at nominal rent that is as durably one's own as a house in the village. The city house is a perquisite of the job, as may be the right to a government car that will overcome the perennial difficulty of transport in a large city. Rice is often dear, but a monthly ration proportioned to the number of the family for many years protected the employee against fluctuations of the rice market as reliably as did possession of a hectare of land. The barter economy of the village, in which cash sale and purchase occur only at the margins, is as far as possible adapted to the city environment. Rural hospitality and generosity are not forgotten by those who have succeeded, and claims and counter-claims among friends and relatives continue to be valid. The urban commercial system in which a cash nexus has replaced traditional bonds surrounds the former villager but remains a somewhat alien world dominated by Chinese and other cultural strangers.

Equally visible to the newcomer, of course, are those of his predecessors who have not done well in this center of the new national life. Not everyone has found a government job, and new hiring is tight. Those who are established want to help others and so become patrons of as many clients as possible, but employee numbers are frozen, and only a few have the influence to arrange for exceptions to be made. So the newcomer must gain his living by pedalling a *betja* (pedicab), by setting up as a petty vendor in the market, by learning a trade, by prostitution, by theft. The life is hard and unpleasant, even compared with the village, but he feels himself in line for what will ultimately lead to full participation in the new national entity.

Harris and Todaro have written on the way in which the newcomer views the poverty of the city, and how he balances the city affluence against it and makes his decision to stay on an expected gain based on estimates of the stakes and probabilities. His calculation of prospects in the city is factual, though possibly influenced by an optimistic distortion of perspective, and he concludes that he is better off to stay.[10]

Helping to make the hardships of life in the city supportable are non-material elements—the symbols of nationhood, the demonstration that here is where history is being enacted. Those who follow a daily newspaper are constantly reminded that the important things all happen in the city. Even crime comes to be dramatically, almost attractively, described. The capital city, Djakarta, especially gives the impression that it is a focus of political power.

Apart from the economic and political aspects of the city is its social attraction. The city is *ramai*—busy; things are going on at all hours of the day and night. There are always places to go and things to do. After finding himself a niche in the city economy, the migrant sees the village only as a place to visit, where he can talk about his adventures and achievements and rest for a further attack on the commanding heights of the city, as a possible refuge against the day when the city might turn against him, and as a place for real estate investment that will shelter him from inflation.

This writer has no way of judging the relative strengths of the economic, political, and social pulls described in the last three paragraphs. They do act in the same direction, however, and so reinforce one another. Perhaps someone will be ingenious enough to devise a means of estimating their separate effects from empirical data.

When contemplating the magnitude of push and pull factors, we must keep in mind that the potential movement into the city is great. Consider Indonesia or any other country that is six-sevenths rural. Suppose that the rural adult population receives a net increment of 3 percent each year. Then this same rural adult increase is equal to 18 percent of the adult urban population. If even half of the rural increment leaves the countryside, the adult population of the cities increases by 9 percent per year, plus its own natural increase. The large number of rural young people is a potential avalanche hanging over the cities. Governments are in a dilemma: whether to restrict movement to the cities and so restrict individual freedom, or face urban overcrowding and confusion.

Youth Mobilization and Employment

Germani has used the word "mobilization" in the special sense of the separation of people from traditional pursuits and their incorporation with the new national entity.[11] They want above all to *participate* in active roles, and "mere" voting does not give the feeling of participation in the same degree as does marching with a rifle, a point exploited by Sukarno during the last years of his rule. Hundred of thousands of young people in the capital had no access to the productive machine, and his problem was to keep them occupied and as far as possible exhilarated by a sense that they were participating in a war against domestic and foreign enemies.

The even larger numbers now coming of age will accentuate the question facing every underdeveloped country: Must its youth be idle, or engaged in offering services that no one wants? The ideal alternative to either is commodity production. Education has expanded rapidly over ten years; the youth are migrating to cities; concentration of a large labor force of educated individuals, mobilized and seeking means to upward mobility, would seem to further the expansion of production.

But one thing needed for productive work is capital. At the present time Indonesia is inviting foreign concerns in oil, tin mining, forest products, and many other fields to initiate or expand investment, and the response has been great. But let us examine with the use of some hypothetical arithmetic the relation of the new entrants into the labor force to the employment created by prospective capital investment.

Suppose that $5,000 worth of capital will give productive employment in perpetuity to one person. The capital requirement is much larger than this in oil and copper, smaller in textiles, but $5,000 could well be the order of magnitude of the average for modern production. To be conservative, disregard all of the older persons now unemployed or unsatisfactorily employed and consider only the prospective new entrants into the labor force. Leave the women entrants to one side and consider only the men. Disregard also all of the islands except Java, on the (doubtful) ground that they can occupy their own labor force by development of their natural resources. Then take only half of the youth cohort in Java, assuming the remainder to be capable of assimilation in their own villages. With these assumptions—so conservative as to embrace only a small part of the problem—we find 500,000 entrants per year into the labor force. At $5,000 per entrant they would require an aggregate annual investment of $2.5 billion to set them up in useful production. This amount is one sixth of the entire national income. It is about three times domestic saving. It cannot in present circumstances be provided by internal resources, and foreign investment is even less likely to contribute any large part of it.

Such calculations will strengthen the present impression that employment is the problem of the less developed countries in the 1970s, just as food was their problem in the 1960s. This shift in the balance of priorities may be assisted by the Green Revolution. With the spread of improved agricultural methods that began to come into use about the end of the decade, higher productivity per acre can be expected; hence a decreasing concern for food production. On the other hand, the peasant who has had to borrow from the bank to buy fertilizers must sell his crop if he is to repay the loan, and he will be less able than before to tolerate inefficient employment of his relatives and other villagers. Depending on how the new methods are brought into use, there may be anything from a slight increase in farm employment to a considerable decrease.

Present discussion among planners and the public, in Indonesia and elsewhere, revolves around whether an intermediate technology can be devised, at least in some industries, that would be more labor-intensive than the use of standard modern equipment. If this cannot be done economically over a sufficiently wide range of industries, an alternative would be to have industry running at the level of technology familiar in the West, and to provide work with simple hand tools or no tools at all to all those who are not absorbed. Hundreds of thousands of men are at the moment engaged in such public works schemes as the construction of roads and irrigation channels, and are paid a bare subsistence wage corresponding to their necessarily low productivity.

Planning still seeks to raise production, but it has become equally concerned with *keadilan sosial* (social justice). This could mean not only that the average income must rise but that the standard deviation of the distribution must decrease. Some ask in effect that the curve of income distribution be truncated on the left or pushed as a whole toward the right and that everyone be provided with a minimum income, either in money terms or in physical terms. But even this does not embrace the whole of *keadilan sosial,* which in current Indonesian discussion seems to include as well participation in production. Thus the aim of the search for intermediate technology is not necessarily to maximize production but to enable all citizens to take part in production as well as in consumption. How to square the concept with economic rationality is another of the dilemmas presented by large population, little land, and a mobile citizenry, all within a state whose claim to legitimacy is its promotion not only of welfare but of economic as well as political participation.

Chapter 8

Students and the Establishment in Indonesia: The Status-Generation Gap *Donald K. Emmerson*

EDITORS' NOTE: In this chapter a political scientist examines the advancing front of the Indonesian youth wave which the demographer Nathan Keyfitz has identified in chapter 7. Professor Emmerson compares significant attitudinal orientations of the elite under training with those of the existing elite and finds that their differences conform to the contrasting perspectives one might expect of the "ins" and the "not-yet-ins" and at the same time constitute a sea change in political culture. That fundamental issue of Indonesian politics, the relation of center to periphery, receives its due share of attention. Finally, the insights derived from this analysis are brought to bear on the current political scene to clarify our understanding of youth protest in Indonesia and forecast the opportunities as well as the quandaries this presents for broad social policy.

It is useful, even urgent, to remind ourselves of the ways our vantage points limit what we see. Kenneth Boulding has argued that Americans live in a "cowboy economy." [1] By contrast, Indonesians live in a peasant economy. Americans look at Indonesians and see the overproduction of persons. Indonesians look at Americans and see the overconsumption of goods. Each of these perceptions is accurate enough,[2] but it is also partial and a solution based upon it will necessarily be incomplete. In Indonesia, those who urge that primary emphasis be placed on slowing rates of demographic growth may underestimate the importance of raising rates of economic growth, whereas well-being obviously involves a balance between the two. Holland is five times more densely populated than her ex-colony yet enjoys a

AUTHOR'S NOTE: I am grateful to James Guyot and Crawford Young for their comments on an early draft of this paper.

standard of living twenty times higher.[3] A view of Indonesia's "problem" as exclusively or even essentially demographic may also, in the eyes of some Indonesians at least, divert attention from and thereby perpetuate her peasant economy and its dependence on investment capital and manufactured goods from abroad. On the other hand, a solution to America's "problem" that attempts to slow the production of consumers—zero population growth as a policy goal, for example—while leaving essentially unregulated the production of consumables threatens to prolong the production-geared structure of a cowboy economy, the costs of whose indulgence—in automobiles, strip mines, and handguns, for example—are already painfully clear.

These solutions are also partial in that their emphasis on production and consumption ignores a third critical process: distribution. In Indonesia, it is much easier to insert IUD's than to transport and resettle families from densely populated Java onto any of the sparsely settled outer islands, which is why redistributive internal migration has never exceeded a cosmetic trickle. But exclusive reliance on contraceptive acceptance rates as measures of success can foster a misreading of the demographic problem as being merely the overproduction of consumers rather than their maldistribution in relation to available sources of life support as well. Similarly, the maldistribution of opportunities to consume and produce may also be neglected in a policy that simply targets hikes in GNP. If and as the underconsuming dependent peasant economy and the wastefully overconsuming cowboy economy eventually turn toward the paradigm of a steady-state system, distributive questions within and between countries should become more visible. Ideally, they will complement questions of production and consumption in a more holistic and ultimately more beneficial view of human problems.[4]

It is from such a perspective that this chapter is written. It is mainly about some distributions in Indonesia—of age, status, opinion, and power—and about some possible relationships between them. Summarized, the argument has seven steps. First, the Indonesian population is observed to be comparatively youthful, and some difficulties of political inference from that demographic fact are noted. Second, the idea of a "status-generation gap" is introduced. Third, a sample of Indonesian university students is found to hold certain opinions that differ from those of a sample of the adult political and administrative elite. Fourth, these differences of opinion are shown to constitute a status-generation gap whose widest distance occurs over the question of the appropriate distribution of power between the center and the regions. Fifth, some possible implications and consequences of the gap are explored. Sixth, a relationship between the gap and urbanization is suggested. And seventh, introducing a behavioral dimension to the gap, recent youth protest is interpreted as a possible outcome of job insecurity, ethnic outgroup status, and culture change.

Compared with the populations of the rest of the world, those of the Third World are markedly more youthful. Indonesia is no exception.[5] And aside from being comparatively youthful at a single point in time, Indonesia's population is also undergoing rejuvenation over time. Specifically, the Japanese occupation (1942–45), and the Indonesian revolution (1945–49), and all the dislocation and suffering those experiences entailed, appear to have had a markedly depressing effect on the rate of population growth during the 1940s compared with that of the preceding decade.[6] Rejuvenation is occurring as the postwar baby boom cohort of the 1950s advances on the sparse ranks of the preceding generation. Thus, a rapid absolute and proportionate increase in the 15–19-year age group in 1967–71 will be followed by a similar expansion among persons aged 20–24 in 1972–76. According to Indonesia's leading demographer, "The creation of employment opportunities for these new entrants into the labor force is clearly essential," while an Australian political economist projects an "apparently fearsome demand for additional employment, housing and social capital" by discontented and politically volatile Indonesian youth in the 1970s. A Djakarta daily predicts that the 15–29 age group will increase from 26 million in 1966 to 42 million in 1978, and that "all of them will be ready to storm the cities." [7]

But young people can also be seen as demand-satisfying producers, of salutary criticism and change as well as of goods. An "excess" of young people need not be a "maldistribution" except in the statistical sense by comparison with the age pyramids typical of industrialized societies. Politically, proportionately large youth segments in Third World nations may herald overdue reforms, while economically they can provide the human energy necessary for growth.

The empirical basis for choice between these perspectives is ambiguous. The relationships of economic and political to demographic variables appear to be highly indirect and contextual. What is needed is an understanding of the effects, limiting or enabling, of different demographic rates and pyramids on the achievement of socio-economic and political goals like well-being, stability, and structural reform.

A further complication in evaluating a youth bulge such as Indonesia's is the heterogeneity of the category of youth itself, encompassing as it does students, workers, and peasants, among others. Which subcategory of youth will have the greater political impact? It is probably generally true that on political issues university students are the most articulate and visible subcohort. And students can play a doubly high-energy role: on the one hand as a force generating more political demands than, say, working or peasant youth, and on the other hand, as an incipient or insurgent elite, being nearer to the positions of power from which demand-satisfying changes could be initiated.

It is also true that objectively, compared with their less educated age-mates, students are an advantaged group. Most of the members of the youth cohort are prevented by some combination of talent and circumstance from even competing for university entrance. Those who do find their way to the lecture hall benches represent only a tiny fraction of the full youth category.

And for not having climbed the educational ladder or for having fallen off it on the way up, non-student youth, insofar as they are employed at all, will tend to get the less prestigious jobs. The extent of this relative disadvantage will of course depend on the state of the economy and on the cultural and monetary valuation of manual vs. nonmanual labor.

Subjectively, however, the sense of relative deprivation felt by the graduates may be greater. Undereducation and underemployment can combine in a low-level stable equilibrium—and so, incidentally, can underconsumption and underproduction, which is why the steady-state paradigm being popularized in the West may seem like a poisoned gift to the leaders of the Third World. But overeducation and underemployment may encourage in a thwarted would-be elite an insurgent frame of mind; witness the Naxalites in India, the People's Liberation Front in Ceylon, and the Kabataang Makabayan in the Philippines, to cite only some recent examples from demographically youth-heavy Asian countries. These movements suggest that the larger the student subcohort in relation to the number of available opportunities for skill-utilizing postgraduate employment and for upward social and political mobility in general, the greater the likelihood of student protest.

The question whether such protest can succeed leads the inquirer still further from strictly demographic variables. One important intervening condition is how deeply the adult establishment is split. When student leaders can ally with one powerful element in the adult political elite in a struggle against another element, as they could in Indonesia in 1965–66, their chances of success will obviously be brighter than if their adult ally is weak or nonexistent, as appears to have been the case in Ceylon in 1971. Whether students are an apprentice or an insurgent elite, their political role is defined in relation to the establishment.

For these reasons, this chapter focuses on the distance between students and the establishment in Indonesia. But there is an initial problem of describing this distance. The term "generation gap" typically refers to the sharply contrasting and outlook-anchoring historical experiences of two generations, experiences that are formative and tenacious in the lives of those who undergo them and become axiomatic as they are used again and again by the two generations to justify two correspondingly different sets of perceptions and valuations.[8] And because these two sets are rooted in historical experiences that cannot be shared across generations—especially not the establishment's experience, which occurred when the younger generation was unborn or politically unconscious—the resulting gap is hard to bridge and may be "resolved" only when the older generation dies out and the outlook of the younger becomes in its turn a model for society as a whole.

To illustrate from the contemporary West, insofar as an experience of scarcity during the Depression sustains a work ethic in a prewar generation and an experience of abundance by a postwar generation supports an ethic of nonmaterial self-actualization, then the coming to power and maturity of the younger generation may parallel a cultural shift in paradigm for the larger society.[9] To close such a gap in favor of the receding ethic, members of an establishment may even attempt synthetically to reproduce their own experience for the younger generation: the Great Proletarian Cultural Revolution, for example, as a surrogate Long March.

But a generation gap in this sense cannot logically be inferred backward from a difference in outlook alone. For the difference may simply be a function of status, disappearing or at least shrinking just as soon as the younger generation replaces the older in positions of responsibility. Whether the exercise of power corrupts or sobers the individual, it may be the critical distinguishing feature of the establishment vis-à-vis the students and one that will outlast the replacement of the former by the latter. According to this purely structural explanation, students can be expected to leave their oppositionist views at the door if and when they enter the establishment's club to accept membership in it, and the "generation gap" is best seen as little more than a phase of elite succession.

A third logically possible explanation is psycho-biological: Youth is an insecure period of transition from the unconscious acceptance of the role of child toward the conscious selection, rejection, and creation of roles for the adult self. Tension with elders is a natural byproduct of this process of self-definition, reflecting neither "generational" nor "status" conflict but a gap between two psychological ages within the same life cycle of personal development.

Because this chapter does not rest on psychological evidence, the term "status-generation" gap will be used and the third interpretation will be discarded. The life-cycle approach also seems prima facie the least satisfactory of the three. For whereas a great range of demographic, economic, and historical patterns can be observed around the world in many combinations—that is, the independent variables in these explanations do vary—the age-phase hypothesis presumes a universal process of youthful individuation—that is, the independent variable does not vary. If all young people undergo a crisis of self-definition in relation to elders and elders' roles, then why are some young people politically active and oppositionist while others are not? A search for the sources of variation in student political outlooks and behavior quickly enters socio-economic and cultural realms beyond the limits of psychology.[10] If the youth crisis described in the works of Westerners like Freud and Erikson is not universal and does not operate in Indonesia—where family structures, sexual mores, and notions of individuation and sociability vary one from another and from the patterns typical of late-Victorian Vienna in particular and the West generally—then one must again look to other variables for sharper explanations.

Before this can be done, the notion of a status-generation gap must first be given operational form and empirical content. To accomplish this, in 1968–69 a small number of members of the politico-administrative elite in Djakarta were randomly selected and interviewed—18 officials in the higher central bureaucracy and 18 members of the national parliament—and their relative agreement or disagreement with a set of scaled orientational statements was compared with that of a much larger convenience sample of university students—2,344 persons in nine institutions of higher education in Java, Sumatra, and Bali.[11]

Intrapsychic motivation could not be inferred from these questionnaire responses; instead they were treated merely as indicators of surface orientations that were politically relevant but that might or might not be rooted in personality. The orientations were seven: support for central authority; support for deference to authority; support for empathy as a social priority; perceptions of normlessness; perceptions of powerlessness; religious tolerance; and trust in leaders.

The adults and the students differed significantly along five of these seven scaled orientations. As Table 8.1 shows, the members of the establishment on the average gave greater support to central authority, to deference to authority, and to empathy as a social priority, showed greater eclectic religious tolerance, and were less inclined to perceive normlessness in the society around them.[12] Although the number of orientations along which these two groups could have been located is in theory infinite; and the number along which they actually were is very small, this preponderence of divergence over convergence already suggests a gap of some importance between the students and the established elite, irrespective of the content of the observed differences. Further evidence of a gap is the consistency of that content: compared with the adult elite, the students were less deferential, and more intolerant and pessimistic.

But before these differences can be called a status-generation gap—that is, a gap attributable primarily to the respectively incumbent and aspirant status of the establishment and the students or to their unique formative experiences—it is prudent to test for other explanations. Consider the most striking difference, that between the tendency of the establishment sample on bal-

Table 8.1 Significant Differences in Outlook Between the Establishment and the Student Samples

Orientation	*Sample and Sample Mean*		*Differ-ence*	*Level of Statistical Significance of Difference*
	Establishment	*Students*		
Support for central authority [1]	higher (3.17)	lower (2.25)	.92	.001
Support for empathy as a social priority [2]	higher (4.03)	lower (3.21)	.82	.001
Perceived normlessness [3]	lower (2.80)	higher (3.50)	.70	.001
Support for deference to authority [4]	higher (3.08)	lower (2.54)	.54	.01
Eclectic religious tolerance [5]	higher (3.83)	lower (3.09)	.74	.02

Note: Each of the items in each sample was scored from 1 (Disagree) through 5 (Agree). Mean scores for each sample on each scale were obtained by summing the individual scale scores on a given orientation for a particular sample and dividing by the number of scalable sample respondents. A respondent was scalable for a given orientation only if he/she answered all its component items. Scalable N's for the establishment on all scales were 36; for students they ranged from 2,109 (perceived normlessness) to 2,325 (eclectic religious tolerance). The level of significance was obtained with a two-tailed *t* test of the null hypothesis. For the formula used, which includes a correction for unequal standard deviations and the extreme disparity in sample size, see William L. Hays, *Statistics* (New York: Holt, Rinehart, and Winston, 1963), pp. 320–21. Information on questionnaire administration, internal consistency, response set, standard deviations, and related matters can be found in my dissertation, "Exploring Elite Political Culture in Indonesia: Community and Change," Yale University, New Haven, September 1972, Table III.32 and Appendices I and II.

[1] "In the event of differing standpoints between center and region, the center's interest should take priority."

[2] "What our society needs a great deal nowadays is people who always try to see things from the other person's point of view."

[3] "It's hard these days to distinguish friend from foe."
"Nowadays most people who do good are really only trying to conceal the evil things they did previously."
"In our present society, evil people have more influence than good people."
"Nowadays it's rare to find a person one can trust."

[4] "A good school is one where the teacher teaches and the pupils listen and take notes without asking a lot of questions."
"A leader's orders must always be obeyed."
"Only the leaders of the state are capable of determining the meaning of the 'national interest.' "
"The best youth is the youth who obeys his parents, obeys his teacher, and respects those who hold high positions."

[5] "Among all the religions in the world, there is only one true religion."

ance to agree that the interest of the central government should take priority over regional interests and the tendency of the students to disagree with the same statement (Table 8.1). The central government is located in the capital city of Djakarta on Java and is staffed mainly by Javanese. Whereas the adminstrative and legislative duties of the adult elite sample required all of them to spend much or all of their time in Djakarta, more than three-fifths of the students were in institutions outside Djakarta and nearly one-fifth were studying outside Java. Perhaps the students were more decentralist because they were physically further from the center. Also, proportionately more students were born outside Java (34 percent) than adults (22 percent), and there was a much higher proportion of non-Javanese among students (64 percent) than among adults (44 percent). The students' greater support for regional interests could simply be a consequence of their greater regional and ethnic dispersion.[13]

But it is not. Even when physical location, regional birthplace, and ethnic affiliation are successively controlled, the difference between the students and the establishment remains. None of these counter-explanations is supported by the evidence.

Hypothetical alternatives to the status-generational interpretation were developed for all five differences, using six control variables to "explain" the dependent variation in outlook. Birthplace (region and community size), ethnicity (identity and intensity), and religion (identity and intensity) were selected as control variables because they seemed important in a nation as culturally and demographically differentiated as Indonesia and because they suggested plausible alternatives to the status-generational explanation of the observed differences in outlook between students and the establishment. Perhaps the students' greater unwillingness to recognize alternative paths to religious truth was a consequence of the apparently greater intensity of their affiliations to a particular faith—58 percent of the students had "strong" religious commitments compared with only 44 percent of the adults, although the two measures used are not exactly comparable.[14] Perhaps the students' lesser support for empathy as a social priority was a consequence of the apparently greater intensity of their affiliations to a particular ethnic group —74 percent of the students had "strong" ethnic affiliations compared with only 56 per cent of the adults, although again the measures used are not exactly comparable.[15] Perhaps the students' lesser support for empathy as a social priority was a consequence of the higher proportion of minority (non-Islamic) religious identities among students—31 percent compared with the adults' 21 percent—in what is statistically an overwhelmingly Muslim nation where a Christian head of state is still unthinkable. Or perhaps the students' greater perception of normlessness in the society around them reflected their more urbanized origins —35 percent having been born in cities with populations of more than 100,000 (as of 1961) compared with only 22 percent of the adults. (The 100,000 cutoff applies to all future references to urban vs. rural birth.)

In all, thirty hypothetical alternatives to the status-generational explanation were generated by applying each of the six control variables to each of the five dependent orientational differences. Yet in only one of these thirty instances did the control variable have a significantly greater and consistent explanatory impact on the dependent variation in outlook than did the status-generational or inter-sample difference between the students and the adult elite. The sole exception was the counter-hypothesis that the greater intolerance of the students toward multiple visions of religious truth (Table 8.1) could better be explained by the apparently "stronger" commitments of the students to their own faith. Statistically, this counter-hypothesis proved over three times as powerful as the status-generational hypothesis.[16] Results for several of the other control variables also served to erode confidence in the status-generational hypothesis that the adults were more eclectically tolerant because of their elite vantage point or because of some prior historical experience the students did not share. Of the five observed orientational differences, it

Table 8.2 Evidence for a Status-Generation Gap

Orientation	*Discriminating Power* [1] *Status-generational variable*		*Discriminating Power* [1] *Control variables*		*Relative Discriminating Power of Status-Generational Variable*
Support for central authority	.85	–	.21	=	.64
Support for empathy as a social priority	.90	–	.28	=	.62
Support for deference to authority	.60	–	.19	=	.41
Perceived normlessness	.49	–	.15	=	.34
. . . .					
Eclectic religious tolerance	.57	–	.62	=	–.05

[1] Average difference of means.

Note: For each orientation, the status-generational variable was crossed successively with each of the six control variables. This procedure generated twelve status-generational and twelve control variable differences of means. A comparison of the average of all twelve status-generational differences of means with an average of all twelve control-variable differences of means yields the relative discriminating power of the status-generational variable for that orientation. On this last figure is based the judgment, indicated by the location of the dotted line, whether the control variables washed out the status-generational variable or not. Consistency as well as size of differences was incorporated into this measure by treating as negative differences that ran against the hypothesized direction. For the full matrix from which this table and Table 8.3 are derived, see my dissertation, Table III.37.

was on eclectic religious tolerance that the control variables were most successful in washing out the status-generational hypothesis, as can be seen in Table 8.2.

There certainly is, then, a gap in outlook between students and the establishment in Indonesia, and it has at least four dimensions. Compared with the adult elite, students show less support for deference to authority in general and to central authority in particular, a greater sense of social breakdown, and less support for social empathy. The reasons for this lie not in any intervening demographic or cultural differences of birthplace, ethnicity, or religion but rather in the superior status and the generational experience of the adult elite. On these four issues at least, the status-generation gap in Indonesia is real.

Of the four, the difference in outlook most plausibly attributable to the status-generation gap—that is, least powerfully explained by the control variables—is the greater inclination of students to place regional interests above those of the central authority. The counter-hypothesis of ethnic identity—that the fact of being Javanese would correlate more highly with support for the interest of the central (largely Javanese-staffed) government than the fact of membership in the establishment—was disconfirmed. Nor was there a relationship between region of birth and support for central authority, disconfirming the counter-hypothesis that those born on Java would be more likely to place the interest of a central government located on Java over those of the regional governments on the outer islands. On the average, the status-generational variable discriminated more than four times more powerfully than the control variables between those who supported the central authority and those who did not (Table 8.2).

What of the two different explanations contained within the status-generation hypothesis? What is the logic of a status gap or a generation gap in relation to our findings, and which accounts better for this difference in attitudes toward central authority?

The generational explanation rests upon the unique historical experience of the adult elite. Most of these men had been active in the revolution of 1945–49 in defense of the idea of a single unitary Republic of Indonesia and in bitter opposition to the proposed "federal solution" of the returning Dutch. The struggle for a unified free Indonesia had been for many of them a deeply moving experience. After the revolution, they had seen the strains between center and region break out again and again in local uprisings and ultimately in a breakaway government and a full-scale civil war. A decade later the leaders and parties implicated in that rebellion—Suharto's trade minister excepted—were still not rehabilitated. Among the adults, several army officers remembered the activities of the separatist Darul Islam movement in the 1950s and the role of the Communist Party in the uprising of 1948 and in the attempted coup of 1965 as equivalent threats to the unity of the Republic. Several civilian politicians who disagreed with Sukarno in important respects could nevertheless endorse his emphasis on the abiding imperative of national unity. Among the administrators, too, there were men who perceived their contemporary roles in part as extensions of their revolutionary experience: Having struggled to create one central government in a unified Republic of Indonesia—fulfilling the ideal of "one country, one people, one language," in the words of the oath of the "1928 generation"—they were now employed by it and saw themselves as defending it from the centrifugal attractions of sectional interest.

More than four-fifths of the adults were born in 1910–29 and none after 1939. The Indonesian revolution was thus an important part of the remembered experience of all but a few of these men. In this sense, they were a revolutionary generation. Several expressly identified themselves with the "1945 generation" label that has come to be applied broadly to those in the politico-administrative elite who took part in the revolution and for whom the revolutionary experience was indelible. One member of the establishment sample was actively involved in a project to impress upon the student generation the unitarian, nationalist ideal of the 1945 generation and the need for vigilance in defense of that ideal against its enemies whether on the "extreme right" or the "extreme left."

But for the students sampled, so it appears, the struggle for unity was over. To them, the oath of 1928 was a history text item, while virtually none had any significant memory of the revolution. Only 3 percent of them were born before 1940 and more than 70 percent were born during the revolution, in 1945–49. (Because the student respondents *preceded* the 1950s baby boom, on demographic grounds alone—holding all other variables constant—the gap observed in 1968–69 might be expected to widen into a gulf in the 1970s as the swollen birth cohort of the 1950s begins to seek matriculation and employment.)

These students probably took for granted what the 1928 generation dreamed of and the 1945 generation fought for.[17] It is likely that Sukarno's record for them was comparatively unadorned by admiration for his role in creating one Indonesian identity. Indeed, if any experience was formative for them, it was the overthrow of Sukarno in 1965–67. The "1966 generation," with which many of them no doubt identified and in whose struggle some had actually taken part, rejected what it saw as the empty symbolism of Sukarno's regime and urged that the abstract idea of the independent, unitarian Republic be given concrete economic content. The nation had been made—that battle was long since over—and now it was high time to develop the nation for the benefit of its citizens.

A status explanation is also possible. The adults were all associated in their work with the central government, either in the upper reaches of its bureaucratic hierarchy or in Parliament. Their elite position, rather than any historical experience of revolution and separatism, may account for their more centralist views. Similarly, the more critical stance of the students toward the central authority may reflect their status as "outs" or at least "not-yet-ins." Those students who in the future gravitate to the center and move upward to incumbencies in administration and Parliament may well be resocialized into an elite-centralist perspective and shed their earlier solicitude toward regional interests.

The data do not allow a test of this argument, but it can be evaluated by internal analysis of the two samples. Those of the elite sample who were administrators found in their bureaucratic status as officials of the central government an integral part of their self-concepts. Most had long civil service careers behind them and all were year-round residents of the capital city. Several had been associated with the *pamong pradja,* the elite corps of generalist administrators whose spokesmen in the past had resisted the decentralization and politicization of a paternalistic, colonially modeled administrative state. By contrast, their status as members of Parliament was much less central to the identities of the politicians, almost all of whom held other jobs or played other roles. Many resided outside Dakarta and came there only to attend legislative sessions. The loyalties of most of the politicians to the central government passed first through whatever party or organization they represented. More diversely recruited than the bureaucrats, their activities bound them less completely into a centralist perspective.

From this comparison, by the logic of the status hypothesis, one would expect the bureaucrats to prefer the center over the regions by a larger margin than the politicians. But on the contrary, the legislators were noticeably more centralist than the bureaucrats.[18] Furthermore, returning to the generational hypothesis, the politicians did have a slightly more intimate and positive experience of the unitarian revolution in 1945–49 than the bureaucrats, and national unity may have been a somewhat more flexible (because less revolutionary) notion in the eyes of the bureaucrats than in the eyes of political leaders who still associated it with an anti-colonial struggle for unconditional freedom.

On the student side, evidence for both the generational and the status explanation is weaker. The students, unlike the adults, were not interviewed, so their reasons for agreeing or disagreeing with any item on the questionnaire can only be surmised. Furthermore, under both hypotheses, it is a *lack* of something—the experience of historic struggle to create and defend a unitarian Republic or the position of a ruling elite at the center of that Republic—that is said to determine the students' outlook. Again, however, at least the logic of the explanation can be pursued.

It is unclear why the students should have discounted the interest of the center if they expected eventually to be associated with that interest. To the extent that they were an incipient central elite, why should they not have defended the center? On the other hand, if their regionalist preference could be interpreted as identification with regional authority by an incipient regional elite, one would expect a positive association between outer island residence and birthplace and non-Javanese ethnicity on the one hand and this decentralizing perspective on the other. Yet none of those associations was found. In fact, Javanese students and students born on Java were by trivial margins *less* centralist than non-Javanese students and those born on the outer islands.

It may be that the students chose not to endorse the center not because they positively endorsed regional interests but because, from a negative oppositionist standpoint, they declined to support deference to authority in general and central authority in particular (Table 8.1). Their stance toward the central government may be less the anticipatory identification of the would-be incumbent than the critical appraisal of the would-be opponent. But if this is so, the reasons for opposition would appear to lie less in the status difference between the two groups than in actual student perceptions of government as relatively corrupt or militaristic—perceptions reinforced both informally and through the media. And yet regional authorities were hardly exempt from such criticism.

What conclusion can be reached? The data do not permit a definitive choice between the status and the generational hypotheses. But, given the ambiguity of the status hypothesis as an explanation of the students' more decentralist orientation, the conclusion does seem warranted that the differing outlook of the two groups on centralism is to a significant degree a product of their differing historical experiences.

Aside from the origins of this difference of views, what about its consequences? An answer to this question depends on the answer to two prior questions: First, how appropriate to objective conditions in Indonesia is the relatively centralizing response of the adult elite? And second, how centrifugally divisive is the relatively decentralizing response of the student generation?

An extreme centralizing response to contemporary Indonesian conditions—to answer the first question—is obsolete, unsuitable, and exacerbating. It is obsolete in that the revolution is, after all, over. It would be premature to say that national unity has been irrevocably won. But the territorial integrity of Indonesia is far less fragile than it was at the time of the rebellions of the 1950s, to say nothing of the period before 1950 when the idea of Indonesian independence itself was contested.

Extreme centralization is also unsuitable in the world's largest archipelagic nation. Indonesia's ecological systems, social structures, linguistic groups, religious cores, and webs of communication and exchange are multiple and diverse. If centralization in the face of armed enemies was a political imperative in the early years of the Republic, decentralization to meet a range of qualitatively varied and spatially dispersed developmental problems may be an economic imperative in the 1970s. Beyond a certain level of centralization to correct gross imbalances and preserve the national frame—a level that is difficult to specify in the abstract but that may be fairly high the more deeply rooted and reform-resistant those imbalances are—the further accretion of prerogatives to the center is likely simply to reduce the responsiveness of the center to local needs. This is especially true of a "soft state" [19] like Indonesia where the capacity of the center to exercise its responsibilities effectively is already sorely tried. At the extreme centralist end of the spectrum, overloads in communication and control approach the breaking point and corrective feedback vanishes. Finally, insofar as the prominence of certain partial if not partisan groups in the constellation of power at the center—the army, the Javanese, and for that matter the 1945 generation itself—reduces the equivalence of the interest of the center with the interest of the nation, to that extent extreme centralization, far from resolving redistributive grievances, may actually exacerbate them.

For many of those who identify most closely with the 1945 generation, this argument is not very persuasive. They have been socialized through dramatic experience into accepting the logic of a different argument. Centralization as a prerequisite for the effective defense of the Republic against external and internal enemies has remained an article of faith for many of the 1945 generation long after the battles that made it axiomatic have been won.

In the adult elite sample, for example, a high-ranking officer in the Department of Defense took pleasure in recalling his experiences on behalf of the Republic in 1945–49; even allowing for some *ex post facto* embroidery, they were unmistakably heroic and a source of great and continuing personal fulfillment. During one interview, he recalled a long discussion he had had with a fellow revolutionary shortly after the 1945 constitutional convention had completed its work. They had both agreed how absolutely essential it was to have a strong central government to defend Indonesia and to advance her historic role as one great independent nation. Both men, this informant recalled with a smile, had been caught up in the nationalist mystique. Now he could see the costs of a unitarian system, its top-heaviness, the way it had enabled clique parties in Djakarta to "sink their claws," as he put it, into the provinces. Yet these afterthoughts were not strong enough to neutralize the earlier, formative paradigm, and he ended by agreeing with the questionnaire statement that the interest of the center should take priority.

Another officer, not among those interviewed, formulated this centralizing paradigm quite explicitly a few years ago. An Army colonel at the time, his participation in the defense of the Republic successively against the Dutch, the Communist Party, the breakaway Sumatran regime, and the Darul Islam on Java typifies the experience of the 1945 generation. He was led by the spectre of enemies on the Left and the Right to endorse a strong central authority:

> Until now Indonesia has succeeded in defeating infiltration both from the Left and the Right. . . . Basically the answer to the threat of infiltration and subversion lies in the existence of a strong and stable government which enjoys the confidence of a large part of the population. A strong government will be able to regulate the political life in the country, establishing a democracy which is not necessarily

Western democracy, and [will be] strong enough to prevent anarchy. The relationship between the central and the provincial government, a very important factor in an archipelago like Indonesia, can only be regulated equitably by a strong government.[20]

It would be unfair to characterize Suharto's government as extremely centralist. In the economic sphere, some steps toward decentralization have been taken. But in the political realm, the unitarian paradigm of the politically incumbent 1945 generation and its distinctive perception of the greater evil as anarchy from below and intervention from without rather than official imposition from above does facilitate a centralizing response. The goal is a strong and stable government which enjoys popular confidence without allowing much autonomous local participation. In 1971–72, the appointment of more than a fifth of Parliament and all governors by the center, the discouragement of party organization below the regency level, and official suspicion toward independent local development efforts as potential foci of opposition to the regime were all reflections of this depoliticizing thrust of centralization in the eyes of its advocates among the ruling elite. Typifying the thrust was the notion of a "floating" rural mass advanced by several high-placed generals, under which villagers would be allowed no permanent political commitments but would instead participate in politics only at the polls where they could exercise their right of choice without being unduly influenced by divisive partisan organizations and disruptive urban ideologies.[21] The likelihood was, of course, that such a "floating" mass could be that much more easily "anchored" by a central government whose authority and personnel would extend unchallenged from the ministries and the military commands right down to the village level.

It would also be unfair to characterize the establishment sample as extreme on the issue of centralization. Only in relation to a more decidedly decentralizing student response could the establishment's position be called "extreme." To evaluate the divisive potential of this difference between the two groups, it will therefore be necessary to interpret the students' viewpoint as well.

The more closely and more cumulatively students' decentralizing views are linked to subnational frames of reference—region, religion, and ethnicity—the greater the behavioral threat posed by those views to the preservation of national unity. Whereas many in the 1945 generation mixed in elite colonial schools with classmates of widely differing primordial backgrounds and came to share with them an Indonesian national identity, the massive expansion of educational opportunity since independence now means that it is possible for an Islamic Atjehnese or a Christian Menadonese, for example, to go through primary, secondary, and higher schools without ever leaving Atjeh or North Sulawesi.[22] If these students prefer regional over central authority, perhaps their motivations are less to decentralize within an assumed national frame and thereby strengthen it than to improve and protect the position of their primordial group in a zero-sum contest over scarce resources with little or no regard for issues of game-wide unity or stability. And if the latter is true, then perhaps the establishment's fears of breakaway rebellion may not be so obsolete after all.

But insofar as the survey data shed light on this question, it is not true that the students were primordially motivated (Table 8.3). Whereas religious identity, for example, did appear to underlie the views of the adults on the question of centralization—Muslim members of the politico-administrative elite were more decentralist than non-Muslim members [23]—neither this nor any other control variable was associated with differences in support for central authority among the students. Ignoring urbanization (size of birth community) for a moment as a demographic phenomenon, primordial variables were significantly linked in eight instances with variation in adult outlooks, whereas only three such links occurred among students and one of these was in a direction contrary to the counter-hypothesis.

It is true that Muslim students were significantly less inclined than non-Muslim students to recognize multiple paths to reli-

Table 8.3 Significant Differences Between the Orientation Scores Generated by Each Control Variable within the Establishment and Student Samples

	Control Variable					
	Birthplace		*Religion*		*Ethnicity*	
Orientation	*(region)*	*(community size)*	*(identity)*	*(intensity)*	*(identity)*	*(intensity)*
	Differences Among Establishment					
Support for empathy as a social priority			.86			.61
Perceived normlessness	−.68					
Support for deference to authority	.91					
Support for central authority		−.74	.66			
Eclectic religious tolerance	1.39			2.40	.60	
	Differences Among Students					
Support for empathy as a social priority		.24				
Perceived normlessness						
Support for deference to authority	−.23	−.25				
Support for central authority						
Eclectic religious tolerance		.38	1.30	.80		

Note: Each of these figures is a difference between two means on a scale from 1.0 through 5.0. Only differences of .20 or higher are shown for the student sample while the cutoff for the adult sample is higher (.60) to allow for the greater variability resulting from smaller sample size. Control variable values are given in the text; signs indicate directions.

gious truth, and that strongly religious students were similarly less eclectic than weakly religious ones. But with the exception of these two counter-hypotheses—which, although impressively confirmed, merely relate religious backgrounds to religious outlooks—the students' views did not vary significantly along primordial lines. To this degree at least, fears of a primordially motivated and therefore politically centrifugal student generation seem unjustified.

The status-generation gap, then, involves not only a difference of opinion between students and the establishment but also a difference in the underpinnings of opinion on either side of the gap. As Table 8.3 shows, the variations in adult elite outlooks were more often associated with region, religion, and ethnicity than were variations in student opinion. This is not to suggest that student views were secular while those of adults were primordially based. Neither student nor adult views, for example, were organized to any meaningful degree along ethnic lines, and despite the greater utility of primordial considerations in explaining variation in adult views, in most instances in Table 8.3 even among adults primordial variables had no marked effect. But a comparison of the single most frequently significant explanatory variable for adult opinion and its counterpart for student opinion does reveal a striking difference.

Region of birth, treated here as a primordial variable, had the greatest impact on adult opinion. Members of the establishment born outside Java perceived greater normlessness, were less likely to support deference to authority, and were less syncretic in their notion of religious truth than their counterparts born on Java. Regionalism obviously involves more than a simple dichotomy of geopolitical core and periphery, but in these limited terms at least, certain outlooks—religious absolutism, personal independence, and disaffection from the social environment—could be roughly predicted from an adult's distant origin and minoritarian identity.

For the students, on the other hand, the most frequently significant explanatory factor was not primordial but demographic—the size of their birthplace. Urban-born students were more likely to support empathy as a social priority, less likely to support deference to authority, and more eclectically tolerant of alternative religious truths than rural-born students. The opinions associated, among students, with urban birth—social empathy, personal autonomy, and religious tolerance—can be said to constitute a broadly "liberal" syndrome, although this term obviously has historical connotations from the Western tradition that do not apply in Indonesia and derogatory connotations in Indonesia that are not intended here.

Why should a "liberal" syndrome be associated with urban birth? As noted earlier, it is not easy to infer a political outlook from a demographic circumstance; the intervening variables are too many and too ambiguous in their possible effects on the causal chain. Consider the extreme possibilities: Does urban life integrate or polarize primordial interests? Are cities melting pots or pressure cookers? Plausible chains of logic could be extended in either of these opposing directions.

One intervening variable that can help resolve the resulting contradiction is socio-economic status. Once again structure is seen to shape experience. Crudely put, the hypothesis would be —*ceteris paribus,* of course—that whereas the urban environment will facilitate the secularization and integration of individuals of higher socio-economic status, it will, by contrast, increase the likelihood of primordial conflict among lower-status individuals. To the slum dweller urban life is more of a contest over scarce resources. The poorer the migrant to the city, the more likely he or she is to band together with others of shared primordial identity for aid and protection in a strange and even threatening environment. And because urban life for these people is more of a struggle over scarce resources, those re-created bases of primordial solidarity are more likely, given some precipitating incident, to collide—in the marketplace or on the streets —and often violently.[24] The more advantaged urbanites, including university students, can almost literally afford to take the more empathic, tolerant, and autonomous "liberal" view.

Urban birth among the high-status adult sample was linked to only one orientation, but in that instance it did appear to have had a "liberalizing" influence—although the data do not strictly justify using causal language to describe this or any other association found. The link occurred on support for central authority (see Table 8.3). Members of the establishment born in cities were more solicitous of the interests of the regions than their colleagues born in the rural sector. This pattern suggests a process whereby persons closest to the countryside—the four-fifths of the adult elite who were born in rural areas—are "oversocialized" into the centralizing perspective of the capital city. Elite individuals born and raised in cities can apparently view the interests of the regions more magnanimously.

Table 8.4 Liberalizing "Effects" of Urbanization on Three Student Views

	Subsample Mean			
Orientation	*Rural (rural-born, rural-raised) N=1,035*	*Immigrant (rural-born, urban-raised) N=425*	*Urban (urban-born, urban-raised) N=760*	*Shift from Rural to Urban*
Eclectic religious tolerance	2.93	3.08	3.35	+.42
Support for empathy as a social priority	3.06	3.27	3.36	+.30
Support for deference to authority	2.55	2.42	2.28	−.27

Note: The causal term "effects" in the table title is necessarily in quotation marks, because no rearrangement of these data can actually generate the missing time dimension.

The data do not permit soundly empirical conclusions about the effects of the *process* of urbanization upon politically relevant opinion because they provide values for the dependent variable at only one point in time, whereas the hypothesis to be tested asserts change in opinions over time. But it is possible to approximate—albeit crudely—the time-series requirement by comparing students who were born and were raised in rural areas with students who were born in the countryside but migrated to the cities to be raised there, and these latter with students who were born and raised in the cities. Table 8.4 supports the expectation that the views of students in each category will be more "liberal" moving from the rural through the in-migrant to the urban group. Length of exposure to an urban climate is consistently associated with the "liberal" syndrome of greater tolerance toward alternative religious truths, more support for the related value of social empathy, and a less deferential outlook on authority.

If urbanization can be linked to certain "liberal" orientations among students, can the chain of inference from demography to politics be extended further to connect with actual behavior? Although it is impossible to know, for example, whether among the students surveyed support for deference to authority was inversely correlated with opposition to the government, independent evidence can be brought to bear at least suggestively on this question.

Since the break-up of the officer-student alliance that brought down Sukarno and the naming of Suharto as acting President in 1967, there have been actions in Djakarta by young people, including secondary and university students, against rising prices, against a Parliament seen as inactive, against corruption, against an election seen as coerced, and against a costly tourism-promotion project initiated by Suharto's wife and regarded as extravagant, to cite the more prominent examples. In Indonesia as elsewhere, cities and universities do tend to be associated with political protest. Why? At least three hypotheses suggest themselves.

Two of the three fall under the general heading of a status explanation, expanding that term now to include any status discrepancy whether drawn along primordial lines or not. They are the "job insecurity" hypothesis and the "ethnic outgroup" hypothesis. The third is an instance of generational explanation; it could be called the "counter-culture" hypothesis. The rest of this chapter will be devoted to these three differing accounts of political protest by educated urban youth.

The "job insecurity" hypothesis moves from demographic preconditions through economic conditions to political outcomes. It pictures too many students chasing too few positions and therefore turning in frustration against the authorities. The editors of the daily *Harian KAMI,* historically the major press organ of the '66 generation in Djakarta, articulated this approach in their February 24, 1972, issue when they interpreted youth protest as a "permanent feature of major cities like Djakarta, Bandung, Medan, and Surabaya," whose population growth rates—Djakarta's they estimated at 4 percent per year—were not being accommodated by any equivalent expansion in educational or employment opportunities. As a result of the 1950s baby boom, they wrote, young people—many of them insufficiently trained—were flocking to the job market and finding only disappointment there. No wonder the cities were turning into "crisis centers" of restless youth.

Even more disturbing are the 1971 census figures, which show that Djakarta has grown on the average by 5.7 percent annually since 1961 to reach a total 1971 population of 4.7 million.[25] Among those aged 15–19, about two-thirds are not in school and many of these are unemployed. According to the Minister of Education and Culture, only about one percent of the pupils in elementary schools reach higher education and more than two-thirds of those who drop out at the primary level do so because of their parents' poverty. The number of jobless young people in Indonesia is estimated to increase by 1.2 million every year.[26]

But do these figures necessarily translate into political opposition? A look at protest actions that have actually occurred casts several doubts on "job insecurity" as an exclusive explanation. First, whereas the hypothesis implies a potential for massive demonstrations by unemployed graduates and about-to-be-unemployed students, the protests of 1967–72 were typically undertaken by small ad hoc groups, sometimes involving only about five individuals. Second, the groups were generally led by occupationally secure persons. Third, their targets were so diverse that only an assumption of widely displaced frustration can link these actions primarily to a motivation as utilitarian and self-interested as unemployment or anticipated unemployment. And the cost of that inserted assumption is that it psychologizes and personalizes protests that at least appear to have been aimed at reforming government not in the interest of the job-seeking individual but in the interest of the nation as a whole. When the short-lived, self-styled "White Group" passed out leaflets in June 1971 urging citizens to exercise their right to abstain in the coming general election, they appear to have been acting in relation to some standard of free choice they felt was not being met, rather than from displaced personal frustration. Those in the ad hoc "Movement Against the Waste of the People's Money" who opposed Mrs. Suharto's tourism project apparently did so despite the fact that it would create employment and because they believed it to be a luxury Indonesia as a whole could not afford.

The second hypothesis emphasizes the disproportionately non-Javanese ethnic make-up of student protest leadership in Indonesia. Again the preconditions are demographic: rapid urbanization and a youth-skewed age distribution. But the intervening variable is ethnicity. Ethnically non-Javanese university students are said to come from cultural backgrounds where hierarchy and deference are less important than they are in Javanese social and political relations. Javanese culture, in part because it flows out of an aristocratic precolonial past and in part because it was bureaucratized by the colonial administrative state, is said to inhibit open criticism of elders by their juniors and of higher-status by lower-status individuals. Ethnically outer island students in Djakarta and Bandung are also physically further from parental constraints than are the Javanese. From this lesser or lessened inhibition against acting in opposition to superordinate authority figures and from the fact that in national politics those figures are mainly Javanese, the inference is made that ethnic outgroup students have been more available for protest leadership than have their Javanese classmates.

The ethnic skewness of protest leadership is not in question. Whereas ethnic Javanese constitute something over half the population of Indonesia and something over a third of the population of Djakarta, they account for only about 10 percent of the leadership of the Indonesian Students' Action Command (Kesatuan Aksi Mahasiswa Indonesia or KAMI) that opposed the Sukarno regime or of the leaders of the various groups critical of the present government.[27] Especially prominent among these individuals are Batak, Minangkabau, and Indonesians of Chinese and Arab descent. Suharto himself is said to have remarked on the absence of any Javanese names on a petition against corruption submitted to him by student representatives from the Javanese core city of Jogjakarta and to have been annoyed at their apparent insensitivity to the Javanese etiquette of respect for one's seniors. Several students reportedly commented in retrospect that it was accidental but fortunate that few Javanese students were in the vanguard of the student struggle of 1966, for otherwise the opposition to the Old Order would have been weakened by their more "feudal" attitude.[28] The "ethnic outgroup" hypothesis asserts that this disproportion was not accidental at all but a product of the more egalitarian background of the outgroups and their greater physical distance from whatever restraining effects their parents might have exercised.

At one level this hypothesis is plausible, but at another it is not. If the dependent variable it explains is the fact of ethnic skewness among youth protest leadership, it is reasonable. But if it is carried further in order to explain why the protests were launched, it is not. This distinction is crucial analytically and because of its meaning for Indonesian politics. If in fact the disaffection of non-Javanese among them has been a major reason for the student's opposition, then once again the fears of the 1945 generation, or at least its Javanese if not Javacentric elements, may be justified: that the student generation's "liberalism"—including the survey findings of the students' more decentralist and authority-critical stance reported herein —could split the nation. Or if it is true, as one foreign observer has concluded, that the predominantly Javanese and politically incumbent military elite in Indonesia is "strengthening Javanese social and political forces and persistently blocking the growth of the more modern, Western-oriented, non-Javanese elements of society," [29] and if it faces an ethnically non-Javanese student opposition to boot, then the outcome could be explosive.

Student political protest leadership in Indonesia may be ethnically skewed, but it is not, by and large, ethnic group-minded. Neither the student movement of 1965–66 nor the far more sporadic and smaller-scale flare-ups of more recent years have been ethnically motivated to any significant degree. Although ethnic sentiments, especially within regionally defined student organizations, do persist among university students in Indonesia, they are not important bases for political mobilization.[30] The issue of corruption, for example, which was raised in 1966 as well as 1970, implicates Javanese and non-Javanese members of the establishment alike. Of any control variable, ethnic intensity and identity were the only ones that had no significant impact whatever on student views and only a minor impact on the corresponding views of the establishment (Table 8.3). Finally, cross-ethnic acquaintance and friendship in Indonesian student circles—including, from admittedly subjective impressions, intermarriage—appear to be comparatively high and probably rising.[31]

If the political protest dimension of the status-generation gap is not satisfactorily explained either by job insecurity on the one hand or by ethnic outgroup status on the other, perhaps what is involved is a basic cultural shift: the internalization by young intellectuals in Indonesia of the value of criticism as a creatively moral act—reflecting the demonstration effect of youth protest in the West and the universality of the gadfly role—a value which then separates this group from a security- and development-minded establishment for whom change is something to be channeled and energies are above all to be harnessed.

This third hypothesis slights economic explanation and pinpoints an emerging "counter-culture" as the indispensable facilitating variable between the demographic facts of urbanization and youthfulness and the political fact of opposition. As the editors of *Harian KAMI* put it, in an editorial whose ironic tone merely exaggerated an empirical argument:

> Almost all the ringleaders of student activities, almost all young demonstrators in Indonesia as well as other countries, come from wealthy parents, have full bellies, fine clothes—because they do have a taste for the latest fashion—and a first-rate education. Hence they face a very bright material future. And yet they make trouble. Why? . . . Its impact may not yet be seen in Indonesia, but in Western countries the young people have generated a tremendous shift in cultural values. . . .[32]

If there is an emerging "counter-culture" among urban, educated youth in Indonesia, something of its shape is suggested by the writing of Arief Budiman, a young psychologist-author-activist who has become a key figure in the intellectual and political dissent of recent years in Djakarta and who was arrested and detained for 26 days in January–February 1972 for his opposition to Mrs. Suharto's proposed tourism project. A basic feature is the act of criticism itself:

> Will we allow the Suharto government to continue making mistakes without at least attempting to make it aware of them? Was not Sukarno toppled because nobody dared criticize his growing mistakes and because he himself did not like criticism? These two symptoms are the consequence of the fact that the function of criticism is not sufficiently developed in our political culture.
>
> —*Kompas,* December 30, 1971

One reason for the low receptivity to criticism in contemporary elite circles, Arief has argued further, is that the military—the mainstay of the New Order—is a vertically and centrally organized command organization which tends to see even the opposition as a mirror image of its own top-down, center-out self. Writing of his experience in detention, Arief recalled that his interrogators had

> asked how I had *instructed* the students to get out onto the streets [and demonstrate against the tourism project]. I said there is no

such word as "instruction" in our dictionary. We are individuals who think for ourselves. I cannot make them obedient with instructions just as I cannot obey anyone else's instructions. We can obey only the logic of our own thinking combined with our own conscience. I explained to [my interrogators] that . . . today's youth movement is a movement in which individuals are horizontally related as equals in worth and dignity. Smiling in disbelief, they continued to ask whom I had contacted so that even the regions would be aroused. [Demonstrations against the tourism project occurred in several regional capitals.] I also smiled, despairing.

At this point I realized that it was rather difficult for me to communicate with my interrogators. We live in completely different worlds. My world is the world of intellectuals and artists in which the living values are creative values. In this world it is taboo to obey an instruction whose truth we do not fully accept. My interrogators, however, live in a military world, in a tight cone-shaped organization. An order is an order. Do not act contrary to orders, do not defy them. Only the leadership has the initiative, subordinates are forbidden to have initiatives. And so on. Can these two worlds communicate with each other?

—*Horison,* February 1972 [33]

Arief does not feel he is opposing the Suharto government. On the contrary, he has said that he supports its efforts to develop the country and recognizes it as "far better than the previous regime." He also recognizes the need for stronger government in Indonesia. But "I do not agree that the government should be too strong. And I consider it my role to make criticisms." [34] From the standpoint of the military authority, criticism outside of official channels like Parliament means tension, and tension means instability. But from the point of view of young intellectuals like Arief, official channels are unsatisfactory because they tend to swallow criticism rather than facilitate an impartial response to it. Demonstrations do create tension but that can be a good thing because, as *Harian KAMI* put it on March 9, 1972, "tension is essentially the whip of development and progress."

Nor is Arief the only advocate of creative criticism. Individuation and the rejection of imposed conformities are exemplified in the purposely shock-effecting, cant-puncturing work of the young poet-actor-playwright W. S. Rendra, the leader of one briefly active group whose pretentious name—the *Gerakan Moril* (Moral Movement)—was intentionally ridiculed by its own acronym—GERMO (PIMP). The re-evaluation and even breakdown of old assumptions can also be seen in the figure of Nurcholish Madjid, a devout but independent Muslim student leader who has publicly renounced the goal of an Islamic state and has promoted discussions with other young Muslims of how Islam can in practice be made more humanistic.[35] Otherwise very dissimilar, Rendra and Nurcholish do share with Arief a critical spirit and a commitment to the autonomous search for answers.

The reaction of the authorities to the criticism directed against them has varied. Face-to-face meetings with students and young people have taken place, for example in Suharto's home during the campaign against corruption and later at a conference convened in Tjipayung expressly to understand the views on either side of the gap and if possible to narrow it. At the same time, demonstrations have been banned and demonstrators have been detained for questioning; in one instance, under uncertain circumstances, a youth protesting the tourism project was stabbed.[36] But neither in dialogue nor in confrontation has the politically incumbent generation shown much inclination to accept the ideas and least of all the styles of its young, urban, educated critics.

Spokesmen for the 1945 generation have tried unilaterally to close the gap by promoting their "own" values as they see them. But those values are often too general to serve as guides to concrete behavior, and the more purely symbolic they are the more their propagation becomes an exercise in rhetoric rather than in resocialization. In 1972 at an army seminar convened in Bandung to promote the "1945 values," for example, President Suharto said that the most important of them all was national independence, "the nation's highest honor and possession." [37] In 1945, national independence was indeed a basis for behavioral choice: To support it meant to join the revolutionary struggle; not to do so meant to opt out of that struggle. But twenty-seven years later it had a rather more abstract ring, and as an imperative to act its meaning was less obviously clear.

This stress on the value of national independence is, nevertheless, made with behavior-changing intent. Its proponents in the 1945 generation mean in part to warn the student generation not to ape Western ways, not to abandon or debase the nation's own cultural identity. Individuation and criticism are perceived to pose a threat to indigenous values of sensitivity to the group, submission to its consensus, and trust in its natural leadership. The students' "liberal" ideas—as President Suharto himself has called them [38]—are seen as originating abroad, in an economically advanced West that has thrown off so many limits on personal freedom that it is undergoing a severe cultural crisis from which the leaders of the 1945 generation would like, if at all possible, to spare their own nation.

Western influences are undeniably present. One student—born and raised in Jogjakarta and only two years old when the independence struggle ended—described himself on his questionnaire as a "100 percent liberal," quoted Thomas Jefferson and Adam Smith from memory, and wrote: 'I want to live like in the West. Rationally, Egoistically, Individualistically, Honestly, honoring *freedom*." But his is an extreme, rare case. In the demonstrations since 1968, symbols of Western youth protest have been taken out of context and used for purposes that bear little relationship to their original meanings. The singing of "We Shall Overcome" by young people in Central Java and the banner of "civil rights" unfolded by students in Bandung in 1970 after a fatal conflict with military cadets do not mean what they did to the movement for integration in the American south.[39] The fact that all these Western symbols are essentially optimistic also suggests the time-lag in their diffusion and the moderate-reformist outlook of their young importers in Indonesia.

In the final analysis, like its predecessors in this discussion, the third hypothesis of an emerging "counter-culture" is unsatisfactory as an exclusive explanation of the status-generation gap and student protest. In the first place, it probably exaggerates the uniformity and breadth of impact of what were after all the ideas and actions of only a tiny few. These protests were highly experimental and not obviously the thin end of any single larger wedge except in the very broadest sense of secularization. For there are at least two different cultures to which these actions and ideas ran counter: the official culture of the urban regime and the "traditional" culture of the rural masses, from both of which the young experimenters were isolated. The "counter-culture" hypothesis, furthermore, emphasizing as it does the force of ideas rather than circumstance—demographic, socio-economic, and political—underplays the role of personal motivation just as the "job insecurity" hypothesis overplays it. If the actions of 1968–72 were not purely self-interested, neither were the actors merely conforming to a new intellectual style. Prices had in fact risen (though not so precipitously as under Sukarno), corruption did exist, coercion did play a role in the government's smashing electoral victory, and the tourism project was estimated to cost over ten billion rupiah. The demonstrators were spotlighting as dramatically as they could what they felt to be genuine ills and wrongs.

The three hypotheses, like the broader status vs. generational modes of explanation they illustrate, are interrelated. None excludes the others. Even if the conditions of job insecurity were to be eliminated through some optimal mix of economic and demographic policies, a potential for generational conflict in the sense of distinctive historical experiences and values would still exist. The ethnic outgroup hypothesis least plausibly explains the status-generation gap today, but if existing high rates of demographic increase, influx, and maldistribution are not accommodated by even higher rates of impartial socio-economic demand-satisfaction, then primordial tensions could open an even more explosive gap tomorrow. And even if the "counterculture" is a passing phenomenon that will decline as its protagonists in Indonesia enter the mainstream or as the preoccupations of young exemplars in the West begin to change, there is still the possibility of a far more massively alienated and radically adversary culture growing up out of personal disillusionment and primordial suspicion as more and more applicants attempt to elbow their way past one another into proportionately fewer and fewer opportunities. These dire prospects are another way of saying that what threatens the regime and, more important, the future of Indonesia is not the status-generation gap but the political demography of that gap—the contexts of structural constraint and imbalance, for example, identified as crucial by the two status hypotheses of job scarcity and ethnic pre-eminence.

Viewed from this broader perspective, the status-generation gap itself is not a portent of major change. Urbanization and centralization have helped to shape the gap, but they have also generated city-village and center-region chasms that encapsulate and overwhelm it. As long as conflict between students and establishment remains a purely urban phenomenon, and assuming the establishment retains its monopoly of force, the status-generation gap will have few if any important system-wide political effects. Only insofar as students can break the official monopoly of force or extend their own political base will they ever present a serious threat to the government. At present, neither prospect is likely or even desired by the still basically reformist young critics of the regime, who appear to be more interested in voicing their consciences than in organizing a following.

But extrapolate the three hypotheses to their levels of maximum disruption: What if job insecurity intensifies and enlarges into job hunger that is felt clear up and down the slopes of the educational pyramid? What if the cities become even more products of rural "push" than urban "pull," so that in-migrants trying desperately to recapture primordial solidarities find themselves more and more often thrown against one another on the basis of those ties as competitors for increasingly scarce resources? And what if the "liberal" values of the student generation begin to spread through the villages? What would happen then?

Among these possibilities, the third one appears to be the least likely. Peasants are simply too far, physically and socially, from urban universities to be easily liberalized, let alone radicalized, by what goes on there.

This is why the talk among some of the government's military spokesmen about the need to seal off the villages from the contagion of "subversive" Western liberal culture that has already "poisoned" the cities and the universities seems so misplaced. The movement of ideas can be seen as a traffic pattern to be redirected, but it is more accurately viewed as a response to local experiences that give those ideas specific meaning and relevance. A policy of roadblocking as yet uncontaminated rural areas is misplaced even by its own rationale of inhibited opposition, for any major rural threat—itself highly implausible under present circumstances—is far less likely to be a movement of ideas than a thrust by concretely disadvantaged groups.

The status-generation gap in Indonesia is not a threat to the incumbent elite. It is an opportunity. It is an opportunity to re-evaluate the centralizing revolutionary paradigm of 1945 and to consider instead a decentralizing, redistributive paradigm for the 1970s—one that will better respond to the need for autonomous citizen participation in development, including political development, to the need for empathic understanding in a time of rapid social change, and to the need for an economic pie that not only grows faster than the mouths surrounding it but is resliced as it expands. These are the lessons of an holistic political demography of Indonesia's status-generation gap.

Chapter 9

Schooling, Youth, and Modernization in India *Cora Du Bois*

EDITORS' NOTE: This essay considers the sources of student disaffection and parental perplexity in the face of numerous incongruities within India's educational experience—between differing family, traditional, and modern norms, and between contradictory elements at the heart of the Westernization process. Geared to passing examinations and echoing the *chela-guru* relationship but without its human warmth and reassurance, the schools do not encourage the independent thought which an innovative, changing life requires, nor do they provide the skills necessary for remunerative jobs beyond the level of clerkship. College students lack paternal guidance, maternal succor, and—all too often—intellectual stimulation. No wonder, then, that students periodically erupt, often in ways quite consistent with the heritage of agitation of their fathers, the members of the independence generation.

These reflections sketch at least part of the challenge facing India's youth and educational system. In her more sanguine moments,

AUTHOR'S NOTE: Acknowledgment is gratefully made to the National Science Foundation Grants (no. 19713, G. S. 141, G. S. 1014), which permitted the writer to make repeated field trips to India between 1961 and 1972 and more specifically to the new state capital and immediately adjacent old temple town of Bhubaneswar in Orissa. The general intent of the enterprise was twofold; a study of the interaction between a new administrative town and a traditional sacred community on the one hand, and, on the other hand, the guidance of Ph.D. research for both Indian and American students.

Inevitably one is indebted to many persons in such an undertaking. The scholars, officials, and private citizens who gave so generously of their time and thought are too numerous to mention. Nor do they require such ancillary expressions of recognition. It is to just a few of the younger Indian and American colleagues that expressions of indebtedness need to be specified: Harish C. Das, Jyotish C. Acharya, Manamohan Mahapatra, Gagan N. Dash, Richard Taub, James Freeman, Susan Seymour, David Miller, and particularly in regard to this paper, Alan Sable.

Although acknowledgment is gratefully extended to all named and unnamed persons, they are in no way responsible for the interpretations offered here.

the author is profoundly impressed by the adaptability and discriminating selectivity displayed by so many Indians confronted with the pressures and opportunities of modernization.

Some General Considerations

This essay is based on the assumption that members of the youth cohort in South and Southeast Asia face problems that, while not unique to them, are nevertheless severe. These problems derive in part from the abrupt and sharp increase in their numbers that has followed the introduction of improved medical practices. It is also obvious that job opportunities are scarce for those who have more than primary schooling. The effects of these two phenomena, however, are intensified by other circumstances. These can be looked upon as congruencies and/or incongruencies between their family situations, their schooling experiences, and the multiple value systems that impinge upon them.

In any socio-cultural or political aggregate there are varying degrees of congruencies. In the nations of the so-called Third World, the political aggregates appear to be the least congruent and the least stable. The more incongruent political aggregates are in socio-cultural terms, the less stable they are as modern states.

In no society are incongruities absent. But one of the remarkable aspects of human beings is the capacity to keep many incongruities out of awareness. Some incongruities, whether in or out of awareness, are relatively innocuous. However, there are others, both in and out of awareness, that seem to precipitate conflicts at either or both institutional and psychological levels. It is a reasonable assumption that such conflict-breeding incongruities will be particularly salient in periods of rapid social and cultural change. We must also not forget that there may be important congruencies between former life styles and newly introduced institutions and values. Before proceeding to a preliminary exploration of such issues, it will be necessary to lay down some possibly idiosyncratic definitions.

"Traditional" versus "modern" is a loose and somewhat mindless dichotomy. Suggested processes are more useful than crude categorical dichotomies. In this essay, certain words will carry specific connotations. In reference to India, "traditional" will encapsulate over two thousand years of adaptation in a remarkably flexible society and absorptive culture (stereotypes to the contrary notwithstanding). The cut-off date for traditional, as I shall use it in this paper, is approximately 1900. The word "westernization" for India will designate the administrative (not the mercantile) period of British encroachment from approximately 1750 to the present. "Modernization" will be used for the adaptive absorption of Western influences associated with Indian politics and society since about 1920. The process of modernization, i.e., adjustment to recent external impacts, has obviously been greatly accelerated in India since independence. The word "contemporary" in what follows will be used as a neutral term with respect to the traditional, Westernizing, and modernizing processes that coexist in India today.

The interactions between traditionalism, Westernization, and modernization constitute our core concerns. But the concern must be further analyzed in terms of the congruities as well as the incongruities among these three processes. Limiting these core concerns to India and to the factors that we are dealing with in this conference, the following sequences of roughly ordered events can be identified.

Western administration courted the indigenous elites as instruments of their administrative and often indirect rule. This was a move congruent with the society into which the British were intrusive. To serve British administrative interests, the traditional elites were encouraged to acquire a Western education. This Western-educated elite, often with the highest motives, became a powerful instrument for implanting in India three dominant Western incongruities.

The first major influence was a humanist philosophy in which I include ideals of a democratic state, universal franchise, and parliamentary government. These ideals resulted in the Western-educated elite's formulation of the Indian Constitution with its heavy emphasis on a welfare state and egalitarian ideals. The second was a technology that has proved less humane than its proponents originally conceived. The third was national self-determination whose effectiveness is increasingly at variance with the growth of technology on a world scale.

It is these Western socio-cultural complexes, whose incongruities are now all too apparent in the West itself, that constitute the major Westernizing processes. India is now reacting to the internal incongruities adopted from the West and to the incongruities between the West and traditional India. It will be India's capacity to create new syntheses that will constitute the core of true modernization.

In my view, the sequence of the impact of such Westernizing influences on the modernization of India runs somewhat as follows. Western health and medical technologies, combined with humanistic ideals, have produced since 1930 massive absolute population increases. The government of India's efforts to cope with a growing and disparate population while instituting "welfare" and egalitarian reforms have spawned a sprawling mass of bureaucracies. With independence these were rapidly recruited and often ill prepared for the tasks assigned them. The ideals of a democratic state with universal franchise and parliamentary government have politicized India to a degree never before conceived. And again, as in the case of bureaucracies, this has led to political activities by persons often ill prepared by education or broad public responsibilities to exercise such functions. Finally, the Western ideal of national self-determination encouraged a variety of minor nationalisms as divisive in India as major nationalisms are in the world at large. That India has so far weathered as well as it has the difficulties engendered by the institutions and values adopted and adapted from the West is a remarkable tribute to its people, its society, and its culture.

In the effort to adopt and adapt to these Western complexes

and fit them to India's own complicated and diverse society and culture, Indians at almost all levels of society have viewed education as the key to unlock the dilemmas which face the nation and its individual citizens. From this point of view, education becomes an ancillary and not a primary factor in contemporary India. Possibly the greatest error is not to recognize that education is a dependent rather than an independent variable. The reason will become apparent in what follows.

Traditional Education

In India, education has long been honored and prized as a value in itself. Traditionally education was a privilege of elites. That it was also instrumental to power and prestige was not generally recognized. Today, among both traditional and Westernizing Indians, the value placed on education is explicitly phrased instrumentally. Also, the base line of accessible education has been broadened and facilitating institutions have multiplied, particularly at the primary and rural levels. Curricula too have altered —but perhaps not as much, particularly at the primary level, as some Indian and Western observers believe. One salient congruence, however, remains between the traditional and the contemporary modernizing view of education: It is "a good thing."

Let me use as an example the State of Orissa where my field inquiries have been centered. Orissa, by contemporary developmental standards, is generally considered traditional and backward. Yet traditionally education, even in "remote" villages of Orissa, was accessible to the upper castes and wealthier families —in other words, to elites. The institution rested on an occupational group, often hereditary, of literate teachers called *abadans. Abadans* were often, but not necessarily, Brahmins. They were hired for board and lodging plus minimal remuneration in kind and/or cash. They taught the three R's to the children of their patrons. Their status at transient hirelings vis-à-vis their patrons was what I suppose we would now call middle-class. The discipline, the curriculum, and the role of the teacher were not markedly different from the present government-sponsored, village primary schools. Usually a three-year course of rote learning was expected. Promising girls and clean caste boys were allowed to attend. But only promising high-caste boys, usually Brahmins, went on to further schooling. In the ideal traditional past, further education for boys was the apprenticeship of a youth (*chela*) to a teacher (*guru*). It is probable that this *chela-guru* relationship was always rare and highly elitist.

With the introduction of the British school system as we know that institution in the West, promising young people were sent off to English language schools. But such opportunities were limited, and education remained an elite prerogative.

Before going further, it is important to distinguish between traditional Indian (and Western) education on the one hand and schooling on the other. Basically education is a socio-cultural adaptive process acquired, or not acquired, through many channels of learning. Schooling is an institution concerned with the mastery of techniques which may, or may not, lead to education. Although this distinction is a purely heuristic device, and although facile dichotomies are more often than not suspect, it may be important to separate the two notions—particularly in India. It may be particularly important because in the West and in international census-taking there is too frequently an inclination to confuse education with literacy acquired in schools. Many illiterate Indian women, for example, were and are deeply versed in their society and culture, including traditional literature which was learned and transmitted orally. These women and often the men are highly educated, even if unschooled and illiterate. They have a profound influence in maintaining the continuity of Indian culture. They also frequently undermine the authority of contemporary schools and even of those fathers who see the future of their sons and daughters primarily in acquiring modern schooling. Sons of the most sophisticated Indians I have met—

sophisticated in the sense of Western schooling and exposure—are, nevertheless, able to move back and forth between these two world views with little apparent sense of incongruity or malaise. At first these transitions baffled me. Later I came to appreciate the intellectual capacities of persons who were free to operate in both the empiric, practical world of Western thought and the legendary, mythical world of Indian tradition. They present an enviable breadth of human perceptions. With greater or lesser degrees of awareness, they are transitional men who hold the key to the modernization of India.

There was, and is, another level of indigenous education that was traditionally of the greatest importance. Many priestly, commercial, and artisan castes of traditional India developed both educated and technically competent sons by the family apprenticeship system. Such sons might be minimally, or not at all, schooled, but they performed in hereditary occupations both the roles to which they were educated and the skills required of such roles. Even today in Orissa I have seen sons who were doing very well in expensive, private English-language secondary schools withdrawn by fathers if a prosperous business enterprise needed their services and skills.

It can thus be said that India had a traditional educational system which served to perpetuate both intellectual and practical preoccupations. The influences of this tradition have not yet been, and may never be, abandoned in favor of the Western school systems. The latter are appropriate for coping with the various levels required in the civil services and technologies introduced by Westernization. They do not supplant, nor in my opinion should they, the qualities of traditional Indian education. The Western school system, particularly at the higher levels, is adaptive, however poorly, to the technologies, bureaucracies, and national aspirations accepted from the West. But the modernization of India will rest on the ability to amalgamate its traditional education with its school system.

The Modern Schools

I shall make no attempt to describe the intricacies of the modern school system of contemporary India, which is exceptionally ornate and varied. Rather, I shall mention only some aspects that bear ultimately on youth and values. Essentially it is based on the system instituted during British rule and modified by later theories of centralization and channels current in Great Britain during the first half of the twentieth century.

Very briefly, and to that extent inaccurately, the schooling gradient is as follows: three years of lower primary, three years of upper primary, three to four years of secondary, and then college with an intermediate degree after two years and a BA on completing four years. State universities are administrative centers that control constituent colleges and also offer graduate training in the humanities, the social disciplines, the sciences; and they usually provide professional schools in law, medicine, and engineering. To this skeletal structure must be added a series of semi-autonomous and prestigious colleges and secondary schools that date from British and often missionary efforts. Both were, and still are, intended to educate primarily a Westernizing English-speaking elite.

There is also a plethora of more recent trade and technical schools, craft centers, special schools for tribal peoples, private schools sponsored by reformist groups, regional military schools supported by the central government, and regional teacher training and agricultural colleges.

Lastly, India has been sponsoring in recent years a large number of advanced institutes or centers that combine research and training in areas such as international affairs, linguistics, community development—*ad infinitum.* These are frequently, although not exclusively, staffed by Indian scholars who have had advanced training abroad or at home and who are too specialized to fit into universities or who find that appropriate university posts are already occupied.

With the possible exception of these institutes the dominant emphasis of this school system, from bottom to top, is to train students to pass examinations. The curriculum is centrally set by the state, and in colleges, at least, so are the examinations. Both teachers and students focus on answering possible examination questions based on prescribed texts.

In my observations, students take by preference only those courses which are geared to such examinations. Also students, by and large, float idly through a semester or year's classes and a week or two before the examinations have anxiety-ladened cramming sessions with or without special tutoring. Outside examiners are paid a fee for grading the papers of students they do not know. This obviates political and personal pressures on teachers but completely depersonalizes both learning and teaching.

Some Implications of Contemporary Schooling

The adoption and adaptation of a centralized Western European system of schooling in India warrant scrutiny as to congruencies or incongruencies with traditional Indian education and relevance for a modernizing (rather than a Westernizing) India. As I said earlier, education, even as schooling, was, and is, prized by most Indians but was, and is, largely accessible only to elite or upwardly mobile groups and individuals.

At the 3 R's level, the traditional *abadan* lived intimately with his students and their families. He was expected, quite literally, to beat discipline and diligence into his students. Today most parents still expect schoolteachers to inculcate discipline. Many Indian parents have said to me, "We are sending X to school to learn how to behave." The implication of such statements for the nature of familial relationships and family discipline are legion but would lead us into by-paths. For the moment it is the similarity with the traditional *abadan* system that I want to stress. In this respect old wine is being poured into new vessels.

However, there are also some marked changes. At the primary level the teacher no longer lives with the family nor is he in their employ. He is more often than not a stranger to the village and a state employee. His lot is not an easy one and in my field notes there is repeated evidence that he tends to hold himself aloof from village affairs—from motives of both discretion and status assertion.

At the primary level we encounter the first symptoms of the depersonalization that I believe pervades the contemporary schooling system in India. When one moved beyond the basic literacy of the 3 R's into the traditional Indian paths to education, two branches were apparent: rare *chela-guru* relationships on the one hand and the family-centered occupational apprenticeship on the other. The former, the *chela-guru,* was highly personalized but was discontinuous in the sense that the youth was separated from his family and authority was to a large degree transferred from father to *guru.* The family apprenticeship system provided a personalized and continuous educational trajectory with an assured occupational role at the end.

The trajectory in the contemporary school system presents no such discontinuities. The system *qua* system is continuous but impersonal. It is not congruent with family supervision or necessarily with occupational skills and assured employment. In this incongruity between occupational opportunities and family authority of the past and the contemporary school system lies a whole range of disaffections felt by both students and parents.

Speaking still at a primary and secondary level of schooling, I have heard parents complain repeatedly about the inadequacy of teachers and often with reason. The teachers at these levels are often ill equipped educationally; they are wretchedly paid and overworked; they are constrained by formal curricula requirements and pressure to pass their students; they are frequently strangers to, and suspect in, the communities in which they teach. Their disaffection is rife. But so also is the dissatisfaction of parents.

Parents consistently complain about the inadequacy of these schoolteachers. In upper caste or upwardly mobile families, either the educated father tutors his children or, when he can afford it, he hires tutors after school hours to compensate for what is, and is felt to be, incompetent preparation to move on to the next grade. Hired tutors may be themselves the classroom teachers, who thereby add to their inadequate incomes; or they may be young college graduates studying for civil service posts. The point is that hired tutors become employees of the family and in so being re-echo the traditional role of the *abadan* as a personalized family-controlled instructor. Whether a competent father or a hired tutor tries to compensate for the inadequacies of the contemporary school system is irrelevant. In the face of such inadequacies, either of the traditional modes of education, the *abadan* surrogate or parental apprenticeship, is resorted to.

Possibly the most interesting similarity between traditional education and modern schooling is that both are authoritarian and neither encourages independence, initiative, and innovation. The traditional education demanded submission to the authority of the father or *guru* but lent in return an assured personal concern and occupational role. The modern school system with its emphasis on examinations also discourages independent thought, initiative, and innovation. It also emphasizes the authority of the teacher, but it fails to provide an assured personal concern or train the student to an immediately relevant occupation.

Population Growth, Status, and Schooling

Although what has so far been said may not obviously be related to population growth, occupational diversities, and social status, these factors are, nevertheless, salient and new in the Indian scene.

It is a truism in public health circles that population growth results primarily from the reduction of infant mortality, producing several successive generations of increasingly numerous young people. This phenomenon in India as elsewhere in the Third World has taxed the traditional economy based on land and agriculture. At the national level the response has been to diversify the economy and to improve agricultural technologies. To the degree that agricultural technologies are successful, they may in the short run absorb rural youth by increasing the kinds of crops, by extending the lands used, and by cropping favorable lands two and even potentially three times a year.

In the past, population growth in India was met by internal migration. That this outlet still exists is suggested by the census estimates of the increasing number of villages. But we are learning that the underprivileged reproduce more prolifically than the privileged despite higher infant mortalities. This seems to be true whether the society is primarily industrial or primarily agricultural, and whether the populations are urban or rural. In India this leads to a disproportionate increase in unskilled labor. The low castes and the poor have no surpluses to risk on innovations. Nor does family occupational apprenticeship linked to patterns of family authority encourage innovations. The underprivileged rural poor either lag in adopting new technologies or go into debt through ill-understood and often ill-managed experiments with them.

It is this hard-pressed and unskilled surplus of India's men who drift into cities in the hope of employment for which they are rarely qualified. They turn to low-grade, underpaid industrial jobs that encourage inefficient, labor-intensive industries; or they turn to service occupations such as carting, rickshaw pulling, small foodstands—all of which constitute little more than taking in each other's wash. This is a factor in Indian urban deterioration that we have also seen in American cities in the last three decades. It is not my task to discuss urbanization. What I am trying to suggest is the rural roots of economic, status, and educational factors that help to create the urban glut in India.

The rapid expansion of the school system at all levels in India has, of course, been a remarkable achievement. Not only universities and secondary schools but village schools as well have shown a notable increase. However, the quantitative growth has been at the expense of quality and immediate relevance to the new technologies. As I have already said, primary and secondary schoolteachers are often undereducated, underpaid, and alien to the village in which they teach. They assume the aloofness that characterizes petty bureaucrats in many parts of the world. These features contribute to the wastage in primary schools that is one of the serious economic and human costs in the contemporary school system of India.

It is estimated that three years of primary vernacular education is required to gain a minimal working knowledge of the 3 R's in Indian vernaculars. But this elementary and limited literacy tends to disappear unless put to constant use—which, of course, it is not by most individuals of lower caste and class.

For the lower castes, attendance in village and town primary schools is sporadic. If my figures for Bhubaneswar are correct, 50 percent of those enrolled in the first grade do not complete the third grade of lower primary. Further, even free schooling is costly for poor families if only in providing the clothing required for children: shorts and shirts for boys and cotton frocks for girls. For example, in one special primary school for tribal children, attempts to encourage attendance were made by the Welfare Department by providing first-year students with the necessary clothes, slates, etc. The first-year enrollment in that school was commensurately large, but the drop-out rate in the next two years of the lower primary was almost 100 percent.

To sum up: at least in relatively traditional areas like Orissa, the families of lower castes or impoverished classes will subscribe in the abstract to the desirability of schooling. Like all other Indians they see it as a possible avenue to occupational opportunities—particularly in the lowest class of government service. However, in practice, they are not inclined to push their children to complete even the primary grades.

Turning now to upper castes: again in Orissa at least, two castes, the Brahmins and Karans, are outstanding in their tradition of education and in their adoption of modern schooling. The Karans, originally reputed to be Sudras and scribes, now compete in Orissa with Brahmins in the upper ranks of the civil service, which are largely staffed by these two castes. In the case of Brahmins or assimilated Brahmin temple servants, an interesting split occurs in the realm of education. Usually one Brahmin son is designated to maintain the traditional temple duties, thereby retaining the perquisites of office and of pilgrim services. The modern schooling of those sons is frequently no more than is required for the discharge of their traditional roles or for additional occupations such as shopkeeping or money lending. They are, however, still educated through the family apprenticeship system in traditional religious ritual and services. Other sons, usually younger ones, are sent to modern schools with the expectation that they will enter Western or modern employments. From a family's point of view this may be an astute way to cover one's bets. But it is not one that tends to consolidate ties between brothers. The Karans, usually having few vested interests in land and none in religious foundations, have steadily improved their position vis-à-vis Brahmins in the modern sector of Orissa.

A third caste, the Khandayats, claims to have a higher status than the Karans in India's traditional four-tiered *varna* caste stratification system. They are predominantly small landholders. Traditionally, land and houses have been, and continue to be, prized both as status symbols and as desirable investments. The Khandayat families are, therefore, unwilling to enter the modern or Western occupational sector until they are assured that these lands will be well managed and retained in the family. Like the Temple Servants, the oldest son is usually assigned this task while the younger sons are given various degrees of modern schooling.

Aspirations, Occupations, and Education

What has already been said clearly indicates that schooling is widely held to be a positive value, but in contemporary terms it is seen as an avenue to the newer occupations provided by Westernization and modernization. Particularly esteemed are office jobs, even when they are at the lowest level of either private or public bureaucracies. They are considered to have higher status —even when the earnings are no greater than in traditional occupations. The appeal is that common to "white-collar" jobs. But an additional appeal is a steady cash income in an economy that is increasingly based on a money exchange and a market that provides more and more seductive, if shoddy, gadgets.

This combination of new occupations that promise to provide white-collar status, regular wages, and the increasing availability of tempting manufactured goods serves as a quite direct stimulus to the schooling of children at all levels of society. To the extent that such opportunities are present in various localities, school attendance increases. However, these opportunities are balanced against the possible loss of traditional economic resources. Where such resources exist, at least two surviving sons—one for the traditional and one for the modern sector of the economy—are thought to be highly desirable.

From the point of view of middle-class households that have no traditional vested interests and where any surpluses can be invested in the schooling of sons, such traditional restraints are not operative and even a single son can be viewed as an economic asset. In such cases a single son may be asked to bear crippling economic burdens that involve responsibility not only for the care of aged parents but also for the dowry of his sisters. I have seen several such young men whose promising careers were crushed by such burdens.

This paper is not focused on household economies nor directly on the intricacies of birth control programs in India, but the implications of what I have just proposed indicate that there are important practical concerns to be explored in a nexus consisting of household economics, status shifts, and family planning. Since I am persuaded that Indians are as practical and worldly in these matters as any people I have encountered, I am inclined to think these micro-social factors more important than the frequently cited opposition to family limitations phrased in terms of having enough sons to assure the death rites of the parents.

So far I have said little about the modern schooling of girls. Without exception girls are expected to marry. At the most Westernized and professionalized levels, girls with any aptitude are encouraged to go through the university and prepare themselves for a profession. Fathers often express a preference for medicine and teaching. The reasons given are that these professions may be practiced wherever their husbands may be posted.

Even when hypergamy is not formally institutionalized, most fathers want to marry daughters up the class (and if possible caste) hierarchy. This means negotiating a marriage with a "schooled" youth who appears to be on his way to a promising career in the modern sector. The girl must, therefore, also be schooled enough to be congenial to such a husband. Needless to say, these aspirations are not always realized. But they guide fathers in providing education for their daughters commensurate with their hopes for a hypergamous marriage. On the whole, however, women's schooling is inferior to that provided for men. Furthermore, wives are still expected to adjust to the demands of their mothers-in-law. As a result, women exercise a conservative, and often markedly traditional, force in raising children, which may be at variance with the aspirations of modernizing fathers.

When asked for preferred occupations for their sons, middle- and upper-class fathers were saying in the 1960s: engineers, doctors, and civil service (in about that order). Engineers are seen as possible employees not only in government but particularly in large foreign and domestic enterprises whose beginning wage scale and opportunities for advancement are presumed to be preferable. Medicine is also perceived as a skill that provides the choice between government and private practice, with urban private practice preferred over government posts. The profession of law, which was so popular in the first decades of the twentieth century, is now rarely mentioned. The civil service, which under the British was considered highly desirable, has slipped down in the ranking of paternal aspirations for their sons. This reflects the general downgrading of the civil service since independence when government and educational bureaucracies were rapidly enlarged with the attendant increase in numbers and decrease in quality as well as the increase in regulatory red tape, frustrations, and corruption. In some cases, of course, the opportunities for corruption may be an incentive. This is an inducement by no means limited to India.

There is, then, a flexible gradient that fathers may express as aspirations for their sons. How the gradient is perceived depends not only on the status of the father himself and on his best estimate of changing occupational opportunities but also on his desire to perpetuate family interests in property and in traditional occupational perquisites. Good housing and land remain important values. Upward mobility at least within the class structure and between castes is not a new idea in India. But the growing population and inflation make the task of fathers in guiding their sons' future far from an easy or obvious one.

Some Possible Sources of Student Disaffection

There are undoubtedly many reasons for student disaffection in India. Some are economic and political. But I shall limit myself to those more directly concerned with contemporary schooling, particularly at the college and secondary level.

So far I have stressed paternal decisions about the amount of schooling their children should receive and the occupational goals for which they should strive, because paternal guidance and authority remain strong in Indian families. Even when fathers pay lip service to letting sons choose their own careers, the expectations are clear and the choices are limited. Inversely and revealingly, a still unpublished study by Alan Sable shows that drop-outs are sons of fathers who do not take an interest in their sons' schooling. The full extent of paternal dominance is apparent when one comes to know at least some college students well and can break through the stereotypic answers they think are required of them. Acquiescence in parental wishes is explicit not only in schooling but also in many other aspects of life. Leeway for divergence from such wishes is extremely narrow without precipitating dramatic disruption of family ties, which in India are not easily flouted.

But there is cognitive dissonance in all this. While fathers may insist on higher education, sons have heard and experienced the parental dissatisfaction with the quality of both the school system and its teachers. Young men see themselves held to an educational system which is disprized—however much education in the abstract is valued. Moreover, sons have all too often heard educated fathers complain of the difficulties and dissatisfactions they themselves face in their occupations. Parenthetically, the degree to which Indians and Indian media are outspokenly critical of their institutions is striking—even to Americans who are also outspoken in these respects.

The investment, both emotional and economic, of fathers in the schooling of their sons is highly personalized. I have heard many fathers say that they have no savings for their old age except the investment they have made in their sons' education. The implications are inescapable. The son is expected to succeed in terms set by his father's sacrifices and to provide for his parents, and often for his brothers and sisters, in return for the privilege of education.

Yet the school system through which Indian youth is moving is, as we indicated earlier, highly depersonalized. There is nothing that links the immediate and personalized authority of the father to the depersonalized authority of the school. Furthermore, most youths have been sent to other areas for a college or university education. They are removed not only from the immediate supervision of the father but also the nurturing warmth of mothers, grandmothers, and sisters—all of which are traditionally affectionate relationships that tend to cater to young men. In most schools, facilities for both board and lodging are meager. This is to be expected in a poor nation bent on a massive increase not only in schooling but also in other developmental and humanistic enterprises. For the individual student, the actual austerities, which he may also have faced at home, are in the college context regarded as hardships—precisely because of the impersonality of these relationships. A repeated theme in conversation with men who left home to attend school is the deprivations, particularly in food, that they experienced as students.

I suspect that the majority of Indian college students experience this sense of deprivation. Whether or not they are able to express it, they also experience a loss of immediate paternal authority and maternal succor with no compensating parental substitutes, few intellectual challenges, and considerable uncertainty as to their occupational future. This experience is intensified by little training for individualism and autonomy in early childhood. It is hardly surprising, therefore, that students make every effort to go home over the many long holidays that break into the academic year and that they extend these long breaks even further with excuses of illness—either their own or illness in the family. It is also not surprising that such students are easy prey to local politicians who befriend them for ends that are frequently unscrupulous.

There now enters another intimate and personalized factor in the life of college students which I did not recognize until I had observed serious rioting precipitated by students. Let me briefly sketch the circumstances of this case and the explanations offered.

In this instance student-led riots resulted in serious disruptions. Before order could be restored by martial law and curfews, the disorder had spread to most of the state, a factory was burned, houses of the highest officials were looted, and some officials stoned. The State Assembly was closed for ten days and the University for a month. The precipitating factor was a quarrel between a bus conductor and a student over the payment of a fare. The remarkable thing was the speed with which crowds gathered, rumors spread, and issues multiplied. Young leaders invaded local colleges and secondary school classrooms to recruit support. A villager who received a minor stone bruise was reported killed by the police. This rumor quickly enlisted the nearby villagers, who had no concern with students and were ignorant of the immediate cause for disorder but who saw in arson and looting an opportunity for excitement and booty.

In terms of student-provoked disorders in India the disturbance I saw in Bhubaneswar was trivial. In discussing the matter with poised and neutral Indian observers, I commented on the effectiveness with which students marshaled crowds, encircled and immobilized police, cut telephone wires, built road blocks that cut off the fire department, co-opted trains, and terrorized the legislators. The explanation given was persuasive. The paternal generation of this 1960 student group were the heroes of the anti-British, independence movement. They were skilled in techniques of disruption. Imprisonment was an honor. With independence many of the men who participated in the "Quit India movement" became admired and powerful political and administrative leaders, while those who held office under the British were subjected to career discriminations.

Sons not only had learned the techniques of anti-government opposition from their fathers but had heard it praised and had seen it rewarded. A new and valued tradition of active opposition to an impersonal authority was created in the struggle for independence. And as we know, traditions in India have considerable durability.

We have again a certain incongruity. The concerned parental authority should not be flouted; but the impersonal authority of institutions is fair game. When conflicting messages are received with attendant rewards or punishment, some individuals take refuge in dissociation.

Of course, as in other countries, only a small percentage of students assume leadership in disorders, but the disorders they precipitate seem to resonate not only among students but in many segments of a population caught in the incongruities between and within Westernizing values, habits, and institutions on the one hand and the traditional ones on the other hand. Such dissociations have been manifest repeatedly in the course of history and in widely varied societies. They occur not only when changes are abrupt but also when they are so rapid as to take place in the course of decades rather than generations. It is the price paid for what nineteenth-century Euro-American theorists and power elites optimistically called "progress." The targets for disorderly protest will be institutions that require the most stringent individual readaptations. Although such attacks are often initially mindless and self-defeating, they sometimes serve the purpose of individual learning and ideological readjustment—even among politicans.

Envoi

After-the-fact analyses are always easier than predictions. On the other hand, there is virtue in learning from past and comparative experiences. If India is to modernize, in my sense of the word, namely to amalgamate constructively its traditional past with Western stimuli and the problems they have precipitated, its leaders must henceforth select and adapt with more insight the Western values and institutions that serve their ends. Like organ transplants in modern surgery, the system must be able to tolerate the new organ or the patient will die—however skillful the operation.

In sanguine moments I sense that this discriminating selection is underway, certainly at least in India. The imitative Westernized Indian elite that struggled to achieve independence and to establish a new nation is being supplanted because of death and political pressures. The thousands of Western advisers who knew little of India and whose vision was rarely broader than their technical specialties are in decreasing favor. This does not imply a retreat into isolation. Indian scholars abroad are more numerous and more variously exposed to different societies and different disciplines than ever before. Those who opt out and stay abroad can be discounted; but many more return. As individuals they may reflect the discontent of transitional men. But, *pari passu,* they will, as a group, if not always as individuals, aid in the difficult task of providing Indian culture with a viable, modern, and more congruent society. This will not be quickly achieved, and not by slavish imitations or by foreign advisers. Only Indians could achieve that country's independence, and only Indians can, in my sense of the word, modernize it. Among other things, this will require serious re-scrutiny, and possibly even a slowing down, of its university system as well as raising the quality and relevance of its primary and secondary schooling.

Chapter 10

Youth Protest in Sri Lanka (Ceylon) *W. Howard Wriggins and C. H. S. Jayewardene*

EDITORS' NOTE: This analysis of the effort of a segment of Sri Lanka's youth to seize power by direct assault in April 1971 demonstrates the complexity of the relationship between demographic changes and a dramatic political event. The paper examines Ceylon's rapid rate of population growth; the moderate increase in the proportion, but sharp increase in actual number, of young people in the population; and the mutually reinforcing educational and political processes that are changing traditional values and rapidly inflating the expectations of the young.

These changes are contrasted with the stagnating economy: the lack of sufficient structural change and the worsening trading position of what was recently a prosperous country. Ceylon's economic troubles have contributed to an extremely high rate of unemployment, particularly among the educated.

But none of these demographic, social, or economic conditions in themselves—either separately or in combination—would have "produced" the political events under review. Dynamic political leadership exploited these cumulating difficulties to mobilize a daring and desperate band of youths willing to take unprecedented risks on behalf of an almost magical faith in the one-day revolution.

On April 5, 1971, in many localities in Sri Lanka, groups of young people attempted to seize police stations and major government buildings, precipitating a "youth rebellion" without precedent in Sri Lanka or Southern Asia.[1]

With a miniscule army and a small, scattered police force, the authorities tackled the dispersed points of resistance. After several weeks of bitter strife and intense government patrolling, thousands of activists were captured, others went into hiding in Ceylon's more inaccessible jungle areas, and many who were less involved turned themselves in. Over 1,000 deaths were reported, and some 14,000 young men remained in internment a year later, although large-scale releases began in the spring of 1972.

On the surface, it would appear that demographic changes were at the heart of the matter. Compared with a number of countries in South and Southeast Asia, Sri Lanka experienced rapid population growth, particularly in the late 1940s and up to the early 1960s. In an area the size of West Virginia, the population had doubled since 1947 and in 1970 was over 12 million. It is commonplace in the literature to note the abrupt change in Sri Lanka's rate of population growth in 1947 following the introduction of a nationwide DDT program to control malaria. To the extent that this acceleration in the growth rate resulted from a sharp decline in infant mortality, one could hypothesize an abrupt increase in the size of successive youth cohorts. Since the beneficiaries of these public health innovations in the late 1940s would, by 1971, be 24 years old and under, and the bulk of activists arrested in 1971 were also in that age group, a startlingly direct relationship could be adduced.

As this paper demonstrates, however, the picture is actually much more complex, demographic change being but one of several significant variables. While our analysis generally confirms the significance of the rise in sheer numbers in the youth age groups, we conclude that this in itself was by no means sufficient to produce such violent and dramatic political consequences. Population growth, compounded by other social, political, and institutional changes; a slow pace of economic growth; and a rapid expansion of the educational and communications systems combined to put great pressure on the political system and provided both the raw materials and the incentives needed by political activists to mount their protest movement.

General Background

The Demographic Setting. Demographic data on Sri Lanka are more accurate than in any other country in the area and show unambiguously that since independence, it has experienced a severe population increase. The mortality rate has dropped sharply, while only since 1960 have fertility rates begun to decline.

In 1945 and 1946, the government undertook measures to correct dietary deficiencies that had become apparent during the closing years of World War II. In 1947 Ceylon began to use DDT in a house-to-house and environmental spraying campaign to control malaria.[2] Expenditures in other areas of public health and medical care nearly trebled between 1948 and 1968. Mortality data demonstrate the remarkably sustained effect of these policies. For example, the crude death rate, averaged for the five years preceding 1946, was 20.7 per thousand; for the five years after 1946 it dropped to 13.1. By 1960 the crude death rate had dropped to 8.6. In the meantime, however, the crude birth rate remained relatively stable, moving downward only 2 points in the course of half a century from an average of 38.6 per thousand for the five years 1900–5 to 36.5 for the five years 1955–60. These trends together caused Sri Lanka's population to double in twenty-five years.[3]

The rate of natural population growth for the period 1942–70 reflects the same phenomenon.[4]

1942	1.8	1952	2.8	1962	2.7
1943	1.9	1953	2.9	1963	2.6
1944	1.5	1954	2.6	1964	2.5
1945	1.4	1955	2.7	1965	2.5
1946	1.8	1956	2.7	1966	2.4
1947	2.5	1957	2.6	1967	2.4
1948	2.7	1958	2.6	1968	2.5
1949	2.7	1959	2.8	1969	2.2
1950	3.0	1960	2.7	1970	2.1 (est.)
1951	2.8	1961	2.8		

This series underlines the dramatic change between 1946 and 1947, for which malaria control is usually given the credit. Its role, however, should not be exaggerated: only a portion of the island was affected by malaria, and the first change in the rate of population growth was recorded a year before the malaria program was well established.[5]

To be sure, birth rates began to decline in the 1960s and by 1969 were estimated to be of the order of 30.5, down 6.2 per thousand in eight years. Later marriages and to some extent the practice of various forms of contraception appear to be the main causes of the decline. But there are now so many women of child-bearing age that the actual number likely to be added to the population during the next two decades may well result in a population of 20 million by the year 2000.

An analysis of the changing age composition of the population shows that the sudden increase in the rate of growth did not produce a massive youth cohort such as Keyfitz found in Indonesia. The overall population increase was a result of reduced mortality among older people as well as among infants. The postwar birth rate did not rise as markedly in Sri Lanka as in Indonesia, which had suffered such enormous social and political disruptions as a result of Japanese occupation and the protracted war of independence. All age groups increased, though admittedly the younger ones grew somewhat more rapidly. For example, during the decade 1950-60, the proportion of the population 25 years of age and younger rose from 56 percent to 60 percent.[6] This increase of 4 percentage points in a decade does not in itself seem enough to precipitate severe political dislocations. But should it continue for a second decade, major difficulties might be expected. Indeed, there are some indications of this already. Thus the proportion of the population 0–4 years old was reported as 12.9 percent in 1946 and also in 1953, confirming that the jump in population growth after 1946 was not concentrated mainly in the youngest age group. But by 1963, the 0–4-year-old group had increased ten times as fast as the 0–25-year-olds, representing 16.2 percent of the total population. This is a much more marked increase in that five-year age group than has been noted before. This large cohort is now entering the 9–13-year-old group and in another five years will be between 15 and 19 years old. It had not yet entered the politically active years and therefore had no role in the 1971 events. But very soon one can expect a much larger youth cohort which will create greater strains unless its needs are more effectively met than were those of its predecessor.

While the proportion of the 25-and-under age group has not shown an abrupt increase since 1946, their actual number has grown substantially, adding considerably to the burdens of the employed population. In 1946 there were 3.8 million under 25; by 1955, 4.9 million; by 1963, 6.5 million; and in mid-1968, 7.2 million.[7] By 1973 it is estimated that there will be between 8.25 and 8.5 million in this age group. This represents an increase of 125 percent in twenty-seven years: over twice as many mouths to feed, young people to educate, and jobs needed to absorb them.

The political significance of such proportionate and absolute numerical changes depends on a number of variables. First, the political consequences would be affected by the expectations of the new youth cohort. These in turn would be related to expectations associated with schooling during the past decades, the effects of expanding schooling opportunities on traditional norms, and the ideas and expectations engendered by the curriculum itself. Expectations could also be affected by non-curricular influences from political life and the mass media. Second, the harmony or incongruity between these acquired expectations on the one hand and the socio-economic reality of social relationships, job opportunities, and adult roles accessible to young people on the other would be crucial in contributing to their sense of grievance, or, as Ted Gurr has spelled out, their perception of "relative deprivation." [8] Third, their reaction to this sense of grievance will be affected by the political alternatives they perceive to be available. Finally, these in turn will be affected by how specific leadership groups and activists go about the task of organizing for political action against or in support of the incumbent regime.

In the absence of detailed data from interviews with the activist students, many dimensions of this paradigm cannot be filled in on the basis of hard evidence. However, a number of observations can be made after a brief review of the dramatic political events we seek to understand.

The Immediate Political Events. Evidence of growing preparation for widespread conspiratorial and violent action had reached the UNP government as early as 1969, and a number of the leaders were arrested some time earlier; but they were released from prison as a result of normal legal processes by the new Bandaranaike government following the May 1970 election. Fortunately for the government—and to the disadvantage of the would-be revolutionaries—a well-coordinated attack on the American Embassy in March 1971 further alerted the security forces to the possibility of an ambitious program of violent direct action. This effort appears to have been organized by a disgruntled, breakaway faction opposed to those who precipitated the action in April. Nevertheless, it gave the authorities an opportunity to move. Arms caches were uncovered including substantial quantities of home-made bombs and weapons in university dormitories. Some 300 young people were arrested.[9] But the timing and extent of the major onslaught appears to have taken the government by surprise when it actually occurred in early April. Although attacks on several police stations took place one night too soon, providing additional warning, over 80 police stations were assaulted simultaneously, a number of major government buildings invested, and several towns were in effect held by the activists.[10]

All of the action occurred in Sinhalese Buddhist areas. Indian and Ceylon Tamils, Hindu, Christian, and Muslim minorities did not participate. Nearly all the young men and women involved were between 18 and 25. They were acting out the

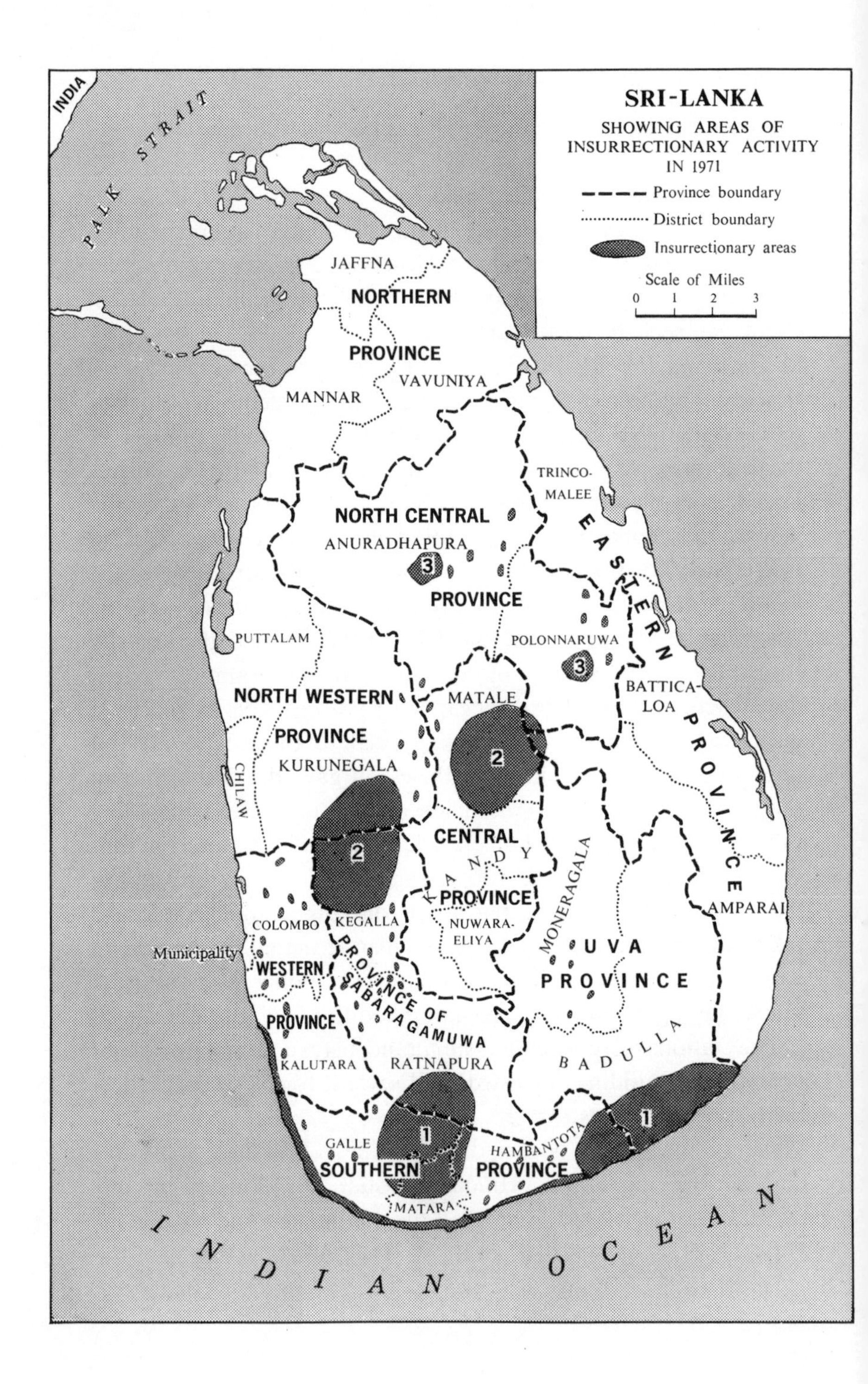
SRI-LANKA
SHOWING AREAS OF
INSURRECTIONARY ACTIVITY
IN 1971
Province boundary
District boundary
Insurrectionary areas
Scale of Miles
0 1 2 3
INDIA
PALK STRAIT
JAFFNA
NORTHERN
PROVINCE
VAVUNIYA
MANNAR
TRINCO-
MALEE
NORTH CENTRAL
ANURADHAPURA
PROVINCE
EASTERN PROVINCE
PUTTALAM
POLONNARUWA
NORTH WESTERN
PROVINCE
MATALE
BATTICA-
LOA
KURUNEGALA
CHILAW
CENTRAL
KANDY
PROVINCE
MONERAGALA
AMPARAI
COLOMBO
KEGALLA
NUWARA-
ELIYA
Municipality
WESTERN
PROVINCE
PROVINCE OF SABARAGAMUWA
UVA
PROVINCE
KALUTARA
RATNAPURA
BADULLA
GALLE
HAMBANTOTA
SOUTHERN
PROVINCE
MATARA
INDIAN OCEAN

revolutionary direct-action slogans of left-wing rhetoric that had been the stock in trade of many of the self-proclaimed Marxists then serving in the government the young people were trying to overthrow. Mao, Ché Guevara, and Kim Il Sung appear to have inspired them, though members of the movement did not refer to themselves as "Ché Guevarists." Students, many of them unemployed, and numerous low-level civil servants, including rural schoolteachers, appear to have been most active. The areas most affected were the Matara and Galle districts of Southern Province, Kurunegala in Northwestern Province, Kegalla in Sabaragamuwa Province, and the agricultural colony areas of Polonnaruwa and Anuradhapura, as shown in the accompanying map. It seems clear that the young people in these areas were more directly involved than were those of the more "modernized" Western Province, although it is probable that a number, though by no means all, of the leaders came from the capital.

The warning signs had all been there. With the benefit of hindsight, Sri Lanka's leaders could perceive growing impatience with the pedestrian pace of change under previous governments, whatever shade of Socialist they might have called themselves. Annual student protests at the University of Ceylon had been taking on a tougher, more radical tone. In the mid-1960s militant students occupied administration buildings and attempted to pressure administrators to improve library facilities and provide better hostel arrangements and smaller classes. The confrontation had seemed to administrators to be so serious that in a determined bid to deter a repetition in the future they called in the police. This sparked a minor battle resulting in the injury of 101 students and 30 policemen. There were a number of confrontations between the students and the administration thereafter, but none was permitted to run its logical course. No sooner would a strike begin than the university administration closed the universities, declaring the premises out of bounds. There were also confrontations at the less prestigious Vidyalankara and Vidyodaya universities near Colombo. Much of this student activity was shrugged off as part of the tradition of student radicalism in the protected—and not quite serious—environment of the university, not unlike the tradition of irresponsible rhetoric at the Oxford Union.

A Tradition of Student Protest? Of course, student protests were not new in South Asia, although student violence in Sri Lanka had been rare. In undivided India, there has been a notable tradition of student involvement in politics since the days of the independence movement. After independence they continued their political involvement, often with encouragement from political organizers of all persuasions, including the ruling Congress Party, to the dismay of university administrators and leading Cabinet members.[11] In Korea, students had been instrumental in challenging the legitimacy of the Syngman Rhee regime, dramatizing its failures to the point where the old man had to step down. Student protest in Turkey also had contributed to the downfall of the government of Adnan Menderes in 1960.[12] The end of Sukarno's rule in Indonesia had been accelerated by widespread student protests. But in Ceylon there had been no such dramatic demonstrations of solidarity or vaulting political goals among young people. Since independence, student university politics had been a close reflection of national politics, each party finding that a group of students formed a student wing which sought to demonstrate "their" party's national strength by the victories they won in campus elections. To be sure, it was usually followers of the Marxist parties that contested most vigorously and won most of the elective posts. Much of the rhetoric called for revolutionary action. But electoral politics were an accepted part of university life and tended to confirm the notion that Sri Lanka's youth were becoming increasingly identified with open, competitive democratic practices, with violence flaring up only occasionally in the heat of campaigning.[13]

The resort to violence in 1971 was all the more unexpected because until then students had participated actively in constitutional politics outside the university. They had usually assisted the opposition at election time before the franchise was lowered to age 18 in 1960. Their activities had mainly been restricted to helping to organize voters against the party in power. Thus, in 1956 many students had actively supported Mr. S. W. R. D. Bandaranaike's Sri Lanka Freedom Party (SLFP) against the incumbent conservative United National Party (UNP).[14] In 1960 the UNP, then in opposition, ran with substantial student backing. Some students supported the UNP once more in 1965 against the incumbent SLFP. In 1970, when the UNP held office, thousands of students enthusiastically backed Mrs. Bandaranaike's opposition party, contributing to her sweeping victory. This time, however, young people who formed the Janatha Vimukthi Peramuna (JVP) expressed support for the Bandaranaike government but warned the Prime Minister that this very active element in her youthful support would turn against her if she did not promptly carry out her ambitious election pledges.

In a remarkable acceleration of the normally rather casual Ceylonese sense of time, this radical element gave her barely a year to fulfill her many promises. And when her efforts failed to satisfy them, they tried to overthrow her by direct action.

Overview of Violence

Personality Stereotypes and the Level of Public Violence. A violent eruption such as Sri Lanka experienced is more likely to occur in a society that stresses individual assertiveness and aggressiveness or has a history of revolution, such as inspired French students in 1848 and in 1968 at Nantes and the Sorbonne. Indeed, there is a sharp contradiction between the 1971 youth rebellion, pre-planned, secretive, and seeking radical change for the future, and the widespread stereotype that characterizes the Ceylonese as affable, easygoing, accepting whatever comes and rarely making a sustained effort to achieve a goal.[15] Explanations for these attributed characteristics vary widely. Oscar Lewis, writing about "the culture of poverty," holds that it induces a kind of short-run hedonism, transcending regional, urban-rural, and even national differences.[16] Ceylonese are often said to share some of these tendencies. The climate is humid and monotonous: temperatures, along the coast at least, vary only slightly throughout the year and do not provide the stimulus to activity that sharp seasonal differences provide in more temperate climates. Theravada Buddhism teaches the transitoriness of this existence and of all worldly objects; non-desire and detachment are commended.

Even these stereotypes, however, are flawed. Sri Lanka is a multi-ethnic society; its people follow four main religions; and weather and natural conditions differ. It has long been apparent to observers that different ethnic groups often approach their life problems in different ways.[17] Thus, the Sinhalese people, living in the more salubrious south, have been characterized as lazy, with little interest in hard work and investment now in hope of a better future. The Ceylon Tamils, on the other hand, living in the more arid north, are conditioned by a culture demanding sustained, disciplined effort for survival. They are said to be more industrious and keenly interested in education for their young people so they can obtain the government employment and therewith the income to maintain a respectable standard and style of living.[18]

However, these stereotypes have not remained fixed along ethnic lines. Training in British-type schools before independence could be seen to have developed in the children of both ethnic groups similar standards of achievement, of application to duty, and of thought for the morrow—a parallel association of characteristics transcending their ethnic and religious differences.[19] The characteristics of complacency, laziness, and unchangeability thus came to be generally attributed to the peasantry, while members of the elite were often considered industrious and future-oriented.

Regardless of these differentiated—and shifting—stereotypes, the country's history would seem to confirm the notion of an easy-going population, able to contain any social, political, and ethnic tensions that existed. There was no militant struggle for independence, as in India. No local anarchist tradition, so important in Bengal, provided indigenous inspiration to young revolutionaries. There was no Northwest Frontier area, where tribal self-defense glorified violent resistance to authority. And there was no precedent for destruction such as the communal slaughter which took place at Partition in India. In fact, there have been only two examples of substantial ethno-religious strife in the last six decades—the 1915 riots triggered by conflicting Muslim-Buddhist religious practices, and the 1958 riots caused by Sinhalese-Tamil differences.[20]

Substantial Private Violence. On the other hand, it must be noted that individual violence plays a significant part in Ceylonese social relations. There is an old Sinhalese saying that both the man who continues to worship when he is being repeatedly and continuously struck and the man who continues to strike when he is being repeatedly and continuously worshipped are fools. It is part of the traditional way that many minor annoyances, discomforts, and disadvantages should be accepted with equanimity. But a number of observers have noted that the Ceylonese have a low individual threshold of anger and are prone to outbursts of personal violence and loss of self-control that often lead to crimes of passion.[21]

Seen as separate incidents, these outbursts often appear to lack justification. But close observers argue that most such incidents represent the final crisis point, the culmination of a series of frustrations, when individuals see no other way out of their predicament than to lash out at whatever or whomever they consider to be the source of their frustrations.[22] Leonard Woolf's classic *Village in the Jungle* depicts this sequence admirably. When the "big man" of the village who has repeatedly wronged his poor neighbor finds himself alone in the forest with his long-suffering victim, he discovers too late that the victim, turning vanquisher, frees himself from his impossible situation by a decisive act of violence.[23]

In this light, the student rebellion was not so entirely alien to traditional norms, even though the mode of action and the advance organization preceding it were totally new. To understand the student protest, it is necessary to consider a number of social and economic conditions that were becoming increasingly severe.

Socio-Economic Conditions

An Expanded School System Raises Expectations. Sri Lanka expanded its school system and succeeded more than any other country in the area, with the exception of Singapore, in providing schooling for a substantial proportion of its school-age children. In 1950, there were some 1.4 million between the ages of 5 and 15 in school. By 1959 the number had increased almost 50 percent to 2.1 million. During the same period the proportion of school-aged children attending school had increased from 76 percent to 89 percent.[24]

University education also expanded rapidly. Sri Lanka provided free university education for all those who could pass the examinations. By the mid-1960s the one university had expanded to four. The Peradeniya campus graduated over 660 B.A.'s in the late 1960s as compared with only 108 in 1949, 262 in 1958, and 311 in 1960. Two former Buddhist seminaries, converted to universities in the late 1950s, virtually exploded in a six-year period. Together they graduated 77 B.A.'s in 1961, 385 in 1963, 826 in 1965, and 1,240 in 1967.[25] But these graduates were not evenly drawn from all fields. In 1969, for example, there were 2,662 arts graduates from the universities, but only 230 in science, 205 in medicine, 90 in engineering, 21 in agriculture, and 18 in veterinary science. In a country where 75 percent of the population is rural, there was only one graduate in agricultural science for every 100 liberal arts graduates.[26]

Although they differed in their views of specific educational objectives, government, teachers, students, and parents all agreed that education was important and deserved the support of government resources and student effort. But their differences contributed to a lack of hard curricular decisions so that the system continued to grow under its own momentum, shaped by elite patterns established early in the colony's history.

It is difficult to be certain about the gains that parents and students expected from their liberal arts education. Until more reliable survey data are available, some general observations will have to suffice. In traditional Ceylonese society, both Buddhist and Hindu, the scholar has been honored. During the British period the man with a liberal education was freed from manual labor and had assured access to prestigious and secure positions in the public service. With independence and the rapid expansion of the public service, many new government jobs opened up, further convincing parents and students that the liberal arts program was the royal road to white-collar security and status.[27]

Despite the fact that substantial acres of jungle land had been given over to peasant cultivation in the 1950s and 1960s, land pressures were intensifying. Paddy holdings in many areas averaged no more than one acre. Although there are hopes that more labor-intensive modern methods will make such holdings highly productive, present methods are rarely sufficient to support a small family. Eldest sons have been inheriting the family's plot, and other sons are increasingly being shut out.[28] Hence, to the peasant, education appears to be a chance for at least one son or daughter to move beyond peasant society and help the family by entering into the civil service or other white-collar employment, with its security, better pay, and higher status.

Others had a different perception of what education was about. Prime Minister S. W. R. D. Bandaranaike spoke for the government and for the liberal education tradition when he declared that education was a process which endowed the individual with a trained and disciplined mind, "a mind trained to think, to think clearly, to think calmly and above all, to think correctly." [29] The important point for this group was the fact that the school system was expanding rapidly and university education was becoming accessible to whoever could pass the examinations.

Teachers, who dispensed the services, had various views. One group tended to adhere to the scholastic model. To them, schooling represented a period during which students acquired given knowledge about the past and traditional ways of thinking about the present. It was the acquisition of knowledge, most often by rote and in the traditional *guru-sishya* relationship that was pertinent, not the use to which the learning would be put after graduation.[30] Another group of teachers, however, were more activist. They stressed the contrast between democratic egalitarian ideals embodied in the "one man, one vote" principle and the reality of the traditional social structure and slow pace of economic growth which hampered the achievement of these ideals.

The political role played by the activists among the teachers also helped to raise student expectations and change traditional acquiescent attitudes toward one's condition. Since the mid-1950s particularly, some vernacular teachers had been seeking to improve their own status within the teaching profession by backing those political leaders who appeared to promise them the most. The efforts of these teachers legitimatized activism and showed the students that it was possible to act in order to improve one's lot in life.[31]

The curriculum offered in the schools and universities was hardly geared to the country's needs and problems. The English stream was still tailored to British practices, and the university required papers similar to those called for by the University of London. The Sinhala stream lacked adequate textbooks for a rigorous wide-ranging education and, at least in the lower secondary schools, often reflected a nostalgia for the heavenly society of early Buddhist kingdoms. On both counts, the schools inflated expectations beyond what the real world of Sri Lanka could provide and neglected vital areas. Little heed was paid, for instance, to improving peasant agriculture, developing economical light industry for home consumption and possible export, and fostering the management skills to put human and resource components together in new, productive, and humanly acceptable ways. As the ILO report stated: "More than 100,000 young people come pouring every year out of the secondary schools with paper qualifications for which the demand is very limited and one wonders about the relevance of the expectations and values they have acquired at school to the real tasks of development that now face Ceylon." [32]

No longer are traditional Buddhist ideas regarding the wheel of life accepted by those who have experienced substantial secular schooling. They do not find it necessary to wait out this present life and follow the path of traditional piety. The social order is not ordained, with certain families and caste groups divinely chosen or legitimatized by ancient law and custom. Men can seize the initiative and concert together to make the necessary—and obviously advantageous—changes. In the April uprising, a number of the students apparently hoped to go much further than this. They too believed they could improve their lot, but one aspect of their time sense had been radically foreshortened. They did not believe in long-term, prudential decisions that bore fruit only decades later. Their political goals had to be satisfied immediately; only vigorous, daring action now would initiate the process of change they regarded as urgent.[33]

The educational system as now established, therefore, has greatly increased the number of students aspiring to white-collar jobs, students who consider manual or industrial labor beneath them. It inevitably separates young people from their illiterate and conservative parents; it accentuates impatience with the status quo.

Frustration among Educated Rural Youth. In rural areas, where most of the activity of April 1971 occurred, several developments had converged to intensify difficulties and resentments among educated youth. The man/land ratio had deteriorated as a result of population growth, and the educated youth in peasant families probably perceived the significance of this deterioration more acutely than those who stayed in the village and experienced it gradually. Roughly 70 percent of the population are dependent on domestic agriculture, but nearly a fourth of agricultural families are landless, while another one quarter own less than half an acre.[34] Detailed, up-to-date data are difficult to obtain, but the following impressions are widely reported.

Average holdings are small and land distribution inequitable though admittedly less so than in most peasant societies. As already noted, the number of young people reaching adulthood has increased, as has the life span. (Thus, life expectancy for a child born in 1967 was 66 years; in 1954, 60 years; in 1946, 43 years; and in 1921, 32 years.) Each laborer must therefore support more dependents. There are more young people to be accommodated on the land each year. And an increasing number from rural areas are graduating from the school system with aspirations unsuited to life in the countryside. Their education has led them to expect white-collar jobs, but these are not locally available. Such jobs are even scarcer in transitional areas between the low-country and hill districts than in Western Province and parts of Southern Province, where there is a more highly developed cash economy. These educated young people from rural areas lack the network of contacts provided by knowledgeable families or close friends that are indispensable for obtaining hard-to-come-by white-collar jobs. Furthermore, many village youth, the first in their family to be educated and still closely linked to the traditional ethos, are more likely to expect near-magic results from education and neither they nor their families realize that formal paper qualifications will not always procure a well-paying, high-status job. The ideals of an equitable and democratic society are not reflected in rural life, where ascriptive standing and unequal distribution of laborious tasks still prevail. So long as only the children of the well-placed went to school, the contrast between ideal and reality was not so sharply noticed. But when increasing numbers of poor rural youths managed to obtain schooling, a new "rural intelligentsia" began to develop, resentful of their circumstances—the lack of opportunities on the land and "connections" in the towns to help get jobs—and educated enough to be sensitive to their disadvantages.[35]

Social Mobilization Opens New Affiliations. A synoptic view of social development would point to Sri Lanka as becoming more and more socially mobilized.[36] The country's transport network is among the area's most developed, so that movement from one area to another is easy and inexpensive. As a result even peasant farmers are mobile and can see for themselves what standards of production and of living are like outside their own home areas. Its people are better served by the mass media than any other Asian country apart from Singapore. While earlier activism tended to consolidate traditional ethnic and ascriptive differences and accentuated communal hostility between Sinhalese and Tamils, present trends suggest that new patterns of mobilization are increasingly along class and not traditional affiliation lines.[37]

A more detailed examination of other data, including the formation of new associations, changing patterns of political affiliations, and the breakdown of traditional patron-client relationships, would tend to confirm the proposition that social mobilization in Sri Lanka has been accelerating. Socially, these changes weaken the legitimacy of traditional stratification patterns. Politically, they mean a new fluidity and unpredictability in the way people perceive their interests and define their friends and prospective opponents in the political arena. They undermine the authority of the more conservative elderly and open up positions of influence to younger men who may be less inhibited in the means they adopt to gain political ends.

Competitive Politics Inflates Demands. Political practices have further increased expectations. Since the early 1930s when Ceylon received the universal franchise, the country's political leaders have had to contend against each other at election time, with most seats hotly contested. To be sure, until the mid-1950s most of the electoral contests were between men of roughly the same social strata and economic standing, often with ascriptive followings who would vote for their patron regardless of promises and policy issues. But there were always marginal votes to be sought. Inherited ascriptive standing became progressively less important in determining who should have the right to rule. As time went on, political organizational skills assumed greater importance, and more and more contests were fought on welfare and other issues of distributive policy. He who promised the most was more likely to win than he whose promises bore some relation to what the economy and polity might be able to provide. The ever greater aspirations of ever larger numbers of people, and an increasing proportion of young people, were stimulated by the political process and focused on a government which was supposed to satisfy these aspirations. What of that government's ability to meet these demands?

Governmental Capabilities To Meet Increased Demands

Promoting Economic Growth and Diversification. Much has depended upon the economy's ability to earn foreign exchange to import goods necessary to sustain a standard of living which, after Malaysia and Singapore, is the highest in South and Southeast Asia. During the early years of independence, the country was prosperous and well supplied with the foreign exchange accumulated during World War II. These balances, rapidly depleted by developmental and consumption imports immediately following independence, were boosted by the Korean War boom, at least temporarily. Although in the 1950s and 1960s tea, rubber, and coconut exports grew substantially, they did not earn commensurately increased foreign exchange except during the brief tea boom of 1955–56. Indeed, earnings of foreign exchange in 1970 were less than 5 percent above the 1954–56 average.[38] Simultaneously, the prices of industrial imports had been rising with increasing costs in the prosperous developed countries, resulting in a severe decline in terms of trade. As a result, the heavy imports of machinery and industrial and agricultural raw materials needed to diversify the economy and expand productivity and job opportunities undermined the country's foreign exchange position.

At the same time government policies which were derived largely from popular demands for welfare and consumption subsidies, coupled with the additional burden of a rapidly growing population, placed increasingly severe demands upon domestic production and the declining foreign exchange surplus. Sri Lanka's net foreign exchange assets have steadily decreased, from $379.5 million in 1945 to $268 million in 1956 to $67.7 million in 1970, while the population has nearly doubled and has become politically more demanding. In recent years the international payments situation has worsened further. To keep the economy going at a politically tolerable level, the government has resorted to extensive borrowing abroad, often on short-term suppliers' credits at a high interest rate. In the three-year period from 1967 to 1970, capital payments to creditors shot up from Rs. 80 million to Rs. 656 million.[39]

If the country's economy were largely self-sufficient, or if its earnings were growing more rapidly than the population, there would be room for economic maneuver to find remunerative work for Sri Lanka's growing and increasingly educated work force. But failing both conditions, the situation is deteriorating.

The government's financial difficulties have been agravated by the generous food subsidies, social security, and medical service allowances already mentioned. Undertaken at a time of greater prosperity and smaller population, they have contributed materially to the quality of life of Sri Lanka's people. But as competitive politics raised aspirations and prevented a reduction in these subsidies as fiscal conditions worsened and as the population grew, these transfer payments also had an inexorable tendency to increase.

To be sure, useful economic and political results have been obtained. The government's effort to produce more paddy has been based on a combination of price supports and improved seeds, water control, and fertilizer subsidies. As a result, annual rice production has improved markedly, and imports of rice have declined from roughly 50 percent of total rice consumed to around 25 percent, despite a doubling of the population since independence and increased real cash incomes. This is a major accomplishment. For a number of additional reasons, a higher proportion of Sri Lanka's peasants participate heavily in the cash economy than any other peasants in South Asia.

This trend may in part explain Ceylon's relatively slow rate of urbanization as cultivators find their rural cash standard of living rising in the villages, even though man/land ratios are worsening as the rural population rapidly expands. The involvement of such a high proportion of the peasantry in the cash economy and the levels of real cash incomes opens a larger national domestic market for light industry consumption goods that may be manufactured domestically. But they have placed a heavy burden on the fiscal system, a burden compounded by another food subsidy measure.

In order to maintain food prices at a low level, particularly in cities and towns, the government also provides a portion of each family's rice absolutely free, lower than the price paid to the farmers to produce it and lower than the price for rice imported from abroad. These food subsidies, plus social security payments and government subsidies for industrial corporations operating at a loss, account for nearly one-half of government expenditures in some years.

Sri Lanka also has a virtually free national medical service which reaches even into many of the more remote areas. Per capita services have improved notably, though there is still much that remains to be done, particularly in safe water supplies in rural areas. The expanded medical services, originally the result of political pressures in the competitive electoral arena, have been one of the major causes of rapid population growth, which in turn has accentuated the total medical service burden. These services are, of course, a blessing to citizens however hard on governments. Improved health helps all strata in the population to be more productive. Public health measures have opened new areas to cultivation. Better health is a widely accepted human right, and an improved medical service can be used to implement a government policy limiting population growth.

The net effect of these policies, however, which became more generous in their application in the late 1950s and have had a tendency to increase since then, under the combined pressure of rising expectations and the rapidly growing population, has been to leave smaller and smaller real resource margins for development investment. This, in turn, has adversely affected the pace of economic growth and the diversification away from heavy dependence on only three export crops.[40]

Under these circumstances, the performance of the economy, particularly its ability to provide increasing numbers of young people with meaningful adult roles and job opportunities, takes on unusual importance. And it is here that the Ceylon economy has been notably deficient.

Unemployment for the Educated Becomes More Severe. Data on unemployment are notoriously unreliable. Underemployment is even more difficult to define with precision than figures reflecting registered unemployment. Accordingly, trend calculations are bound to be inadequate. This is particularly true where, as is typical, the definitional base for either unemployed or underemployed has shifted over time.[41]

As early as the mid-1950s a consumer survey by the Central Bank indicated that some 10–12 percent of the employables were without jobs. Unemployment and underemployment have both grown since then. Based on a preliminary socio-economic survey done in 1969–70, an ILO study concluded that nearly 15 percent of the total work force was *openly* unemployed, i.e., had applied to unemployment exchanges in the search for employment. And underemployment was even more marked. Unemployment was particularly serious among the young, nearly 40 percent of the 15–25-year-olds being without work. The problem was becoming particularly severe among those with higher education. While only 5 percent of those without education were unemployed, over 50 percent of young men between 20 and 24 who had gone through tenth grade were still unemployed, even though they had been out of school six to ten years! Of those who had completed the twelfth-grade equivalent 40 percent were without work. Those with tenth or twelfth grade education in rural areas were finding it still more difficult to find work than those in the cities.[42]

An earlier World Bank study of education showed that between 1953 and 1963, employment chances for those without schooling improved; the proportion of elementary school leavers who were unemployed declined from 16.4 percent to 10.5 percent. However, secondary school education apparently produced a reverse trend. In 1953, 18 percent were unemployed, while in 1963, 23 percent could find no jobs. High school graduates fared even worse: 25 percent of them were unemployed in 1953; in 1963, 39.7 percent, or over one-third, were without jobs. Those with higher degrees, while generally better off, experienced the same trend. Only 3 percent were unemployed in 1953, but by 1963 nearly 14 percent were jobless.[43]

Income data demonstrate clearly that those with higher educational degrees received high incomes by local standards. This no doubt encouraged both students and parents to carry education as far as possible, even if to fall short of a university degree was to run grave risks of being without employment at all.[44] No doubt, status considerations contributed to unemployment among the educated since even a high school diploma raised sights sufficiently to make many jobs unacceptable. Put another way, education still did pay dividends when it was coupled with the good fortune of employment, and the best returns went to those who obtained the most education. Yet by no means all of those who got advanced degrees received jobs—and even those who were willing to take ordinary jobs were often not hired because employers feared they would be intractable workers and sources of unrest in the labor force. Indeed, by 1970 there were reportedly some 14,000 university graduates without jobs, as many as 4,000 having been added to that number each year.[45]

Another indicator of deterioration during the 1960s was the marked decline in the proportion of registrants in every category at labor exchanges who succeeded in finding work.[46]

A review of overall social and economic data and political practices therefore suggests that a combination of general social and economic conditions revealed a sharp incongruity between what young people had come to expect and what in fact they found in seeking the remunerative and respected openings they considered appropriate.

Areas of Maximum Unrest

Another approach to the events of April 1971 would be to examine in greater detail three areas of Sri Lanka where social unrest appeared to be most severe at the time. It is, of course, possible that the distribution of violent expressions of unrest resulted more from the strategy of the movement's leaders than from any unusual social or economic conditions in those areas. The island is small; linguistic differences in the Sinhalese areas are few. Individuals could therefore be assigned to actions away from home where they would not be known. On the other hand, the type of action associated with the uprising suggests that the leaders had to depend in major part upon local supporters to implement their strategy.[47] Accordingly, these actions would be likely to be in areas where "relative deprivation" was felt to be most severe.

The most intense activity during the uprising appears to have taken place in three different areas: (1) the coastal areas south of Colombo, particularly the inland village areas of Galle and Matara districts; (2) the transitional areas from low country to middle upcountry subsistence village areas in Kurunegala and Kegalla districts; and (3) the areas reclaimed from jungle and settled by agricultural "colonists" under government auspices during the past thirty years, mainly in such centers as Anuradhapura and Polonnaruwa. The three contrasting areas show differing characteristics, all of which could intensify a sense of relative deprivation as compared with residents of most other Sinhalese areas.

In Area 1, characteristic hypotheses about the strains of modernization could apply to the towns. This area was subjected to foreign rule longer than most others, and is the most Westernized apart from Colombo itself and surrounding Western Province. For several generations the economy has been more cash-oriented than in most other parts of the island, apart from Western Province and the estate areas. Educational facilities in the towns have been considerable and long-standing, so that whatever contribution education makes toward dissatisfaction could be expected to have been at work in these towns longer than in most places.

Some violence occurred along the coastal strip. But a good bit of the activity in Southern Province occurred inland in rural village areas. Here land pressures are intensifying. Traditional family dependency and social stratification patterns still persist. Lower castes are numerically important, including Vahumpura, Durava, and Radha communities. It would be an easy error to overstress caste issues as being at the heart of the rebellion. The analysis thus far should make clear that many other issues appeared to be at stake. Many Goyigama youth were involved. But it is probably correct to say that communities other than the highest-status Goyigamas were proportionately more involved. And it is probably not entirely coincidental that one of the identifiable leaders of the movement belonged to the Karava community and that a number of his fellow community members were at the core of the movement. Members of this community are known for their energy and drive in business and the professions. Although many of them claim descent from South Indian Kshatriya warrior castes, and therefore should be thought of as superior to farmers in the traditional Indian stratification system, the "cultivator" Goyigamas consider themselves to be the highest status and the Karavas of lower social rank.

New schooling opportunities for rural children, particularly those of Vahumpura, Durava, Batgam, and Radha families, would generate a sharpened sense of the incongruity between traditional village ways and the egalitarian ideas found in the schools.[48] Moreover, radical political appeals have been the stock in trade of prominent political personalities in this area more than in most, so that a direct political action program would be less surprising to prospective recruits there than most anywhere else.

One would also anticipate that in such an area lower-level public servants, including vernacular schoolteachers, long in touch with the more Westernized aspects of Sri Lanka and impatient with their highly stratified service and blocked career opportunities would have joined the activists.

In Area 2, ecologically transitional between the low country and the hills, as in Kegalla and Kurunegala districts, similar incongruities between ascriptive and achieved status would be particularly apparent in the rural areas. And for those who had come fresh to educational opportunity only recently made available in rural central schools, these contrasts would be particularly galling. In these areas, too, lower castes are numerous.

As in Area 1, the man/land ratio has been declining with the rising population, particularly the young entrants to the labor market resulting from the baby boom in the 1940s and early 1950s. Rural overcrowding due to rapid population growth is becoming more severe in these traditional village areas in both the south and the intermediate areas under consideration. Few alternative job opportunities would exist because the economy has not yet begun to change its structure. Parents would find it increasingly difficult to place more than one son on the land. And being on the margins of the more politically organized and mobilized Western Province, political organization focused on the movement's objectives in both Areas 1 and 2 would be easier and the young populace likely to be more responsive than in the upcountry Kandyan districts, where land hunger is often thought to be more severe in fact.

Some of the above propositions are confirmed by more detailed regression analysis and cross tabulation of economic and socio-ecological data. They show that most intense and dramatic unrest occurred where the amount of paddy land per rural male was declining most severely. Both these affected areas also showed a larger net out-migration of rural males than was typical for other Sinhalese areas of rural Ceylon.[49]

In Area 3, life was quite different from that in the traditional village. North Central Province is marked by elaborate irrigation colonies established by heavy government investment during the past four decades. Although caste identifications have been important in mobilizing local support for elected representatives, in such government-supported colonies human relationships are not embedded in a complex nexus of inherited familial or other traditional structural networks as in usual Sinhalese villages, but are more impersonal, utilitarian and, one might say, modern.[50] While originally, individual plots varied roughly according to the size of the colonist's family, each man's plot soon became too small, with established technologies, to accommodate all his children. To be sure, many agro-industrial services have developed in the area of these productive colonies—tractor repair shops, fertilizer and pesticide distributors, etc.[51] But few of these occupations were considered to be sufficiently dignified to accommodate school leavers. And by the time desperate students were prepared to take such jobs, there were by no means enough to absorb the numbers. Moreover, the structure of colony life and the relative impersonality of colony relationships in contrast to traditional village structures have favored political organization. Village elders have had little influence on the young people. There is a looseness of social integration and an individual autonomy outside traditional norms. These characteristics were likely to have made it easier to organize young people for radical political activity than in the more integrated, traditional village areas.

If these conclusions have validity, one can say that for a variety of socio-economic reasons, certain areas proved to be more fertile ground for a radical youth movement than others.

Lack of Apparent Political Alternatives

In the paradigm suggested near the beginning of this essay, we identified political alternatives as a significant element in defining the likelihood of such a radical upheaval as Sri Lanka experienced.

The youth of the country saw little possibility that the economy would be able to absorb them. Successive governments had made promises, and services had been expanded. But the numbers unable to find a worthwhile adult role were growing. Mrs. Bandaranaike had made more radical promises than her UNP opponents, but the innovations she was introducing were too slow and did not seem likely to provide answers to the problems of young people. Foreign aid from Communist countries had been paltry despite notable political gestures in that direction. Western sources of support appeared to be drying up, and short-term credits were threatening to bankrupt the country with ever larger interest payments. The effect of the Cuban Revolution, the Korean students' success in overthrowing Syngman Rhee, and the dramatic protests of the Turkish students against Adnan Menderes were not forgotten. As a member of that rapidly expanding youth cohort, could one expect substantial change without resort to radical means?

The conventional political parties did not seem promising. The United National Party, though in power several times, had failed to fulfill many of its major popular promises. Mrs. Bandaranaike's coalition of center and moderate Leftist elements, including important leaders of Ceylon's Trotskyist party, the Lanka Sama Samaj Party (LSSP) and the Communist Party, had attempted to bring about changes. But like her predecessors, she was stymied by lack of available economic resources and by differing and irreconcilable views among members of her diverse Cabinet about what should be done. The same political leaders, all too familiar, argued over stale issues. There were few new public faces in the ranks of the Left. Leaders of the Left parties continued their sterile quarrels, which had divided them for the past two critical decades. The Communist Party itself had split in 1963, one wing now oriented toward Peking, the other appearing to many to be closer to Moscow. Moreover, the UNP, at least, did not provide many opportunities for younger members to participate in responsible positions. They were given chores at election time, but after elections the permanent structure of the main parties generally remained impermeable to the more enthusiastic and dedicated young people. And the opportunities that did open up were far too few in relation to the numbers who wanted to participate.

The fact that several leading spokesmen for Left parties were in the coalition contributed some talented men to the government bench. But by joining the Cabinet, they dramatized to the impatient young people their swing away from revolutionary action to parliamentary participation. Their collaboration with the regime made it seem all the less likely that the established Leftist parties could produce the changes some of the young people so desperately desired.[52]

It is possible that the professional politicians of whatever party increasingly came to be seen as representatives of the same class and economic interests, and as profiting equally from their prominence and influence as elected members of Parliament. They became identified with the capital, where many of them had served so long, alienated from the countryside they were supposed to represent, increasingly cut off from the urgencies of hard-pressed rural life by the perquisites and preoccupations of ministerial administration or parliamentary maneuver.

Leadership and Organization of the Eruption

Even with all these psychological, social, and economic conditions providing the raw materials for a radical political movement, such a dramatic effort to seize power could not have been mounted without careful political organization. The core of the enterprise was a youth movement already referred to, the Janatha Vimukhti Peramuna (People's Liberation Front), founded in 1967–68. Several names of the JVP's leadership are known, including Rohana Wijeweera, an ex-member of the Peking-oriented faction of the Communist Party, a 32-year-old Karava and former student at Lumumba University in Moscow. Chinese complicity was first suspected, and most Peking-oriented political leaders were promptly arrested. Some blamed the CIA. Kim Il Sung's collected works were widely available in Sinhale well before the uprising. Shortly after the events, the government expelled the North Korean diplomatic mission, whose representatives reportedly had been active in the countryside prior to the eruption. And subsequently, the government implied that Moscow was involved in some way. In sum, the leadership, detailed command, and foreign influence (if any) of the events of April 1971 remain obscure.

The Peramuna nevertheless showed obvious political skills. It recruited sufficiently large numbers of disgruntled young people from both factions of the Communist Party and from widely scattered rural constituencies prior to the 1970 election so that Mrs. Bandaranaike's coalition was ready to accept support from elements of the JVP.[53] Wijeweera, though recommending support to Mrs. Bandaranaike's coalition during the election, continued to advocate within the JVP a non-parliamentary strategy of "the one-day revolution" or seizure of power by direct action in a concerted, one-day coup.

Before and after the election, the leadership played up persisting inequities in rural areas and sought to build a base of followers, not on urban workers as the Marxist Left had done until then, but on the 75 percent of the Sinhalese population who were rural. We have seen that the educational system was turning out increasing numbers of young people from rural areas who were no longer suited to village life but could find no suitable employment either there or in the towns or cities. Educated unemployed rural youths appear to have formed the numerically most important part of the movement, although many participants were employed. Lower-level civil servants, indigenous language schoolteachers, and even peasant youths were also active.

The leaders organized secret study classes and group cells, with only minimal links between them to maximize the chances of maintaining secrecy. Unlike the Marxist leaders who seemed incorrigibly oriented to the urban trade unionists, to concepts defined abroad, and to issues drawn from international experience, the JVP's ideology was carefully constructed on indigenous, rural concerns. It included such issues as the continuing dominance of up-country tea estates by foreigners, the displacement of Kandyan peasantry by British estates and Indian Tamil estate workers, the "threat of Indian imperialism," rural indebtedness, inequitable land distribution, floods, drought, soil erosion, caste resentments, and other "remnants of feudalism" in rural Sri Lanka.[54] These ideas were simplified into "five lectures," and given wide currency in secret meetings of young recruits. The lectures were often obscure, it seems, but they tended to conclude with simple, memorable slogans, the last one calling for revolution by a one-day assault on centers of effective power. These presentations appear to have been enormously exciting, moving thousands of young people to enlist secretly in the movement, ready to risk their lives if ordered to do so by the organizers.

Clandestine assault training classes were held in remote jungle areas. Explosives were concocted, weapons inconspicuously gathered, a communications network developed, part of it reportedly built on obituary notices read over Radio Ceylon. The movie *Battle of Algiers* may have provided some ideas on how to mount a secret organization, but returnees from training programs in the Soviet Union, North Korea, or China were probably more important in bringing such skills. The cell-like character of the protest effort no doubt assisted in sustaining the remarkably high degree of secrecy achieved.

Within a year of Mrs. Bandaranaike's sweeping electoral victory, enough opposition to the United Front's rule had been generated that even some of the more conservative elements reportedly were prepared to close their eyes to the JVP's preparations.[55] Some may even have supported the movement to embarrass Mrs. Bandaranaike's government. Certainly a number of the movement's leaders must have been known to those parliamentarians within the government who had profited from its organized support in the 1970 election.

In the event, when the orders went out for action in early April, the assault brought the government briefly into disarray. In the end, however, the assault failed. In certain areas of Matara Province, the movement held control for three or four weeks while government troops and police were busy elsewhere. But there too, it withered. And where it had held control, the JVP provided few innovations which would lead large numbers of people to support its return to local power should there be a second effort.

The overwhelming majority of the Ceylonese people were simply not interested. They were not persuaded that a group of young people, however well organized, could seize and hold the commanding heights of political power and turn that power to the country's advantage. The trade unionists, a number of whose leaders were in the Cabinet, assisted the government in maintaining order and the flow of production and logistical support. Port workers did not join the revolt. Foreign assistance in the form of military equipment, cash gifts, and loans came to the government from all quarters including India, the Soviet Union, China, and the United States.

As a result of these events, the military and police budgets have been doubled; development investment has been further retarded. No longer can the Ceylonese take it for granted that politics, while bitter and intense, will never lead to organized violence.

In sum, therefore, one sees profound political problems developing, primarily out of a sharply increased rate of population growth fifteen to twenty years ago and expanding expectations in a situation of competitive politics, limited economic growth, and sharply increasing unemployment, particularly among the young and better educated. Without careful political organization the assault of April 1971 could not have taken place. But without the worsening socio-ecological circumstances, as these affected the moderately and better educated in particular, the political organizers would have had relatively little to build on.

Epilogue: The Population Crisis—No Quick or Simple Answer *Kenneth Thompson*

Dramatic demographic changes are building up to one of history's most urgent crises. While recognizing that analogies are hazardous, I nevertheless believe that in the demographic sphere boundaries are set and possibilities defined that are not entirely unlike those that have beset us elsewhere. Or, in the words of Montaigne: "As no event and no shape is entirely like another, so also is there none entirely different from another: an ingenious mixture on the part of Nature. If there were no similarity in our faces, we could not distinguish man from beast; if there were no dissimilarity we could not distinguish one man from another."

Mankind has faced other crises that cried out for early and authoritative solutions, and it may be illuminating to reconstruct broadly past attempts to resolve crises in other spheres. I wish to consider how the search for ways of controlling the population explosion is in important respects analogous to the continuing effort to manage and contain international conflict.

In the study of international relations, we have been beset by a recurrent fallacy. Robert Hutchins used to proclaim that world government was necessary, and therefore possible. Champions of world disarmament sent out a similar rallying cry. Woodrow Wilson inspired millions of men and women to organize themselves around the cause of the League to Enforce Peace and to make democracy the common cause of mankind everywhere.

The nobility of these great purposes was somehow never matched by commensurate advances and progress. It is sobering to observe that for most problems the "necessary therefore possible" formula has proven unrealistic and fallacious. In the aftermath of each crusade, successors have asked: Why did it fail? How can we account for the shattering experiences confronting men who tried to legislate change or solve a great and tangled problem with one institutional innovation or one legislative or technological gimmick? What went wrong?

More often than not, at least in the study of international relations, the first impulsive reaction was to blame "a handful of evil men," a small group of recalcitrant Senators, a band of simple-minded optimists or paranoid militarists. Then gradually, with the passage of time, more dispassionate scholarship showed that the fault was more widely shared, that there were deep-rooted forces at work. It became clear that what was possible or impossible was inextricably bound up with the realities of the human condition. The far-reaching changes that seemed so obvious to their proponents were hedged about and confined by factors inherent in existing groupings and structures, both national and international. To be more specific, nationalism stood in the way of world government as mankind everywhere put national or group interest first. Or, the newly independent societies found themselves, within their own borders, at a stage of political development in which the imposition of the full panoply of Western democratic institutions or political practices intensified existing divisions and incapacitated already feeble governments. World government remained a long-term goal for mankind; but in the absence of effective world community it remained distant and remote. Democracy, which may be the best existing form of government, proved not to be the best attainable government for all nation-states. The human condition was more intractable than the reformers acknowledged; the great crises could not be so easily wished away; intangible factors were more resistant to change.

The simple proposition that world government was necessary and therefore possible was immensely appealing; it appeared to brush aside and to resolve all the baffling and intractable problems that had led earlier scholars to consider world government to be impracticable. The impossibility of creating a world government without the foundations of world community was dismissed, given the necessity for it. An astounding amount of human intelligence and energy was devoted to creating world constitutions and new structures, all carried on simultaneously with growing rivalry between the great powers and the rise of new centers of assertive nationalism in Africa and Asia. In the meantime, the hard business of keeping the peace continued, less in the halls in which world government was discussed than in national chancelleries and in the chambers of an imperfect international body, the United Nations. The urgent necessity of managing and containing conflict has never waited on the creation of perfect instrumentalities.

To move from international politics to population planning at this point is admittedly a debatable venture. The history of science and medicine makes clear that major breakthroughs are possible in areas as complex as human reproduction. The ideal solution scientifically may be just around the corner. But for the present, given an imperfect technology, two conclusions seem inescapable. First, the argument that because it is necessary it is possible can be positively harmful if it leads to a reduction of effort in the area of immediate, if limited, possibilities. There is work to be done in the here and now while men await more ideal solutions.

Second, the argument that necessity guarantees the possibility of a clear-cut solution can also lead to rash, extravagant, and quite often futile reallocations of national resources. Technologies which justify only limited and experimental resource allocations scarcely warrant all-out national and global efforts, however urgent the need. Yet invariably in national and international endeavors this is the course which is followed.

A case in point is international studies and programs, which received substantial emphasis by both the private and the public sectors following World War II. Domestic problems were correspondingly neglected. Similarly today, there are those who believe that eradicating the ghetto or transforming education or conquering disease is a simple matter of reallocating massive resources. Yet if experience in these spheres teaches anything, it is that progress is the result of a complex and somewhat mysterious blending of human and material resources; the two stand in some catalytic relation to one another.

The twin questions worth asking are: (1) What is the human condition as it affects solutions to the population problem? (2) Can we anticipate persistent obstacles and roadblocks *before* rather than after "solutions" are undertaken? Is it possible to avoid the disillusionment, malaise, and lack of commitment which often follow slow-paced, incremental progress as against dramatic advances?

An inquiry regarding population control or the relationships between demographic changes and politics is more complex and perplexing than explorations in most other fateful areas of human endeavor, for it must touch on those deep-running questions involving human life and death. It is not only that the variables are more numerous and less susceptible to legislative and institutional change. It is also that penetrating the innermost motivations and emotional lives of individuals is an even more baffling and problematic task than penetrating the boundaries of national sovereignty. For the individual's choices about family, children, and the creation and sustaining of the most intimate human community are stubbornly and jealously guarded. Identity, prestige, and the will to live all come into play. And these, particularly the latter, lie beyond the realm of usual behavioristic observation.

The fear of death lies heavily upon us all, though we do not often admit it these modern days. In an age of widespread uncertainty, the one empirically vertifiable certainty is that of death. The nightmare of death by nuclear holocaust has haunted all of us and particularly the young since 1945; they have never known a world without the bomb. For millions of the world's poor, the specter of death through disease and famine hangs over their brief lives despite improvements in life expectancy in many places. This prompts us to ask: Does not the fear of death provoke an opposing assertion of the will to live, a mysterious assertion affecting responses to the would-be family planner? With the waning of institutionalized religion and the weakening of the hope for personal immortality, is not the search for a broader immortality through children and heirs brought more consciously to the fore? If the individual cannot live on, what he stands for can live on through others, and all this may go on in an age where the whole concept of immortality is formally rejected.

From religious and quasi-religious motivations it is not too great a distance to other deeply felt emotional needs and aspirations. For example, those who returned from World War II observed that after participating in the destruction and suffering that conflict brought upon us, they yearned for the moral warmth and personal security of family life. After the deprivations and inhumanities of war, their aim was to rediscover humanity through the mystery and majesty of building a family. They sought to assert their relationship to life after having, for many years, dealt with death.

I further suspect that, more than we know, family choices link up with deep-running sensitivities of men and women who feel lonely and even abandoned in a profoundly isolating and insecure world. Modern urban life provides ever fewer truly human primary contacts. Particularly for persons living on the margins of the larger society, those for whom failures and deprivations have been the greatest, family life or the love of progeny may be the only source of reassurance. Is it far-fetched, therefore, to question whether the very sense of loneliness, anomie, and personal insecurity which so marks the more "modern" sectors of our world may be leading to a drive to recreate the warmth and security of a family group, however defined? There are echoes of this abroad in such books as Octavio Paz's *Labyrinth of Loneliness;* at home some of the writings of militant blacks reflect similar compulsions. Proposals, therefore, for reducing the size of families must take into account these deeper psychic needs of men and women living in an insecure and sometimes threatening world.

Another analogy between population and foreign policy programs merits at least passing reference as it touches on psychological and political variables. One great problem in surmounting the challenge of recurrent war has been the lack of effective institutions and techniques that could assure to each member state its national integrity and a continuing state of peace in the world at large. Doubting that either the League of Nations or the United Nations could insure peace, each state has been unwilling, for the most part, to trust its security and sovereignty to the new instruments of international security. In an earlier period, nations demonstrated similar doubts about the balance of power or the Concert of Europe. And lacking confidence, each took steps on its own behalf which intensified the dangers for all.

The instruments and technology of population control suffer from a similar crisis of confidence. Men and nations are suspended between a now dissipated confidence in the IUD, the pill, and other much-heralded techniques and the presently awaited breakthrough that some predict from expanded research on the physiology of reproduction. Thus, confidence must be maintained among the world's people despite the discouragements that followed early exaggerated and unrealized expectations. And the re-establishment of credibility for a widely scattered and educationally diverse population around the globe can come only when results become tangible and real.

In the interim, progress depends on movement and initiative by national and international agencies despite widespread skepticism, and this requirement is one not wholly unknown to international relations. Peacemakers for centuries have had to pursue their efforts in the face of a crisis of confidence. No student of the international system could argue that international institutions in the nineteenth and twentieth centuries have assured peace and security. Yet institutions that objectively were deficient have for relatively long periods been "sufficient unto the day." The League, and more recently the United Nations, especially in certain periods, commanded sufficient confidence and respect to contribute to peace. In an analogous fashion, present technologies in the population field may serve limited purposes however much they fall short of objective needs.

Economists are quick to add that the economic variable is another profoundly important force in the making of family choices. When infant mortality was high and life expectancy low, as is still the case in many agrarian societies, the case for a family to have double the desired number of children in order to maintain the family economy exerted what amounted to deterministic force. Subsequently, as medical knowledge and changing agricultural and industrial technologies freed men and women from such necessities, prospective parents began to make choices regarding the number of children they preferred. Economic theory has been put to work with new concepts and hypotheses about "family formation." Briefly put, this theory sees family-size decisions occurring within the household as a series of rational choices analogous to other economic decisions. Children can be viewed as an economic asset whose benefits or satisfactions are realized in the form of direct monetary or in-kind contributions to the income of the household and/or means of old-age insurance in the absence of government programs. On the other hand, children are also viewed as giving rise to certain family costs including financial costs associated with birth and rearing, as well as the opportunity costs associated with the loss of potential earnings of the wife during pregnancy, confinement, and subsequent child care. Thus, it may be that we have been placing too much research emphasis on the technology of population control and too little on psycho-cultural and economic behavior factors affecting family-size decisions.

While the development and dissemination of contraceptive

technology is necessary for lower fertility, perhaps the answer to the population crisis lies more in the enhancement of human dignity and individual security through meaningful educational and employment opportunities and an environment of adequate order and political participation in the developing world. I am impressed—and my curiosity is piqued—by the fact that Singapore's population growth rate has fallen from 3.7 percent to approximately 1.5 percent over the past two decades, concurrently with a rapid increase in job opportunities for both men and women.

Historical evidence has revealed again and again that there appears to be a set of preconditions which must be satisfied before any new technology can be successfully adopted. The technology of "death control" was clearly in the best immediate interests of all humanity and was, therefore, readily accepted. But can we say the same for the technology of "birth control" under contemporary social, political, and economic conditions prevailing in those developing nations, where two-thirds of the world's population reside? The limited success of family planning programs in Asia may not be entirely due to internal inefficiencies of program design and implementation. It may simply be due to the absence of the necessary social and economic preconditions for lower fertility, which in turn fosters only a limited interest on the part of the individual in reducing family size.

Accordingly, we need to understand a good deal more about the eschatological, social, economic, and political aspects of the human condition in Southern Asia. An improved technology is essential. But the motivations for the use of that technology must also be understood. Until we can grapple effectively with these fundamental aspects of the human condition, I fear that, unlike the people who are being urged to limit family size, discussions of the population crisis could tend to become sterile and perhaps even barren.

Notes

1. DEMOGRAPHIC CHANGE AND POLITICS: AN INTRODUCTION

1. D. R. Galle, et al., "Population Density and Pathology," *Science,* 176 (April 7, 1972), 23–30.

2. We are indebted to his paper "Political Demography: An Inquiry into the Political Consequences of Population Change," prepared for the National Academy of Science, November 1969, for early suggestions on many of these points.

3. Herbert Moller, "Youth as a Force in the Modern World," *Comparative Studies in Society and History,* 10, No. 3 (April 1968), 237–60.

4. For a discussion of this general trend, see James C. Scott, "Patron-Client Politics and Political Change in Southern Asia," *American Political Science Review,* 66, No. 1 (March 1972), 91–113.

5. Joseph LaPalombara, "Distribution: A Crisis of Resource Management," in Leonard Binder, ed., *Crises and Sequences in Political Development* (Princeton: Princeton University Press, 1971), pp. 233–82.

6. Ted Gurr, *Why Men Rebel* (Princeton: Princeton University Press, 1970), chs. 2, 3, 4, and 5.

7. Francine Frankel, *India's Green Revolution: Economic Gains and Political Costs* (Princeton: Princeton University Press, 1971).

8. For a vivid example see Alan R. Beals and Bernard J. Siegal, *Divisiveness and Social Conflict: An Anthropological Approach* (Stanford: Stanford University Press, 1966).

9. Ralph Braibanti, et al., *Asian Bureaucratic Systems Emergent from the British Imperial Tradition* (Durham, N.C.: Duke University Press, 1966).

10. For a careful discussion of this problem in Sri Lanka, see International Labor Office, *Matching Employment Opportunities and Expectations, A Programme of Action for Ceylon* (2 vols.; Geneva: International Labor Office, 1971).

11. Lester B. Pearson, *Partners in Development* (New York: Praeger, 1969), ch. 4.

12. Ansley J. Coale, "Population and Economic Development," in Philip Hauser, ed., *The Population Dilemma* (Englewood Cliffs, N.J.: Prentice-Hall, 1963).

13. For a discussion focused on this political objective, see Howard Wriggins, *The Ruler's Imperative* (New York: Columbia University Press, 1969).

14. Gayl D. Ness and Hirofumi Ando, "The Politics of Population Planning in Malaysia and the Philippines," *Journal of Comparative Administration,* 3, No. 3 (November 1971). See also Jason L. Finkle, "Politics, Development Strategy and Family Planning Programs in India and Pakistan," *ibid.*

2. POPULATION CHANGE AND DEVELOPMENT IN SOUTHERN ASIA: AN OVERVIEW

1. *Demographic Yearbook, 1969* (New York: United Nations, Department of Economic and Social Affairs, 1970), Table 2, pp. 119–20. These calculations exclude Singapore, with a density of 3,471 persons per square kilometer.

2. *Ibid.,* Table 2, pp. 116–28. Among less developed countries mainland China was reported with an extremely low annual rate of growth averaging 1.4, but such an estimated figure reflects guesswork more than reliable population data. Some African countries also grew at rates well under 2.0, for example Congo-Brazzaville (1.3), Gabon (1.0) and Angola (1.3). Again, the data on which these estimates rest are partial and unreliable. Certain islands, small kingdoms, and other special cases show extremely high growth rates which have been excluded here.

3. In this chapter, South Asia includes Afghanistan, Sri Lanka (Ceylon), India, Iran, Nepal and Pakistan. Southeast Asia is composed of Burma, Cambodia, the Federation of Malaya (or Malaysia), Indonesia, Laos, the Philippines, Singapore, Thailand, and North and South Vietnam. This follows the United Nations designation. After 1971 Bangladesh would be added.

4. At a rate of population increase of 2.5 percent, India would take twenty-eight years to double its population and would reach 1.074 billion in 1997.

5. The proportion of the population under 15 seldom exceeds 25 percent in developed countries but is frequently as high as 45 percent in those which are less developed. A high proportion of dependent children in a population places an additional burden on those in the labor force who must support them.

6. These are also the young adults who are entering the labor force in greatly increased numbers and demanding jobs. For a discussion of this population consequence, see the paper by Nathan Keyfitz.

7. These figures are estimates for the period 1965–70 from United Nations, *Monthly Bulletin of Statistics,* 25–4 (April 1971), Special Table D, pp. xxx–xxxiv.

Life expectancy at birth for both sexes combined is around 70 years in the more advanced countries, including Japan. Life expectancy is generally 3 to 6 years more for women than for men.

8. The ability of a country to provide for a stable system of payments to any sizable proportion of the population is, of course, ultimately dependent on productivity. Political motivations underlie the establishment of some kind of social security program in specific countries. The outlook for the success of these programs once benefits come due in substantial amounts is bleak in the absence of an effective economic base.

9. These general conclusions are not intended to denigrate in any way the efforts or accomplishments of public health programs, which have increased substantially in almost all Asian countries since the 1940s. Rather, they reflect the enormity of the task such organizations face with rapidly rising populations and limited gains in average living conditions.

10. Both Singapore and Hong Kong are special cases because of their special status as metropolitan cities. Their crude birth rates in 1969 were 22.2

and 20.7 respectively. By 1969 Taiwan had reduced its rate to 25.6 during a period of rapid economic growth and modernization.

11. The results of the 1971 Census of Population showed India with a population of 547 million—some 13 million less than had been projected. This could indicate a drop in the birth rate slightly greater than anticipated. It could also result from a slower decline in mortality or, theoretically, from a higher rate of underenumeration than in the 1961 census. The reason is not yet clear. See Pravin Visaria, "Provisional Data from India's Census," *Population Chronicle,* 6 (September 1971), 8. A publication of the Population Council.

12. Since the accuracy of population data tends to improve only as development progresses, birth and death rates reported for the less developed countries must be treated with great caution.

Figures used in this paper are primarily those published in the *Demographic Yearbook,* an annual volume prepared by the Statistical Office of the United Nations.

13. In addition to those shown in Table 4, Poona, India, was added. Poona's 1960 population was 725,000 and rose to 878,000 in 1969.

14. The additions were Nagpur (670,000) and Lucknow (640,000), India; Dacca (690,000), Pakistan; and Hanoi (650,000), North Vietnam.

15. The certain additions are Varanasi (Banaras), India (643,000); Lyallpur (854,000) and Multan (597,000), Pakistan; and Quezon City, Philippines (545,000). These are 1968 and 1969 populations shown in the *Demographic Yearbook, 1969,* Table 7, pp. 198–201. Kuala Lumpur, Malaysia, and Phnom-Penh, Cambodia, probably had populations over 500,000 in 1970, but no recent census data are available.

16. In Thailand metropolitan Bangkok accounted for 61 percent of the growth in the urban population between 1947 and 1960. Sidney Goldstein, "Urbanization in Thailand, 1947–1967," *Demography,* 8–2 (May 1971), 209. See also Sidney Goldstein, "Demographic Change in the Bangkok Area" in this volume.

17. United Nations, *Growth of the World's Urban and Rural Population, 1920–2000* (New York, 1969), Table 56, p. 124, presents percentages for all regions of the world.

18. Except for the Republic of Singapore.

19. *Ibid.,* Table 4, p. 14, Table 5, p. 15, and Table 44, pp. 104–5. If the 1960 population in places of over 20,000 is used, India had 14 percent, the United States 58.5 percent, and the Soviet Union 36 percent urban.

20. Unless otherwise stated, "urban" is defined as places of 20,000 and more persons. In United Nations terminology these are agglomerations.

21. Extracted from United Nations, *Urbanization: Development Policies and Planning* (New York, 1968), Table 5, p. 12. Southern Asia here refers to Southeast Asia and South Asia, as used in the remainder of this paper, plus Southwest Asia.

22. Even in 1950–59 higher urban growth rates than those for South Asia occurred in East Asia (52 percent), the Soviet Union (56 percent), Latin America (67 percent), and Africa (69 percent). *Ibid.*

23. Extracted from United Nations, *Urbanization: Development Policies and Planning,* Table 6, p. 12 (see footnote 21 for special definition of Southern Asia).

24. Urban growth also occurs because of annexation of formerly rural territory, because of the growth of smaller places to a size where they are classed as "urban," and because of changes in the definition of "urban," which result in increases in places included. All of these factors together are less important causes of urban growth than are natural increase plus net in-migration.

25. Ansley J. Coale, "How a Population Ages or Grows Younger," in Ronald Freedman, ed., *Population: The Vital Revolution* (New York: Anchor Books, Doubleday, 1964), pp. 48–49.

26. It is not certain to what extent the relatively small cohort currently in their twenties is simply an artifact of age misreporting in the census, but this is certainly not the entire explanation. For further discussion, see chapter 7 in this volume, by Nathan Keyfitz.

27. For a more detailed treatment and bibliography, see Warren C. Robinson and David E. Horlacher, "Population Growth and Economic Welfare," *Reports on Population/Family Planning,* February 1971, pp. 1–39.

28. One of the first, and still one of the most useful, demonstrations will be found in the case study of India presented in Ansley J. Coale and Edgar Hoover, *Population Growth and Economic Development in Low Income Countries* (Princeton: Princeton University Press, 1958). For a summary of this and subsequent models, see Robinson and Horlacher, "Population Growth."

29. A $2 a year increase in per capita income represents only a 0.2 percent increase in a country with a per capita income level of $1,000. Most Western economies will grow at a consistently faster rate than this.

30. Economic Commission for Asia and the Far East (ECAFE), *Economic Survey of Asia and the Far East, 1970, Part II: Current Economic Developments,* February 22, 1971, pp. 11–17, limited distribution. See also Harry Oshima, "Income Inequality and Economic Growth: The Postwar Experience of Asian Countries," *Malayan Economic Review* (October 1970), pp. 7–41.

31. This idea is based on three main assumptions: (1) savings as a proportion of current income increase as incomes rise; (2) it is easier to "capture" part of the incomes of the higher-income groups by taxation for purposes of capital formation than of low-income groups; (3) any investible surplus between consumption and disposable income is more likely to be invested in productive projects in the case of high-income groups than in the case of low-income groups.

32. E.g., Simon Kuznets, *Modern Economic Growth, Rate, Structure and Spread* (New Haven: Yale University Press, 1966), ch. 4.

33. Oshima, "Income Inequality," p. 7.

34. ECAFE, "Economic Survey of Asia," pp. 11–18.

35. United Nations Food and Agriculture Organization, *Provisional Indicative World Plan for Agricultural Development* (Rome, 1970), I, 15. For additional information, see p. 60.

36. These calculations are actually for non-Communist Asia, excluding Japan. Enrollments were related to the population aged 5–12, which is slightly wider than the official primary school age groups.

37. William Seltzer, "Environmental Issues," *Concerned Demography,* 2 (March 1971), 53–59.

38. ECAFE, *Review of the Social Situation in the ECAFE Region* (Bangkok, February 1970), p. 9.

39. The range of the share of social services in current expenditures is much the same: from 7 percent in Pakistan to 30–32 percent in Nepal, the Philippines, and Singapore (all figures for 1968). See United Nations, *Statistical Yearbook for Asia and the Far East, 1969, passim.*

40. Educational planning is ideally a more complex process than merely adjusting enrollment rates, but the most complex assumptions about trends in repeater, dropout, and promotion rates can nevertheless be translated into trends in enrollment rates.

41. Gavin W. Jones and Vallobh Tantivejakul, *The Effect of Alternative Population Trends on the Attainment of Educational Goals in Thailand: A Preliminary Investigation* (Bangkok: Manpower Planning Division, National Economic Development Board, 1971), mimeographed.

42. For a detailed country case study where such savings are spelled out, see Gavin W. Jones and S. Selvaratnam, *Population Growth and Economic Development in Ceylon* (Colombo: Hansa Publishers, 1971).

43. The status of each country and brief comment on existing programs will be found in Dorothy Nortman, "Population and Family Planning Programs: A Factbook," *Reports on Population/Family Planning: 1971–2* (June 1971), Table 6, pp. 20–22. A publication of the Population Council, New York.

44. Demographers have developed various techniques for estimating fertility and mortality in areas where the data reported cannot be considered reliable. See United Nations, *Methods of Estimating Basic Demographic Measures from Incomplete Data* (New York, 1967). Issued as Population Studies, Number 42.

45. Saw Swee-Hock, *Singapore Population in Transition* (Philadelphia: University of Pennsylvania Press, 1970).

46. The situation in the People's Republic of China is unknown in any detail. Contraceptives and clinical services are available at least in all the larger cities and much public encouragement has been given to delaying marriage beyond the early twenties.

47. Widjojo Nitisastro, *Population Trends in Indonesia* (Ithaca: Cornell University Press, 1970). The assumptions and working out of the projection from base year 1961 are found in ch. 11.

48. Singapore illustrates the combination of factors favorable to smaller completed families and therefore to "successful" family planning programs. When explanations for declines in fertility are sought, changes in other demographic variables which can account for substantial proportions of such changes must first be considered. Ordinary period fertility rates may rise or decline in specific years because of a change in the proportion of women in the peak marital years, for example. See Saw Swee-Hock, *Singapore Population in Transition,* ch. 10. For a careful examination of the proportion of the fertility decline attributable to family planning in a parallel case, see Ronald Freedman and Arjun L. Adlakha, "Recent Fertility Declines in Hong Kong:

The Role of Changing Age Structure," *Population Studies,* 22–2 (July 1968), 181–98.

49. Ceylon is not an exception to this statement even though fertility has declined moderately over the past few decades from high to medium levels. Other factors such as the increase in the proportion of young persons at advanced educational levels and the not unrelated rise in the average age of marriage for both men and women have been influential in the decline of fertility. There has not been any large-scale government program in effect over most of this period of gradual decline.

50. Kirk argues that in several countries, including Pakistan, fertility may actually have increased as economic and social prospects have brightened. Dudley Kirk, "Natality in the Developing Countries: Recent Trends and Prospects," in S. J. Behrman, Leslie Corsa, and Ronald Freedman, eds., *Fertility and Family Planning, A World View* (Ann Arbor: University of Michigan Press, 1969).

51. United Nations, *Monthly Bulletin of Statistics* (April 1971), special table C, pp. xx–xxi.

52. For an optimistic view of the probabilities of early declines in fertility in the less developed countries, see Donald J. Bogue, "The Demographic Breakthrough: From Projection to Control," *Population Index,* 30–4 (October 1964), 449–54. More cautiously optimistic is the paper by Ronald Freedman, "The Transition from High to Low Fertility: Challenge to Demographers," *Population Index,* 31–4 (October 1965), 417–30. Freedman specifically denied that he was ". . . predicting that *major* fertility declines are inevitable in the large populations of Latin America and Asia" but did expect "large declines" in some areas. Italics in original.

53. Norman B. Ryder, "The Character of Modern Fertility," *Annals of the American Academy of Political Science,* 369 (January 1967), 26–36; especially 31–35.

54. Because of space limitations we shall hide behind the notion that every one knows what is meant by "modernization." But certainly one major component of modernization is economic development, customarily but inadequately measured by an increase in (assumed) per capita income, and another is social development, for which no standard measurement exists. One study notes that "There is, possibly, a common underlying structure among the demographic, economic and social barometers that can be called 'modernization.' " United Nations, *Urbanization: Development Policies and Planning,* p. 33.

55. We recognize that individual countries in the region will score high, or reasonably high, on specific indexes of modernization. For example, Ceylon and the Philippines would do so with respect to educational enrollment rates. See Dudley Kirk, "A New Demographic Transition," in *Rapid Population Growth: Consequences and Policy Implications* (Baltimore: Johns Hopkins Press, 1971), pp. 138–45.

56. James T. Fawcett, "Thailand: An Analysis of Time and Distance Factors at an IUD Clinic in Bangkok," *Studies in Family Planning,* 19 (1967), 8–12.

57. See, for example, John A. Ross and David P. Smith, "Korea: Trends in

Four National KAP Surveys, 1964–67," *Studies in Family Planning,* 43 (June 1969), 7; and John Y. Takeshita, et al., "West Malaysia: 1969 Family Planning Acceptor Follow-up Survey," *Studies in Family Planning,* 51 (March 1970), 20–21.

58. Sidney Goldstein in his study of Thailand concludes that "urbanization may be linked to modernization and general economic advancement. However, the empirical interrelationship among the different variables examined here by no means demonstrates that increased urbanization in itself will transform or improve the social and economic conditions that characterize the various regions of Thailand." Goldstein, "Urbanization in Thailand, 1947–1967," p. 219.

59. Many aspects of this complex set of relationships were discussed at the second World Population Conference, held under United Nations auspices in Belgrade, Yugoslavia, in 1965. A brief, non-technical summary of conference reports and conclusions is given in *World Population: Challenge to Development* (New York: United Nations, 1966). More detail is provided in the four volumes of *Proceedings,* also published in 1966.

60. It is superficially encouraging to note that the last annual report of the United Nations Food and Agriculture Organization found food production in the Far East to be rising "at a rate comfortably ahead of population growth" (*New York Times,* August 23, 1971, p. 5). But further examination shows that only in the Far East among the developing nations was there any increase in the past year in per capita food production.

Norman Borlaug, the agronomist who in 1970 won a Nobel Peace Prize, concluded in his Laureate address, "There are no miracles in agricultural production. . . . The Green Revolution has won a temporary success in man's war against hunger and deprivation; it has given man a breathing space. *If fully implemented,* the Revolution can provide sufficient food for sustenance during the next three decades." Norman E. Borlaug, "The Green Revolution: For Bread and Peace," *Science and Public Affairs: Bulletin of the Atomic Scientists,* 27–6 (June 1971), 8 and 48. Italics added.

61. See United Nations, *Urbanization: Development Policies and Planning.*

62. Unless we accept the argument that this increasing pressure will in itself trigger more rapid increases in productivity per hectare in agriculture than would have occurred with slower population growth.

63. See M. Todaro, "A Model of Labor Migration and Urban Unemployment in Less Developed Countries," *American Economic Review,* 59–1 (March 1969), 138–48.

64. A number of studies in developing countries have shown this to be the case. For a recent analysis, see H. A. Turner and D. A. S. Jackson, "On the Determination of the General Wage Level—A World Analysis; or 'Unlimited Labour Forever,' " *Economic Journal,* 80–320 (December 1970), 827–49.

65. For a detailed analysis, see David Turnham, *The Employment Problem in Less Developed Countries: A Review of Evidence,* O.E.C.D. Development Centre, Paris, June 1970; and Ronald G. Ridker and Harold Lubell, eds., *Employment and Unemployment Problems of the Near East and South Asia* (New Delhi: Vikas Publications, 1971), 2 vols.

66. Excluding the countries of Southwest Asia (i.e., those west of Iran).

67. One exception is United Nations, *1967 Report on the World Social Situation* (New York, 1969). It is argued (p. 129) that ". . . development should constitute an objective quite different from the kind of economic growth now taking place, which is seen as inherently self-limiting and inequitable. True development is seen as, *inter alia,* a process of social change involving far-reaching shifts in the roles and power relationships of different groups. . . ."

3. THE DEMOGRAPHY OF BANGKOK—THE CASE OF A PRIMATE CITY

1. The following discussion of the world's urban-rural population distribution is based on United Nations Population Division, *Urban and Rural Population: Individual Countries, 1950–1985, and Regions and Major Areas, 1950–2000,* ESA/P/WP.33/Rev 1 (New York: United Nations, 1970).

2. United Nations, *Growth of the World's Urban and Rural Population, 1920–2000,* Population Studies No. 44 (New York: United Nations, 1969), Table 35.

3. See Norton S. Ginsberg, "The Great City in Southeast Asia," *American Journal of Sociology,* 40 (March 1955), 455–62; Donald W. Fryer, "The 'Million City' in Southeast Asia," *Geographical Review,* 43 (October 1953), 474–94.

4. See, for example, Kingsley Davis, *World Urbanization 1950–1970, Vol. 1: Basic Data for Cities, Countries, and Regions,* Population Monograph Series No. 4 (Berkeley: Institute of International Studies, 1969).

5. Norton S. Ginsberg, *Atlas of Economic Development* (Chicago: University of Chicago Press, 1961), p. 36; Surinder K. Mehta, "Some Demographic and Economic Correlates of Primate Cities," *Demography,* 1 (1964), 136–47.

6. This discussion of urbanization in South and Southeast Asia is based on United Nations Population Division, *Urban and Rural Population.*

7. United Nations, *Growth of World's Urban and Rural Population,* Tables 12, 13, and 14.

8. John C. Caldwell, "The Demographic Structure," in T. H. Silcock, ed., *Thailand, Social and Economic Studies in Development* (Canberra: Australian National University Press, 1967), pp. 33–40; United Nations Population Division, "Estimates of Crude Birth Rates, Crude Death Rates, and Expectations of Life at Birth, Regions and Countries, 1950–1965," ESA/P/WP/38 (February 22, 1971), mimeographed.

9. Gordon W. Perkin, et al., "Thailand," *Country Profiles* (New York: The Population Council, 1969), pp. 2–3.

10. *Population Growth in Thailand* (Bangkok: National Economic Development Board, 1970), p. 23.

11. Chula Chakrabongse, *Lords of Life: A History of the Kings of Thailand* (London: Alvin Redman, 1960), pp. 70–80; T. G. McGee, *The Southeast Asian City* (New York: Praeger, 1969), pp. 72–73.

12. Mark Jefferson, "The Law of the Primate City," *Geographical Review,* 29 (1939), 227.

13. In the absence of an official definition of "urban population" in any of the six Thai censuses between 1911 and 1960, the nearest equivalent to an urban place is the locality designated as a "municipal area." There are three types of municipal areas: (1) cities (Nakhorn), of which there are three—

Bangkok, Thonburi, and Chiengmai; (2) towns (Muang), which consist of the provincial administrative seats, regardless of size—there are 68 muang, one for each of the remaining 71 provinces; (3) communes (Tambol)—communities designated as municipal areas by the Ministry of the Interior. All municipal areas have some characteristics generally regarded as urban, but some of these areas are geographically extensive with a population more rural than urban. In the 1947 census, 117 places were designated as municipal areas. By the 1960 census only 3 additional places had been so classified; and this number has remained constant at 120 through 1970. The legal character of the designation means that other places which may have reached urban levels of concentration are not necessarily included on the list. As a result, measurement of change is very largely restricted to the same units, and to this extent gives a somewhat misleading picture. Since, however, most additions would presumably be in the very smallest size categories, the overall effect of the omission, except for the analysis based on areal units rather than population, may not be great.

The two largest municipal areas in Thailand, Bangkok and Thonburi, are twin cities divided by the Chao Phraya River; together they constitute the capital city area of Thailand. For purposes of this analysis, they are treated as a single urban place, referred to as Greater Bangkok. Following this procedure reduces the total number of urban places in 1947 to 116 and the number in 1960 and 1967 to 119.

14. For a fuller discussion, see Sidney Goldstein, "Urbanization in Thailand, 1947–1967," *Demography,* 8 (May 1971), 205–23.

15. The 13.1 percent of the population classified as urban in 1960 is based on registration statistics and refers to December 31. The 12.5 percent cited earlier is the census figure which refers to April 1960.

16. *Report of the Survey of Population Change, 1964–1966* (Bangkok: National Statistical Office, 1969).

17. Following publication of the 1960 census, and before destruction of the IBM cards on which those tabulations were based, a 1 percent sample tape of the census was made in order to preserve a sample of the data and to permit special tabulations. Since the published census statistics did not provide information on the characteristics of the municipal and non-municipal (urban-rural) population, the availability of the 1 percent tape, which contained information on 1960 municipal and non-municipal residence, provided a unique opportunity for gaining insights into compositional differences between the urban and rural populations.

Utilizing the dichotomy between municipal and non-municipal areas as a starting point and combining this with membership in agricultural and non-agricultural households, a five-category classification of the population along an urban-rural continuum was prepared. At the most urban level are those living in the metropolis of Bangkok in non-agricultural households. At the most rural extreme are all rural, agricultural households. Intermediate categories are (1) other urban, non-agricultural; (2) urban, agricultural; (3) rural, non-agricultural. The placement of the last two in the continuum is somewhat arbitrary; if priority were given to household type rather than residence, the order would be reversed.

In all of the analyses in this paper in which the composition of the Bangkok and the urban-rural populations is examined, the data are derived from special tabulations of the 1 percent tape.

For a fuller discussion of these data, see Sidney Goldstein, "Religious Fertility Differentials in Thailand 1960," *Population Studies,* 24 (November 1970), 327–28.

18. *Ibid.,* pp. 329–33.

19. United Nations, "Urbanization: Development Policies and Planning," *International Development Review,* 1 (New York: United Nations, 1968).

20. For a fuller discussion of the sources of data and of migration patterns, see Sidney Goldstein, "Migration Differentials and Urbanization in Thailand," paper presented at the annual meeting of the Population Association of America, Washington, D.C., April 1971.

21. See Everett S. Lee, Ann R. Miller, Carol P. Brainerd, and Richard Easterlin, *Population Redistribution and Economic Growth: United States, 1870–1950, I: Methodological Considerations and Reference Tables* (Philadelphia: American Philosophical Society, 1957); United Nations, *Methods of Measuring Internal Migration, Manual VI* (New York: United Nations, 1970).

22. Ashish Bose, "Migration Streams in India," *Report of the IUSSP Sydney Conference, Internal Migration and Urbanization,* (n.d.) pp. 597–606; Alden Speare, Jr., "Urbanization and Migration in Taiwan," *Taiwan Population Studies,* Working Paper No. 11 (March 1971).

23. International Labour Organisation, *Report to the Government of Thailand on Internal Migration* (Geneva: International Labour Organisation, 1965), p. 72.

24. Goldstein, "Migration Differentials and Urbanization in Thailand," pp. 13–26.

25. Cf. Rhoades Murphey, "Urbanization in Asia," *Ekistics,* 21 (January 1966), 8–17; Robert H. Weller, John J. Macisco, Jr., and George R. Martine, "The Relative Importance of the Components of Urban Growth in Latin America," *Demography,* 8 (May 1971), 225–32.

26. For a fuller discussion of this estimate, see Sidney Goldstein, "Urban Growth in Thailand, 1947–1967," *Journal of Social Science,* 6 (April 1969), 104–15.

27. Kingsley Davis, "The Urbanization of the Human Population," *Scientific American,* 213 (September 1965), 40–53.

28. Amos H. Hawley, James T. Fawcett, and Visid Prachuabmoh, *The Potharam Study,* Research Report No. 1 (Bangkok: Institute of Population Studies, 1970).

29. See Evaluation Unit of Family Health Project, "Monthly Report on Family Planning Acceptors" (Bangkok: Ministry of Public Health, June 1969 through April 1971).

30. See James T. Fawcett, Aree Somboonsuk, and Sumol Khaisang, "Thailand: An Analysis of Time and Distance Factors at an IUD Clinic in Bangkok," *Studies in Family Planning,* 19 (May 1967), 8–12.

31. Larry Sternstein, *Greater Bangkok Metropolitan Area Population Growth and Movement, 1956–1960,* Research Report No. 3 (Bangkok: Institute of Population Studies, 1971).

32. *Ibid.*, p. 9.

33. McGee, *The Southeast Asian City*, pp. 106–38; Gerald Breese, ed., *The City in Newly Developing Countries* (Englewood Cliffs, N.J.: Prentice-Hall, 1969), pp. 331–406.

34. For a fuller discussion of standardization, see George W. Barclay, *Techniques of Population Analysis* (New York: Wiley 1958), pp. 161–66. Readers interested in detailed age data are invited to write the author for copies of specific tables.

35. See McGee, *Southeast Asian City*, p. 115.

36. International Labour Organisation, *Report to the Government of Thailand on Internal Migration*, pp. 69–70; K. C. Zachariah, "Bombay Migration Study: A Pilot Analysis of Migration to an Asian City," *Demography*, 3 (1966), 383.

37. McGee, *Southeast Asian City*, p. 123.

38. Janet Abu-Lughod, "Migrant Adjustment to City Life: The Egyptian Case," *American Journal of Sociology*, 67 (July 1961), 22–32.

39. See, for example, Philip M. Hauser, ed., *Urbanization in Asia and the Far East* (Calcutta: UNESCO, 1957); Kingsley Davis and Hilda Hertz, "The World Distribution of Urbanization," *Bulletin of the International Statistical Institute*, 3 Part 4 (1951), 227–42; T. G. McGee, "The Urbanization Process: Western Theory and Southeast Asian Experience," *SEADAG Papers*, No. 59 (New York: The Asia Society, 1969).

40. N. V. Sovani, "The Analysis of Over-Urbanization," *Economic Development and Cultural Change*, 12 (January 1964), 113–22.

41. United Nations, *The Determinants and Consequences of Population Trends* (New York: United Nations, 1953), pp. 124–26; International Labor Organization, *Report to Government of Thailand*, pp. 79–98.

42. Robert H. Weller, "The Employment of Wives: Role Incompatibility and Fertility," *Milbank Memorial Fund Quarterly*, 46 (October 1968), 507–26.

43. *Statistical Yearbook of Thailand, Vol. 28, 1967–69* (Bangkok: National Statistical Office, 1970), p. 454.

44. *Bangkok Post*, January 19, 1971, p. 1.

45. Zachariah, *Migrants in Greater Bombay*, pp. 162–205; Speare, "Urbanization and Migration in Taiwan."

46. Caldwell, "The Demographic Structure," pp. 29–33.

47. G. William Skinner, *Chinese Society in Thailand: An Analytical History* (Ithaca, N.Y.: Cornell University Press, 1957), pp. 17–18.

48. *Statistical Yearbook of Thailand*, pp. 97–98.

49. Caldwell, "The Demographic Structure," p. 33.

50. McGee, *Southeast Asian City*, p. 114.

51. *Statistical Yearbook of Thailand*, p. 266.

52. *Ibid.*, pp. 420–22.

53. *Ibid.*, p. 417.

54. United Nations, *1967 Report of the World Social Situation* (New York: United Nations, 1969), p. 119.

55. Allan E. Goodman, "The Political Implications of Urban Development in Southeast Asia: The 'Fragment' Hypothesis," *SEADAG Papers*, No. 61 (New York: The Asia Society, 1969).

56. United Nations, *1967 Report of the World Social Situation.*

57. *Bangkok Magazine,* April 11, 1971, p. 6.

58. Faculty of Social Administration, *Social Work Survey of the Squatter Slum at Klong Toey, Bangkok* (Bangkok: Thammasat University, 1971).

59. See United Nations, *Report of the United Nations Interregional Seminar on Development Policies and Planning in Relation to Urbanization,* Pittsburgh, October 24–November 4, 1966 (New York: United Nations, 1967), pp. 41–44.

60. *Bangkok Post,* Financial Section, July 30, 1970.

61. Litchfield, Whiting, Browne and Associates, *Bangkok-Thonburi City Planning Project,* Technical Monograph (Bangkok: Ministry of the Interior, 1959 and 1970).

62. As reported in *Bangkok World,* March 24, 1971.

63. Manpower Planning Division, National Economic Development Board, "Urban Problems," May 1971, mimeographed. For an earlier set of projections of the urban-rural population and labor force, see Halvor Gille and Thip Chalothorn, "The Demographic Outlook of Thailand and Some Implications," *Proceedings of the First National Population Seminar* (Bangkok: National Research Council, 1963), pp. 113–39.

64. *Ibid.*

65. Cf. United Nations, "Urbanization: Development Policies and Planning," pp. 71–106; *Urbanization in the Second United Nations Development Decade* (New York: United Nations, 1970), pp. 21–39; United Nations, *Planning of Metropolitan Areas and New Towns* (New York: United Nations, 1967).

66. See, for example, Hauser, *Urbanization in Asia and the Far East,* pp. 33–39.

67. United Nations Economic Commission for Asia and the Far East, *Report of the Expert Working Group on Problems of Internal Migration and Urbanization.* Conference held at Bangkok, May–June, 1967, pp. 127–30.

68. Abu-Lughod, "Migrant Adjustment to City Life: The Egyptian Case" and Richard L. Meier, "Relation of Technology to the Design of Very Large Cities," in Roy Turner, ed., *India's Urban Future* (Berkeley, Calif.: University of California Press, 1962), pp. 299–323; Karen K. Peterson, "Villages in Cairo: Hypotheses vs. Data," *American Journal of Sociology,* 77. (November 1971), 560–73.

4. URBAN TENSION IN SOUTHEAST ASIA IN THE 1970S

1. The concept of pseudo-urbanization has been advanced by T. G. McGee in *The Southeast Asian City* (London: G. Bell, 1967); that of overurbanization by Bert F. Hoselitz, in "Urbanisation and Economic Growth in Asia," *Economic Development and Cultural Change,* Vol. VI, 1957, and by Philip M. Hauser, *Urbanization in Asia and the Far East* (Calcutta: UNESCO, 1957); while "subsistence urbanization" was defined by Gerald Breese in *Urbanization in Newly Developing Countries* (Englewood Cliffs, N.J.: Prentice-Hall, 1969).

2. The idea of dualism is basically an economic one, though it has been extended to other aspects of urbanization as well. See, for example, Bryan

J. L. Berry, "City Size and Economic Development," in Leo Jacobson and Ved Prakash, *Urbanization and National Development* (Beverly Hills: Sage Publications, 1971), p. 137. The concept of creeping urbanism was proposed by James F. Guyot in "Creeping Urbanism and Political Development in Malaysia," in Robert T. Daland, ed., *Comparative Urban Research* (Beverly Hills: Sage, 1969), pp. 124–61.

3. Sidney Goldstein, in Chapter 3 of this book.

4. Robert W. Oliver, "Greater Djakarta: The Capital City of Indonesia" (Washington: International Bank for Reconstruction and Development, Economic Staff Working Paper No. 105, 1970), mimeographed, pp. 15 and 34.

5. A. A. Laquian, *Slums and Squatters in Six Philippine Cities,* a monograph from a project supported by the Southeast Asia Development Advisory Group, The Asia Society.

6. *Ibid.*

7. Sidney Goldstein, in chapter 3 of this book.

8. A. A. Laquian, "Urban Insurgency: New Communist Strategy," *Solidarity,* April 1969.

9. James F. Guyot, "Creeping Urbanism and Political Development in Malaysia," p. 124.

10. Frederick L. Wernstedt and Paul D. Simkins, "Migration and the Settlement of Mindanao," *The Journal of Asian Studies,* XXV, No. 1 (November 1965), 101.

11. *Ibid.,* p. 102.

12. See, for example, A. A. Laquian, ed., *Rural-Urban Migrants and Metropolitan Development* (Toronto: Intermet, 1971).

13. Edward M. Bruner, "Medan: The Role of Kinship in an Indonesian City," in William Mangin, ed., *Peasants in Cities* (Boston: Houghton Mifflin, 1970), p. 126.

14. *Ibid.,* p. 127.

15. *Ibid.,* p. 128.

16. Man Gap Lee, "Social Organizations," in Man Gap Lee and Herbert Barringer, eds., *A City in Transition, Urbanization in Taegu* (Seoul: Hollym Corporation, 1971), p. 353.

17. A. A. Laquian, *The City in Nation-Building* (Manila: School of Public Administration, UP, 1966), ch. 3.

18. Man Gap Lee, "Social Organizations," p. 357.

19. Bruner, "Medan," p. 130.

20. Donn V. Hart, "Philippine Rural-Urban Migration: A View from Caticugan, a Bisayan Village," *Behavior Science Notes,* 6, No. 2 (1971), 129.

21. Ali bin Esa, "Kuala Lumpur," in A. A. Laquian, ed., *Rural-Urban Migrants and Metropolitan Development* (Toronto: Intermet, 1971).

22. James M. Anthony, "Urban Politics in Malaysia," unpublished Ph.D. dissertation, Australian National University, 1971, p. 14.

23. Sidney Goldstein, in chapter 3 of this book.

24. *Ibid.*

25. Allan Goodman, "The Political Implications of Urban Development in Southeast Asia: The 'Fragment' Hypothesis," *Economic Development and Cultural Change,* 20, No. 1 (October 1971), 117–30.

26. G. M. Desmond and Ved Prakash, "Financing Housing and Urban Development in the ECAFE Region." Paper read at the SEADAG Urban Development Panel Seminar, University of Wisconsin, October 13–14, 1971.

5. MIGRATION, URBANIZATION, AND POLITICS IN PAKISTAN

1. Definition of an urban area as adopted by the Pakistan Census Commissioner. See Government of Pakistan, *Population Census of Pakistan, 1961,* Bulletin No. 2 (Karachi: Ministry of Home Affairs, 1961), p. 13.

2. Ved Prakash, *New Towns in India* (Durham, N.C.: Program in Comparative Studies on Southern Asia, 1969), p. 3, Table 1.

3. Government of Ceylon, *Ceylon's Population* (Colombo, 1965).

4. Kingsley Davis, "The Origin and Growth of Urbanization in the World," *American Journal of Sociology,* LX, No. 5 (March 1955), 427.

5. Kingsley Davis, "The Urbanization of the Human Population," in Sylvia Feis Fava, ed., *Urbanization in World Perspective* (New York: Thomas Y. Crowell, 1968), p. 42.

6. D. J. Dwyer, "The Problem of In-Migration and Squatter Settlements in Asia Cities: Two Case Studies, Manila and Victoria-Kowloon," *Asian Studies,* II, No. 2 (August 1964), 151.

7. M. G. Kutty, "Calcutta: Problems and Plans," *Asia,* No. 2 (Summer 1968), p. 57.

8. United Nations Secretariat, Bureau of Social Affairs, *Report on the World Social Situation* (New York, 1957), p. 113.

9. Robert I. Crane, "Urbanism in India," *American Journal of Sociology,* LX, No. 5 (March 1955), 463.

10. Gustav F. Papanek, "The Location of Industry," *Pakistan Development Review,* X, No. 3 (Autumn 1970), 300.

11. Prakash, *New Towns in India,* p. 5, Table II.

12. Forthcoming publication entitled *Political Groups and Development in Pakistan.*

13. Nirmal Kumar Bose, "Calcutta: A Premature Metropolis," *Scientific American,* 213, No. 3 (September 1965), 91.

14. Government of Pakistan, *Census of Pakistan, Vol. 3, West Pakistan* (Karachi: Ministry of Home Affairs, 1961), p. ii–121.

15. Government of India, *The Imperial Gazetteer of India, Vol. XVI* (Oxford: The Clarendon Press, 1908), pp. 106–8.

16. For a detailed discussion of the anti-Ahmadya movement, see *Government of the Punjab, Report of the Court of Inquiry Constituted under Punjab Act II of the 1954 Enquiry into the Punjab Disturbances of 1953* (Lahore: Government Printing Press, 1954).

17. Shahid Javed Burki, "Social and Economic Determinants of Political Violence—A Case Study of the Punjab," *Middle East Journal,* 25 (Autumn 1971), 465–80.

18. Government of India, *The Gazetteer of India, Vol. XXIII* (Oxford: The Clarendon Press, 1908), p. 406.

19. For a fuller report see my forthcoming volume already referred to.

20. Sultan S. Hashmi, Masihur Rahman Khan, and Karol J. Krotki, *The People of Karachi* (Karachi: The Institute of Development Economics, 1964), pp. 208–9, Table 5.01.

21. Farhat Hussain, "Population Growth and Problems of Rawalpindi and Islamabad," in Shafik H. Hashmi and Garth N. Jones, eds., *Problems of Urbanization in Pakistan* (Karachi: National Institute of Public Administration, 1967), pp. 107–10.

22. Ruth Glass, *Urban-Rural Differences in Southern Asia* (Delhi: UNESCO Research Centre on Social and Economic Development in Southern Asia, 1962), p. 3.

23. Government of Pakistan, *Census of Pakistan, 1951, Vol. I* (Karachi: Ministry of Home and Kashmir Affairs, 1951), p. 43.

24. J. Russel Andrus and Azizali F. Mohammad, *The Economy of Pakistan* (Stanford: Stanford University Press, 1958), p. 314.

25. Gerald Breese, *Urbanization in Newly Developing Countries* (Englewood Cliffs, N.J.: Prentice-Hall, 1966), p. 88.

26. Andrus and Mohammad, *The Economy of Pakistan,* p. 467.

27. Hashmi, et al., *The People of Karachi,* pp. 220–25.

28. Donald J. Bogue and K. C. Zachariah, "Urbanization and Migration in India," in Roy Turner, ed., *India's Urban Future* (Berkeley and Los Angeles: University of California Press, 1962), p. 27.

29. The net international immigration during the census decade 1951–61 was only 0.8 million. See Government of Pakistan, *Population Census of Pakistan, 1961, Vol. I* (Karachi: Ministry of Home and Kashmir Affairs, 1961), pp. 11–17.

30. Government of Pakistan, *Population Census of Pakistan, Vol. I,* pp. ii–16.

31. Including the 1951 and 1961 censuses, a demographic survey of Karachi, a survey of 13 towns in West Pakistan, a survey of 27 villages in the Punjab, and a survey of 5 villages in Hazara district.

32. Imtiazuddin Husain, Mohammad Afzal, and Syed Amjad Bahadur Rizvi, *Social Characteristics of the People of Karachi* (Karachi: The Pakistan Institute of Development Economics, 1965), p. 44.

33. Joan M. Nelson, *Migrants, Urban Poverty and Instability in Developing Nations* (Cambridge: Center for International Affairs, Harvard University, 1969), *passim.*

34. Data taken from Sultan S. Hashmi, et al., *The People of Karachi, passim.* In this respect the survey towns resemble some of the cities surveyed in India. Thus for Kanpur: "Migrants who are either from the same district or from the neighboring districts constitute 54.68 percent." Majumdar, et al., *Social Contours of an Industrial City* (London: Asia Publishing House, 1960), p. 71. However, in the case of the city of Lucknow it was noted that "very few of them [migrants] . . . belong to the district of Lucknow itself. The proportion of these latter is only 13 percent of the rural immigrants, 2 percent of the urban immigrants, and 10 percent of the total." Nearly one-tenth of the migrant population had come from outside the state of Uttar Pradesh. Mukerjee and Singh, *Social Profiles of a Metropolis* (London: Asia Publishing House, 1961), pp. 49–50.

35. In the case of the migrants to Agra, Chauhan found that about 80 percent of the households made only one move, 12 percent made two moves, and the remaining 8 percent made more than two moves. *Trends in Urbanization in Agra* (Bombay: Allied Publishers, 1966), p. 308. In the Kanpur study it was

noted that nearly 13 percent of the migrants reached the city after having first settled in another urban area. Majumdar, et al., *Social Contours of an Industrial City,* p. 80.

36. See William H. and Charlotte Viall Wiser, *Behind Mud Walls, 1930–1960* (Berkeley and Los Angeles: University of California Press, 1969); Oscar Lewis, *Village Life in Northern India* (New York: Vintage Books, 1958); and Zekiye Eglar, *A Punjab Village in Pakistan* (New York: Columbia University Press, 1960). Also sèe Prakash Tandon's biography, *Punjab Century, 1857–1957* (Berkeley and Los Angeles: University of California Press, 1968). Muhammad Rafique Raza in his sociological study of two villages in the Punjab found some occupational instability, but makes no reference to population turnover as an important characteristic of modern-day rural life. See *Two Pakistani Villages: A Study in Social Stratification* (Lahore: University of the Punjab, 1969), p. 31.

37. Shahid Javed Burki, "Rural-Urban Migration: A Case Study of Hazara Migrants in Karachi," *Government College Economic Journal,* III, No. 2 (June 1970).

38. Government of Pakistan, *Fourth Five-Year Plan, 1970–1975* (Islamabad: Planning Commission, 1970), pp. 55–57.

39. For a detailed discussion see ch. 6 of my forthcoming book.

40. Robert LaPorte, "Succession in Pakistan: Continuity and Change in a Garrison State," *Asian Survey,* IX (November 1969), 853. There are other political scientists who support this view. Thus: "With the twenty-twenty vision of hindsight, my informants this week have pinpointed the beginning of Ayub's decline on the India-Pakistan War of 1965." Phillips Talbot, *Pakistan Turns a Corner* (PT-1-69), Field Staff Reports, South Asia Series, XIII, No. 1 (1969), 5.

41. Government of Pakistan, *Monthly Statistical Bulletin* (Karachi: Central Statistical Office, 1969), various issues. Azizur Rahman Khan, "What Has Been Happening to Real Wages in Pakistan?" *The Pakistan Development Review,* VII, No. 3 (Autumn 1967), 317–47.

42. Wayne Wilcox, "Pakistan in 1969: Once Again at the Starting Point," *Asian Survey,* X, No. 2 (February 1970), 73.

43. Talukdar Maniruzzaman, "Crisis in Political Development and the Collapse of the Ayub Regime," *Journal of Developing Areas,* V (January 1971).

44. Government of Pakistan, *Services Reorganization Committee: Composition and Terms of Reference* (Rawalpindi: Printing Corporation of Pakistan Press, 1969), p. 1. See also Lawrence Ziring, *The Ayub Khan Era, Politics in Pakistan, 1958–1969* (Syracuse, N.Y.: Syracuse University Press, 1971), pp. 197–98.

45. W. M. Dobell, "Ayub Khan as President of Pakistan," *Pacific Affairs,* XLII, No. 3 (Fall 1969), 307.

46. As compared with a total of 46 administrative districts.

47. Joan M. Nelson, *Migrants, Urban Poverty and Instability in Developing Nations.*

6. SOCIO-POLITICAL CONSEQUENCES OF INTERSTATE MIGRATIONS IN INDIA

1. The 1931 figure is from K. C. Zachariah, *A Historical Study of Internal Migration in the Indian Sub-Continent, 1901–1931* (Bombay: Asia Publishing

House, 1964); the 1961 figure is from the *Census of India 1961*. The figures are not, however, exactly comparable because of changes in state and international boundaries, but they do provide a crude indication that internal migration in India, though still modest by European and American standards, has substantially grown.

2. *Constitution of India,* Article 19.

3. Article 29 of the constitution specifies that "any section of the citizens residing in the territory of India or any part thereof having a distinct language, script or culture of its own shall have the right to conserve the same"; Article 30 says that "all minorities, whether based on religion or language, shall have the right to establish and administer educational institutions of their choice" and "the State shall not, in granting aid to educational institutions, discriminate against any educational institution on the ground that it is under the management of a minority, whether based on religion or language." Article 350A stipulates that "it shall be the endeavor of every state and every local authority within the State to provide adequate facilities for instruction in the mother tongue at the primary stage of education to children belonging to linguistic minority groups; and the President may issue such directions to any State as he considers necessary or proper for securing the provision of such facilities." Article 350B creates a Special Officer to be appointed by the President of India to ensure the protection of linguistic minorities.

4. National migration data are published in Volume I (India), Part II-C (iii) and Part II-C (iv) of the *Census of India 1961*. There are also separate migration volumes for each of the states. In this paper all the migration data arranged by district have been taken from the state volumes. In the state series these volumes are generally published as Part II-C and are titled "Cultural and Migration Tables" containing both language and migration data. There is also a separate volume (for Greater Bombay), published as Part X (i–c), *Special Migration Tables.*

5. It is, of course, impossible from the census data to distinguish among female migrants as to who migrates to the labor force, to marry, or to accompany their migrant husbands.

6. Obviously this is a very crude estimate. For a more precise estimate we would need to know the mortality rate for each migrant age group.

7. We can, however, report where in India Pakistani migrants settled (as of 1961). Of the 8.3 million migrants from Pakistan, 5.2 million lived in the Punjab and West Bengal while 3.1 million lived in other states of India. The largest number (mainly Bengalis) now live in Assam (with 775,000 migrants from Pakistan), followed by Delhi (508,000, mainly Punjabis), Tripura (395,000, mainly Bengalis), U.P. (335,000), Rajasthan (305,000), Maharashtra (273,000), Madhya Pradesh (179,000), Gujarat (139,000), and Bihar (101,000). After the Bengalis and Punjabis, the largest single migrant community from Pakistan are the Sindhis. Though the specific number of Sindhi migrants from Pakistan is not known, we do know that there are 1,371,000 persons who reported Sindhi as their mother tongue in the 1961 census. Sindhis are often shopkeepers in the textile trade in many Indian cities; there are substantial Sindhi concentrations in Jaisalmer and Barmer districts in Rajasthan (near the Sindhi border) and in Thana district outside Bombay.

8. For a mapping of migration flows see the Census Atlas, part IX of Vol-

ume I of the *Census of India 1961,* edited by Dr. P. Sen Gupta, especially maps 60, 61, and 62.

9. Bihar has 418,000 migrants from the other five Hindi states, Madhya Pradesh 890,000, Punjab 575,000, Rajasthan 576,000, Uttar Pradesh 952,000, and Delhi 872,000.

10. See S. C. Sinha, Jyoti Sen, and Sudhir Panchbhai, "The Concept of Dhiku Among the Tribes of Chota Nagpur," *Man in India,* XLIX, No. 2 (April–June 1969), 121–137.

11. For an account of the Telengana nativist agitations, see Hugh Gray, "The Demand for a Separate Telengana State in India," *Asia Survey,* XI, No. 5 (May 1971); and Duncan B. Forrester, "Sub-regionalism in India: The Case of Telengana," *Pacific Affairs,* XLIII (Spring 1970). A history of the *mulki* movement and the various restrictions in Hyderabad and later in Telengana on the employment of non-*mulkis* can be found in K. V. Narayana Rao, *Telengana Regional Committee* (New Delhi: Indian Institute of Public Administration, 1970).

12. For studies of the Chota Nagpur region and its tribes, see F. Ivern, *Chotanagpur Survey* (Ranchi: Indian Social Institute, 1969): R. O. Dhan, *These Are My Tribesmen: A Study of the Oraon* (Ranchi: G. E. L. Church Press, 1967); Narmadeshwar Prasad, *Land and People of Tribal Bihar* (Ranchi: Bihar Tribal Research Institute, 1961); Suresh Singh, *Duststorm and Hanging Mist* (Calcutta: Firma K. L. Mukhopadhyaya, 1966), an account of a late-nineteenth-century millenarian movement against outsiders; S. P. Sinha, *The Problem of Land Alienation of the Tribals In and Around Ranchi* (Ranchi: Bihar Tribal Welfare Research Institute, 1968); L. P. Vidyarthi, *Cultural Configuration of Ranchi: Survey of an Emerging Industrial City of Tribal India* (Ranchi, n.d.); L. P. Vidyarthi, *Leadership in India* (Bombay: Asia Publishing House, 1967), part II, "Tribal Leadership" (especially the papers by L. P. Vidyarthi, and S. P. Sinha); Sachidandanda, *Profiles of Tribal Culture in Bihar* (Calcutta: Firma K. L. Mukhopadhyaya, 1965). For earlier studies of the Oraons and Mundas, see the classical studies by the famous ethnographer, S. C. Roy.

13. For an account of the history of migration to Assam, see the *Census of India, 1951,* XII, Part I-A, Assam, Manipur, and Tripura by R. B. Vaghaiwalla, pp. 31–33, 66–83, and 356–60; See also the *Census of India, 1961,* III, Part I-A, Assam, by E. H. Pakyntein. For a brief account of the growth of the tea industry, see P. C. Goswami, *The Economic Development of Assam* (Bombay: Asia Publishing House, 1961), pp. 22–31, 141–57. The problem of Pakistani "infiltration" is described by B. P. Chaliha, *Infiltration and Deportation of Pakistanis,* The Directorate of Information and Public Relations, Government of Assam, n.d. Accounts of the anti-Bengali movements can be found in H. N. Barua, *A Glimpse of Assam Disturbances* (Gauhati, 1960); Charu Chandra Bhandari, *Thoughts on Assam Disturbances* (Rajghat: Kashi, 1961); Sahitya Sabha, *Assam's State Language* (Assam: Jorhat, 1960). The standard history of Assam is by Sir Edward Gait, *A History of Assam* (Calcutta: Thacker Spink, 1933; first published in 1905). For a popular introduction to Assam, see Hem Barua, *The Red River and Blue Hill* (Gauhati: Lawyer's Book Stall, 1954), revised edition, 1962.

14. For an account of government policy toward preferences to local population in employment, see the *Report of the National Commission on Labour,* Government of India, Ministry of Labour, Employment and Rehabilitation, 1969, pp. 74–78.

15. These restrictions in scheduled areas are enumerated in the Fifth Schedule of the constitution for all states, excluding Assam, and in the Sixth Schedule for the Tribal Areas in Assam.

16. Subsequently declared unconstitutional.

17. In West Bengal, for example, the state with the largest proportion of immigrants from outside, there has been a steady rise in immigrants, from 2.2 percent of the population in 1881 to 6.6 percent in 1901, 8.9 percent in 1921, 9.5 percent in 1941, and 15.9 percent in 1961. (This latter increase is largely the result of refugees from East Bengal.)

7. THE YOUTH COHORT REVISITED

1. Kozo Ueda, "Analysis of Results of the One Percent Sample Tabulation of the Population Census of Indonesia, 1961" (Djakarta: Central Bureau of Statistics, 1964), mimeograph, p. 31.

2. Widjojo Nitisastro, *Population Trends in Indonesia* (Ithaca: Cornell University Press, 1970), p. 237.

3. Etienne Van de Walle, "Some Characteristic Features of Census Age Distributions in Illiterate Populations," *American Journal of Sociology,* 71, No. 5 (March 1966), 549–55.

4. Ansley J. Coale and Paul Demeny, *Methods of Estimating Basic Demographic Measures from Incomplete Data* (New York: United Nations ST/SOA/Series A/42, Manual IV, 1967), pp. 17–22.

5. Nathan Keyfitz and Wilhelm Flieger, *Population: Facts and Techniques of Demography* (San Francisco: Freeman, 1971).

6. Nathan Keyfitz, "Age Distribution as a Challenge to Development," *American Journal of Sociology,* 70, No. 6 (May 1965), 659–68.

7. *Statistical Pocketbook of Indonesia* (Djakarta: Central Bureau of Statistics, 1963), p. 31.

8. J. Wiramihardja, *Civics* (Bandung: Dhiwantara, 1963), p. 48.

9. *Statistical Pocketbook of Indonesia,* p. 77.

10. J. R. Harris and M. P. Todaro, "Migration, Unemployment and Development," *American Economic Review,* 60, No. 1 (March 1970), 126–142.

11. Gino Germani, *Politica y Sociedad en Una Epoca de Transicion* (Buenos Aires: Editorial Paidos, 1962), p. 151 and *passim.*

8. STUDENTS AND THE ESTABLISHMENT IN INDONESIA: THE STATUS-GENERATION GAP

1. Boulding coined this term to symbolize the seemingly limitless resources and reckless behavior characteristic of open societies. He contrasted the cowboy economy with a spaceman economy of the future when, if man is to survive, the earth will have to be treated as a closed, steady-state, resource-recycling spaceship. See his "The Economics of the Coming Spaceship Earth," in Henry Jarrett, ed., *Environmental Quality in a Growing Economy* (Baltimore: Johns Hopkins Press, 1966).

2. Indonesia's crude birth rate and population growth rate are approximately double those of the United States, whereas Americans annually spend on recreation alone roughly three times Indonesia's GNP. *World Tables* (Washington, D.C.: International Bank for Reconstruction and Development, January 1971), Table 2; *East Asia: Economic Growth Trends* (Washington, D.C.: Agency for International Development, May 1972), p. 10; *Information Please Almanac Atlas and Yearbook 1971* (n. p.: Dan Golenpaul Associates, 1970), p. 130.

3. These figures are approximate. *Britannica Book of the Year 1972* (Chicago: Encyclopaedia Britannica, 1972), pp. 353 and 572.

4. Elements of such a view can be found, for example, in Barry Commoner, *The Closing Circle* (New York: Knopf, 1971), pp. 237–49. There is a temptation, of course, to overemphasize distribution, especially in a nation as bifurcated as Indonesia with its sparsely settled outer arc and densely packed core. When the editors of the Djakarta daily *Merdeka* in an editorial on "Production and Population" (September 23, 1971) downgraded the goal of slowing future consumption through family planning in favor of redistributing the population and increasing its productivity through technology, they failed to mention the high cost per transmigrant of resettling people, the possibly maldistributive effects of capital-intensive production (high-capital-input "miracle" rice, for example) on employment and income, or the long-run importance of also attempting to reduce the rate of natural increase.

5. *Demographic Yearbook 1969* (New York: United Nations, 1970), Table 6; Widjojo Nitisastro, *Population Trends in Indonesia* (Ithaca: Cornell University Press, 1970), p. 164.

6. Nitisastro, ch. 7. The actual extent of rejuvenation, however, may have been exaggerated by errors in the 1961 census. See the chapter in this volume by Nathan Keyfitz.

7. *Ibid.*, pp. 237–38; J. A. C. Mackie, "Indonesia in the 1980's," *Australian Outlook,* 25 (December 1971), 336–37; and *Harian KAMI,* September 15, 1972.

8. This usage is comparable to Karl Mannheim's notion of an "actual generation," that is, not an age-set or biological generation but a cohort whose members also share some concrete historical experience. See "The Problem of Generations" in his *Essays on the Sociology of Knowledge,* ed. by Paul Kecskemeti (London: Routledge and Kegan Paul, 1952), esp. pp. 302–4.

9. For evidence in support of a similar hypothesis relating the generational experience of economic insecurity vs. security to the endorsement of "acquisitive" vs. "post-bourgeois" values, see Ronald Inglehart, "The Silent Revolution in Europe: Intergenerational Change in Post-Industrial Societies," *American Political Science Review,* 65 (1971), 991–1017.

10. Consider, for example, a study of political socialization and the students' "revolt" in 1965–66 in which Stephen Douglas has argued that "Indonesians generally do not have their Oedipal tensions very firmly repressed, and they need to express their father-hatred from time to time." Even if the assertion were true, the Oedipus complex must have been a part of Indonesian psychology before October 1, 1965, when students did not actively oppose the regime, as well as afterward, when they did. When he inserts the notion that

the father-hatred pent up before 1965 erupted into militant opposition at that time because of the failure of certain unspecified societal "defensive mechanisms," Douglas directs attention away from Freudian categories toward external conditions of incentive and constraint—for example, the economic crisis and the balance of power between the Communist Party and the Army. These conditions changed drastically with the attempted coup, and they are much more useful in explaining student political behavior before and after that event than intrapsychic speculation. Stephen A. Douglas, *Political Socialization and Student Activism in Indonesia* (Urbana: University of Illinois, 1970), pp. 170 and 38.

11. Stratified sampling of the politico-administrative elite ensured a roughly even spread across government departments dealing primarily with political, economic, and socio-religious affairs, and across the governing non-party civilian-military alliance, the Islamic parties, and the non-Islamic parties in Parliament. Eleven of eighteen departments and seven of eight legislative groups were represented in rough proportion to their numerical strength and political importance. Some three-fourths of the students were, by institution, from the University of Indonesia in Djakarta, the Institute of Education and Pedagogy in Jogjakarta, or Padjadjaran University in Bandung. Another three-fourths, by faculty, were in law or a social science, especially economics. The 36 adults and 2,344 students represent roughly 3 percent samples of the senior central bureaucracy and of the nation's university student population, respectively. For further information, see my doctoral dissertation, "Exploring Elite Political Culture in Indonesia: Community and Change," Yale University, New Haven, September 1972, Parts III.A and III.D.

12. The two orientations on which students and adults did not differ significantly were perceived powerlessness and trust in leaders. Even when perceived normlessness was combined selectively with perceived powerlessness, the resulting scale of perceived anomie failed to distinguish significantly between the two groups. For a full discussion of the scales and the responses, see my dissertation, Part III.C and Appendix II.

13. For example, on June 21, 1972, a Djakarta daily, *Kompas,* published a letter from a student at the Technological Institute in Bandung—apparently not a Javanese—complaining that "these days it is more difficult for people from the regions than for people from Java . . . to find employment in some state enterprises and government departments," despite the fact that "the sources of foreign exchange for the salaries of the employees lie mainly in the regions." To illustrate, the student cited the state oil corporation, more than 90 percent of whose revenues originate on Sumatra, yet whose employees "are almost all Javanese" and where "non-Javanese have a hard time getting jobs." The student wondered whether this employment bias might be due to the greater size of the Javanese population, to its greater political power, or to a Javanese view of people in the regions as politically unreliable. Whatever the accuracy of such perceptions, this letter suggests that regional and ethnic differences are likely to become explosive when they are seen to be a basis for discrimination in the allocation of a particular good, in this case jobs. And the scarcer the good, the more explosive the perceptions.

14. The "strongly" religious adult was operationally defined as someone

whose self-definition, revealed in his verbal and nonverbal behavior, rested wholly or in important part on his religious affiliation. Those for whom religion was an unimportant source of identity were placed in the "weak" category. Extended personal acquaintance and interview evidence could be relied upon in deciding which category best described an individual. Such means were unavailable for the students, who were categorized according to their own answers to a question on religiosity in a self-administered questionnaire. The "strongly" religious students were those who reported that they "regularly" practiced the observances of their religion (prayer and so forth), while those who reported they "did not," "seldom," or "irregularly" observed such requirements were considered "weakly" religious. In the anti-Communist atmosphere of the New Order, students may have exaggerated their religiosity, but probably not much since they were not asked to write their names; or the most frequently used response category—"regularly"—may not have discriminated finely enough even though three other possible responses were offered across which respondents could spread themselves. All in all, it is likely that among the 1,359 who answered "regularly" there were a number who would have been classified as only "weakly" religious under the more independent and comprehensive measure of piety applied to the adults.

15. Adult elite respondents whose ethnic affiliation was an important source of personal identity were considered "strongly" ethnic; those for whom it was not were classified "weak." An exact counterpart measure of strength of ethnic identity was unobtainable in the questionnaire format used on the university students, especially given the sensitivity of questions about one's *sukubangsa* (ethnic group). Therefore a less obtrusive, linguistic measure was used. Asked separately in which regional language their mothers, fathers, and themselves were most fluent, students reporting the same language for all three instances were classified as having "strong" ethnic identities. Students who spoke no regional language at all or whose regional language differed from that of one or both parents were considered "weakly" ethnic. As with the student measure of religious intensity, the student measure of ethnic intensity may exaggerate somewhat the strength of ethnic identity.

16. That is, the counter-hypothesis was supported: "Strongly" religious adults were indeed less tolerant than "weakly" religious adults by a difference of means of 2.40 (on a scale from 1.0 or extreme intolerance to 5.0 or extreme tolerance) and "strongly" religious students were likewise less tolerant than "weakly" religious students by a difference of means of .80 (on the same scale). At the same time the status-generational hypothesis was washed out: although the "weakly" religious adults were more tolerant than the "weakly" religious students by a difference of means of 1.33, the "strongly" religious adults were on the contrary *less* tolerant than the "strongly" religious students by a difference of means of .27. The average control variable (religious intensity) difference of means $(2.40+.80)/2=1.60$ is more than three times as large as the average status-generational difference of means $(1.33-.27)/2=.53$. The last difference of means (.27) was subtracted because it ran counter to the hypothesized direction of the relationship. For the full matrix of controls and results, see Table III.37 in my dissertation.

17. For example, an editorial in the October 28, 1971, issue of the Djakarta

daily, *Harian KAMI,* exponent of the 1966 generation, cited the complaint of a spokesman for the 1928 generation that if in their youth he and his friends had been like today's young people—who, he alleged, prefer talking and smoking marijuana to mixing with the peasants in the villages—Indonesia would never have won its independence. Such men have mythicized their own youth, the student editors wrote in rebuttal, and they "fail to realize that 26 years of independence have bred a new generation that is not impressed by the 'pioneering [1928] generation' or the '1945 generation of founders' [of the Republic]." The editors minimized the current danger of a generation gap, but warned that if the older generation were to go on banning young people's discussions and trying to deflect youth's energies away from participation in decisions and toward the mere passive carrying out of apolitical development plans, then a real split could result.

18. On the 1.0–5.0 scale of increasing preference for central over regional interests, the administrators' mean was 2.9 compared with 3.4 for the politicians.

19. The term is Gunnar Myrdal's. See his *The Challenge of World Poverty: A World Anti-Poverty Program in Outline* (New York: Vintage Books, 1971), ch. 7.

20. Sajidiman Surjohadiprodjo, "The Defence of Indonesia," in K. K. Sinha, ed., *Problems of Defence of South and East Asia* (Bombay: Manaktalas, 1969), p. 232. Sajidiman has since been promoted to major general.

21. For these issues, policies, and hints of policy, see the Djakarta press generally over this period. One illustration is an editorial in the official *Suara Karya* of September 18, 1972, arguing that students do not need permanent political organizations.

22. On August 8, 1972, *Harian KAMI* wrote that unlike the Indonesians of differing regional origins who studied together in elite colonial schools, who could see the colony as a whole, and who went on to unify and free the nation, the contemporary student generation might cherish national unity less for having in large part been educated entirely in their home provinces. Nor was this editorial the first expression by intellectuals in the capital city of the possibility of rising parochialism in the regions as a consequence of the decentralization and democratization of higher education.

23. This may be because the non-Muslim (Christian) minority perceived the central government—itself led mainly by secular or nominal Muslims—as a buffer between them and extreme Muslim elites in the regions. But since there were only four non-Muslims in the establishment sample, both the observed difference and this explanation may exaggerate the importance of religious affiliation.

24. For a vivid portrayal of ethno-economic conflict in Djakarta's underworld—triggered by trivial incidents but reflecting both contemporary poverty and the heritage of colonial Batavia where particular ethnic groups dominated particular fields of activity and resided in particular neighborhoods—see Richard Critchfield's report on Djakarta through the experience of a pedicab driver, *Hello, Mister! Where are You Going?,* Part Two (New York: Alicia Patterson Fund, [1971]).

25. The 5.7 percent overall growth rate is made up of two component rates:

net immigration (3.3) and natural increase (2.4). The latter rate alone is higher than the 2.1 percent annual growth rate estimated for the country as a whole. The comparison helps explain why in August 1970 Djakarta was declared by its Governor a closed city to any immigrant who could not prove permanent employment and lawful residence there within six months of arrival. This Draconian step appears to have had some effect on cutting down the influx. *Kompas,* June 9, 1971 and June 15, 1972.

26. *Nusantara,* October 15, 1971: *Harian KAMI,* October 28, 1971.

27. These estimates are based for 1966 on an examination of the membership of the executive bodies of KAMI and of its Djakarta and Bandung branches, of *Harian KAMI*'s Board of Editors, and of the leadership of the KAMI-associated Arief Rachman Hakim Regiment, and for the more recent period on the signatories of the famous "Overcast January" statement of January 6, 1972, in which youths who had protested Mrs. Suharto's tourism project reluctantly "surrendered" to the sheer armed might of the military. *Harian KAMI* published the latter statement the following day.

28. Peter Polomka, *Indonesia Since Sukarno* (Ringwood, Victoria: Penguin Books Australia, 1971), pp. 202–3.

29. *Ibid.,* pp. 203–4.

30. For an interpretation that de-emphasizes the ethnic dimension even more, see Douglas, *Political Socialization and Student Activism in Indonesia.*

31. In a survey of 545 students at Gadjah Mada University in Jogjakarta conducted by Joseph Fischer in 1960, for example, 74 percent reported they had "regular contact in the university" with members of ten or more different ethnic groups. The figure among Javanese students was 70 percent. Only 13 students—all Javanese, incidentally—said they associated only with members of their own ethnic group. Even shrinking these figures to eliminate students who answered according to the ideal of cross-ethnic integration rather than some less palatable reality, the impression of substantial and widespread inter-ethnic communication remains. These figures were obtained through secondary analysis of Fischer's data, and his generosity in making them available is gratefully acknowledged.

32. March 14, 1972. Youth unrest, the editorial concludes, is not a "problem of the stomach."

33. Arief is not suggesting that the world of order be dismantled in favor of the world of creation—he is in no sense an anarchist—but simply that there should be communication and understanding between them and that the one should not overwhelm the other. Arief also associates the lack of a tradition of criticism in official culture with a failure to adhere to the scientific method. He has charged, for example, that intelligence agencies in Indonesia "don't operate phenomenologically on the basis of a 'null hypothesis' " but instead seek facts to fit a prepared script. (*Proklamasi,* January 18, 1972.) Insofar as university graduates have acquired in the classroom an empiricist or experimentalist outlook, they may come in conflict—at least when sensitive political questions are involved—with the more norm-affirming agents of an official hierarchy.

34. *Tempo,* February 26, 1972.

35. On Rendra, see H. B. Jassin, *Angkatan '66: Prosa dan Puisi* (Djakarta:

Gunung Agung, 1968), p. 301, and the special issue of *Basis,* XXI (January 1972), pp. 122–33 and the cover photographs. On Nurcholish, see the cover story in *Tempo,* July 29, 1972.

36. *Pedoman,* December 31, 1971.

37. *Merdeka,* March 17, 1972.

38. *Tempo,* March 11, 1972.

39. On the singing of "We Shall Overcome," see *ibid.;* on the Bandung incident, see Polomka, pp. 197–200.

10. YOUTH PROTEST IN SRI LANKA (CEYLON)

1. Ceylon *Observer,* April 6, 1971.

2. O. E. R. Abhayaratne and C. H. S. Jayewardene, *Fertility Trends in Ceylon* (Colombo: Colombo Apothecaries, 1967), Table VI, p. 22.

3. *Ibid.,* Table 7, p. 24.

4. From Government of Ceylon, *Report on Vital Statistics,* Administration Reports, Registrar General; United Nations, *Demographic Yearbook, 1966;* Department of Census and Statistics and Provisional Figures by Dr. N. H. Wright.

5. For the debate over the consequences of the anti-malaria campaign and the exact sources of the 1946–47 change in population growth rate, see H. Cullimbine, "An Analysis of the Vital Statistics of Ceylon," *Ceylon Journal of Medical Science* (July 1950), pp. 92–272; P. Newman, *Malaria Eradication and Population Growth* (Ann Arbor School of Public Health, University of Michigan, 1965); H. Frederickson, "Determinants and Consequences of Mortality Trends in Ceylon," *Public Health Reports* 75 (1960), 865–68; and J. M. May, "The Ecology of Malaria," in his *Studies in Disease Ecology* (New York: Hafner, 1961).

6. Table IX, 1966, p. 18 and Table XII, *Statistical Abstract, 1969,* p. 26.

7. United Nations, *Statistical Yearbook;* for 1968, *Statistical Abstract, 1969,* p. 26; for 1946, *Statistical Abstract, 1954,* p. 12; for 1955, *Statistical Abstract, 1956,* p. 18; for 1963, *Statistical Abstract, 1965,* p. 24.

8. Ted R. Gurr, *Why Men Rebel* (Princeton: Princeton University Press, 1970).

9. For the government's view, see Prime Minister Bandaranaike's report to Parliament on July 20, 1971, mimeo.

10. For contemporary accounts see Richard Rahula, *Washington Post,* April 22, 1971; *The London Economist,* April 17, 1971; Mervyn deSilva, *Washington Post,* May 23, 1971.

11. Myron Weiner, *The Politics of Scarcity, Public Pressure and Political Response in India* (Chicago: University of Chicago Press, 1962), ch. VII; also Philip G. Altback, "Student Politics and Higher Education in India," in S. M. Lipset, ed., *Students in Revolt* (Boston: Houghton Mifflin, 1969), pp. 235–56.

12. For a brief discussion, see Howard Wriggins, *Development and Protest in Ceylon and South Asia,* Occasional Paper Series No. 1, Centre for Developing Societies, McGill University, Montreal. For a contrasting view, see Leslie Ross, Jr., Noralou P. Roos, and Gary R. Field, "Students and Politics in Contemporary Turkey" in Lipset, *Students in Revolt,* pp. 257–82.

13. For a discussion of political culture and the processes by which young

people become socialized into one or another type of political orientation, see Lucian Pye, ed., *Political Culture and Political Development* (Princeton: Princeton University Press, 1965), particularly the Introduction.

14. Howard Wriggins, *Ceylon: Dilemmas of a New Nation* (Princeton: Princeton University Press; 1960), ch. IX.

15. E. Tennent, *Ceylon: An Account of the Island. Physical, Historical and Topographical* (London: Longmans, Green, 1859); A. G. Ranasinha, *Census of Ceylon. 1946 Report* (Colombo: Ceylon Government Press, 1950).

16. O. Lewis, *La Vida* (New York: Vintage Press, 1966).

17. E. Tennent, *Ceylon: An Account;* T. L. Green, "The Cultural Determination of Personality in Ceylon," *School and Society,* LV (March 15, 1952), 164–66; Murray A. Strauss and Solomon Cytrynbaum, "Support and Power Structures in Sinhalese, Tamil and Burgher Student Families," *International Journal of Comparative Sociology,* III (September 1962), 138–53.

18. S. J. Thambiah, "Ethnic Representation in Ceylon's Higher Administrative Services, 1870–1946," *University of Ceylon Review,* XIII, No. 2 and 3 (April–July 1955), 113–34.

19. S. Arasaratnam, *Ceylon* (Englewood Cliffs, N.J.: Prentice-Hall, 1964).

20. For a detailed account of growing labor strife, usually left unnoticed in political accounts of Ceylon, see Visakha K. Jayawardena, *The Rise of the Labor Movement in Ceylon* (Durham: Duke University Press, 1972).

21. H. A. Bloch, *Research Report on Homicide, Attempted Homicide and Crimes of Violence* (Colombo: Ceylon Police, 1960).

22. C. H. S. Jayewardene and H. Ranasinghe, *Criminal Homicide in the Southern Province* (Colombo: Colombo Apothecaries, 1963).

23. Leonard Woolf, *Village in the Jungle* (London: Chatto and Windus, Phoenix Edition, 1951), pp. 223–30.

24. Abhayaratne and Jayewardene, *Fertility Trends,* pp. 29–30.

25. Government of Ceylon, *Statistical Abstract* for appropriate years.

26. Data from National Council of Higher Education, *The Framework of a Plan for the Development of Universities in Ceylon* (1969–78), cited in International Labor Office, *Matching Employment Opportunities and Expectations: A Programme of Action for Ceylon,* II, 1964.

27. *Ibid.,* I, 1972; Murray A. Strauss, "Childhood Experience and Emotional Security in the Context of Sinhalese Social Organization," *Social Forces,* 33, No. 2 (December 1954), 152–60.

28. See, for instance, *Report of the Kandyan Peasantry Commission* (Government of Ceylon, Sessional Paper XVIII, 1951).

29. G. E. P. de S. Wickramaratne, *Towards a New Era: Selected Speeches of S. W. R. D. Bandaranaike* (Colombo: Government Press, 1961).

30. W. R. Muelder, *Schools for a New Nation* (Colombo: K. V. H. G. deSilva, 1962).

31. Wriggins, *Ceylon: Dilemmas,* chs. VI and IX.

32. International Labor Office, *Matching Employment Opportunities,* p. 5.

33. Lipset sees similar changes in other countries. See his essay, "Students and Politics in Comparative Perspective" in his *Students in Revolt,* pp. xv–xxxiv.

34. Politicus, "The April Revolt in Ceylon," *Asian Survey,* XII, No. 3

(March 1972), 259–74, especially 261; based on Government of Ceylon, *Land Ownership in Ceylon,* Sessional Paper XI, 1954.

35. For a discussion of the new "rural intelligentsia," see Hector Abeyawardhana, "The April Insurgency," *The Nation* (Colombo), April 7, 1972.

36. Karl W. Deutsch, "Social Mobilization and Political Development," *American Political Science Review,* XV, No. 3 (September 1961), 493–514.

37. For the first tendency, see Wriggins, *Ceylon: Dilemmas* and S. and L. Rudolph, *The Modernity of Tradition* (Chicago: University of Chicago Press, 1967), Part I; for the latter see Robert N. Kearney, *Trade Unions and Politics in Ceylon* (Berkeley: University of California Press, 1971).

38. For a discussion of the traditional exports and the role they play in Ceylon's prosperity, see D. R. Snodgrass, *Ceylon: An Export Economy in Transition* (Homewood, Ill.: Erwin, 1966). For recent earnings, see International Labor Office, *Matching Employment Opportunities,* II, 244.

39. International Labor Office, *Matching Employment Opportunities,* I, 244–46.

40. For a detailed discussion, see Snodgrass, *Ceylon: An Export Economy,* pp. 139–98.

41. International Labor Office, *Matching Employment Opportunity,* I, 23–26.

42. *Ibid.,* I, 21–30.

43. International Bank for Reconstruction and Development (IBRD), *Ceylon Preliminary Report on Education* (Colombo: Ministry of Planning and Economic Affairs, n.d.).

44. *Ibid.*

45. Numerous newspaper reports, April 1971; see particularly *Washington Post,* from Colombo, April 27, 1971.

46. Central Bank of Ceylon, Annual Report, 1971, p. 205.

47. A careful review of the testimony of Rohana Wijeweera suggests that the leaders were indeed sensitive to the necessity of enlisting a wide following, which would depend significantly on local conditions as perceived by local recruits. Rohana Wijeweera, *Transcript,* translation of Tape Recorded Statement (mimeo, n.d.), 366 pp.

48. Geraldine Gamburd, "The Seven Grandparents: Locality and Lineality in Sinhalese Kinship and Caste" (Ph.D. dissertation, Columbia University, 1972).

49. We are indebted to Frank Ceo, a research assistant associated with the Southern Asian Institute, for the analysis behind these observations. Cross tabulations were performed for levels of paddy land / non-estate rural male population for 1963 and changes in this ratio for the period 1953–63. Data were taken from the 1954 and 1963 censuses. Other variables examined for comparison district by district included: birth rates, population growth rates, age ratios, increases in school buildings, school attenders and graduates per district. None of these proved to be statistically significant except paddy land per rural male and male out-migration from areas (1) and (2). Of course, it may be that changes between the 1963 and 1971 censuses have been marked; this part of the analysis must therefore remain tentative until results of the 1971 census are available.

50. James Guyot, "Creeping Urbanism and Political Development in Malaysia," in Robert T. Daland, ed., *Comparative Urban Research* (Beverly Hills: Sage, 1969), pp. 124–61.

51. For a discussion of similar by-product effects of agricultural change, see Francine Frankel, *India's Green Revolution: Economic Gains and Political Costs* (Princeton: Princeton University Press, 1971).

52. Politicus, "The April Revolt in Ceylon," p. 265.

53. *Ibid.*, p. 268.

54. *Ibid.*, p. 262.

55. *Ibid.*, p. 271.

Index